Exploring God's Word

# Teachers Guide

## Grade 1

Concordia Publishing House

Series editors: Carolyn S. Bergt, Clarence F. Berndt, Rodney L. Rathmann

Project editors: Karen Arnold, Edward E. Grube

This publication is available in braille and in large print for the visually impaired. Write to the Library for the Blind, 1333 S. Kirkwood Rd., St. Louis, MO 63122-7295; or call 1-800-433-3954.

Scripture quotations taken from the HOLY BIBLE: NEW INTERNATIONAL VERSION®. NIV®. Copyright © 1973, 1978, 1984 by International Bible Society. Used by permission of Zondervan Publishing House. All rights reserved.

Copyright © 2001 Concordia Publishing House
3558 S. Jefferson Avenue, St. Louis, MO 63118-3968

Manufactured in the United States of America

1   2   3   4   5   6   7   8   9   10                    10   09   08   07   06   05   04   03   02   01

# Contents

# Introduction

## About Your Role as a Teacher of the Faith

God has given you the opportunity to share the Good News of His love and grace with the young people in your class. As you plan to live out your role as a Christian teacher, consider the following suggestions:

- Make your daily personal Bible reading and devotional time a priority. Through God's Word the Holy Spirit builds you up in faith, guiding and equipping you for the important work God has given you to do.
- Be regular in your attendance at worship; partake in the Sacrament often. Through the means of grace God nurtures our relationship with Him and with all others who love and trust in Jesus as their Savior.
- Plan your religion lessons prayerfully and thoughtfully. You will find your students at various degrees of depth and understanding in their spiritual life. Aim at meeting your students where they are, bring them to the Word of God, and trust in the power of the Holy Spirit to work the results.
- Look for ways to connect lesson objectives throughout the day, extending the influence of God's Word and love beyond the class designated specifically for Bible study.
- Remember, you teach about Jesus in everything you say, do, and are as a teacher in a Christian school. By God's grace your students will see God at work in the attitudes you project, the decisions you make, and the words you say.
- Begin your teaching day with a private prayer. Pray for individual children by name. Ask God to bless them at this stage of life and to guide and direct them as they grow into adulthood.
- Don't try to go it alone. Seek out the support and encouragement of your brothers and sisters in Christ—your principal, fellow teachers, and staff as well as your students' parents. Do all you can to make the spiritual growth and development of your students a Christian community effort, involving all who contribute to establishing and nurturing the mission and objectives of your school.
- Evaluate each day in light of your spiritual goals for your class. Celebrate successes. Ask for and receive forgiveness for failures, trusting in the saving and restoring power Jesus continues to provide. Then look forward to tomorrow, mindful that God's mercies "are new every morning" (Lamentations 3:23).

## About Christian Education

This curriculum has been designed to assist those teaching in Christian classrooms so that through the Word and Spirit of God, people of all ages

- may know God, especially His seeking and forgiving love in Christ;
- may respond in faith and grow into Christian maturity;
- see themselves as the reconciled, redeemed children of God and individual members of Christ's body, the church;
- live happily in peace with God, themselves, and their fellow human beings;
- express their joy in worship of God and in loving service to others;
- value all of God's creative work in His world and the church;
- witness openly of Christ as the Savior of all people;
- participate actively in God's mission to the church and the world;
- live in Christian hope with the blessed assurance of eternal life in heaven through Christ Jesus, our Lord.

To focus on these goals the Voyages curriculum is Christ-centered so that students will have optimal opportunity to grow in their relationship of faith and life with God. "We proclaim to you what we have seen and heard, so that you also may have fellowship with us. And our fellowship is with the Father and with His Son, Jesus Christ" (1 John 1:3).

## About Your Students

What are first-grade students like? Although God has given each person a unique pattern of growth, individuals generally follow growth patterns characteristic of their age group. Consider some of the common physical, emotional, social, intellectual, and faith-development characteristics of children between the ages of 6 and 7.

But remember that no child will display all the characteristics listed. You must know your students as individuals in order to help them grow toward becoming independent and mature individuals. Your students are growing in different areas at different rates. A person who is exceptionally gifted in social skills may have difficulty with physical development. Others may seem intellectually gifted but lack spiritual maturity. Some days you will question whether an individual or the entire class is growing at all. On such days, let the Holy Spirit fill your heart once again with His love. Ask God to help you trust in His power to work faith in the hearts of these individuals He loves and for whom He died.

## Physical Development

Students in grade 1 may be

- improving their use of small muscles (though large muscle development progresses faster);
- increasing adeptness at hopping, running, and jumping;
- improving eye-hand coordination;
- very active and energetic;
- easily tired when overactive, but recover quickly;
- demonstrating an improvement in their sense of rhythm.

## Emotional Development

Students in grade 1 tend to

- want to be accepted and liked by their peers;
- be proud of their accomplishments;
- desire praise and recognition;
- accept the authority of rules without question;
- want to please and cooperate with the teacher;
- be developing self-sufficiency and can work alone or in groups;
- be responsible for their possessions;
- show excitement about learning.

## Social Development

Students in grade 1 often

- accept diversity among people;
- have an increasing awareness of the feelings of others;
- think primarily in terms of "I" and "my";
- enjoy playing with groups and in games with rules.

## Intellectual Development

Students in grade 1 can usually

- think primarily in concrete and literal terms;
- think of parts and wholes independently;
- classify, compare, and contrast;
- begin to see pictures as symbols;
- work with sequencing and cause and effect;
- more readily distinguish between fantasy and reality;
- engage in exploration and experimentation.

## Spiritual Development

Students in grade 1 generally

- recognize Jesus as their Savior, God's Son;
- are growing in understanding forgiveness;
- express their love of Jesus;
- trust God's ability to help them;
- recognize sin and that it needs to be punished;
- pray for others;
- recognize that God gives us everything;
- want assurance of God's unconditional love;
- worship joyfully.

## About Voyages: Exploring God's Word

These units, designed to be taught to students in grade 1, will involve the use of the Teachers Guide, nine Student Books per child, the Teacher Resource Book, and the Bible. Key elements of Luther's Small Catechism are available for quick and easy reference in the Teacher Resource Book.

There are nine units in this course (approximately one per month). The Bible stories in each unit are connected by a common theme. All stories and units are presented in chronological order to survey God's story of love and salvation for His people as found in the Old and New Testaments and continuing on to touch our lives today. Each of the nine units is divided into four weeks of lessons, and each week consists of four daily lesson plans.

The first-grade materials of the Voyages curriculum are designed primarily to help you teach students about key concepts of faith such as Law and Gospel, confession and repentance, forgiveness and grace, while focusing specifically on the person, attributes, and work of our triune God. The lessons (1) confront us with the Law, showing us our sin and need for a Savior; (2) lead us to see God's grace in sending Jesus to redeem us from sin, death, and the power of the devil; and (3) encourage us as we daily live in Christ, empowered by the Holy Spirit. Each lesson centers on the cross of Christ and is grounded in the Word of God through which the Holy Spirit works to create, strengthen, and sustain saving faith.

In the Teacher Kit you will find a collection of large classroom posters. These posters are referenced periodically in the lessons and have been especially designed to enhance and reinforce lesson presentations. You will also find a music CD set included in the Teacher Kit. The CDs contain instrumental accompaniment and also vocals to assist your class in learning songs of praise to God. All songs on the CDs can be found in the printed songbook *Little Ones Sing Praise (LOSP)*, available from CPH. The kit also contains the puppets Jenna and Jake, flannelgraph materials, and a set of "Fold 'n' Tell" story pictures.

## The Importance of Committing God's Word to Memory

A graded memory curriculum for kindergarten through grade 8 has been especially developed for use in Christian schools. This series consists of the Six Chief Parts of Christian Doctrine, selected Bible verses, prayers, and great hymns of faith. The use of the memory book for grade 1 with the Voyages curriculum is strongly recommended. A sample has been included in the Teacher Kit.

In addition, each Voyages lesson concludes in the Student Book with a selected portion from God's Word highlighting the lesson's theme; this section is appropriately titled "Words to Remember." You may draw attention to this theme verse, assign it for memory work, or review and discuss it with the class.

The Teacher Resource Book contains reproducible Unit lists of the "Words to Remember" Bible verses, so that you can inform and involve parents in this learning activity. As you can see, you have several options for developing your memory work program.

# Student Books

Each of the nine units in this Bible course has an accompanying Student Book. At the end of each unit, send the book home so that parents and children can share what they have learned about God's message. Urge children to collect the series of nine books to make one complete Bible storybook by the end of the year. These books contain illustrations and narratives of Bible stories and also activities to focus on Bible truths and their life application. These books complement the lesson, but the primary vehicle is your sharing of God's Word and your discussion of it in class and through personal witness of your faith in Christ Jesus.

Note: The Teacher Resource Book includes blacklines for nine parent letters. Send a copy of the letter home at the beginning of each unit and send the Student Book home at the end of the unit. This will help parents keep in touch with what their children are learning about Jesus.

# Teachers Guide

Each daily lesson plan is presented on a two-page spread with student material reductions provided, complete with answers written in where appropriate. All lessons follow the same easy-to-teach 3-step pattern (introduce, develop, respond). Sidebars frame each lesson, providing a focus, objectives, materials list, worship ideas, background information helpful for teaching the lesson, ideas for using the memory verses, and suggestions for extending the lesson.

Use the Teachers Guide together with the Teacher Resource Book (TRB). The latter contains the blacklines referenced in each lesson, together with a host of other resources to assist you in teaching the faith.

The Teachers Guide also contains a helpful overview at the beginning of each unit to help you focus on, develop, and extend the unit theme for the next four weeks.

## Unit Overview

Review this section as you begin your planning for each unit. This two-page spread includes the following unit applications:

- *Worship Connections:* activities for applying unit concepts to some aspect of Christian worship.
- *Community Building:* games and activities to help teachers and students celebrate the oneness that God's Spirit desires to build in us through Christ Jesus, our Lord.
- *Tools for Witness:* craft projects that may be undertaken to create a reminder of God's grace and to assist in sharing the faith with family and friends.
- *Service Projects:* activity suggestions to help young people

demonstrate their faith in acts of kindness toward others.
- *Reaching Every Individual:* suggestions or strategies aimed at addressing individual needs and challenges.
- *Integrating the Faith:* suggestions for extending unit themes and concepts into social studies, science, language arts, fine arts, mathematics, and technology are displayed on a concept map to equip and inspire you as you look for ways to extend and apply the teachings of God's Word in every aspect of your curriculum.

## Lesson Overview

Each weekly plan consists of four days (assuming that a chapel service is held one day of the week). Two Bible stories are presented each week; two days are spent on each story in order to reinforce and expand concepts. Routinely, a blackline activity (found in the Teacher Resource Book) is included on the first day a story is taught, and two pages of the Student Book are used on the second day.

The core of the lesson is a 3-step process involving activities, visuals, relationships, and always a Christ-centered focus. The *Introduce* section sets the stage for the lesson, engaging student interest in the information about to be presented. The *Develop* section provides the lesson content. The final section, *Respond*, encourages students to react to and apply the concepts they have learned during the lesson presentation.

In addition to the 3-step lesson plan and the reduction of the student material for each day, the Teachers Guide contains sidebars with pertinent information. Sidebars give you the focus for the week and objectives for teaching individual Bible stories. They list any extra materials you will need to gather. (It is assumed that you will have pencils, paper, scissors, crayons, a Bible, *Little Ones Sing Praise*, and the music CDs accessible at all times.)

Another sidebar suggests worship ideas that can be used on either of the two days a story is taught. Student involvement in worship, though sometimes difficult to accomplish, will help make the worship experience meaningful to them.

A Bible background section encourages your personal Bible study, providing additional insight and enrichment of the text.

Sidebars also list the Bible words to remember and give ideas on how to learn or how to use the passage. You should always consider the abilities and needs of your class and the individual in this regard. Use the Bible words frequently throughout the lesson and in worship so that children see its meaning and purpose, not just an assignment.

Ideas for extending the lesson are also included in sidebars. These may be activities to expand and enrich the concepts taught. They may be suggestions for carrying the lesson theme into other curricular areas throughout the day.

It is important to make this guide your own, adapting it to the needs of your students. This is a guide, not a prescription. Pick and choose what works for you. Do not feel compelled to cover all the material presented. What is most important is to focus on Christ, using a Law/Gospel perspective in each lesson. The Law shows us our sin and our need for a Savior; the Gospel shows us who our Savior Jesus Christ is and leads us to repentance and faith. Then, through the power of the Holy Spirit working through God's Word, we are led to a new life lived for Him, now and eternally.

## Teacher Resource Book (TRB)

This resource is a valuable companion to your Teachers Guide. It contains information and ideas to assist you as you plan your lessons and as you teach Voyages: Exploring God's Word. This information is also available in CD-ROM format so that you can adjust, delete, or add to the material to customize it and suit the needs of your individual situation. General curriculum information is included as well as lesson-specific helps. These are some of the things you will find.

*Voyages Bible Story Sequence:* a complete listing of Bible stories taught in the curriculum and the level at which they are taught.

*Catechetical Connections:* a scope and sequence chart that includes references to sections of the catechism included in sessions throughout Voyages. In addition to those sessions cited in the index, other lessons also teach portions of the catechism, in some instances with even greater emphasis. This index insures that references to all sections of the catechism are made regularly and not only in conjunction with more obviously related Bible accounts.

*In This Together:* a collection of articles by Christian educators to motivate, inspire, and equip teachers in living and teaching the faith we profess.

*Catechism Enchiridion:* a handy listing of the key elements of Luther's catechism.

*Blacklines:* reproducible pages to be used for teaching and extending lesson concepts.

*Unit Assessment:* group and individual activities to review and reinforce learning.

*Parent Letter Blacklines:* reproducible pages that are to be distributed at the beginning of each unit to make parents aware of what their children will be learning about God's Word, so that they can support and encourage their children's faith development in the home. Accompanying these are the Unit Bible verses to remember.

*Poster Key:* a reduction of all the posters provided in the Teacher Kit so that you can quickly identify the poster you need.

*Supplemental Ideas and Helps:* a variety of information, activities, recipes, and reproducibles that can add to your classroom study of the Bible and worship of the Lord.

*May God bless you and the children in your care as you share the Good News we have in our Savior, Christ Jesus!*

# UNIT 1
# Beginnings

## Unit Overview

There are many beginnings taking place at this time of the year—beginning a new school year, beginning new friendships, perhaps even beginning in a new school itself or in a new city. We are also focusing on the beginning of the Bible, the beginning of creation, the beginning of our relationship as sinful people with our loving Lord, and the beginning of God's covenant and promise to send a Savior. Beginnings can be frightening when facing the unknown, but they can also be exciting when facing new opportunities. Whatever the beginning being made, we have the comforting assurance of the presence of our gracious God. Encourage the children with this confidence during this unit of *Beginnings*.

Send home copies of the family letter and Bible verse list for Unit 1 as you begin. (See Teacher Resource Book.) This will let parents know what their children will be learning during the next few weeks. At the end of the unit, let the children take their *Beginnings* books home. Encourage them to show their parents what they have learned. Tell them they will be getting nine of these books throughout the year. Suggest that they collect these to make one big Bible storybook that will show God's loving plan for us through the Old Testament, New Testament, now, and eternally. Also consider adding some of the following activities to your curriculum to make related connections between God's message of love and all that you do throughout the day.

## Worship Connections

At this beginning of the school year, begin with attention to your worship center. It can be as simple as a small table with a Bible or cross on it. Additional items can be added, if you wish, such as an altar cloth with Christian symbols painted on it. Perhaps you might vary the altar cloth colors according to the season of the church year. You might have a religious bulletin board display or poster behind the altar or place *unlit* candles and silk flowers on it. What is important is to have a focal point that remains constant throughout the day and throughout the year, reminding us of the constant presence of our Lord. Comment on any similarities between your worship center and the one in your church (whether physically or in function). This will increase the children's awareness of what they see in the church.

At this time, also begin to establish classroom worship procedures. We can worship at any time, as we live lives of worship in the Lord. Closing your Bible time with worship is important as you respond to what you have learned about our loving God. These can be experiences that involve a variety of responses and opportunities. At the same time, children also learn from and enjoy the comfort of repetition and tradition. So it is good to begin the day with a simple common liturgy. You may use the following example, adapt it, or develop one of your own. Perhaps you can involve individuals in leading the Invocation and Benediction. All children could join in making the sign of the cross at those two points in the worship.

- **Invocation:** We begin in the name of the Father and of the Son and of the Holy Spirit. Amen.
- **Song of Praise**
- **Bible Verse**
- **Prayer**
- **Benediction:** The Lord bless you and keep you. The Lord make His face shine on you and be gracious to you. The Lord look upon you with favor and give you peace. Amen.

## Community Building

- Take a class trip to a zoo, with the explicit purpose of identifying the many things God has made. Speak often of the wonder of God's creation and His many blessings as you walk through the zoo. You can be a model to the children for natural, Christian conversation, worshiping God in all we do.
- Right from the start of the school year, lead the children in praying for each other. Each day pray for one or two children specifically. It will mean a lot to the children to hear their teacher praying for them, and it will remind the class of their bond in Christian community.

## Tools for Witness

- Always encourage the children to share the activities they work on during Bible time. These can be tools they use to witness to family members. Help the children understand that we can witness to people who already know about Jesus. God can work through our conversation about His Word to strengthen and comfort others in their faith in Jesus.
- Consider having children make special containers for collecting the nine Student Books they will be using throughout the year. For example, cut off one narrow side of a large cereal box and seal the top with tape to make a book collection holder. Cover the box with gift wrap or adhesive paper. Use marking pens and stickers to decorate the boxes. (Note: It is all right if the books extend beyond the edge of the box, just so it serves to gather the books together.) Another possibility for holding the books is to purchase plain canvas bags at a craft store and decorate them with fabric paint and iron-on transfers.

## Service Projects

Consider planning a service project that involves the care of God's creation, which He has entrusted to us. Point out that God has not given us this world to use selfishly or wastefully; instead, He has *entrusted* the world to our care, to use wisely and for a good purpose and to glorify God.

Projects could include environmental care in the areas of cleaning (antipollution) or preserving (conserving) the land, the water, or the air God has given us.

Or, you may choose a project to protect and care for the animals God created. Check with a local humane society about their needs. Or ask if they have guest speakers who could talk to the children about pet care.

Another project could involve a classroom garden, indoors or outdoors. (Note: An indoor garden could be placed in a wagon bed or in several large plastic buckets so that the gardens are portable and so children can easily gather around them to take care of them.)

## Reaching Every Individual

Your beginning readers should not be pressured to read during Bible time. The printed pages can always be read aloud by teachers and parents. Be sure to give clear directions so children know exactly where you are on a page and what to do. It is always best to do the printed activities as a group. The activities are meant to encourage discussion and response, not to test skills.

## Social Studies

Display a world map or globe. Use removable tape to attach two large red arrows, one pointing toward Israel and the other pointing to the country in which you live. Emphasize that the Bible stories you are studying took place on the other side of the world. Thank God that He has blessed us by spreading His message of the Good News of salvation through Jesus around the world to far-off places like where we live.

## Science

You can't ignore the fact that children are exposed to ideas of evolution even at this early age. It is best to make them aware of differing viewpoints in a simple way so that the children are equipped to handle issues they may face. For example, display children's books about dinosaurs. Explain that God created dinosaurs and all animals. But it did not take millions of years as the book may say. God's power is great—He created all things in just six days.

## Mathematics

Display several labeled charts, each numbering from 1–10. Charts can be labeled *Flowers*, *Fruit*, *Dogs*, *Fish*, *Birds*, or other choices. Children can dictate their ideas to you to see if they can think of 10 different types for each category. You may want to go beyond 10. Praise God for the abundance found in His creation.

Integrating the Faith

# Beginnings

## Language Arts

Work together on a Big Book project that describes the world we are blessed by God to be living in. In advance, prepare 26 pages by writing a describing word (adjective) on each page in alphabetical order (such as amazing, beautiful, cuddly, delicious). Tell the children what each word says and let them volunteer to draw a picture of something described by that word, something created by God or man-made (such as a space shuttle, flower, puppy, ice-cream cone).

## Fine Arts

Listen to, sing, act out, and enjoy the song "God's Creation" from *Songs Kids Love to Sing 2*, (p. 20; also available on audiotape or CD from Concordia Publishing House). This song has a calypso rhythm that is fun to sing and celebrates the joy we have in the Lord.

## Technology

As you learn about Abraham looking at the stars, you may want to use a video, CD-ROM information, or even a piece of paper with holes in it and placed on an overhead projector to show constellation patterns. Point out that people have made up stories about the patterns of stars they saw in the sky. When Abraham looked at the sky, he knew the truth about God's creation and trusted in the promises of God.

## Discovery Point

God showed His love for us by creating this beautiful world and by sending Jesus to be our Savior from sin.

## God Makes the World

Genesis 1–2

## Objectives

That by the power of the Holy Spirit working through God's Word, the students will
• believe that God created them, loves them, and cares for them;
• know that God created and continues to care for all of heaven and earth and that He entrusts us with responsibility for its care;
• thank and praise God for His creation, for His continued love, and for His forgiveness when we fail to do His will.

## Day 1 Materials

• Globe
• Jake and Jenna puppets
• Bag containing "God-made" and "not God-made" items
• Two Hula Hoops
• Blackline 1-A

## Day 2 Materials

• *Beginnings* Student Book
• Beginnings poster, Sections 1 and 2
• Finger foods, napkins, cups
• Picnic basket, blankets or tablecloths

## Special Note

Throughout the year, each time you begin a new unit send home the Unit Family Letter and Bible verse list. Reproducible copies of these are in the Teacher Resource Book and on the CD-ROM. These letters and lists will help parents become informed and involved.

# Day 1

## INTRODUCE

Ask, **Can you think of what makes today such a special day?** Lead thoughts to the first day or week of school. **The first day is a *very* special day. It is a new beginning, a gift from God, called a blessing. God gives us the blessings of many beginnings, like the beginning of a new day, the beginning of a new school year, a new class, a new teacher, and maybe new classmates. What other beginnings can you name?** After the children respond hold up the Bible. **The Bible is our most important beginning, and our world starts in the beginning of the Bible. Listen, "In the beginning God created the heavens and the earth"** (Genesis 1:1).

## DEVELOP

Hold up each puppet as it "speaks." Introduce the puppets, saying, **Jake and Jenna are first- and second-grade puppets. This is a beginning for them too. It's their first day of school, and Jenna is new at the school. Let's listen to them.**

**JAKE:** *(looks around his new classroom)* Cool room. Hi, Teacher.

*Jake is welcomed by the teacher and invited to join the class. Jake notices a girl alone near the globe. He moves toward her and starts a conversation.*

**JAKE:** Hi, I'm Jake. What's your name?

**JENNA:** *(timidly)* My name is Jenna.

**JAKE:** *(looking at the globe)* Hey, Jenna! Cool ball! Are we gonna use this when we play?

**JENNA:** *(timidly)* I don't know. *(Looks from Jake to teacher.)* That's a strange-looking ball, Teacher.

**TEACHER:** You're right. But it's not an ordinary ball. This is a globe. It is a model of our planet, the earth.

**JAKE:** Why is it all different colors?

**TEACHER:** I wonder? Does anyone have an idea about the blue color?

*Allow responses from the class and have the puppets add additional information.*

**JAKE:** Teacher, this globe is great, but if it isn't a ball, what will we use it for?

**TEACHER:** Well, Jake, it will help us think about God's love for all of us when He made the world.

**JAKE:** You mean God made that globe for us?

**TEACHER:** Even better, Jake, God made the real thing! He made the whole earth and everything in it!

**JAKE:** Wow! Everything? When did God do all that?

**TEACHER:** In God's Word *(hold up Bible)* we learn that in the beginning God created the heavens and the earth.

**JAKE:** That's the Bible?

**TEACHER:** Yes, it is, and the Bible is God's Word. Everything in God's Word is true, so we know that God created the world and everything in it.

JENNA: *(studies the globe)* Even the big mountains and oceans and the North Pole and the lakes and …?

JAKE: The leaves and fish and little bitsy bugs?

TEACHER: Yes, Jake and Jenna. Boys and girls, what else do you know that God made in the beginning?

## R E S P O N D

In the beginning, God made the world and everything in it. With everything God made He said, "It is good." When this perfect world was changed by sin, God gave us a new beginning through Jesus, who died on the cross to take away our sin and rose from the dead so that we may live in heaven someday. God made this world for people. He also made people with a mind to think and make things from God's creation. Sit around two Hula Hoops. Explain that these will help us think of things made by God and things made by people from God's creation. Label the Hula Hoops "God-made" and "not God-made." Model the decision-making process by saying thoughts aloud, such as, **God made leaves**, or **God did not make toothpicks**. Have each student take an item and place it into the appropriate hoop. (Dividing items into *is/is not* or *has/has not* areas is called binary classification.) Point out that the items not made by God were made from raw materials that were originally made by Him. Also point out that God created people with the ability to use His creation to make things. Blackline 1-A continues this activity.

### Blessings from God

Use a green crayon to circle things God created.
Use an orange crayon to circle things made by people.
Think about this: What things from God's creation
do people use in order to make man-made things?

## Worship Ideas

- Practice and then use these words to praise God.

**For sun and moon and skies of blue,**
**We clap to show our praise to You!**
*(Clap 3x.)*
**For trees and mountains, oceans too,**
**We stamp our feet in praise to you.**
*(Stamp feet 3x.)*
**For puppies, owls, and kangaroos,**
**We stand and cheer our praise to You.**
*(Stand and shout, "Yeah, God!" 3x.)*
**For all You made and care for too,**
**We do all three to say thank You.**
*(Clap, stamp, and cheer.)*

- Finger-paint a large mural, making pictures of creation. Later, gather around the mural for prayer to thank God.

- Sing and celebrate God's creation with action songs of praise. "He's Got the Whole World in His Hands" and "The Butterfly Song" (*LOSP*, pp. 101, 72, and on the Voyages CD).

## Bible Background

The creation story is not only a story of how God created the world, but it also reveals truths about our God. It reveals that He is a personal God: He has a will, He reasons, and He shows emotion. God is active and present in His creation. He is good and gracious. He did not have to create, but He chose to create that He might demonstrate His love. Creation is God's first act of grace. It is also His first gift. He gives us the gift of life not only here on earth, but also in heaven in Jesus Christ. What a beginning!

## Words to Remember

*God saw all that He had made, and it was very good. Genesis 1:31*

- Have the children listen, then join in, as you hum the tune "Jimmy Crack Corn." Now add the words from the Bible verse. Later add clapping hands.

**God saw all that He had made,**
**God saw all that He had made,**
**God saw all that He had made,**
**And it was very good.**

- **Jake wanted to play ball with the globe. We will play with a bouncing ball as we learn the Bible verse.** Demonstrate bouncing the ball to a partner saying the first word of the verse. Then have your partner return the ball, adding the next word. Complete the entire verse.

## Extending the Lesson

- Take a creation walk and gather objects for a "God-Made" book or bulletin board. See the *Teacher Resource Book (TRB)* for supplemental activities for each unit.
- Manipulate plastic animals, plants, trees, and people to count, pair, classify, pattern, or make one more and one fewer word stories.

## INTRODUCE

*Note: When working with or serving food always remember to check for food allergies; have everyone sanitize hands; work in a sanitized area; wear plastic gloves to handle food; use clean utensils; and check with your school and state education department regarding the preparation and serving of food in the classroom.*

This lesson works well indoors or outdoors. Spread tablecloths or blankets on the ground. Have the children clean their hands. Set the "God-created" finger foods on plates. Distribute napkins, paper plates, and cups of water. Sing "God Is Great," the "Johnny Appleseed Prayer," or pray: **Dear God, thank You for loving and caring for** (name each student). **Thank You for creating this food we are about to eat and this water we will drink. Thank You for always being with us. Amen.**

As the children eat, discuss how God made the food grow and how the food makes us grow too. The water we drink keeps bodies healthy; it also makes the food plants grow. Explain that when we

# God Makes the World

*(Genesis 1–2)*

**Day 1:** God said, "Let there be light." And there was light, daytime and night.

**Day 4:** God made the sun to shine by day and the moon and stars at night.

**Day 2:** God separated the sky from the waters below, and it was good.

**Day 5:** God created animals to fill the sky and the waters below.

**Day 3:** God created the dry land by His word and covered it with grass, trees, and other plants. And it was good.

**Day 6:** God filled the earth with animals. A man, Adam, and a woman, Eve, were God's special creations.

*On the seventh day God rested. Every seven days (Sunday) we celebrate in worship all that God has done to care for us and to save us through Jesus.*

1

read the Bible and hear God's Word, God strengthens our faith and helps us grow spiritually. After cleanup, gather and say, **Help me fill in the blanks. God loves us and made such a wonderful world for us. He gives us everything we need to live: air to _____ , light to _____ , food to _____ , parents and friends to _____ . God does even more! He gives us His love. He gives us Jesus. Jesus is the Son of God. God is great!**

## D E V E L O P

Cut the Beginnings poster into the indicated sections and laminate. Roll and tape the sides of Section 2 so Adam is visible on one side and Eve on the other. Use as puppets for the dialogue.

Hold up Adam. **My name is Adam. I was the very first person to ever live on the earth. After God created this fantastic world, He made me from the dust of the ground. Then God breathed into me, and I became alive! God loved me and named me Adam. He gave me a wonderful body and a mind so that I could think and learn. I was holy and perfect, just like God.**

**God told me to live in the Garden of Eden and take care of it. There were juicy berries growing on bushes, and delicious fruit hung from the tree branches. Everything blossomed and grew.**

**God gave me the job of naming each animal. So, one by one, I named them: the alligator, the panda, and the cricket. I named the worm, the dog, and the horse. I loved living in the**

**garden and being close to God. The animals were my friends. God wanted me to be happy. God said that He would make a helper for me.**

Turn puppet to Eve. Say, **God made Adam fall into a deep sleep, and while Adam slept, God took one of his ribs and made a woman. That's me, Eve! Adam named me.**

**Adam and I lived in the garden. We always had food. We were never sick or sad. God loved us and took care of us. He was our best friend. Everything was perfect.**

**God made each of you too. He looks at you and says, "You are My creation. I love you." God is your best friend. He loves and cares for you all the time.**

## R E S P O N D

God gave Adam and Eve the job of caring for His perfect creation. But the world is not perfect anymore. People have not cared for the world as God intended. That is just one of the many things we as sinners do wrong. Praise God that He loves us so much He created a plan to save us through Jesus.

Display Section 1 of the Beginnings poster on a bulletin board. Throughout this unit you will add other sections of the poster to form a cross shape. (The Student Book, page 16, shows an example of the completed display, which you can use as a reference.)

**As children of God, we live for Him. I wonder what we can do to take better care of His creation?** Allow for discussion, leading the class to understand how they can help right now, right here. Use page 2 of the *Beginnings* Student Book to extend discussion on environmental concerns. Focus always on the great gifts God has entrusted to our care.

# Caring for God's Creation?

*Directions: Mark an X where you find litter and pollution. Draw a smiling face where someone is caring for the earth or something is helping prevent pollution.*

Words to Remember
*God saw all that He had made, and it was very good. Genesis 1:31*

2

## Discovery Point

God showed His love for us by creating this beautiful world and by sending Jesus to be our Savior from sin.

## The First Sin

Genesis 3:1–24

## Objectives

That by the power of the Holy Spirit working through God's Word, the students will

- know that God sent Jesus to be the Savior for all people;
- become aware of their own sin and look to Jesus for forgiveness;
- praise God for His gift of Jesus as their Savior from sin.

## Day 3 Materials

- *Beginnings* Student Book
- Jake and Jenna puppets
- Blackline 1-B
- Beginnings poster, Section 2

## Day 4 Materials

- Beginnings Student Book
- Pan of hydrogen peroxide
- Water-soluble markers
- Clip clothespins
- Paper and newspapers

## INTRODUCE

Review "God Makes the World," using a mixed-up version of the story of creation. If children hear something that is not part of the story or is not correct, they should raise their hands and give the correct response. Make obvious mistakes, such as God forming animals from trees, birds swimming under the water, or whales flying in the air. Use *Beginnings*, page 1, as a story guide. Emphasize, **God really did make a perfect world for Adam and Eve, and you and me. I wonder what happened … Oh my, I wonder what's going on? Jake and Jenna seem to have a problem.**

## DEVELOP

**JAKE:** *(pushing Jenna)* Look out! It's time for the Bible story. Get out of my way, Jenna!

**JENNA:** *(pushing Jake)* Look out, yourself! Stop pushing!

**JAKE:** Hey, slowpoke, don't you push me!

**JENNA:** You pushed me first, you big bully! *(Puppets wrestle.)*

**TEACHER:** Jake! Jenna! Stop. What happened?

**JENNA:** *(near tears)* That mean ol' Jake called me a slowpoke!

**JAKE:** Well, she called me a bully!

**JENNA:** You pushed me!

**JAKE:** You pushed me too!

**TEACHER:** Just a moment, both of you. You are blaming each other. It seems that both of you made some mistakes. Let's talk about this. *(If time allows use problem-solving skills, including "I feel" words and peaceful conflict resolution with the puppets. Or have the puppets huddle and murmur for a short time.)*

**JENNA:** *(softly)* Sorry, Jake. I was wrong to push you and call you a bully.

**JAKE:** *(softly)* I forgive you, Jenna, and I am sorry for pushing you and calling you a slowpoke.

**TEACHER:** It is good that you both recognized your sin and forgave each other.

**JAKE:** Sin?

**TEACHER:** Sin is the bad things we do—like pushing and name-calling.

**JENNA:** Oh!

**TEACHER:** *(removes puppets and turns to class)* Sin makes God sad. Sin hurts others, and sin hurts us.

# RESPOND

Display Section 2 of the Beginnings poster. Place it *below* Section 1. Say, **Sin came into the world when Adam and Eve made a wrong choice. People weren't the only things in creation that changed because of sin. Now all of God's beautiful world became changed by sin. What sins did we hear about from Jenna and Jake?** Discuss the puppets' actions and help the children understand that God forgives us through faith in Jesus, our Savior.

**God forgives our sins because of the Promised One. God promised Adam and Eve that He would send a Savior to save people from their sin. That Savior is Jesus. When Jesus took away our sins on the cross He made it possible for us to be forgiving of others.** Use Blackline 1-B and connect the dots. Draw a cross in the empty circle to remember that Jesus, our Savior, took away our sins. He gives the help no one else can give.

Refer to the prayer Jesus gave us—the Lord's Prayer. Point out that right in the middle of the prayer, we ask God to forgive our sins (trespasses). We also ask Him to help us be forgiving of others. Say the prayer as the children pray silently. Ask them to raise their hands during the "forgiveness part" of the prayer.

## See Our Savior

*Directions: Connect the dots to find the code letters that mean "help." These letters can also remind us of the one who gives us the most help of all. The letters can stand for (S)See (O)Our (S)Savior! In the center circle draw a cross to show how Jesus helps us.*

# Worship Ideas

- Sing about God's love, goodness, and forgiveness in "God Is So Good" (*LOSP*, p. 57). Add stanzas such as "He forgives me" and "I'm His dear child," always ending with the phrase "He's so good to me." The song "I'm Sorry" (*LOSP*, p. 27) teaches confession and forgiveness of sin. Both songs are on the Voyages CD.

- Form an outside circle and an inside circle with pairs of students facing each other. The partner on the inside circle says, "I've got bad news. We are sinners." The outside partner responds, "I've got good news. Jesus died for us." Direct each person to step to the right and repeat the words to the new partner. Repeat the process until the children return to their starting point.

- Stand in a circle with hands joined as you pray. Invite each child to thank God for His creation. Then add a silent time for children to confess their own sin and ask forgiveness. Give thanks for God's gift of the Savior, Jesus, who came for Adam and Eve and all people. Rejoice that we are His own dear children.

- Let the children see how God makes each individual unique—one of a kind. Make thumbprints and then use a magnifier to compare prints with those of their classmates. Praise God for making each individual special and for the forgiveness given for each individual's sin. Jesus died on the cross for every individual's sin. Make individual thumbprints to form a cross.

# Bible Background

The real focus of the story is not on Satan or even on Adam and Eve, but on God and His mercy. God could have chosen to destroy Adam and Eve and begin all over. Emphasize God's choice of grace and His promise. Only God's promise of a Savior would reverse the results of sin's judgment and death. Here the story of the fall in the Garden of Eden points ahead to the stable in Bethlehem, where Christ Jesus is born. In His death and resurrection Christ Jesus wins God's victory over sin and death for us.

## Words to Remember

*God so loved the world that He gave His one and only Son [that whoever believes in Him shall not perish but have eternal life]. John 3:16*

- Use bright markers to print the first phrase of the Bible words on a poster. Say the words together. Post the rest of the verse by phrases as each section is mastered. Ask, **What do these words tell us about Jesus?** Develop statements such as **Jesus is the Son of God. God loves us so much that He sent Jesus into the world to die on the cross. God punished Jesus for all the bad things we do. Now God will take us to heaven someday to live with Him forever.**

- Chant John 3:16 by phrases. Each time, after you clap, children are to echo your words and clap.

**God so loved** (clap), **the world that He** (clap), **gave His one** (clap), **and only Son** (clap), **that whoever** (clap), **believes in Him** (clap), **shall not perish** (clap), **but have eternal life** (clap, stomp, cheer).

## Extending the Lesson

- Consider visiting a recycling center, water purification plant, or landfill. Begin a recycling project in your classroom.

- Begin a compost in an appropriate outside area or in a vented trash can. Use discarded lunchroom items such as vegetable and fruit peels, skins, and cores. Some soil is needed. Do not use meat or dairy products. Discovery Works, Concordia Edition, Grade 1, Lesson 9, provides an individual milk carton compost activity.

# Day 4

## INTRODUCE

Reproduce a simple paper-doll pattern so the children can create a paper doll of themselves. Form small groups to act out classroom situations of sin, confession, and forgiveness. Some groups might volunteer to share a situation with the class. Explain, **It is only because of God's love for us that we can forgive one another in love. God kept His promise to Adam and Eve when He sent a Savior to take away sin. Our Savior is God's Son, Jesus. Jesus died on a cross for all of our sins. He came alive on Easter! Faith in Jesus changes our lives, so now we can live for Him.**

# The First Sin

*(Genesis 3:1–24)*

Adam and Eve lived in the beautiful Garden of Eden God had made for them. Every day God talked with them. God told Adam and Eve, "I love you." God also said, "You may eat fruit from all the trees—but not from the tree in the middle of the garden."

One day Eve walked near the tree in the middle of the garden. The devil was there, hiding in the shape of a snake. He talked to Eve. He told her that she would be like God if she ate from that tree.

Eve disobeyed God and ate the fruit. Then she gave Adam some too. Now Adam and Eve felt ashamed. They knew they had sinned.

God knew what had happened. God asked, "Adam and Eve, why are you hiding? Did you eat the fruit I told you not to eat?"

Adam answered, "It's all Eve's fault. She gave me a bite."

Eve answered, "The snake tricked me."

God was sad. All the world was spoiled by sin. Adam and Eve had to leave the Garden of Eden. They had to work hard. Now they would get sick and have troubles. One day they would die. God said to Adam and Eve, "You sinned, but I still love you. One day I will send My Son. He will suffer, but He will destroy the devil's power. He will be the Savior."

Many years later, God sent Jesus, who died on the cross and became alive again. Because of Jesus, we are children of God and we will live in heaven someday.

3

Read *Beginnings*, page 3, which provides the Bible story account of the first sin. First give these instructions: **Listen for God's promise to Adam and Eve as you hear the story. Draw a cross in the air with your fingers when you hear the words of God's promise.**

At the end of the story write *God, devil, Adam, Eve* on the board. Ask, **Who said, "You may eat fruit from all the trees—but not from the tree in the middle of the garden"? Who said, "You will be like God if you eat from that tree"? Who said, "Adam and Eve, why are you hiding? Did you eat the fruit I told you not to eat?" Who said, "It's all Eve's fault"? Who said, "The snake tricked me"? Who said, "You sinned, but I still love you. One day I will send My Son. He will suffer, but He will destroy the devil's power. He will be the Savior"?**

> ### God sent us a Savior, Jesus.
> ### He wraps His love and forgiveness around us
> ### and makes us able to live for Him.

Words to Remember

*God so loved the world that He gave His one and only Son, [that whoever believes in Him shall not perish but have eternal life]. John 3:16*

4

Assign locations where each child can privately draw with water-soluble markers to illustrate where, how, or what they have done wrong. Clip two clothespins on one end of the paper. Use the clothespins to place the paper, face down, in a pan of hydrogen peroxide. (Teacher supervision is required.) Gently move the paper in the solution and slowly count to 10. Carefully lift the clothespins and drip off the excess solution before placing the paper on newspaper to dry. Ask, **What happened to the paper? How does this remind us of what Jesus did when He died on the cross?** (When Jesus died, He took away my sins. Jesus wants me to tell Him I'm sorry about my sins. Jesus wants to forgive my sins. And you know what? Jesus does!)

Sing "Jesus Loves Me." Have the children stand in a circle, the shape of the world. Say, **God created the world and everything in it. God said, "It is good."** Now rearrange the children into the shape of a cross. **Adam and Eve sinned, but God made a promise to send a Savior who would save us from sin.** Last, form a heart shape. **Jesus died on a cross to forgive all our sins. He came alive again and defeated the power of Satan. God, through Jesus, loves us so very much.**

Conclude with *Beginnings*, page 4, which reviews the concept that the Savior came to redeem and change our sinful lives. His love and forgiveness wraps around us so that with forgiven hearts, in faith, we can live new lives for the Lord.

## Discovery Point

God loves all people. He shows His love and mercy through Jesus, who offers forgiveness and salvation. We respond to God's love in worship and praise.

## The Flood

Genesis 6:9–8:14

## Objectives

That by the power of the Holy Spirit working through God's Word, the students will

- grow in the peace and love of God as they realize His forgiveness for them in Jesus;
- know that God has the power to rescue them from danger, evil, and temptation;
- thank God for His great love and care for them.

## Day 1 Materials

- Pan of dirt or sand, toy boat
- Noah picture, tissue tube or craft stick
- Blackline 2-A
- Beginnings poster, Section 3

## Day 2 Materials

- White crayon, white paper
- Blue wash and sponge applicator
- *Noah* (book in Teacher Kit)
- Beginnings Student Book

## INTRODUCE

Put a boat in a pan of dirt (or sand). Look at the pan curiously and say, **Hmm, I wonder if this is right. The boat isn't floating. It just stays in one place. What do you think I should do to make the boat float?** (A boat needs to be in water before it can move.)

**This makes me think of Noah. He built a boat on dry land, where there was no water to float it. But he had faith because God had told him what to do. Let's hear his story.**

## DEVELOP

Take a picture of Noah (from a leaflet or book) or use a figure from the flannelgraph set in the Teacher Kit. Attach it with tape to a tissue tube or wooden craft stick to make a puppet. Use this dialogue between the reader and Noah.

**READER:** Hello, Noah. You have been working so hard for such a long time. Why did you decide to build this enormous boat?

**NOAH:** Well, this idea was a surprise to me! It wasn't something that I decided. One day I was doing my work when God talked to me! God told me to build a boat. So I did. God called the boat an ark.

**READER:** Why did you build the ark so large and with so many rooms?

**NOAH:** God told me to build it this way. So I did. He even told me what materials to use and how to build it. So I did what God told me to do. It took many years to build!

**READER:** Did God tell you why you were to build this ark?

**NOAH:** Yes. God told me that He was angry at the terrible things that the people were doing. They didn't believe in God or show kindness to each other. They were wicked. God said that He was going to put an end to the wickedness. But He promised He would take care of me and my family. I believed that God would keep His promise to me.

**READER:** Because of God's love, you trusted in Him. God gave you faith. What happened when you finally finished building the ark?

**NOAH:** It was most amazing! God sent pairs of animals from all over the world. They just walked right onto the ark. God told me to put food on the ark for my family and the animals, and I obeyed. Then God told me to take my wife and family and go on the ark. We did. God shut the door of the ark, and it started to rain. It rained and rained like I had never seen before.

**READER:** How long were you on the ark?

**NOAH:** About a year. You see, it rained for 40 days and 40 nights, covering even mountaintops. Then the ark floated until the water went down enough for it to rest on a mountain. It was still many more days before the land was dry enough for us to leave the ark.

**READER:** Were you ever afraid?

**NOAH:** Who wouldn't be? But through all that time, God kept His promise. We were safe inside the ark.

Stand and sing with motions "Rise and Shine" (*LOSP*, p. 66). Then say, **God loves us and takes care of us too. God can rescue us from danger, from evil, and from temptation. God sent His Son, Jesus, to save us, not from a flood, but from punishment for our sins. He rescues us through the forgiveness and eternal life He offers.**

## R E S P O N D

Display Section 3 of the Beginnings poster, along with the sections from last week. Note the placement: it should not be placed directly below the other two pictures. It should be below and to the left so that eventually a cross shape will be formed by the end of the unit. (See page 16 of the Student Book as a reference.) Say, **God was sad that the people forgot how much He loved them. But God's love continued. God saved His creation, rescuing it with the ark. God is sad when people do bad things today and sin. But God's love continues. He rescues us through the cross of Jesus.** Remind the children that everyone is sinful, even Noah. Also remind them that only God can take away our sins. Say, **We are God's children, so we can talk about our sins with God. Because Jesus took the punishment for our sins we can ask God to forgive us, knowing He will listen and forgive us.** Use Blackline 2-A to make a rainbow book. As the children work, talk about the enormous job Noah had. **How did he get the wood? cut the wood? put the pieces together? The Bible doesn't tell us how Noah did this, but we know God was there the whole time!**

## Make a Book

*Directions:*
1. *Print several copies of this page for each child.*
2. *On each page, have the child draw a picture of an animal God made and watches over.*
3. *On the last page, have the child draw pictures of people.*
4. *Cut out each ark picture.*
5. *Place the pictures on top of each other to make a book.*
6. *Staple the pictures together at the top.*

*Let each child show and read their story to the rest of the class.*

**God Watches Over**

## Worship Ideas

- Write the names of animals on slips of paper. Make sure there are two of each animal. Each student picks one slip and then finds a partner with the same animal. Children are to draw, color, and cut out pictures of their animals. Gather in a circle around a simple drawing of the ark. Invite each pair to place their pictures near the ark and encourage them to add their own prayer thoughts about how God cares for them.
- Sing praise with "Psalm 8," "My God Is So Great," or "He's Got the Whole World in His Hands" (*LOSP*, pp. 50, 64, 101, and on the CD). "The Butterfly Song" (*LOSP*, p. 72) and "Rise and Shine" (*LOSP*, p. 66) are action songs of praise.
- Imagine being inside the ark. What would you see, smell, hear, and touch? Thank God for loving and saving Noah. Thank God for loving and saving us.

## Bible Background

"The Lord is faithful to all His promises." This message is so important to our lives. Yet, daily we sin and go against God's plans for us. God calls us to repentance through His Word and promises to love and forgive us through Christ Jesus.

Emphasize God's love and care for Noah and his family. Clearly teach God's displeasure toward sin and His desire for grace and mercy for all people. Praise God for the salvation He gives us through Christ's cross and resurrection.

## Words to Remember

*The wages of sin is death, but the gift of God is eternal life in Christ Jesus our Lord.* Romans 6:23

- Use visuals to help children understand this verse. A paycheck stub represents the concept of earning and deserving wages. A wrapped gift shares the concept of freely giving out of love. The cross inside the gift is a reminder that Christ died to earn the gift of salvation for you and me and all people.

- Stoop down and cover your head with your arms. Chant in a whisper, *The wages of sin is death.* Jump up and say, *but the gift of God is eternal life.* Raise arms high and shout, *in Christ Jesus our Lord.*

## Extending the Lesson

- Use animal crackers to graph and compare *(more than, less than,* and *equal to),* count and add, pair up and count by twos. Estimate how many fit in one hand. Thank God for this fun activity and thank Him for the food. Enjoy the crackers.

- Push back the furniture or go to a gym area or outside to participate. Sing the following song to the tune "The Farmer in the Dell." Designate a Noah and have that child stand away from the rest of the class. As you sing each stanza of the song, have each child, in turn, name an animal and pantomime its action as he or she joins Noah in a line. Keep the line moving around the room until all the children are attached. (Allow animal types to be repeated.)

**Noah in the ark, Noah in the ark,
Oh, how the rain did flow, with Noah in the ark.**

**Noah took a [turtle]. Noah took a [turtle].
Oh, how the rain did flow, as Noah took a [turtle].**

# Day 2

## INTRODUCE

Print the word *faith* in large letters with a white crayon on each of six pieces of white paper. At the indicated time have a student paint a blue paint wash over the word with a sponge brush. Read together the word as it appears.

Say, **Faith in Jesus is knowing and believing that He died for your sins and gives you eternal life.**

Ask, **What does God make stronger as you hear His Word in church and school?** Paint and read.

Ask, **How do you know that God still cares for you even when you sin?** Paint and read.

Ask, **When we are afraid or sad, how do we know Jesus is still with us?** Paint and read.

Ask, **Why can we always celebrate God's goodness and praise Him for His love?** Paint and read.

Ask, **Why did Noah and his family build the ark and care for the animals?** Paint and read.

# The Flood

*(Genesis 6:9–8:14)*

Noah and his family loved and obeyed God. They knew that God loved them too. The people who lived near Noah were very wicked. They didn't love or obey God.

One day God told Noah, "I want you to build an ark." God told Noah how big to build the ark and what materials to use. Noah did as God said.

Noah's neighbors watched Noah and his sons build the ark. They laughed at Noah and called him crazy. But Noah trusted God.

When the ark was ready, God sent animals to Noah. They walked onto the ark. Noah, his wife, his three sons, and their wives got into the ark.

God shut the door. It rained and rained. The whole earth was covered with water. After 40 days the rain stopped. The sun came out. It took almost a year for the floodwaters to dry up.

After a year God told Noah and his family and the animals to come out of the ark. They knew that God would let them begin a new life on the earth.

God rescued Noah and his family from a terrible flood. God rescued us from sin. He sent Jesus to die on the cross for us. Now we are saved to be God's children. We tell others that God saves them too.

5

Say the words of the First Article of the Apostles' Creed together. **I believe in God, the Father Almighty, Maker of heaven and earth.** Ask, **How are we able to say and believe these words?** Paint and read.

**Because we live by faith, we thank and praise God. Let's sing together.** Sing "Father, I Adore You" (*LOSP*, p. 13, and on CD).

## DEVELOP

Gather the children around you in a semicircle and read the book *Noah* (in the Teacher Kit). Children may enjoy hearing this from several other versions such as the Arch Books.

Note: If you purchase the classroom set for the Hear Me Read Big Book *Drip Drop* (available from CPH), you will also receive a Teachers Guide pamphlet with additional ideas and activities for the story of Noah.

Ask the children, **What was the first thing Noah did when he left the ark? Did he …**

1. **count the animals?**
2. **build a new home?**
3. **get a suntan after being cooped up so long?**
4. **clean up the mess the animals left in the boat?**

The answer to all four ideas is *no*. Emphasize instead that the first thing Noah did was to praise and thank God.

## RESPOND

Together look at pages 5–6 in the *Beginnings* Student Book. On page 6, discuss the life situations pictured. Point out that in a world filled with sin, God rescued Noah and gave him a new and different life. We live in a sin-filled world too. God's love and forgiveness continue for us as they did for Noah. God rescues us through Jesus, forgiving us so that we can now live a new and different life as people of God, led by faith in Him, empowered by the Holy Spirit.

Note: Take a look at the Close of the Commandments (see the catechism section of the Teacher Resource Book). These words show us that God's anger about sin is indeed very serious. But praise the Lord that His love and mercy is also truly great—so great that He gave His only Son to save us (John 3:16), the ultimate sacrifice.

# God's Love
## Makes All Things New

*Directions: Draw arrows connecting pictures to remind us that the love of God in our hearts can change envy to goodness, hate to love, and unkindness to joy.*

**Envy**

**Joy**

**Hate**

**Goodness**

**Unkindness**

**Love**

Words to Remember

*The wages of sin is death, but the gift of God is eternal life in Christ Jesus our Lord.*

*Romans 6:23*

6

21

## Discovery Point

God loves all people. He shows His love and mercy through Jesus, who offers forgiveness and salvation. We respond to God's love in worship and praise.

## God's Promises to Noah

Genesis 8:15–9:3

## Objectives

That by the power of the Holy Spirit working through God's Word, the students will
- grow in their love for God, who faithfully keeps His Word and promises;
- trust that God is faithful to His promise to redeem us through our Savior, Jesus Christ;
- praise and thank God for all His goodness to them.

## Day 3 Materials

- Blackline 2-B
- Brown paper
- Gold or yellow pipe cleaners

## Day 4 Materials

- *Beginnings* Student Book
- Jake puppet
- Beginnings poster, Section 4

## INTRODUCE

Point out that the ark was a big floating box, one designed by God to save everyone and everything inside. Distribute Blackline 2-B and follow the directions to make a box. Next point out that God had an even greater plan—a plan to save the whole world. Have children make a small cross by twisting two gold or yellow chenille strips (pipe cleaners) together. Put the cross inside the box. **This wonderful gift is ours by faith in Christ Jesus, the promised Savior.** (You will use the boxes again later in the lesson.)

## DEVELOP

Use this action echo pantomime to review the story. The children will copy your actions and echo your words at the asterisk (*).

**God said,** *(Point up.)** **"Noah, Noah.** *(Hands cup mouth.)** **Build an ark."** *(Pretend to pick up wood.)** **Hammer, hammer.** *(Pretend to hammer.)** **"Gather the animals.** *(Stretch on toes with hand above eyes to look far away.)** **Come, come.** *(Use hands and arms to signal come.)**

**"Close the door!"** *(Hit desk.)** **Drip, drop.** *(Clap two times.)** **Down came the rain.** *(Fingers wiggle.)** **Pitter, patter.** *(Tap legs.)** **40 days and 40 nights.** *(Flash four sets of 10 fingers.)** **Rock, rock.** *(Rock side to side.)**

**Out came the sun.** *(Arms make overhead circle.)** **Shine, shine.** *(Spread fingers and push arms out to the side.)** **Down went the water.** *(Squat down.)** **Dry, dry.** *(Pat the floor.)**

**Then Noah came out.** *(Take a step forward and stretch out.)** **Out, out.** *(Add two steps.)** **To thank the Lord.** *(Fold hands, bow head.)** **Praise, praise.** *(Lift hands up.)**

**God said,** *(Point up.)** **"Never again."** *(Shake head no.)** **And into the sky He put a rainbow.** *(Make an arch with an arm.)** **Promises, promises.** *(Hug self.)**

Adapted from *Fingers Tell the Story*, © 1989 CPH.

# R E S P O N D

Briefly recall that as soon as Noah came out of the ark, he built an altar to the Lord to thank God for His protection and care. **Remember God kept His promise to Noah and his family. He saved them and the animals from the flood. They were safe inside the ark. God keeps His promise to us also. He kept His promise to send Jesus to take the punishment of our sin. Like Noah, we can thank and praise God for His love.** Have the children sit in a circle and have them, one child at a time, add the boxes they made earlier to build a small altar. Sing a song of praise to God. Then rearrange the boxes into the shape of a cross. Thank God for His greatest gift to us, a promise fulfilled in Christ Jesus, who offers forgiveness of our sins and eternal life with Him in heaven.

Conclude with the Lord's Prayer. Invite children to pray along silently, speaking aloud any of the words they know. Suggest that they especially listen for two parts of the prayer that speak of God's protection from temptation and evil. (You may want to explain those two words.) When you get to those sentences—the Sixth and Seventh Petitions—speak those words louder to emphasize them.

## Make a Box

*Directions:*
1. *Color the shape brown.*
2. *Cut out the shape and fold on the dotted lines.*
3. *Tape the edges of the box together.*
4. *Tuck in the lid.*

## Worship Ideas

- Ask the children to write a one-sentence prayer of thanks or praise to God for one thing that God has done for them or has given to them. Place on the classroom altar or in the boxes made from the blackline activity.
- Open your Bible and read Mark 10:45. Give God a praise cheer! **Repeat the letters as they are called out. Give me a P! (P!) Give me an R. (R!)** … Continue until you have spelled the word *promise.* **What does it spell! (Promise!) Who always keeps His promises? (God!) Who is the best promise of all? (Jesus!)**
- Sing a song of joy and praise such as "If You Feel Happy" or "I Have the Joy" (*LOSP*, pp. 60, 62, and on the Voyages CD).
- Listen to the stanza of the song "Promises" that tells the story of Noah and the flood. Learn the refrain, which reminds us of the great promises of God. This song is in *Songs Kids Love to Sing,* (p. 46) and on the accompanying CD, available from CPH.
- If there is a movable altar in the classroom, ask several children to help you move it to the center of the room. Arrange the room around the altar for the day. During the day the children can pause and quietly say a short prayer.

## Bible Background

After the flood, even though the ark rested on dry land, Noah trusted in God and waited to leave the ark until he had word from the Lord. Then God said to Noah, "Come out of the ark." By faith, Noah's first action was to respond to God in thanks and praise. Noah built an altar and made sacrifices to God. Just as Noah praised and gave thanks to God for His promise of deliverance from the flood, so we worship God for delivering us through Christ, who promises forgiveness of sin and eternal life. God will keep this promise and all His promises to His children, including you and me.

## Words to Remember

*The LORD is faithful to all His promises.*
*Psalm 145:13*

- Write the memory verse on the shape of a rainbow. Lightly color the bands. Have the children touch the words as they read the verse aloud.
- Sometimes when you shake hands with someone you are giving your word on something. That is a sign that you will be faithful to what you say. Have the students shake hands and say the memory verse to each other, reminding one another of the faithfulness of God. You have His word on it!

## Extending the Lesson

- Study rain and rainbows. Keep track of the weather this week. Chart it on a bulletin board or poster.
- Make a promise bag and fill it with pieces of rainbow-colored yarn or ribbons. Let the children wear clusters of these ribbons as a remembrance of God's promises to them.
- On a large raindrop shape have children draw a picture of what they would see if they were raindrops falling to the ground.
- Make praise poms using 12-inch lengths of rainbow colors of tissue or crepe paper. Have small groups work together to measure and cut the colors. Another group collects one of each color, and another group twists one end and holds the pom for the last group to tape together with masking tape. Shake the poms to the beat as you sing songs of praise.
- Make color wheels, first using the primary colors, then mixing the secondary colors. Note that this shows the colors of the rainbow. Use paint to make an individual or a group rainbow.

## INTRODUCE

Hold up the puppet each time Jake speaks in this dialogue.

**TEACHER:** Jake, I'm glad to see you this morning.

**JAKE:** *(looking away)* Humph!

**TEACHER:** *(surprised)* That was quite rude. What's wrong with you today?

**JAKE:** What's wrong with me? I'm angry! That's what's wrong with me. I'm really angry. It just isn't fair! Yesterday you promised that I could play with the soccer ball. And I never got to play with it once. You didn't keep your promise. How can I ever trust you again?

**TEACHER:** Jake, didn't it rain during recess yesterday? You couldn't have played with the soccer ball anyway. The rain kept me from keeping my promise.

**JAKE:** It seems like everybody has an excuse for not keeping promises.

# God's Promises to Noah

*(Genesis 18:15–9:13)*

The first thing Noah and his family did when they left the ark was thank God. Noah built an altar to God. Noah and his family knelt before the altar. They praised and thanked God for taking care of them. They knew that God loved them very much.

Noah and his family saw beautiful colors in the sky. God told them, "I have set My rainbow in the sky. Whenever you see the rainbow, remember Me. It is a sign of My love for you. Never again will water cover the earth. Remember My promises of love."

God always keeps His promises. And Jesus is the best promise of all. Because of Jesus we are now children of God who have forgiveness and eternal life.

**TEACHER:** You're right, Jake. Sometimes things do happen that keep us from keeping a promise. Sometimes people just forget. Sometimes people just don't want to keep a promise they have made. People are weak and sinful and live in a world that is not perfect. I'm really sorry that I couldn't keep my promise to you, Jake. Will you forgive me?

**JAKE:** Sure, I'll forgive you. Are you angry with me?

**TEACHER:** No, and I forgive you for being so angry at me. I'm so glad that we both know about Jesus, who forgives us and leads us to be forgiving. We can be happy, knowing that nothing can stop God from keeping His promises. (Read aloud Romans 8:38–39.)

## DEVELOP

Display Section 4 of the Beginnings poster. Point out that we all know the story of Noah and the flood. But the ending of the story is especially important. At the end we see that

1. God's promise is fulfilled as the earth has a new start;
2. Noah and his family give thanks to God;
3. God gives them a special sign and promise.

Review the ending of the story (animals and people leave the ark, Noah and his family worship God, God gives a promise and a rainbow) by drawing simple sketches on the chalkboard or displaying a purchased "Noah and the Ark" figurine set. Rather than retelling the story, ask the children questions so that they are retelling it. Focus on Noah's faith and God's faithfulness to His promises.

Then point out that the Bible compares this story to our Baptism. (See 1 Peter 3:20–23.) In the waters of Baptism these things happen:

1. God gives us the promise of salvation as He gives our lives a new start as His very own children.

2. We have the promise of forgiveness and eternal life through Jesus and His death on the cross.

We praise and thank God for the blessings we have in Baptism through Jesus.

## RESPOND

Direct the children to *Beginnings,* pages 7–8. Emphasize that God did not forget Noah. He remembered Noah's faithfulness and saved him and his family in the ark. God did not forget them during the year they floated on the waters. God remembered at the right time to call Noah from the ark onto dry land. Color in any unfinished sections of the rainbow.

God also does not forget us. He remembered to save us through Jesus Christ. He remembers each day to care for us and be with us. Ask the children to think of something they remember about God. Draw a picture of it in the blank space on the ark. Share ideas with one another after completing the drawings.

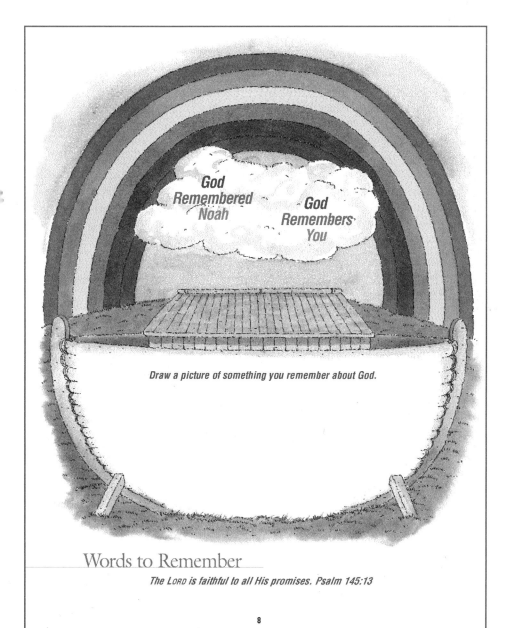

*God Remembered Noah*

*God Remembers You*

*Draw a picture of something you remember about God.*

Words to Remember

*The LORD is faithful to all His promises. Psalm 145:13*

## Discovery Point

God keeps His promises to His people. He promises to be with us always, to bless us, and to forgive our sins through Jesus.

## God Blesses Abraham

Genesis 12:1–9; 13:14–18; 15:4–6; 22:17

## Objectives

That by the power of the Holy Spirit working through God's Word, the students will

- be assured that God's promises are certain;
- rejoice that God promises to be with them always;
- share the joy of Jesus, our promised Savior, with others.

## Day 1 Materials

- Bible story figures (Teacher Resource Book)
- Road map and blank paper folded like a map
- Blackline 3-A

## Day 2 Materials

- *Beginnings* Student Book
- Suitcase or bag with beach items
- Jake and Jenna puppets
- Small colorful stickers
- Beginnings poster, Section 5

# Day 1

# INTRODUCE

Open a large road map and look for a specific destination. Say, **I'm looking for the best way to get to** [name specific area]. **Here it is!** (Mark the spot.) **That's where I'm going.** Ask about different places the children have been and how they got there.

Open the blank map. Say, **Here is another map. If you had this map could you tell where to go? One man received directions much like this map. He was told to go. But he wasn't told where to go or how to get there.**

# DEVELOP

Put the blank map on the floor. Have helpers put the Bible story figures on the map. (Use either the figures from the Supplemental Ideas Section of the Teacher Resource Book or use flannelgraph figures from the Teacher Kit.) Tell the Bible story, using words such as the following.

God chose and loved Abraham. And Abraham trusted and loved God. God told Abraham to pack up his family and everything he owned and move to a faraway land. God said, "I will show you where to go, and I promise to take care of you." God helped Abraham to trust in Him and gave Abraham faith to believe God's promise. So, Abraham, his family, and his many helpers, along with all his animals, started out. They didn't know where to go or how to get there or how long it would take. But there was one thing Abraham did know. God loved him.

God made wonderful promises to Abraham. He said, "I promise to make your name great, and you will be a great nation." Abraham wondered how, but Abraham trusted God to keep the promise. God said, "I promise that you will be a blessing to many people. All people on earth will be blessed through you." Abraham wondered how, but Abraham trusted God to keep the promise. God was saying that the Savior would someday be born into Abraham's family. This promise is also for you and me and all people. Jesus, God's Son, came to earth and died on the cross and rose from the dead at Easter. Jesus gives us the blessings of forgiveness and eternal life .

It was a long time before Abraham arrived at the beautiful land God had promised. God told Abraham, "All the land you see will be yours." Abraham thanked God for bringing him safely to this new home.

God said to Abraham, "I promise that your family will number as many as the stars in the sky." God also said, "Your children [grandchildren, great-grandchildren] will be as many as the grains of sand at the seashore." Abraham wondered how, because he and Sarah had no children. But he was certain that God would keep His word. God's promises are true.

# R E S P O N D

Sometimes people make special promises to us. We especially look forward to those. **On the chalkboard draw something you were promised, like an ice-cream cone.** Draw the cone on the board and invite the children to draw promises made to them. **The problem with people's promises is that people don't always keep their promises. Also, some promises don't last very long.** Erase promises that are in this category. Candy gets eaten; toys get broken; things wear out or are used up or lost. Talk about the difference between people's promises and God's promises.

Have the children color Blackline 3-A, cut out the three shapes, punch holes, and tie one symbol below the other with colorful pieces of yarn to make a mobile. On the back of the rainbow print *Noah.* On the back of the star print *Abraham.* Print your own name on the back of the cross. Talk about God's promise that relates to each symbol, emphasizing the greatness and certainty of the promise of salvation through Jesus.

# Worship Ideas

- Use various colors of play dough as symbols: gray (for worries, problems, sin); red (hearts, love, forgiveness); and yellow (new things, sunny new day, new life that Jesus gives us). Point out that faith in Jesus affects the way we now live. Say, **I live as a child of God because I have Jesus' love in my heart** (display red play dough) **and because Jesus gets rid of my sins** (discard gray) **and makes me a new and changed person** (display yellow). **I am forgiven and thankful and joyful!** Mix the red and yellow to make a third color (orange) for joy.
- Sing a song of joy and happiness such as "Rejoice in the Lord Always" (*LOSP,* p. 52, and on CD).
- Use a bell (*) to signal the response "Help us trust You, Jesus." Ring the bell two times for the Amen. Pray, **Lord, You always keep Your promises. * You have promised to love us always. * You have promised to be with us always. * You have promised to bless us. * We thank You, and we love You. * We trust You because of Your love for us. * Amen. * ***

# Bible Background

As you teach the story of Abraham's call, keep the emphasis on God's plan of salvation for all people. The story of Abraham is also our story. We find that God deals with us in the same way He dealt with Abraham—on the basis of faith. This faith is not something we have accomplished. It is a gift from God. Abraham did not choose God; God chose Abraham. Faith is the gift of a gracious God, working in us to bring about our salvation through Jesus, His Son.

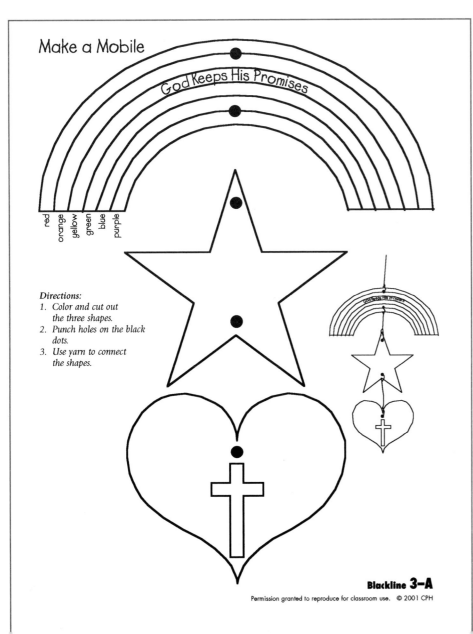

Make a Mobile

God Keeps His Promises

red orange yellow green blue purple

*Directions:*
1. Color and cut out the three shapes.
2. Punch holes on the black dots.
3. Use yarn to connect the shapes.

**Blackline 3-A**

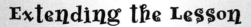
## Words to Remember

*Trust in the LORD with all your heart.*
Proverbs 3:5

- Use crayon to write the Bible verse on a piece of sandpaper. Draw star shapes around the words.
- Say the verse together several times. Stand in a circle for a beanbag toss. The person who catches the bag says the verse, then tosses the beanbag to a new person. Circulate the beanbag until everyone has had a turn.

## Extending the Lesson

- Have the children take turns drawing an aerial view of the classroom to make a map on the chalkboard. **Pretend you are in the middle of the ceiling. Look down and draw what you see in the center of the map. Add doors, windows, the altar, desks, and any other pieces. God is with us here and everywhere.**
- Use a compass to find and label the north, east, south, and west walls in the classroom. **Our God created the north, east, south, and west. God gives us faith to trust Him wherever we go.**
- Make large stars. On one side, decorate with bits of foil, shiny paper, and glitter glue. On the other side print today's Bible verse in glue, then sprinkle with sand mixed with glitter. Recall that God made a promise to Abraham that his descendants would number more than the stars in the sky and grains of sand at the beach. (See Galatians 3:7.)

# Day 2

## INTRODUCE

Hold up a suitcase or bag in which you have packed a number of beach items (beach towel, sun visor, suntan lotion, bucket and shovel, swimsuit, sandals). Tell the children you are going on a trip. See if they can guess where you are going. Ask how your trip would be different than Abraham's. (You know where you are going, what to pack, and how to get there.) Recall how the trip would be the same. (You are with other people and God is with you.)

## DEVELOP

Display Section 5 of the Beginnings poster. (Note: Retain the previous pictures posted. The display will eventually form the shape of a cross, reminding us that the grace of God in Christ was present from the beginning and extends to eternity.)

Review the Bible story using the *Beginnings* Student Book, page 9. Then draw three large squares on the chalkboard and say, **The**

# God
## Blesses Abraham

*(Genesis 12:1–9; 13:14–18; 15:4–6; 22:17)*

Abraham and his wife, Sarah, lived in a faraway land. One day God said to Abraham, "Pack up all your things. I want you to move to a new land. It will be a wonderful place to live." Abraham did not know where they were going. But he trusted God to take care of him.

As Abraham looked at the sky, God said, "I will make you a great nation. The number in your family will be as many as the grains of sand at the seashore and the stars in the sky."

God gave Abraham this special promise, "I will bless all people on earth through you." God meant that someday Jesus would be born into Abraham's family. Jesus would die for the sins of all people.

Finally Abraham and Sarah arrived in the new land. It was just as beautiful as God had promised. Abraham knew that God always did what was best for him. He knew God would always be with him.

We can trust that God will always do what is best for us. He will be with us wherever we are. He has blessed us and all people through Jesus, our Savior.

9

story of Abraham makes me think of the word *promise.* (Write *promise* above the squares.) **It makes me think of** *trust.* (Write *trust* below the squares.) **God promised to take Abraham to a new homeland, but He didn't say where they were going. Abraham trusted God's Word.** (Draw hills, grass, and trees in the first box.) **God promised that there would be as many people in Abraham's family as there were stars in the sky and grains of sand at the seashore. Abraham trusted God's Word.** (Draw stars and dots for sand in the middle box.) **The next promise God made to Abraham was also to you and me. God promised that all people on earth would be blessed through Abraham's family. God kept His promise when He sent Jesus to take away our sins.** (Draw a cross in the last box.) **God's love and faithfulness lead us to trust His promises.**

## R E S P O N D

Jenna and Jake will help the children know that God is with us all the time, and He helps us to trust Him. You can hold up the puppet that is "speaking" or have two children manipulate the puppets as you read the script.

**JAKE:** *(excitedly)* Hi, Jenna! Hi, Teacher! Hi, kids! I'm so happy today.

**TEACHER:** Jake, you do sound happy. Did something special happen to make you so happy?

**JAKE:** I'll say! Yesterday I got lost. I was with Mom and my big sister at the mall.

**TEACHER:** That doesn't sound like fun. Why did that make you happy?

**JAKE:** At first I was really scared, and I didn't like it at all! But then I saw my sister! Wow! Was I happy! I'm still happy!

**TEACHER:** Sometimes we do worry and get scared, especially when we don't know what will happen next. What about you, Jenna? Did you ever feel that way?

**JENNA:** *(nodding her head)* Remember my first day at school? I was so afraid. I stood by the globe and worried that I wouldn't have any friends.

**JAKE:** I remember that. But I was your friend, and I helped you.

**JENNA:** Yes, you did, Jake. And you are still my friend.

**TEACHER:** God was with you yesterday, Jake, even when you were lost. And God was with you, Jenna, when you worried. Boys and girls, have you ever felt this way? *(Response time.)*

**JENNA:** Teacher, the story about God and Abraham will help me remember that God is always with me.

**JAKE:** Me too.

Give everyone small colorful stickers to put on their arms, shirts, or shoes to remember the joy we have in Jesus. **The stickers you wear on the outside will remind you of the joy you have on the inside because you have the love of Jesus in your hearts! He is always with you wherever you go.** Sing the familiar song "I Have the Joy" (*LOSP,* p. 62, and on CD).

Refer to the pictures on page 10 of *Beginnings.* Talk about the different yet familiar places. Model a story using the pictures. Partner the children to make their own stories from the situations on page 10. Create a map by drawing a line from the entrance opening of one place to another as they share their ideas. Remind the children that God is with them in all these places. They may add a new chapter to the story in the empty box. Thank God for being with us wherever we go and in whatever we do.

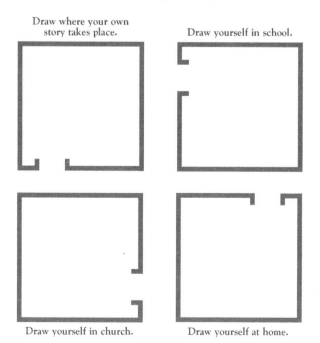

A
Map Story by _____

*As you complete the pictures and share your story, draw a line from place to place. Who is always with you wherever you go? Can you find the cross? Remember, God led Abraham to a promised land. Through Jesus' death and resurrection we have a promised place in heaven.*

Draw where your own story takes place.

Draw yourself in school.

Draw yourself in church.

Draw yourself at home.

Words to Remember

*Trust in the LORD with all your heart. Proverbs 3:5*

## Discovery Point

God keeps His promises to His people. He promises to be with us always, to bless us, and to forgive our sins through Jesus.

## Abraham and Sarah Have a Son

Genesis 17:17; 18:1–15; 21:1–8

## Objectives

That by the power of the Holy Spirit working through God's Word, the students will

- grow in their joy in the Lord because of His many blessings, especially the blessings of family;
- know that God takes away the sadness of sin and gives them gladness in Christ;
- share the happiness God gives them with their families and friends.

## Day 3 Materials

- Grapes, cheese, crackers
- Jake and Jenna puppets
- Blackline 3-B

## Day 4 Materials

- 8 sheets of paper
- *Beginnings* Student Book
- Costumes and props
- Beginnings poster, Section 6

## INTRODUCE

Have the children think about something that they really wanted but had to wait for. Discuss how they felt as they waited. **God made a special promise to Abraham. Abraham had to wait 25 years. But God kept His word.**

## DEVELOP

Gather the children around you, seated on the floor (perhaps even seated on a blanket). In your own words, tell the story of Abraham and the three visitors. When you talk about the feast Abraham had prepared for his visitors, pass around platters of grapes, cheese, and crackers or other food that would have been eaten in biblical times.

Continue with the story and conclude with the celebration feast that was held to thank God for Isaac when he was about a year old. Again pass around the food in celebration as you remember that God kept His promise to Abraham and Sarah when they had a baby boy. God also kept His promise when, hundreds of years later, He sent another very special baby boy. This baby was named Jesus. Jesus came to be our Savior so that we can live as God's children and someday go to heaven. Jesus was the blessing for the whole world that came from Abraham's family!

# RESPOND

Children come from many different family situations. Build on the blessings God gives to each child. Talk about God's desire for happiness in families. Recall the words of Joshua 24:15, "As for me and my household, we will serve the LORD." God wants our families to be happy, but that doesn't always happen. Because all people—including kids and adults—sin, we all have sadness and troubles. Discuss a few of the things that can go wrong in a family (e.g., arguments, hurting others through actions or words, getting hurt feelings). Point out that the Sixth Commandment (as well as the Fourth) shows God's will for families. Read the explanation of the Sixth Commandment from the catechism. Point out that the commandment shows God's will that husbands and wives love and honor each other. But it also includes showing respect between men and women and boys and girls in all things.

Remind the students that God wants to help us. He loves our families. He will forgive us for Jesus' sake. He will help us live as His children. Blackline 3-B provides a follow-up activity for families. Provide enough copies so that children have one for each person in the family, including themselves. Read these words from Philippians 2:15–16, "Shine like stars in the universe as you hold out the word of life."

## Worship Ideas

- Write *Abraham* vertically. Point out that God used Abraham's family as part of His plan for our redemption. You can use the word *Abraham* to share concepts about God's grace. After the **A** write **Always** and use the word in a sentence such as **God always forgives us.** Continue with the words **Blesses, Remembers, Answers, Helps, Acts,** and **Makes.** (These sentences can be used to accompany the words: God blesses us each day; God remembers His promises; He answers our prayers; He helps and protects us; He acts with loving-kindness; and He makes us His own through Jesus.)
- Recall that God said Abraham would have a great family and that the Savior would come from his family. Open your Bible to Matthew 1 and share parts of the long list of the people in Abraham's family. Share the list from a large-print Bible if possible. (Check with your church office to see if one is available.)

## Bible Background

"The Lord did what He had promised." Abraham learned not only to trust in God's promises but also to trust that God would fulfill His promise in His way and time. The birth of Isaac is evidence of God's faithfulness. It also presents the next step in God's gracious plan, which we see as we trace the family line from Abraham to Isaac and Jacob and Judah, through David, and eventually to Jesus. Jesus was from Abraham's family line, a Son of David, and most important, He truly is the Son of God!

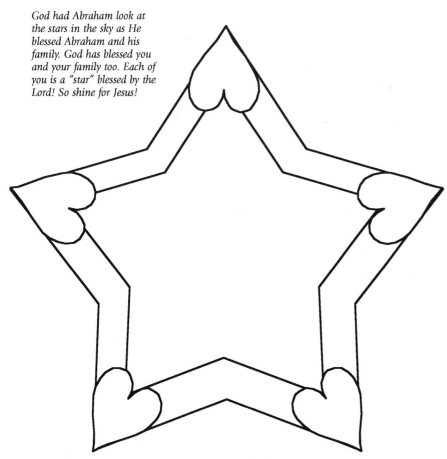

*God had Abraham look at the stars in the sky as He blessed Abraham and his family. God has blessed you and your family too. Each of you is a "star" blessed by the Lord! So shine for Jesus!*

*Directions:*
1. *Make a star frame for each family member.*
2. *Color the hearts.*
3. *Cut out the star.*
4. *Tape a photo of each family member inside each star (or draw a picture or write his or her name).*
5. *Display the stars above a doorway in your home.*
6. *Remember how God has blessed each of you.*

## Words to Remember

*Rejoice in the LORD and be glad. Psalm 32:11*

- Write each word of the memory verse on a large star shape. Shuffle and then hand the stars to eight children. Make sure the children hear the word on each star. Then let the class rearrange the words in correct order. Let everyone have a turn to be a "star."
- Practice the Bible verse, singing it to the tune of the refrain "B-I-N-G-O."

**Re-joice in the Lord,**
**Re-joice in the Lord,**
**Re-joice in the Lord,**
**Rejoice … and be glad! Yeah!**

## Extending the Lesson

- Names are important to God. God tells Abraham, "I will make your name great" (Genesis 12:2). Isaac means "he laughs." Jesus means "He will save His people from their sins." Bring in a name book and let the children find and record the meaning of their names.
- Use magazines, scissors, paper, and glue to make a "God Blesses Families" collage. This project can be done by individuals or by groups.
- Create a "star center." Provide books on creation and stars. Make star pictures. Copy constellations onto dark blue paper and add star stickers. Find a story about one constellation and have the class design a biblical constellation.

# Day

## INTRODUCE

Write each letter of the word *promises* on a separate sheet of paper. Scramble the order of the letters and place some of the letters upside down and sideways. Ask the class what is wrong with this word. (Allow response.) Read Hebrews 11:11. Say, **Abraham knew that God was faithful to keep His promises.** Put the letters of the scrambled word in order and say, **This word says *promises*. We never have to wonder about God's promises. God's promises are never scrambled up. We don't have to try to figure them out. He tells us about each promise in His Word, the Bible. God promises to love us, to forgive us, and to be with us always. His promises are very clear.**

# Abraham and Sarah Have a Son

*(Genesis 17:17; 18:1–15; 21:1–8)*

**Abraham** was almost 100 years old, and his wife, **Sarah,** was 90. They did not have any children. **God** had promised that they would have a family. **Abraham** trusted **God**'s word. **Abraham laughed** to think that people as old as he and **Sarah** could have a **baby.**

One day **Abraham** sat by his **tent. Three men** walked toward him. (It was really **God** and two angels.) **Abraham** said to them, "Rest under these trees. I will bring you food."

**Abraham** served the **three men.** They asked where his wife, **Sarah,** was. **Abraham** answered, "She is in the **tent.**"

**God** said, "When I come again next year, **Sarah** will have a son."

**Sarah** was listening at the **tent** door. **Sarah laughed.** She thought, I am too old to have a **baby.**

**God** knew that **Sarah laughed.** He asked, "Is anything too hard for **God?**"

About a year later **God**'s promise came true. **Abraham** and **Sarah** had a **baby** boy. They named him Isaac, which means "he **laughs**." **Sarah** said, "Now I will **laugh** because **God** made me happy." The servants and friends danced and clapped for joy. **God** had kept His promise.

**Abraham** and **Sarah** knew that **God** would also keep His promise to send a Savior for all people. **God** sent Jesus to die on the cross for your sins. **God** loves you.

11

## DEVELOP

Read the Bible story from Beginnings, page 11, with actors playing key roles. Designate and dress a child as Abraham, Sarah, three men, two to six tent holders, two sign holders, and a person to hold up a doll (Isaac). As you read the story, each person will step forward when their character's name or part is read. Use towels, sheets, and material scraps to costume the children. The tent holders can hold up a bedsheet or large towel. Write the words *God* and *laugh* on posters for the sign holders. The key words in the story are in bold type.

## RESPOND

Add Section 6 of the Beginnings poster to your display of this unit's pictures. Ask, **Did you notice how often we said the word *laugh* in this story? This reminds me that God wants us to be happy in Him. Our Bible verse today says, "Rejoice in the LORD and be glad." But often we are sad and have problems. Sin brings sadness into our world and into our hearts. What did God do to change our sadness into gladness?** (He sent Jesus to take away our sins. We are happy that we are forgiven.) **God helps us to live happier lives by living for Him.** Sing "Happy All the Time" (*LOSP*, p. 59, and on CD) as a response to God's love.

Discuss page 12 of *Beginnings*. You may very well have children in difficult home situations who do not feel their families are a blessing. In a general way, point out that even when we have troubles, God can use us to be a blessing to others in our family. The bottom portion of the page provides the comfort of knowing that God extends our "family" to include people in our school, church, and neighborhood to make an extended family that can help us and guide us.

# God Blesses Us
## with Families

*Directions: Draw your family. Include yourself in the picture.*

### Dear Lord, Bless My Family!

*God gives us many people who help us besides our immediate family. We could say we have a school family and a church family too. In what ways might God use these people to bless your life?*

_____

_____

_____

Words to Remember

*Rejoice in the LORD and be glad. Psalm 32:11*

## Discovery Point

God has a plan for the good of His people. He sometimes works through family and other individuals to carry out His will.

## The Birth of Moses

Exodus 2:1–10

## Objectives

That by the power of the Holy Spirit working through God's Word, the students will
- know that God has a plan for their salvation through Christ Jesus;
- rejoice that God has plans for good in the lives of His people;
- grow in goodness and a desire to love and serve others out of their love for and faith in the Savior and Redeemer, Jesus Christ.

## Day 1 Materials
- Baby doll in basket
- Simple Miriam costume
- Beginnings poster, Section 7

## Day 2 Materials
- Jenna puppet
- Alarm clock
- Rhythm instruments
- *Beginnings* Student Book

## INTRODUCE

Before class, hide a baby doll in a basket in the classroom. Allow the students to find the baby. After the baby is found discuss if it would be easier or harder to hide a real baby? Why? (The real baby might move around, cry, need to be fed.) Explain that Miriam was the sister of a real baby, who was put in a real basket that was hidden in a real river. Say that Miriam will share the wonderful story of God's care for her family and her baby brother. Dress as Miriam or arrange for an older student or volunteer to play the role. If you have a guest, provide a script in advance.

## DEVELOP

My name is Miriam. Long ago my people, the Israelites, moved to Egypt because there was no food in our land. That was part of God's plan for His people. At first we were welcomed by Pharaoh (the king). God blessed us. We lived well, and our families grew. Soon there were many people of Israel living in Egypt. After a new man became ruler, things changed. He was afraid because there were too many of us. He made my people work very hard as slaves. He made a law that all of our boy babies must be thrown into the river to die. (The king was especially afraid of the boys growing up and fighting his army.)

When we heard Pharaoh's law, we were afraid. Our family had a new baby boy! Mother hid him in our house until he grew too big and cried too loud. We just couldn't hide him at home anymore.

Then God gave Mom a good idea! She made a basket and painted it with tar to make it waterproof. It was just the right size for my brother. We walked down to the river. It was so hard for Mother to watch the baby float away. I hid in the river grass to keep watch. No one could see me, but I could see the basket.

The plan seemed to be going well until Pharaoh's daughter came to the river. When she heard crying and saw the basket, I held my breath. The princess opened the basket and saw my brother. Then God made a wonderful thing happen. Even though the princess knew the law and that the baby was an Israelite, she still wanted to keep the baby as her very own.

God helped me be brave and go to the princess. God helped me ask if she needed someone to care for the baby. "Yes, go," said the princess.

I brought my own mother to the princess. She told my mom to care for the baby until he was old enough to live at the palace. The princess named my brother Moses. Not only did God save my baby brother, but also we were able to keep him with our family for several more years. God had a plan for Moses, but we didn't know that until Moses was all grown up.

## RESPOND

Point out God's plan: He chose Moses to lead the Israelites to the Promised Land. Say, **God has a plan for each of you too. One way God helps you is through special people who love you, teach you, and help you.** Talk about who these people could be.

Discuss God's greatest plan to save us. Instead of a baby in a basket, God sent a baby in a manger. **It was God's plan that Jesus die on the cross to forgive all our sins. When Jesus rose from the dead He completed God's plan for us. We are forgiven now, and someday we will live in heaven! What a wonderful plan God has for us.** Add the Beginnings poster, Section 7, to your bulletin board display, emphasizing the cross that is beginning to take shape. Note that the love of Jesus—past, present, and future—is unchanging.

# Worship Ideas

- The princess named the baby *Moses* because she "drew him out of the water." Sing these words to the tune "Here We Go 'Round the Mulberry Bush." Then have the class make up other verses.

**How did Moses get his name, get his name, get his name?**
**How did Moses get his name? Tell me how it happened.**

**From the water, where he came, where he came, where he came.**
**From the water where he came, when the princess found him.**

**Praise the Lord for all His care, all His care, all His care.**
**Praise the Lord for all His care, for Moses, you, and me.**

- God's plans for us are always for our good. They are never for evil or harm. Talk about the plans God has already shown you by looking at the blessings the children have now. Discuss what plans God might have for them in the future. Mention the possibility of vocations in the church.

# Bible Background

The family of Israel was greeted in Egypt with a warm welcome because at that time Joseph was a ruler in Egypt. The Israelites prospered, and they grew from a clan of about 70 into a nation of more than two million. As the Israelite nation grew, so did the fear of the Egyptians. A new pharaoh enslaved them to keep them under his control.

God had a gracious plan of deliverance for His people. A baby boy is born, and by an act of faith, his parents defy Pharaoh's order. They prepare a basket to hide the baby in the water along the riverbank.

The baby is discovered and adopted by Pharaoh's daughter. This remarkable event is another part of God's plan. Moses grows up knowing the ways of the Egyptians, and yet his own Hebrew mother is his caregiver. God's presence makes what seems impossible become possible.

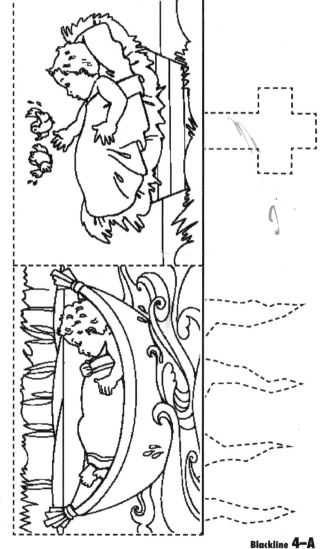

Directions:
1. Color the picture.
2. Cut on the dotted lines.
3. Color the cross yellow on the front and the back.
4. Fold the sections up over part of the picture.
5. Remember that God sent baby Jesus to be our Savior. He protects us from the power of sin and Satan. This is God's plan for you!

Directions:
1. Color the picture.
2. Cut on the dotted lines.
3. Color the cut-out sections green on the front and back.
4. Fold the sections up over part of the picture.
5. Remember that God protected baby Moses as he floated in the basket in the river, with weeds and reeds all around. God had a plan for him.

**Blackline 4-A**

## Day 2

## Words to Remember

*"I know the plans I have for you,"* declares the LORD. Jeremiah 29:11

- Write the Bible words and the reference on separate index cards. Before class tape the 12 cards under 12 chairs. Direct the class to find the 12 cards, then arrange them in order. Have each child make a copy of the verse to keep on their desks.
- Make another set of 12 cards with a different color of print or paper. Mix the two sets of cards and place them upside down in a pile. Form two teams and assign one set of cards (by color) to each team. Make up a relay game that suits your classroom situation. The first team to have all their cards and put them in order gets a cheer. The second team gets one too!
- Have each student complete Blackline 4-A.

## Extending the Lesson

- Take two small baskets. Coat one on the inside and outside with a water-resistant clay. Early in the day put both baskets in a container of water. Check periodically to see which one sinks and which one floats.
- Place several baby items such as a rattle, bib, squeeze toy, small stuffed animal, bottle, pacifier, clean disposable diaper, baby T-shirt, and baby-food jar in a cloth bag or box that has an opening only large enough for a child's hand to fit through. Have students identify as many items as possible by touch alone.
- Use a globe to find Egypt and the Nile River.

## INTRODUCE

Display an alarm clock and bring out the puppet Jenna.

**TEACHER:** Here is the clock you wanted me to bring, Jenna. We are all very curious. Why do you need this?

**JENNA:** *(almost in tears)* I … I don't need it anymore.

**TEACHER:** Why not?

**JENNA:** I was going to get a new puppy. We read that the ticking sound of the clock would help the puppy feel safe because it sounds like the mother dog's heartbeat.

**TEACHER:** What happened, Jenna?

**JENNA:** We found out that dogs and cats aren't allowed in our apartment building.

**TEACHER:** Oh, I'm so sorry, Jenna. You were really looking forward to a new puppy.

**JENNA:** I had such good plans. Now they're all messed up.

## The Birth of Moses

*(Exodus 2:1–10)*

The people of Israel were slaves in Egypt. They had to work hard. But God protected His people. He made them strong.

The king Pharaoh said, "These slaves are too strong. There are too many of them. They might try to rule our land." So Pharaoh said, "Throw all their boy babies into the river."

One family hid their baby boy in their house. Soon the baby got too big and noisy. So the mother put the baby into a basket and set it in tall grass in the river. The baby's sister, Miriam, hid nearby to watch.

Pharaoh's daughter came to the river. She saw the basket. She said to a servant, "Bring that basket to me." The princess saw the baby. She said, "I want this baby to be my son. I will name him Moses."

Miriam ran to the princess and asked, "Do you need help?"

"Yes," the princess said.

Miriam ran home and brought her own mother. The princess said, "Please take care of this baby. When he is older, bring him to me."

God had plans for Moses. God has plans for you too. He helps you grow in faith and to do kind things for others. He loves you and sent Jesus to be your Savior.

13

**TEACHER:** It is hard when plans change. But I know someone whose plans are always good. God wants only good things for you. That's why He sent Jesus to be your Savior.

**JENNA:** *(gives big sigh)* I'm sure glad to know that God's love for me doesn't change.

**TEACHER:** Let's hear about the good plans God had for baby Moses.

## DEVELOP

Provide rhythm instruments for sound effects for the Bible story. Use sand blocks or hands gently rubbed together to sound like the rustling river grasses. Tambourines, a rain stick, or a container of slowly poured water can be used for the sound of the water trickling over the rocks. Assign a sound for each of these characters: Miriam ("Shhh"), Mother (hum a lullaby line), princess (a royal "Ta da!"), and the baby ("Waa, waa"). Use *Beginnings*, page 13, to tell the story.

## RESPOND

Point out that Pharaoh's plan for baby Hebrew boys was evil. In the Fifth Commandment, God says that we should not kill. In fact, God does not want us to hurt or harm people in any way. Breaking the Fifth Commandment is sin.

When people sinned and messed up God's plan for a perfect world, God planned a Savior. Jesus was born and died for our sins and was raised from the dead at Easter. Through faith in Jesus we are forgiven, and the Holy Spirit works in us to live as children of God. With God's help, we honor the Fifth Commandment by helping and protecting others from harm (as Miriam did for her baby brother). Read the explanation of the Fifth Commandment from the catechism (see the Teacher Resource Book).

Direct the children's attention to *Beginnings*, page 14. Explain that this is a page from a weekly planning calendar like many grown-ups use. Start with whatever day of the week it is and follow the instructions. For a week refer back to this page at the beginning of each day. Remind the children, **God has plans for you. He helps you live as His child. God helps you grow in faith. With God's power, we serve others when we do loving things for each other.**

---

# These Plans Belong
## to God and _____

**Sunday**   Date: _____

*Remember the Sabbath Day by keeping it holy.*

**Monday**   Date: _____

*Smile at the teachers and say, "Jesus loves you."*

**Tuesday**   Date: _____

*Pray for missionaries and all who share Jesus' love.*

**Wednesday**  Date: _____

*Tell your classmates, "I'm glad you're here today."*

**Thursday**   Date: _____

*Invite someone you usually don't play with to join in your recess activity.*

**Friday**   Date: _____

*Make cards for others who might be ill, not able to leave home, or in a nursing home.*

**Saturday**   Date: _____

*"I know the plans I have for you," declares the LORD.*

Jeremiah 29:11

*Draw how you can share Jesus' love by helping someone at home.*

14

## Discovery Point

God has a plan for the good of His people. He sometimes works through family and other individuals to carry out His will.

## The Exodus

Exodus 12:31–39, 50–51

## Objectives

That by the power of the Holy Spirit working through God's Word, the students will
- know that God gives them leaders to help them, to guide and protect them, to care for them;
- know that their greatest leader is Jesus, who loves them so much that He died for all their sins;
- pray that their leaders may guide with wisdom blessed by God.

## Day 3 Materials

- Flannelgraph people, palace and desert scenes
- Blackline 4-B

## Day 4 Materials

- Newspaper want ads
- Beginnings poster, Section 8
- *Beginnings* Student Book

# INTRODUCE

Abruptly make this announcement: **We are leaving right away. Take one book with you and line up as quickly as you can. Follow me.** Allow no discussion. Make your leaving seem urgent. Get the class outside the classroom as quickly as you can. Lead them around the playground, gym, or hallway for a short walk and then return to the classroom. Discuss how students felt about having to leave so quickly with no explanation, not knowing where they were going. **The people of Israel must have had questions, too, when Moses and Aaron told them to pack up quickly and leave Egypt in a hurry before Pharaoh changed his mind.**

# DEVELOP

Use the flannelgraph to tell today's Bible story. In advance place as many biblical characters on the board as you can. (Do not use Jesus.) Over the people place half of the palace scene beside half of the desert scene.

Point to the palace scene and explain that Moses spent almost the first 40 years of his life in the Egyptian palace. This was part of God's plan so that Moses would know the Egyptian language, the royal family, and the way people did things at the palace.

Next point to the desert scene, where Moses spent the next 40 years of his life. This was part of God's plan, too, so that Moses would know how to travel through the desert and how to live in the desert when it came time for him to lead God's people out of slavery. Moses did not know God's plan at this time, but we can see now how wise God was.

Point again at the palace and briefly review how God sent Moses and Aaron to say to Pharaoh, "Let my people go." But the king kept saying no. God showed His great power over and over again until finally Pharaoh commanded the people to leave.

Now it was time to hurry and head for the desert and to the Promised Land. The people packed up their things to follow Moses.

Pull off the two scenes to reveal the many people. About two million people left. They knew that God would be leading them. God used a pillar of cloud by day and a pillar of fire by night to show the way.

# RESPOND

Point out that leaders are important and necessary. God calls pastors and elders to be leaders of churches, principals to be leaders of schools, teachers to be leaders of classrooms, presidents and prime ministers to be leaders of countries, and mayors to be leaders of towns. Leaders help people live together and work together. Distribute copies of Blackline 4-B. Let children choose leaders they would like to write, thanking them for the work they do and saying you will pray for them. (It might be good to write a model for this letter on the chalkboard to relieve any anxiety about spelling, etc.)

Ask God to bless us and our nation with good leaders who are also God's people and follow His ways. Discuss our response to the leaders God places over us. (We are to honor, obey, respect, and serve them.)

Say, **God has given us the best leader of all. That leader is Jesus. Jesus told those people who love Him, "Follow Me." As our leader, Jesus even died on the cross for us. We love Jesus and want to follow Him and do His will. God helps us be good followers through the power of the Holy Spirit.**

# Worship Ideas

- Pray that God will help us be good followers of Jesus. At the asterisk have the children respond, "so will I."

**Jesus loves all people. With God's help ***
**Jesus forgives those who hurt Him. With God's help ***
**Jesus shows kindness to people. With God's help ***
**Jesus brings peace between people. With God's help ***

- From a church bulletin or directory read the names of your church leaders. Look in a school directory and read the names of the principal, teachers, and staff. Consider other programs sponsored by the church such as Sunday school, vacation Bible school, and midweek school. Make a word web that includes the names or jobs of all these people. The web helps children "see" all the leaders they can include in a prayer.

# Bible Background

Forty years after Moses was sent to the desert, God calls him to carry out His plan. God said, "So now, go. I am sending you to Pharaoh to bring My people the Israelites out of Egypt" (Exodus 3:10). Moses responds to God's call, "Why me?" Moses goes on to offer reasons he can't, but for each one God has a loving and right answer for Moses and for us.

- *Moses* (to paraphrase): "Why would they listen to me?" (3:11). *God*: "I will be with you" (3:12).
- *Moses:* "They don't know who You are—and neither do I!" (3:13). *God:* "I AM who I AM. Tell them 'I AM has sent me to you.' "
- *Moses:* "They won't listen to words alone" (4:1). *God:* "This is so that they may believe" (4:2–9).
- *Moses:* "Lord, I'm not a good speaker" (4:10). *God:* "I will help you and teach you what to say" (4:11–12).
- *Moses:* "I'm scared. Please send someone else" (4:13). *God:* "Aaron will speak to the people for you" (4:14–16).

God had a plan for Moses, and He has plans for you. "Show me Your ways, O LORD … guide me in Your truth and teach me" (Psalm 25:4–5).

Dear
(name of a leader)
,

I prayed for you today.

I asked God to

Sincerely,

(your name)

## Words to Remember

*Show me Your ways, O LORD ... guide me in Your truth and teach me. Psalm 25:4–5*

- Before witnesses speak in a trial, they put their hand on a Bible and promise to tell the truth. Make a Bible shape by folding a piece of paper in half. Write "Bible" on the cover and today's Bible verse on the inside pages.
- Show your lesson plan book to the class. Tell them that as their leader you write down your plans for them every day. Sit in a circle. Pass the lesson plan book child to child. Have each child say a word from today's Bible verse as they pass it on. Continue around the circle, speeding up each time the verse is completed.

## Extending the Lesson

- Imagine how many shoes followed Moses out of Egypt. How many shoes are in your class? Talk about different kinds of shoes. Point out that God's people did not wear out their shoes while they were in the wilderness for 40 years. See Deuteronomy 29:5. This was another of God's blessings to His people.
- Make "Hurry Up Bread." Note: Do not allow students near the hot oven. Mix together 1 cup flour, 1 teaspoon salt, 1 tablespoon vegetable shortening, and ¼ cup cold water. Knead the dough for 5–10 minutes. Roll it thin and cut it in circles. Press each circle with a fork two times to make a cross shape. Place on a cookie sheet and bake at 350 degrees for about 10 minutes. Talk about the Passover as the bread cools. Eat and enjoy!
- Explain the term *exodus* by comparing it to an *exit* sign. The two words begin the same and both mean *to leave.*

## INTRODUCE

Display the newspaper want ads. Open to the employment opportunities section and show the page to the class. Explain that businesses wanting to hire someone for a job list in the ad what they want the person to be like. **What might be important?** (The person should be honest, smart, have skills, work hard … See if the children have other suggestions.) **When Moses was chosen for the job of leading the people of Israel, there was only one thing that was most important—God was with Him. Everything depended not on Moses, but on the Lord!**

# The Exodus

*(Exodus 12:31–39, 50–51)*

The people of Israel were finally free. Almost two million of them were ready to leave Egypt. They brought animals with them—donkeys, sheep, and goats! What a big parade came out of Egypt! God had plans for Moses to lead the people away from Egypt and into the Promised Land, called Canaan.

Moses had a big job. Leading the people of Israel would not be easy.

But God was with Moses and would help him. God would show the way with a towering cloud by day and a huge pillar of fire at night.

God helped Moses be a good leader for Israel. God gives leaders to help us. The best leader is Jesus, our Savior. Jesus not only shows us the way to heaven—He *is* the Way! By faith in Jesus we have eternal life!

15

## DEVELOP

Review, using this action story. The students are to listen carefully and act out the words when you pause at each asterisk.

**It's nighttime in Egypt. God's people are sound asleep in their beds. Show me how they are sleeping.\* The people quickly jump to their feet.\* They stretch and rub their eyes\* because they are still sleepy. Moses tells the people to pack up quickly.\* Animals are gathered together and belongings are tied to donkeys.\***

**Inside the houses, the people pack up food.\* They roll the bread dough into balls.\* There is no time to add yeast and let the bread rise. They must hurry up.**

**Soon everything is packed up and ready to go. God's people come together\* to leave Egypt. There are many, many people, so they must walk slowly and carefully.\* Children stand on tiptoes\* to look ahead and behind.\* There are people everywhere as far as you can see.**

**God's people celebrate\* because they do not have to be slaves anymore. God will help Moses lead the people to their new land. Wave to Moses\* leading the people. God loves His people. He will help Moses guide them safely home. We are God's children too. He shows His care when He gives us leaders to follow. He gave us Jesus as a special leader, who even died for all people. We celebrate\* because of Jesus. He not only leads us to heaven— Jesus is the *way to heaven!*\***

## RESPOND

Complete the display of Bible story pictures, adding Section 8 of the Beginnings poster to complete the shape of the cross. Have children turn to page 16 of their *Beginnings* book to see a similar display of pictures. Use the questions on the page to review the stories. Emphasize that through all these situations, God was there with His promise to send the Savior. We know that Savior is Jesus, who died on the cross to take away our sins. This is a victorious cross, however, knowing that we and all the saints before us will live in heaven because of Jesus.

# Beginnings

Who is always with us?

Who spoke to make the world?

Who led the people out of Egypt?

Who made the rainbow?

Who was promised a big family?

What did Abraham and Sarah name their baby?

Who watched her baby brother?

Who cared for animals during the flood?

Who were the first two people to disobey God?

## Words to Remember
*Show me Your ways, O LORD ... guide me in Your truth and teach me. Psalm 25:4–5*

16

# Moving On

## Unit Overview

*Moving On* is an appropriate title for the new unit as we learn about the people of Israel traveling to their new homeland. There were setbacks along the way. But God was with His people wherever they went, offering His grace, provision, and deliverance.

Throughout this unit remind the children in your classroom about parallels to their own lives. God is with us wherever we go. We, too, will have setbacks, troubles, and errors. But God is there with us offering provision, deliverance, and above all, His grace through Christ Jesus.

Send home copies of the family letter and Bible verse list for Unit 2 as you begin. At the end of the unit, let the children take their *Moving On* books home. Encourage them to show their parents what they have learned. Remind them to add this book to a growing collection of Bible storybooks that will show God's loving plan for us through the Old Testament, New Testament, now, and eternally. Also consider adding some of the following activities to your curriculum to make related connections between God's message of love and all that you do throughout the day.

### Worship Connections

Throughout this unit we learn about things that helped the people of Israel remember who God is, what He has done, and how He is always near. The stone tablets of the Ten Commandments, the tabernacle, the ark of the covenant, and the stone monument at the Jordan River all helped the people remember. Reminders are needed because people then and now have a tendency (because of our sinful nature) to forget God when they are caught up in their own personal concerns.

- Visit your church sanctuary. Ask the children to look around during a five-minute period of silence. Then ask them to identify things they see that tell them something about God.
- Say, **When someone walks into this classroom, we want them to know right away that this is a Christian school. What things in our room remind people of that?** Also ask what things they have in their homes that help family members remember Jesus. Note that perhaps we can identify ourselves as people of God by wearing certain jewelry or T-shirts with a Christian message. But Jesus tells us an even better way. Read John 13:35. By the forgiveness and grace of God, we can live each day to worship Him.

- While the church sanctuary is designed to help us remember much about the Lord, our God, it has another important purpose—to give honor and glory to Him. Visit the sanctuary again. Discuss in what ways the surroundings honor God's majesty, greatness, and merciful love.

### Community Building

- In a reading or activity center, drape a length of fabric over two chairs that are several feet apart to make a tent where children can go to read or work silently. Remember that the people of Israel lived in tents during the 40 years they lived in the wilderness.
- Take a journey (much shorter, though, than the Israelites traveled). Having secured parental and school permissions, lead the children to a nearby park or open area to eat lunch. Talk about what would be fun and what would not if you had to live in a tent and wander in the desert for 40 years.

### Tools for Witness

- As you use any activity in this curriculum, always evaluate its effectiveness. Do the children just know how to do the activity, or do they understand what it means and how it relates to their faith and their lives? Can they verbalize its significance to others? Talking to their parents about what they have learned about Jesus is an important witness to families.
- As a group project make a long mural that says, "We Are Traveling to the Promised Land." Toward the right side of the mural draw a rectangular sign that has the word *Heaven* printed on it with yellow rays of light extending from it. A little distance from this, show Jesus on a path, walking toward the sign. Have the children draw themselves following after Jesus. Suggest that they sign their names under their self-portraits. Hang this in a hallway of your church or school. Or display it outdoors for all passing by to see.

## Service Projects

- As you study God's provision of food and water to the Israelites in the wilderness, consider the abundance we have today. Share some of this by having a food collection for a homeless shelter. In a note to parents, explain the project and its connection to what you are learning in your study of the Bible at school.
- As you learn about the rescue at the Red Sea and Jordan River, discuss the damaging affects of raging and flooding waters. Check with a national relief agency about their needs. Then help by making flood relief kits for the agency. Ask particularly about the possibility of making kits for children staying in flood relief shelters. **God can use you to help and be a blessing to others.**

## Reaching Every Individual

Keep in mind that the Student Book is not meant to teach reading. Because your children are emerging readers, you will want to focus on the meaning of the message and read the words to them (unless you have volunteers with good reading skills). Suggest that parents read the Bible stories to the children when the books are sent home. Encourage the children, as their skills are developing, to look forward to the day when they can read these Bible stories all by themselves!

## Mathematics

Give children several illustrations to help them develop a concept of the vastness of the number of people of Israel—approximately two million. For example, display a paper coin holder containing 100 pennies. Show 10 coin holders to make a 1,000 pennies. Then say you would need not 2 times as many, but 2,000 times as many to have two million pennies. Or make comparisons to the number of people in a stadium or city with which the children are familiar.

## Science

Watch a video clip of a waterfall, ocean waves, or the outlet at a dam. Discuss the power of water to help or to harm. Then consider God's greater power. As He demonstrated at the parting of the Red Sea and Jordan River, God can control the waters because He made them and all things.

## Social Studies

Camping is fun, but how would you feel about it as a way of life every day? Discuss this. Learn about the Bedouin way of life in the Sinai area today. In what ways is their lifestyle similar to the lifestyle of Israel during their 40 years in the wilderness?

## Integrating the Faith
## Moving On

## Language Arts

Have the children paraphrase the Ten Commandments in their own words. List their ideas on chart paper.

## Fine Arts

Have the children march around the room as they listen to recordings of music by John Philip Sousa. Contrast this to the silent marches of Israel around Jericho.

## Technology

If you have CD-ROM capabilities, display a map of the Sinai wilderness, highlighting locations and moving the mouse to show the movement of the Israelites. This can be done in small groups or teach one child to teach the next and so on.

## Discovery Point

God delivers His people. We praise and thank Him for His loving care.

## Rescue at the Red Sea

Exodus 14:5–15:21

## Objectives

That by the power of the Holy Spirit working through God's Word, the students will

- grow in joyful awareness of all that God has done for them;
- express their trust in God's care, especially thanking Him for the rescue they have through Jesus Christ;
- worship God with songs of praise and thanksgiving.

## Day 1 Materials

- Blackline 5-A
- Box or bag
- Wooden dowel or yardstick
- Bible costumes and tambourine (optional)
- Crepe-paper streamers
- 2 long rolls of blue paper
- 1 sheet of paper
- Paper plates
- Heavy tape
- Unpopped popcorn or dried beans

## Day 2 Materials

- Colored or poster paper
- *Moving On* Student Book

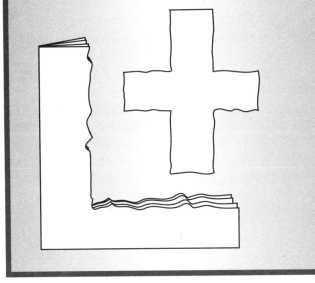

# Day 1

# INTRODUCE

Distribute Blackline 5-A, pointing out that, like the character represented, we all have fears we face. As children name their fears (e.g., storms, darkness), they can begin slowly tearing the picture. **Sometimes we are so busy remembering our fears that we forget God is near, taking care of us. We can either let our fears tear us apart or we can get rid of them.** Assure the children that God is there forgiving and helping them even when they don't remember He is near. Have the children crumple up the papers and throw them in a box or bag as you say, **Let's get rid of those fears. Give them to God. He will take care of our worries by taking care of us!** Pray that God will forgive our weakness, and praise Him for promising to make us strong in faith through His Word. **Let's hear how God helped the people of Israel when they were overwhelmed with fear.**

# DEVELOP

Act out the crossing of the Red Sea in an open play area. Select four helpers to be in charge of the "sea" (two long rolls of blue shelf or wrapping paper, stretched out side by side in the center of the area). Each helper will be in charge of one end of a roll. At your signal the helpers will pick up the paper to stand it on end, forming a long blue "wall of water" on both sides, which children can pass through.

Costumes help children get into their roles; even a crepe-paper streamer tied around the forehead of each child and streaming down the back of the neck helps. The person playing Moses will also need a yardstick for a walking stick. All other children will be Israelites. Ask them to follow you and imitate your actions as you play the part of Miriam (or Aaron).

Rush from the doorway to the edge of the sea and sit down to rest (with children doing so too). **Everyone is so tired. We rushed to escape from Egypt, where we were held captive as slaves. Now we are in this hot desert.** Stand up and point in the direction you came from while acting frightened. **Oh, no! Look! Our enemies are behind us. The sea is in front of us. We are trapped. Why did God bring us out here to die? Nothing can save us.** Be seated and quietly ask "Moses" to walk to the edge of the sea and stretch out his walking stick. **Look at what Moses is doing. He says we should not be afraid. God has helped us before. God will help us again. Only God can rescue us.** Quietly ask the four helpers at the sea to stand the paper on end to form two walls of water. **God has sent a powerful wind. It split the deep waters and dried the ground at the bottom of the sea. Praise God, we can escape to the other side.** Quickly lead the children between the walls of water to the other side of the area, turn, and look back. **Look, the Egyptians are following us! But God will help us again. The waters are going back in place.** Have the helpers place the paper strips back in place on the floor. **The soldiers, horses, and chariots have been tossed into the sea. They can't hurt us anymore. God has saved us! Praise the Lord!** Together sing a song of praise such as "My God Is So Great" or "Hallelujah! Praise Ye the Lord!" (*LOSP*, pp. 64, 58, and on CD). Perhaps play a tambourine and march around as you sing. Dramatically read Exodus 15:1–11.

## R E S P O N D

Ask the children to sit quietly around you. Say, **Did you know that God has rescued you and me? Our enemy is much worse than Pharaoh and his soldiers. Our enemy is the devil himself. But God's power is greater than any evil.** Fold a piece of paper in fourths and tear once vertically as in the illustration, saying, **God rescued us from sin.** Tear once horizontally, saying, **God rescued us from death.** Open the paper to reveal a cross shape. **God rescued us by sending Jesus to take the punishment for our sin when He died on the cross. Jesus conquered death when He became alive again at Easter. Jesus rescued us. He won the victory. We are saved! Let's praise the Lord!**

Praise God by repeating the song(s) sung earlier or other favorite praise songs. Add to the celebration by having the children make tambourines to praise God as the people of Israel did (see Exodus 15:20). Have each child fold a paper plate in half and place unpopped popcorn or dried beans inside it. Seal the edges of the tambourine with heavy tape. Attach long streamers of colored crepe or tissue paper to the rounded edge. Children can wave and tap the tambourines as they sing, march, and praise the Lord.

Afraid? What Do You Fear?

**Blackline 5–A**

## Worship Ideas

- Explain that the Book of Psalms, in the very middle of the Bible, was the songbook of God's people long ago. Point out that we have the words but not the melodies. Invite the children to listen as you read Psalm 150 and decide what word is used most often *(praise)*. **Praise is telling how great and powerful and loving God is.** Read the psalm again, asking the children to shake their tambourines (or clap their hands) whenever it mentions a way to praise and worship God.

- If your church uses the song "Thank the Lord and Sing His Praise" as part of its worship liturgy, play a recording of it taped at a Sunday morning service or sing the song. See if any of the children recognize the song and where they have heard it before. Begin learning the song to help the children actively participate in Sunday worship.

- Learn the refrain of "Earth and All Stars" (*LOSP*, p. 57, and on CD). Have the children sing this in response to praise statements you make such as these:

**Praise God for His greatness and power!** *(Refrain.)*
**Praise God for sending Jesus to forgive my sins.** *(Refrain.)*
**Amen and amen!**

## Bible Background

The exodus became for Israel the banner event of God's salvation. Over and over, they would call to mind this demonstration of His might, used to save His people (Joshua 4:23; Nehemiah 9:11; Psalm 66:6; 78:13; Hebrews 11:29). God worked through the course of history to accomplish His will. Though Pharaoh looked for victory as the world's premier military power, God had planned his defeat. In Pharaoh's disaster God's name would be glorified throughout the world. So mighty was God's miracle that news soon spread to the surrounding nations. Just as important, God's miracle fortified the faith of His own people. At least for now, they were certain God would lead them safely to the Promised Land. The people sang of victory of life over death. We know the ultimate victory in Christ's resurrection and that no enemy can separate us from the love of God (Romans 8:38–39).

## Words to Remember

*Wor*ship the LORD with **glad-ness; come** be*fore* Him with **joy**ful **songs.** *Psalm 100:2*

- Begin clapping a slow, basic four-count rhythm. Have the students clap with you. Then add the words of the first half of the Bible verse, clapping on the syllables printed in bold. Repeat the words several times. Then do the same with the second half. Finally, try the whole verse.
- Try the Bible verse again rhythmically, substituting the clapping with stomping feet, snapping fingers, or tapping tambourines.
- Sing the words of the Bible verse to the tune of "The Farmer in the Dell."

**Worship the Lord with gladness.**
**Worship the Lord with gladness.**
**Come before Him with joyful songs.**
**Worship the Lord with gladness.**

## Extending the Lesson

- Schedule an appointment with your church organist to demonstrate how the instrument works as it adds to the joyous music during the worship service. Perhaps children could play one or two notes on the organ or sing along to a familiar hymn accompanied by the organ.
- Music played an important part in the Bible story. Play a game of "cooperative" musical chairs. Set up chairs in a circle. In each round, remove a chair. As the music plays, children march around the circle, playing their tambourines. When the music stops, children rush to sit down. Children without a chair may sit on someone's lap. Play until everyone seated has someone on their lap.
- Write a class praise poem prayer together. First print the following couplet repeatedly on chart paper:

    Thank You, God, for _____ .
    Thank You, God, for _____ .

    Have the children complete each couplet with pairs of words that rhyme *(bees, trees; ducks, trucks).* Encourage children to illustrate each line. Read the prayers together during worship.

# Day 2

## INTRODUCE

Give a "thumbs up" sign and say, **Yesterday we heard how God rescued His people. Then the people praised God for His mighty power.** Give another "thumbs up" sign. Then ask the children to give a "thumbs up" or "thumbs down" to indicate if the things you mention are times they would praise the Lord. **Your team wins a trophy. Your best friend is moving to another town. You get a new bicycle. Your pet cat or dog dies. Your grandmother is sick. Your aunt gives you five dollars. Someone pushes you down on the playground. Your mom and dad have an argument. The weather is perfect for a picnic.** Next read aloud Philippians 4:4 and 1 Thessalonians 5:16–18. These verses tell us to praise God at *all* times, not just the good times. Keep in mind that some children may confuse *praise* and *thanks.* We are not thanking God for our troubles. (Troubles are a consequence of sin in this world.) Instead, by praising God, we recognize that He is with us and has the power to help us. **Praise God no**

# Rescue at the Red Sea

*(Exodus 14:5–15:21)*

God's people had been slaves in Egypt. They had to work hard for their enemies. They prayed to God for help.

God set His people free. He chose Moses to lead them out of Egypt. But their enemies came after them. They were trapped at the Red Sea.

God sent a wind to separate the waters and to make a dry path. The people hurried to safety on the other side. When the king and his chariots followed them, God made the waters return to drown all the enemies.

Moses and the people sang a song of praise to God for His goodness. Miriam and some of the women played tambourines and danced to the music.

They sang:  *The Lord is my strength and my song.*
*He has become my salvation.*
*He is my god, and I will praise Him.*
*Sing to the Lord.*
*The horse and its rider*
*He has hurled into the sea.*

God saves us from our enemies too. He chose His own Son, Jesus, to be our salvation from sin and death. He is strong to save us.

1

matter what happens. **We can trust that He will work out every-thing for our good and in the time that is best.** You may want to sing "Rejoice in the Lord Always" (*LOSP*, p. 52, and on CD).

# DEVELOP

Print each of the following numbered words on separate sheets of colored or poster paper: *(1) Egypt; (2) Moses; (3) Red Sea; (4) fear; (5) wind; (6) dry path; (7) safety; (8) chariots; (9) tam-bourines; (10) God.* Distribute the word cards to pairs of children (adjusting the size of groups to the number in your class). Give the partners a few moments to talk to each other about their word and what it has to do with the Bible story of the rescue at the Red Sea. Then have the children sit in a circle in numerical order of their words. Call off the numbers in order, having one partner read the word and the other partner tell the part of the Bible story that includes the word. Review the story further by reading aloud the narration on page 1 in the *Moving On* Student Book. Ask partners to listen closely and hold up their word card when they hear you read their word.

# RESPOND

Continue with the activities on page 2 of the Student Book. Refer to the title at the top of the page. **What do you think is missing? Listen to these Bible verses for a clue.** Read the first portion of Psalm 138:1 ("I will praise You, O Lord, with *all* my heart") and Luke 10:27 ("Love the Lord your God with *all* your heart"). **What do you think "halfhearted" wor-ship is like?** (Examples: not listening as God's Word is read; a "do-I-have-to?" attitude about singing praise.) **What does it mean to do something with *all* your heart?** (To think about what you are saying and doing; to mean it honestly, completely, and enthusiastically.) Pray together that God would for-give us when we are halfhearted in worship and ask Him to strengthen our faith to worship Him whole-heartedly.

Emphasize that we can worship God anywhere. **We worship God together here at school. You can worship God in a car when you pray for a safe trip; you can worship God on the playground when you thank Him for a nice day. You can worship at your house or at God's house.** Point out that the circle on the activity page has a scrambled list of three of the many ways we can worship in God's house. Follow the directions indicated. Then close by wholehearted-ly singing one or two favorite praise songs.

# Worship God with ____ Your Heart

snig
veig
seirap

**give**

1. Unscramble the words in the circle.
2. Write the correct words in the blank boxes.
3. Draw a line from each Bible verse to the matching picture.

**sing**

They faithfully brought in the … gifts.
2 Chronicles 31:12

We … will lift up our banners in the name of our God.
Psalm 20:5

I will sing a new song to You, O God.
Psalm 144:9

God Is Great

**praise**

Words to Remember

*Worship the Lord with gladness; come before Him with joyful songs. Psalm 100:2*

2

## Discovery Point

God delivers His people. We praise and thank Him for His loving care.

## God Gives the Ten Commandments

Exodus 20:1–17

## Objectives

That by the power of the Holy Spirit working through God's Word, the students will
* realize that the Law shows us our sin and our need for a Savior;
* ask God for forgiveness of sin and thank Him for His deliverance and salvation through Jesus;
* grow in a desire to obey God's commands as they see that He wants only good for their lives.

## Day 3 Materials
* Blackline 5-B

## Day 4 Materials
* *Moving On* Student Book

# INTRODUCE

Ask the children to close their eyes. **In your mind, picture a tall mountain. The bottom of the mountain is surrounded by tents. And walking between the tents are more than a million people!** Have the children open their eyes and imagine the confusion and troubles that could happen with that many people. **So often even two people can't get along together. So God gave the Law to help people live together in peace and respect.**

# DEVELOP

**God gives us 10 rules. We call them the Ten Commandments.**

1. *(Hold up your index finger.)* **The First Commandment says, "You shall have no other gods." The number 1 also reminds us that God is to be first in our lives.**

2. *(Indicate two fingers and then hold them over your lips.)* **The Second Commandment says, "You shall not misuse the name of the Lord your God." We should not speak God's name to curse. We should say His name to pray, praise, and tell of His love.**

3. *(Hold up three fingers. Then use them to make the sign of the cross in front of you as the pastor does in church.)* **The Third Commandment says, "Remember the Sabbath day by keeping it holy." God wants us to set aside one day of the week to worship Him and learn His Word."**

4. *(Hold up four fingers and place them over your heart.)* **The Fourth Commandment says, "Honor your father and your mother." Always love and obey your parents and others in authority.**

5. *(Indicate five fingers. Use them to push forward as if hitting someone, and then use your other hand to restrain it.)* **The Fifth Commandment, "You shall not murder," also means we should not hurt other people in any way.**

6. *(Indicate six fingers. Then clasp your hands together as if shaking hands with yourself.)* **The Sixth Commandment is, "You shall not commit adultery." That means husbands and wives should be faithful to each other. But this is not just for married adults. It means that boys and girls, men and women should treat each other with respect and dignity.**

7. *(Indicate the number 7. Then pretend to reach out and grab something as if stealing. Then "slap" the hand.)* **The Seventh Commandment says, "You shall not steal." God wants us to help people keep and protect what belongs to them and not try to get it from them, even by tricking them or not returning something.**

8. *(Hold up eight fingers. Then use both hands to cover your mouth completely.)* **The Eighth Commandment says, "You shall not give false testimony against your neighbor." We should only say nice things about people. We should not lie or gossip about them.**

9. (*Hold up nine fingers. Then raise your hands high in praise.*) **The Ninth Commandment says, "You shall not covet your neighbor's house."** Covet means to want what belongs to someone else. **God wants us to be happy with what He has given us.**

10. (*Hold up 10 fingers. Then fold them in silent prayer.*) **The Tenth Commandment says that we should not covet the friends, family, or even animals that belong to someone else.** Instead of being jealous of someone else, give thanks to God for what you have.

## R E S P O N D

Emphasize that God gave us the Law for our good. But we have big problems. The problem is not the Law; the problem is that we are sinners. Because we disobey God's commandments we deserve to be punished. **But God is love. Because of His love, He sent Jesus to take the punishment in our place. Because Jesus died on the cross for us, we are forgiven.** Point out that Jesus forgave our disobedience, but there is more. He also changes our hearts and lives so that we can now live in obedience. He does this through the power of the Holy Spirit working through God's Word. Because of Jesus, we can now look at the Ten Commandments as our guide for our Christian lives. Distribute copies of Blackline 5-B and use the activity to look at the commandments from this point of view (not as rules telling us what not to do, but as guides to what we can now do because of Jesus).

### God's Will for Us

*Draw a line to connect each circled word to the answer blank where it is needed.*

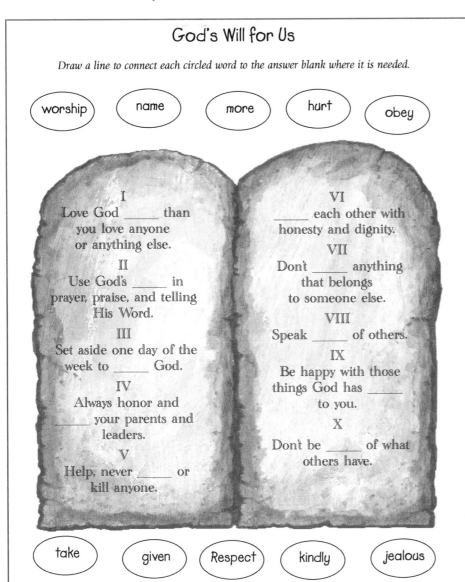

worship   name   more   hurt   obey

I
Love God _____ than you love anyone or anything else.

II
Use God's _____ in prayer, praise, and telling His Word.

III
Set aside one day of the week to _____ God.

IV
Always honor and _____ your parents and leaders.

V
Help, never _____ or kill anyone.

VI
_____ each other with honesty and dignity.

VII
Don't _____ anything that belongs to someone else.

VIII
Speak _____ of others.

IX
Be happy with those things God has _____ to you.

X
Don't be _____ of what others have.

take   given   Respect   kindly   jealous

**Blackline 5–B**
© 2001 CPH  Permission granted to reproduce for classroom use.

## Worship Ideas

- Introduce two important words: *confession* and *absolution.* Point out that we begin every church service this way. As we come before God, we admit we are sinners and confess our sins. Then we hear the words of absolution, which tell us we are forgiven through Jesus Christ. Demonstrate this portion of your worship liturgy so that the children can become familiar with hearing these words. Perhaps the teacher can read the words of confession and the pastor can read the words of absolution. Suggest that the children listen for these words in church and pray along silently, even if they are unable to read the words.

- Sing "I'm Sorry" (*LOSP*, p. 27, and on CD). This song has several important concepts related to Law and Gospel. Stanza 1 focuses on admitting a sin; stanza 2 asks for forgiveness from the person wronged; and stanza 3 gives assurance of God's love and forgiveness.

- Read aloud all of 1 John 4:9. Jesus forgives us and empowers us so that we now live through Him! Because of Jesus we can live in obedience and joy. **Each of us can rejoice and say, "Christ lives in me."** (Have each child repeat those four powerful words from Galatians 2:20.) Sing "Happy All the Time" (*LOSP*, p. 59, and on CD). This is a fun song with a powerful message right in the middle of the stanza telling why we are so happy— because Jesus is in us and has given us a clean heart.

## Bible Background

In just the third month out of Egypt God's people reach Mount Sinai, which rises abruptly 2,000 feet above the neighboring plains. The location provided an ideal campsite for the huge throng, as well as a stunning "pulpit" from which God could speak.

The covenant God establishes is the Ten Commandments. But because all people are sinners, breaking their part of the agreement, the Son of God has become the Mediator, keeping the Law for us and taking our punishment for sin. Jesus has reconciled us with the Father and reestablished us as the people of God!

## WEEK 5-B

### Words to Remember

*Blessed is the man / who fears the LORD, / who finds great delight / in His commands.*
Psalm 112:1

- The slashes printed in the Bible verse divide it into four sections. Divide your class into four groups and teach one portion of the verse to each group. Put the verse together by pointing to one group at a time to have them stand, raise their arms high, and say their assigned words. Then try the verse without pointing to individual groups. As each group stands, in turn, to speak, they will be doing "the wave."

- Explain the difficult words: blessed = receiving God's gifts; man = person; fears = respects; delight = joy; commands = commandments.

- Play a different tone (on a xylophone, piano, or with tone bells) before each group says its portion of the Bible verse. Assign different phrases to different groups; then have the whole group say the whole verse together.

### Extending the Lesson

- At an activity center, let children use play dough to shape tablets of stone to represent those on which the Ten Commandments were written. They can use a toothpick or pencil to carve numerals 1–10 or Roman numerals I–X. Provide a sample to be used as a guide.

- Teach the following counting song to the tune of "Ten Little Indians."
  **One little, two little, three little Christians.**
  **Four little, five little, six little Christians.**
  **Seven little, eight little, nine little Christians,**
  **Ten who trust the Lord.**
  Ask 10 children to stand in front of the class. As everyone sings the song, have one child squat down per number. On the word *Lord* all children should jump up. Repeat this several times so that all children have a chance to participate.

## Day

### INTRODUCE

Ask several children to "give me five" or to give a "high five." Then raise an open palm and say, **We are learning about the *Ten Commandments*. But the number 5 can also teach us about God's will for our lives.** Point out that obeying the commandments is really about love and respect (which means to honor, care for, treat with kindness). Hold up your index finger and have the children do the same. Say, **First, above all, the commandments are about respect for God. In fact, the first three commandments are specifically about our respect for God.** Hold up a second finger, with the children continuing to imitate you by holding two fingers high. **The commandments continue by asking us to respect our family.** Hold up a third finger, **We are to respect other people.** Hold up a fourth finger, **We honor the commandments when we respect things— things that belong to ourselves and others and the things that are part of God's creation.** Then extend a thumb and use it to point to your chest, **God also wants us to respect ourselves, for we are pre-**

# God Gives
## the Ten Commandments

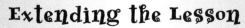

*(Exodus 20:1–17)*

The people of Israel were on the way to the land God had promised them. They came to a high mountain named Mount Sinai. The people camped there.

God came down in fire and smoke. The whole mountain shook. Trumpets sounded. God called Moses to come up the mountain.

God wrote the Ten Commandments on two flat pieces of stone. He gave them to Moses. God said, "Teach My Law to the people. Learn these commandments and do what they say."

God gave His Law to us too. But we are sinners. We do not obey in all things. We need a Savior. So God sent Jesus to show us how to live. He died for us and rose again at Easter. Because of Jesus, we have forgiveness. Because of Jesus, we have new hearts to live each day for Him.

3

cious to Him because we are His redeemed children through Christ Jesus. Let the children give each other "five" or "high fives." From talking 5, we are going to move on now and talk 10.

# DEVELOP

Review the story of God giving the Law by distributing the *Moving On* Student Book and reading page 3 aloud to the children. Emphasize why God gave us the Law: to protect us, to show us how to love and serve Him, to help us get along with each other, to show us how to have a better life. Expand on these details of the Bible story: a thick cloud came over Mount Sinai; there was lightning, thunder, and the sound of a loud trumpet; the whole mountain smoked and shook; God called Moses up to the top of the mountain; the people of Israel watched and waited; God wrote the Ten Commandments on two flat pieces of stone; God asked Moses to teach these laws to His people (that includes us).

When we follow God's ways, our lives and relationships are better. The problem is that we are sinners, and we can't follow God's ways perfectly. **Thank God that He has the answer for our problem—Jesus. He forgives the things we have done wrong. He cleans our hearts to make us strong so that through Jesus, we can do what is right. His forgiveness, love, and help never end.**

Note: Have a special project to encourage the children to learn the Ten Commandments. Rather than making it an assignment, make it a challenge, so that children can work according to their abilities. Set a one-week goal. Provide copies of the commandments (see the Teacher Resource Book), and announce prizes (such as 10 pennies or 10 treats) for saying them all. Each child may choose when they are ready to recite them to you. If a child can say only one commandment, that is fine, and the child receives one penny (or one treat). For saying six commandments correctly, the child receives six prizes (six pennies or six treats), and so on. No one has to enter the contest (but most children will feel challenged to learn as many as they can).

# RESPOND

Use page 4 of the Student Book to discuss application of the commandments to our lives. First have the children identify what is happening in each picture and which commandments are being broken. (The girl is placing her stubborn will first and is not using God's name in worship and praise, commandments 1, 2, 3; the boys are disrespectful of the girls, commandment 6; the boy is ignoring his mother's call, commandment 4; the girl is destroying the property of the boy, commandment 7; the girls are speaking unkindly of someone because they are jealous of that person, commandments 8, 9, 10; the boys are hurting each other, commandment 5.)

Next, place an *X* over each picture that shows something wrong. (All of them.) **The Law shows that we are sinners. But that is not enough. Admitting that something is wrong does not change the sin. We need a Savior from sin. Only Jesus can change the picture.** Have children draw a large yellow cross in the open spaces at the center of the page. **Jesus takes away our sin by forgiving us. He cleans our heart and makes us strong to follow God's will.** Discuss each situation again, this time describing what would happen if the people were led by the power of Jesus in their hearts.

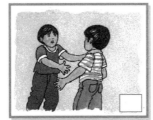

*Blessed is the man who fears the LORD, who finds great delight in His commands. Psalm 112:1*

4

## WEEK 6-A

### Discovery Point

God graciously provides for all our needs.

### Israel in the Wilderness

Exodus 16–17

### Objectives

That by the power of the Holy Spirit working through God's Word, the students will

- recognize that God knows and provides for their physical and spiritual needs;
- grow in faith, trusting in God's mercy and provision;
- thank and praise God for His love, especially as it is shown through Jesus, our Savior.

### Day 1 Materials

- Blackline 6-A
- Small paper plates

### Day 2 Materials

- *Moving On* Student Book

## Day 1

## INTRODUCE

Distribute a small paper plate to each child. Ask, **What is missing from this wonderfully tasty lunch?** (There's no food on it.) **If you were hungry, how would you feel about this empty plate?** (Unhappy.) Have children use a marker or crayon to draw a sad face on the plate. **In today's Bible story we'll see how God provided food and more to His people. He changed their sadness into joy.** Have children draw a happy face on the other side of their paper plates.

## DEVELOP

Ask the children to use their happy/sad plates to help you tell the story. **Moses led God's people away from their hard life of slavery in Egypt. The people were so happy to be free.** (Show happy face.)

**The people walked through the hot, dry desert. They didn't see fruit trees or berry bushes. They just saw sand and stones.** (Sad face.) **The people grumbled and complained, "Why did we leave Egypt? At least we had food to eat there!"**

**God heard His people crying for help. God said, "I will send food for My people."** (Happy face.) **That night God sent many quail. They flew into the camp. The people caught the birds and cooked them for supper. What a good meal.**

**The next morning the ground was white as snow with wafers of bread. The people said, "What is it?" They called it** *manna.* **It tasted good, like honey cake.**

**Moses said, "This is bread from God. Take as much as you need for today. God will send more food tomorrow. Trust Him."**

**Soon the people began to grumble and complain again.** (Sad face.) **They said, "Moses, we have no water to drink. Why did you lead us into this desert to die?"**

**Moses prayed to God for help. God answered, "Hit that rock with your stick. Water will come out of it." Moses did so, and cool, fresh water flowed out of the rock, just as God had said.** (Happy face.) **God is all-powerful. As the people moved on to the Promised Land, God was with them, and He took good care of them.**

# RESPOND

Ask, **In what ways are we like the people of Israel from long ago?** (We need food and water too. We often grumble and complain when things don't go our way.) **When we grumble and complain we are not trusting God to know what is best for us and to give us what we need. We might think we need lots of toys or electronic gadgets or new clothes. But what we need most of all is forgiveness for sinfully grumbling and complaining. God gives us Jesus for what we need most—salvation. God also provides what we need and much more each day.** Discuss how God does this: instead of through quail, manna, and a rock, God provides for our needs through the rain and sunshine that make food plants grow, through parents who work at jobs to earn money, through food producers and grocers who prepare the food we will use. God's hand of blessing is in all this.

Conclude with the activity on Blackline 6-A. These are reminders to praise and thank God for all He gives us.

# Worship Ideas

- Sing "It's Good to Give Thanks" (*LOSP*, p. 61, and on CD). Let the children make up new songs by changing stanza 1. For example, "It's good to give thanks for hot dogs." Adjust the timing for longer or shorter words.
- Read aloud these words from Luther's explanation of the First Article of the Apostles' Creed. Tell the children that this is a brief list of the things God provides for us.

**[God] gives me clothing and shoes, food and drink, house and home, wife and children, land, animals, and all I have. He richly and daily provides me with all that I need to support this body and life.**

Also from the explanation of the First Article, read *why* God does this for us and what is our response: **All this He does only out of fatherly, divine goodness and mercy, without any merit or worthiness in me. For all this it is my duty to thank and praise, serve and obey Him. This is most certainly true.**

# Bible Background

The northern and southern regions of the Sinai Peninsula, where the people of Israel wandered for 40 years, does have some vegetation and clusters of springs. But it is by no means a hospitable environment for a mass of more than a million people in need of food and water. Understandably then, this land seemed a poor exchange for the well-watered Nile delta they had just left. Less understandably, the people forgot the power God had shown so recently again and again, and they began to grumble. Loving Father that He is, God is incredibly patient and answers Israel's ungratefulness with generosity.

It has been noted that the Sinai's tamarisk trees give off a honeylike substance somewhat like manna. But again we see God's miraculous hand because the tamarask trees give off this substance for just a few weeks in the year, never in quantities to feed millions and not with a regularity of six days, skipping the seventh, for 40 years! God took elements of His creation and blessed them in remarkable ways to care for His people.

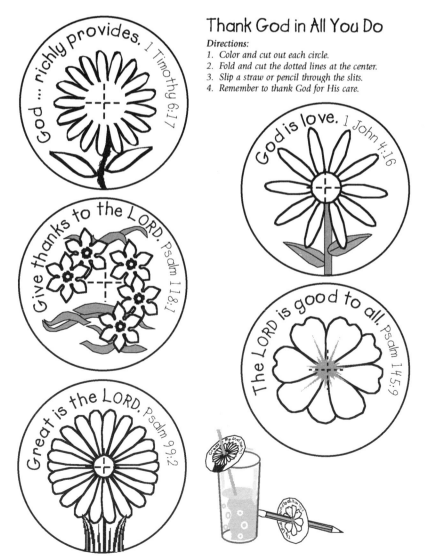

## Thank God in All You Do

**Directions:**
1. Color and cut out each circle.
2. Fold and cut the dotted lines at the center.
3. Slip a straw or pencil through the slits.
4. Remember to thank God for His care.

God ... richly provides. 1 Timothy 6:17

God is love. 1 John 4:16

Give thanks to the LORD. Psalm 118:1

The LORD is good to all. Psalm 145:9

Great is the LORD. Psalm 9:2

## Words to Remember

*God / will meet / all your needs.*
*Philippians 4:19*

- Brainstorm a list of things you need each day. Then evaluate the list. **Are there things on this list that we may *want* but don't really *need?*** Cross off those items. Consider what needs to be added to the list. (These are likely to be spiritual things that are not easily observable, such as forgiveness, faith, Jesus, etc.) **God doesn't promise to give us everything we want, but He does say He will give us what we need and at the time that is best.**

- Note that the Bible verse is divided into sections. The first section has one word, the second has two, and the third has three. Phrase the words accordingly. Add tone blocks to accompany the count of each phrase (1 beat, 2 beats, 3 beats). This will add interest as the children practice the words.

## Extending the Lesson

- Provide each child with a thank-you card. **If we wrote a thank-You note to God, what could it say?** List the children's ideas on chart paper. Let them choose phrases and sentences to copy on their cards. Use the cards as prayer starters. Note: Children may enjoy designing their own cards on a computer.

- Study the desert environment. Find out about adaptations—ways God provides for desert plants and animals to survive. Talk about people's need for water. Use an encyclopedia or the Internet to find out how long a person can survive without water. Let children make models of different types of cactus plants, using toothpicks stuck into self-hardening clay.

- Estimate the total number of people God led through the desert to the Promised Land. Approximately 600,000 men left Egypt. If each man was married, the number would be doubled. If each husband and wife had at least two children, the number would double again.

# Day 2

# INTRODUCE

To introduce today's Bible story review, introduce this new song sung to the familiar tune "Happy All the Time" (*LOSP*, p. 59, and on CD).

> I'm inright, outright, upright, downright
> Grumpy all the time.
> I'm inright, outright, upright, downright
> Grumpy all the time.
> When things don't go my way
> I stomp my foot and say,
> "I'm inright, outright, upright, downright
> Grumpy all the time."

Repeat the song, singing it slower and slower with a sad, grumpy pout. Then say, **It's hard to sing this song without smiling, isn't it? It's also hard to be grumpy when you remember that God loves and cares for you! Let's find out how this song fits our story today.**

# Israel in the Wilderness

*(Exodus 16–17)*

The people of Israel continued moving on to their new homeland. God had helped them in amazing ways. But sometimes the people forgot to trust Him. When they were hungry they grumbled and complained. Some said, "We were better off in Egypt. At least we had food to eat there."

Moses prayed. God answered in amazing ways. God sent quail into the camp. People could easily catch them and have meat for supper. Every morning the ground was covered with a honey bread called manna.

The people had much to be thankful for, but again they grumbled and complained. Some of them said, "Why did we leave Egypt? We will die of thirst in this desert." But God's power is great. He sent water pouring from a rock.

God takes care of His people in many ways and with more than we need. He even forgives us, for Jesus' sake, when we are not content with what we have. God is so good!

5

## D E V E L O P

Read aloud page 5 of the *Moving On* Student Book. Then ask review questions: **Why did God bring the people of Israel out of Egypt?** (To save them from slavery and to take them to the Promised Land.) **Why did God's people grumble?** (They had no food or water. They blamed God.) **What did Moses do when the people complained?** (Moses prayed to God for help.) **How did God provide for them?** (He sent quail in the evening and manna in the morning; God caused water to come from a rock.) **Grumbling and complaining are wrong. When we complain, it's a sign that we are not trusting God to take care of what's bothering us. When you feel like grumbling, try talking to God about it instead. God will help you trust in Him.**

## R E S P O N D

Say, **For Jesus' sake, God forgives us when we grumble and complain. But God does even more! He gives us an "attitude of gratitude."** The illustrations on page 6 show many of the things for which we can be thankful. Ask the children to follow your directions on this page.

**God gives you a place to live and a place to learn. Draw a line to connect these two blessings.**

**God gives you good things to eat and drink. Draw a line to connect these two blessings.**

**God blesses you with friends and family who care about you. Draw …**

**God gives you clothes to wear and toys for fun. Draw …**

**Now look at the lines you've drawn. You have a picture of God's greatest blessing of all. Why do we need this blessing so very much?** (Through His death on the cross Jesus brings us forgiveness of sins and life eternal. He is the only way to receive these blessings.) Let children color in the cross shape to emphasize it.

# Connect
## the Blessings!

*Look at some of the blessings God has given you. Then listen as your teacher tells you what to do.*

## Words to Remember

*God will meet all your needs. Philippians 4:19*

# WEEK 6-B

## Discovery Point

God graciously provides for all our needs.

## The 12 Spies

Numbers 13:1–14:25

## Objectives

That by the power of the Holy Spirit working through God's Word, the students will
- contritely confess when they fail to appreciate God's care and protection;
- know that God forgives them through Jesus and continues to give them the care they need;
- praise God that He provides for life on earth and life forever in the promised land of heaven.

## Day 3 Materials

- Blackline 6-B
- Jenna puppet
- Small plate of cookies
- Overhead and transparency

## Day 4 Materials

- *Moving On* Student Book
- Jake puppet
- Promised Land poster, Sections 1–4

# INTRODUCE

Introduce the story with the puppet Jenna, who is holding a plate of cookies. Have her go by with her nose high in the air.

**TEACHER:** Hi, Jenna. Where are you going with those cookies?

**JENNA:** I offered these to Jake and he said, "No thanks, they look gross." So I'm going to eat them myself.

**TEACHER:** Don't you think he was teasing you?

**JENNA:** I know he was just teasing. But he teased me one too many times. I will not forgive him.

**TEACHER:** You won't even give him another chance?

**JENNA:** No more chances. That's it. I'm out of here.

**TEACHER:** It's a good thing God doesn't treat us that way.

**JENNA:** What do you mean?

**TEACHER:** Well, in today's Bible story we will hear that once again the people of Israel grumbled and did not trust God. God could have said, "That's it. I'm out of here. They did wrong one too many times. No more chances for them." But God did not abandon the people.

**JENNA:** It's a good thing God isn't like us. I'm going to pray God will help me be more forgiving like Him.

# DEVELOP

Display on an overhead projector a transparency you have made from Blackline 6-B. Use a transparency marker to connect the numbered dots as you tell and trace the path the Israelites took on their journey from Egypt to the Promised Land.

(1) People of Israel were slaves in Egypt. (2) They cried to God for help, and He sent Moses to be their leader. (3) God rescued the people at the Red Sea. (4) God led them with a cloud by day and fire at night. (5) God gave them water in the desert. (6–7) He provided manna and quail for the people to eat. (8–9) God gave them the Ten Commandments to show His will for their lives. (10–11) He told them how to make a tent church called the tabernacle to take with them wherever they went. (12) He told them to make a gold box, the ark of the covenant, to carry reminders of God's love and care wherever they went. (13–17) Quite often the people complained, but God still took good care of them on their journey.

(18) **Finally the people came close to Canaan. Moses chose a man from each of the 12 tribes of Israel. The men were sent as spies to see what the land and the people living there were like.**

(19) **The 12 spies explored the land for more than a month. When they returned, they said the land was beautiful. They brought a cluster of grapes so large it took two men to carry it on a pole between them.**

Everyone should have been happy. But 10 of the spies grumbled. They were afraid. They said the people in the land were powerful giants living in walled cities. Two of the spies, Joshua and Caleb, were not afraid. They said, "God has been with us in the past. He will help us again." But the people wouldn't listen to Joshua and Caleb. They did not trust in the Lord.

Moses asked God to forgive the sinfulness of the people. God is slow to anger; He forgave His people. But He said they must wait to enter the Promised Land. The people had much to learn about the faithfulness of the Lord.

(20–27) The people wandered in the desert for the next 40 years. God took care of them during those years until it was the right time to enter the Promised Land.

# RESPOND

Point out that the people in the Bible story grumbled and complained because they were afraid. Have children help you make a list of things people fear. **What good does it do to grumble and complain about these things?** (That doesn't help anything.) **What good does it do to be afraid of these things?** (That doesn't help either.) **What can we do? We can turn these fears over to God. We can ask Him to take away what we fear or make us strong to face our fears and live with those concerns. We can do what Moses did—talk to God about it and trust His plans for us.**

Lead the children in prayer, asking God to forgive us because of Jesus, who died and rose again for our salvation. Thank Him that we need never be afraid of our worst enemies—sin, death, and Satan—because Jesus has conquered them. Ask God to make us strong in faith to trust Him in all things.

# Worship Ideas

- Read aloud these Bible verses, which remind us to trust our faithful God: Psalm 126:3; Psalm 128:1; and Psalm 130:7.
- How do we change from "grumbling" to "grateful"? First, we confess our sins and ask for the forgiveness we have in Christ Jesus. Then with renewed hearts, we look not at what we want but at what we have. Thank God for these many blessings by singing several favorite songs of praise.
- Use a "baby name book" to find out the meaning of the names of several children in your class. Then say, **I'm thinking of an important name that is not in this book. The name is "Jehovah-Jireh." It's a name for God. The reason I like this name is because it means "God is my Provider." Jehovah-Jireh means God gives me what I need.** Pray to God, our Jehovah-Jireh, thanking Him for all His blessings, especially for His love and forgiveness through Jesus, our Savior.

# Bible Background

The 12 spies exaggerated the strength of the Canaanites, saying the people of Israel were like grasshoppers compared to the giants of the land. But they did not exaggerate the fruitfulness of the Promised Land. They brought clusters of grapes that had to be carried by two people. To this day bunches of grapes weighing up to 20 pounds are found in this area.

In rebelling against Moses, God's chosen leader, the people were also rebelling against God Himself. In their fear and lack of trust, they had forgotten God's destruction of the Egyptian army, the strongest military in the world at that time. God is forgiving and slow to anger. But He is also a just God. He could not let the people continue in their sinful ways. They must be punished to help them learn about God's will and ways. Other than Joshua and Caleb, no one older than 20 years would enter the land. Israel would be a new people on their return to Canaan, a people ready to follow God's command.

## Words to Remember

*The LORD is slow to anger, abounding in love and forgiving sin. Numbers 14:18*

- As you say the Bible verse together, suggest that children stretch out the word *slo-o-o-o-w* to emphasize it. Explain that *abounding* is very much like the word *overflowing*. To demonstrate that, place your hands over your heart, raise them above your head, and extend them out to the side to represent an overflowing fountain of God's love. To emphasize *forgiving* have everyone make the sign of the cross on themselves as a reminder that we have forgiveness because of the cross of Jesus.
- Have children say the verse while standing and facing a partner. As one person says the first half of the verse, the partners shake hands. Then, continuing to hold right hands, do a left-hand handshake as the second person says the second part of the verse. Point out that in doing so, they have crossed their arms, which reminds us that God shows His love and offers forgiveness through Jesus, who died on the cross to save us.
- Always keep in mind that many of the ideas for using the memory verse can also be used as part of your worship time.

## Extending the Lesson

- God led the people of Israel to an abundant land, flowing with "milk and honey." On a map or globe locate that land and also the land in which you live. Talk about how God has blessed your country with climate, resources, freedom to worship, and so on.
- Discuss the blessings God has given you in your local community such as industry, farming, natural resources, scenery, transportation, health care, and so on.
- Have students write three words that describe what they like best about their land. Then ask them to write three describing words that tell what they think they will like about heaven, which is promised to us through the salvation Christ offers us.

## INTRODUCE

Use the puppet Jake to introduce a main concept of the Bible story. Jake looks droopy and sad.

**TEACHER:** Hi, Jake. You look like you need cheering up. Maybe we can play a new game at recess. Would you like that?

**JAKE:** I don't really like new games.

**TEACHER:** You don't? Why is that?

**JAKE:** New things can be kind of scary. Like with a new game or a new math skill, I'm afraid I won't do it right. Or like making a new friend or moving to a new town, I'm afraid I won't know what to say or I'll be lonely.

**TEACHER:** I understand now. The people of Israel felt that way too. They were going to a new land and were very frightened. They forgot that God was always with them. He never changes. Let's review what happened.

# The 12 Spies

*(Numbers 13:1–14:25)*

When the people of Israel came near the Promised Land, God told Moses, "Send 12 spies to see what the land is like." The spies searched for 40 days. When they returned, they gave this report: "The land is good and has lots of food. It is a land flowing with milk and honey." They showed the people the huge bunches of grapes from the land. This seemed so much better than the desert, where they had been traveling for so many months.

But the spies were afraid of the people who lived in the new land. They said, "The people are powerful and live in great cities with high walls. We seemed like small grasshoppers next to them."

Joshua and Caleb, two of the spies, said, "Don't be afraid. God is with us. He has helped us in the past. He is stronger than any enemy." But the people would not listen. They wanted to choose a new leader instead of Moses.

God said to Moses, "Will these people never learn to trust Me?" Moses asked God to forgive the people. God did forgive them, but the people who complained would not get to go into the new land. Only their children and Joshua and Caleb would one day enter it. In the meantime, the people lived in the desert for 40 more years.

The people were sorry they had sinned, but they were glad that God forgave them. God forgives our sins, too, because of Jesus, our Savior.

7

## DEVELOP

Cut apart Sections 1–4 of the Promised Land poster. Gather the children close so they can see the pictures well. Ask the children to tell what is happening in each picture. (1—Spies check out a walled city in Canaan. 2—To show it is a land "flowing with milk and honey," they bring back huge clusters of grapes. 3—The people angrily complain that they were brought to a land with powerful enemies. 4—God continues to provide for the people as they wander in the wilderness for 40 years as punishment for not trusting God.) Display these pictures on a bulletin board so that in future lessons more pictures can be added. Distribute the *Moving On* Student Book and use page 7 for further review.

## RESPOND

Turn to page 8 in the Student Book. Ask, **Why were the Israelites afraid to go into the new land?** (Ten spies said that the people in the land were fierce giants.) List, with the children's help, some of the things we fear today. Have the children copy some of these words in the sharp-edged shape.

Ask, **What did Joshua and Caleb tell the people?** (They reminded the people of God's power, His help in the past, and His promise to give them this land.) **God kept all His promises to His people, including His promise to send the Savior, Jesus, to rescue us from our worst enemies—sin, death, and Satan.** Talk about how we can go to Jesus in prayer, asking Him to take away what we fear or to take away our fear and make us strong in Him. List some of the things we have because of Jesus—faith, trust, forgiveness, comfort. Have children write some of these words inside the outline of Jesus.

**Instead of looking at the things we fear, let's concentrate on the many blessings we have from the Lord. We have these things because we have been forgiven and made children of God through Jesus.** Ask the children to help you build a "word web" on the chalkboard. At the center print the word *blessings* and circle the word. Draw lines extending from the word to indicate categories of blessings. Draw lines from these categories to indicate specific blessings. (See sample diagram.) Use these words in a thank-You prayer during your worship time.

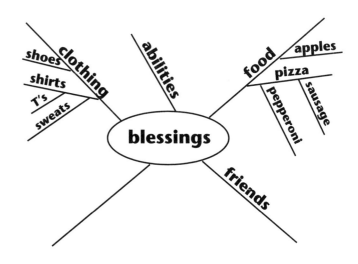

# Fear
## and Faith

*Directions: Circle the missing words in the puzzle and draw a line to show where the words belong.*

The Lord is _____ to anger,

_____ in _____ and

_____ sin.  Numbers 14:18

```
o c (s l o w) f d o g
e k l z d p h a t q
(a b o u n d i n g) x
q z w m e o t i m e
w p (l o v e) h g e t
s (f o r g i v i n g)
```

Words to Remember
*The LORD is faithful to all His promises. Psalm 145:13*

8

59

## Day 1

### Discovery Point

God is with us always, wherever we go.

### Joshua Becomes the New Leader

Deuteronomy 31:1–8; Joshua 1:1–9

### Objectives

That by the power of the Holy Spirit working through God's Word, the students will
- grow in joyful trust and confidence in God's promise to be with them wherever they go;
- rely on God's protection and strength at all times;
- rejoice that because of Jesus, their journey in this life is covered by His grace and will one day lead to life with Him in heaven.

### Day 1 Materials

- Blackline 7-A
- 3 signs
- Promised Land poster, Section 5

### Day 2 Materials

- *Moving On* Student Book
- 3 signs

## INTRODUCE

Ask, **Can you name something that is too difficult for a baby to do?** Listen to responses. Then follow the same line of questioning, asking, **Can you name something that is too hard for you to do? What might be too difficult for even a grown-up to do? Is anything too hard for the Lord?** Help the class understand that God is all-powerful. Read aloud Matthew 19:26b. **We can trust God in all things. Today we will hear that the people of Israel learned that God is faithful. They learned from Him to trust Him always to do what is best for them. We can ask God to help us grow in faith and trust too.**

## DEVELOP

In advance make three signs saying *Egypt, Desert, Promised Land*. Use Section 5 of the Promised Land poster to tell the Bible story. Fold the picture in half to show just Moses. Walk over to the *Egypt* sign and review how God chose Moses to lead the people out of slavery. Walk past the *Desert* sign to the *Promised Land* sign, reviewing the events of the 12 spies and revealing the picture of Joshua along with Moses. Return to the desert for 40 years of wandering. Point out that during that time Joshua and Caleb helped Moses in many ways and learned from him. Return once more to the *Promised Land* sign. Explain that **During 40 years many changes took place. Some people were born, some grew older, and others died. During this time God showed His faithfulness to His people. Once again they were near the Promised Land. This time they were eager to go in, ready to trust in the Lord.**

Point out that Moses was now 120 years old. He gathered the people together and told them he was too old to continue as their leader. God had chosen a new leader—Joshua. Read aloud the words that Moses said to Joshua in Deuteronomy 31:6.

Fold the picture in half to show just Joshua. Point out that Moses had been the leader of the people all their lives. It was sad that he would no longer be with them. But they trusted that God would always be with them. Read aloud God's words from Joshua 1:9. **As God was with Moses He was also with Joshua. Joshua trusted God's faithfulness in all things.**

# RESPOND

To emphasize that God's promise to Joshua is also His promise to us, walk around the class, placing your hand on each child's head, saying the child's name and this blessing from Joshua 1:9: "_____ , the Lᴏʀᴅ your God will be with you wherever you go."

Continue, **Jesus loves us so much that He came to earth from heaven to live here with His people, to die for us, and to rise again at Easter. When Jesus returned to heaven on Ascension Day, He gave a special promise to us.** Distribute copies of Blackline 7-A to find the words of that promise (Matthew 28:20). Remind children that even though we can no longer see Jesus in His body, He is true God, and though invisible to us, He is always near to help and bless us, just as He promised.

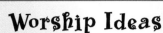

## Worship Ideas

- Point out that the people of Israel must have been sad that Moses would no longer be their leader. He was 120 years old, and they had known him most of their lives. He must have seemed like a father or grandfather to them. But Moses pointed the way to God, our true Father who cares for us in all things. Because Jesus forgives our sins and makes us children of God, we can now go to Him, as in the Lord's Prayer, saying, "Our Father, who art in heaven." Have the children say that sentence with you and any other parts of the Lord's Prayer that they know as you speak the prayer in its entirety. Remind them that they can pray silently in their hearts even if they don't know all the words to say aloud.
- Sing "My God Is So Great" (*LOSP*, p. 64, and on CD). The song "God Is with Me" is especially appropriate to use. It is available from Concordia Publishing House in *Songs Kids Love to Sing 2*, (p. 13) and on its accompanying CD.

## Bible Background

After 40 years of wandering, it was now time for Israel to enter Canaan, and it was also time for Moses to die. He gathered the people—a new generation—to remind them of all that God had done and all that God commanded. Moses turned over his leadership publicly to prevent any controversy after his death. Joshua was installed in a formal ceremony of laying on of hands. Joshua had shown himself to be (1) a devout servant of the Lord, (2) "full of the Holy Spirit and wisdom," (3) a faithful helper to Moses, and (4) endowed with talents needed for leadership.

Moses also reminded them of the Messiah to come, who would be born from the tribe of Judah. He urged them to listen to the Savior and cling faithfully to Him (Deuteronomy 30:20). God the Father would echo these words centuries later on the Mount of Transfiguration (where Moses appeared with Elijah), where the Father said of Jesus, "This is My Son, whom I love; with Him I am well pleased. Listen to Him!" (Matthew 17:5).

---

## A Promise for You

*Cut out the decoder at the bottom of the page. Carefully cut on the dotted lines to cut out the spaces on the decoder. Place the decoder over the box of letters. Read Jesus' promise to you.*

Matthew 28:20

```
B O Q S N R T O V D A E L O N M U W
E I A M F O B S R E B X O P Z R S X
V A R S E L I O F G D S Z O T I L M
I O F B W I T H X R N I Y O U R T U
S R X O E V B A E O U C E G H C Y C
L N T P A L W A Y S E Z M C B A E Q
Z T S V X Z M P E B L D N R Z V I X
```

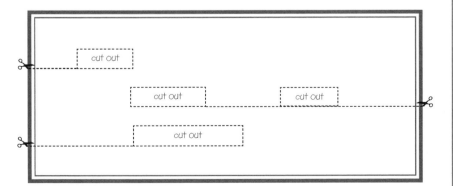

cut out

cut out          cut out

cut out

**Blackline 7-A**

## Words to Remember

*The LORD your God will be with you wherever you go. Joshua 1:9*

- Print the Bible words in large letters and duplicate a copy for each child. Children may trace over the letters with a glitter pen or puff paint and add decoration to the background. Suggest that they enlist a parent's help to display this above a doorway leading out of their home. This will be a constant reminder that God goes with them everywhere.
- The Bible words this week are used in worship, the Bible story presentation, and the Student Book. Continue to find appropriate times in various settings to refer to these words. Help the children to see that God's Word is fitting in many (any) settings.

## Extending the Lesson

- See if the children can create sentences about the Bible story, using pairs of opposite words such as *come/go; in/out; young/old; men/women; boys/girls; land/water; desert/farmland.*
- Suggest that children use the decoder from Blackline 7-A to create new messages about God, such as *Jesus hears your prayers; The Lord loves you; Jesus forgives your sins.*
- Identify your government leaders in local and national offices. Pray that God would touch the hearts of the leaders to follow God's ways and faithfully to trust in Him.

## Day 2

## INTRODUCE

Sing together "I Am Trusting You, Lord Jesus" (*LOSP*, p. 24, and on CD). Then say, **We've been talking about trusting God, and we just sang about trust. What does *trust* mean?** Listen to responses and then summarize that trusting means you feel safe and secure that the person will do what they say and you will be able to rely on their honesty and ability. Demonstrate *trust* by calling on two volunteers (one should be a smaller child, perhaps even someone from a younger class, and the other a larger child). Stand next to the smaller child, and say to the larger child, **If I asked you to turn around, close your eyes, and fall backwards, whom would you trust to catch you, me or her/him? Why?** Then explain that we can put much greater trust in the Lord not only because of His almighty power, but also because He has always kept His word. Take another look at the faithfulness of God.

## Joshua Becomes the New Leader

*(Deuteronomy 31:1–8; Joshua 1:1–9)*

The people of Israel traveled in the desert for 40 years. Finally it was the right time to enter the Promised Land. Moses gathered the people to remind them once again of all that God commanded them and of God's faithfulness to them.

The people listened as Moses said he would no longer lead them. "God has chosen Joshua to be your new leader. Trust in the Lord. God will go ahead of you across the Jordan River. He will defeat your enemies. Be strong and full of courage."

Then God told Moses to go up on a mountain. From there, Moses could see the beautiful Promised Land. God had kept His promise. Moses died there on the mountain. God buried him there.

The Lord was with Joshua, the new leader. God is with you too. He is with you wherever you go.

9

## D E V E L O P

Display again the *Egypt, Desert, Promised Land* signs from yesterday. Move from one sign to the next, asking the children to identify how God faithfully blessed His people in each location. **As the people looked at all the ways God took care of them, they began to grow in trust in the Lord.**

Turn the three signs over and write *School, Home, Playground* on the back. Ask the children ways that God is with them and blesses them in each location. **When you have troubles or fears at school, home, on the playground, or wherever you may be, talk to God in prayer. Trust that He is near and can help you.** Distribute the *Moving On* Student Book and use pages 9–10 to review the lesson concepts.

## R E S P O N D

Take the children outside for this closing activity. If weather does not permit that, use a large flashlight indoors. Let children explore moving with their shadows. Ask, **Can you outrun your shadow? Can you make yourself so small that your shadow disappears?** Take the children to a shaded area to sit down. Ask, **What has happened to our shadows?**

Say, **Our shadow experiment reminds me of some things I know about God. God has promised to be with us always. Whenever I see my shadow, I think to myself, God is just as close as my shadow. That helps me feel happy and safe to know that God is with me.**

**Other times, like now, when I cannot see my shadow, I still think about God's promise. I know that even though I do not see God, He is still right beside me.** Read aloud God's promise to us from Hebrews 13:5b. Sing "I'm with You" (*LOSP*, p. 32, and on CD).

---

## A Special Promise

*Jesus said, "I am with you always." He is with us each day. And one day He will take us to be with Him in heaven. Start with the picture of the children and draw a line to connect the pictures of places where God is with you. Color each picture you come to.*

Words to Remember

*The LORD your God will be with you wherever you go. Joshua 1:9*

10

## Discovery Point

God is with us always, wherever we go.

## Entering the Promised Land

Joshua 1; 3–4

## Objectives

That by the power of the Holy Spirit working through God's Word, the students will
- feel confident that God will provide for all their needs in their life on earth;
- rejoice in the gift of Jesus, our Savior, and His promise to take us to the promised land of heaven;
- praise God for His guidance and care in all things.

## Day 3 Materials

- Blackline 7-B
- Large box
- Gold paper or paint
- Long blue rolls of paper

## Day 4 Materials

- *Moving On* Student Book
- Pictures of famous monuments
- 12 bricks or bags
- Long blue rolls of paper

# Day 3

## INTRODUCE

In advance prepare a large box (about two feet by three feet in size) to represent the ark of the covenant. Cover it with gold gift wrap or spray paint it gold. (You can add gold winged angels at the top and wrapped cardboard tubes for poles, but this is not necessary. You can tell the children about details of the real ark, which was so much grander than your gold box.)

Begin by asking, **What reminders do we have in this room that God is here and that He loves us?** (Children may refer to pictures, crosses, Bibles, etc.) Bring out the gold box you have prepared and say, **The people of Israel had reminders of God and His love. They put these reminders in a very special gold box called the ark of the covenant. In the box they placed things like the Ten Commandments and a bowl of manna to remind them of God's will and God's care. This box, the ark of the covenant, will have an important part in today's Bible story.**

## DEVELOP

Say, **The people of Israel were walking in the desert. But they had to stop. In front of them were deep and raging waters. They could go no farther.** In an open area set out two long strips of blue paper or two blue blankets side by side. Ask, **Doesn't this sound familiar? Didn't we already have a Bible story like this?** See what the children remember about the story of the crossing of the Red Sea. Then point out the differences in this story. **Forty years have gone by; Joshua is now the leader of the people; this was the Jordan River, not the Red Sea; and instead of grumbling and complaining to God that they would die, the people now trusted that God had a plan and would save them.**

Act out the Bible story. Have two children be the priests holding the gold box. Have one of them touch the waters with his toe, then you can pull one section of the blue material aside to make a "dry path" in-between. (Do not make a wall of water as at the Red Sea. Just show that the flooded river stopped flowing.) The priests should stand in the middle of the river as all the children pass by to the other side. Then push the blue sections together again. (You will use them again tomorrow.)

Say, **God had helped His people at the Red Sea at the beginning of their journey. And He helped them at the end of their journey at the Jordan River, just as He had been with them everywhere in-between.**

*Option:* If you made the transparency map for Week 6-B, you may want to refer to the map again and complete the crossing of the Jordan River into the Promised Land.

# RESPOND

Display the gold box you made to represent the ark of the covenant. Point out that the box itself had no power; it was a reminder of God's presence and contained reminders of His help in the past. **If today we placed reminders of the love of Jesus into this box, what might they be?** (Perhaps a red paper heart, a cross, a Bible.) Point out that reminders can be helpful, but all we need to know about Jesus is in God's Word. Hold up a Bible and thank God that in this one place we have all the reminders we need of God's love, forgiveness, power, and grace. But continue to thank God for all the additional things that help us focus on Him and His grace.

Distribute copies of Blackline 7-B. Follow directions to make a miniature ark of the covenant as a reminder of today's Bible story. Children may "update" their arks by placing in them paper cutouts of a heart, cross, and Bible.

## The Ark of the Covenant

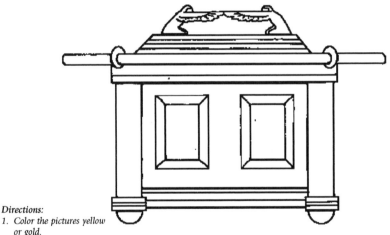

Directions:
1. Color the pictures yellow or gold.
2. Cut out both pictures.
3. Cut the top off a half-pint milk carton.
4. Tape the pictures to opposite sides of the carton.

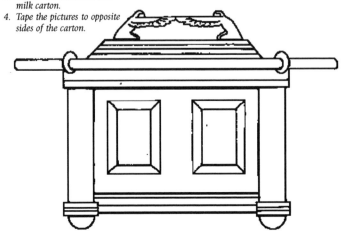

# Worship Ideas

- God gave His people a land "flowing with milk and honey." In other words, food was plentiful. There was an abundance of fruit and other things to eat. Recognizing the plentiful abundance we have today, praise God with tangerines. As the children examine, peel, and eat the tangerines, stop to consider how all your senses can be involved in thank-You prayers to God. Thank God for the bright color of the fruit (sight), the firm thumping sound it makes as you toss it up and catch it (sound), the texture of the skin as it easily pulls away from the wet and stringy pulp (touch), the fragrance that fills the room (smell), and the juicy flavor (taste).
- Give a cheer for Jesus, asking the children to respond.
  **Give me a J.** (J)
  **Give me an E.** (E)
  **Give me an S.** (S)
  **Give me a U.** (U)
  **Give me another S.** (S)
  **What does that spell?** (Jesus.)
  **Who is with us right here, right now?** (Jesus.)
  **Who is always with us, wherever we go?** (Jesus.)
  Sing "Jesus! What a Name" (*LOSP*, p. 47, and on CD). Sing other favorite songs that begin with the name *Jesus*.

# Bible Background

As the children of Israel approach the Jordan River for the second time, it is spring-time—the days of Passover and the early grain harvest. Because of the spring rains and snowmelt from Mount Hermon, the Jordan is at flood stage. It is time for another miracle.

The priests are instructed to carry the ark of the covenant ahead of the people. Fittingly they will be the first to reach the Promised Land, for the ark represents God's presence. God Himself will lead His people into their new homeland.

The miracle at the Jordan River recalls the miracle 40 years earlier at the Red Sea. But this is a new generation of people with a new leader. The message of deliverance is not to be forgotten, so the people are told to build a memorial of stones from the riverbed. It will be a visual statement of God's care in that place.

## Words to Remember

*I will never leave you nor forsake you.*
*Joshua 1:5*

After the Bible story lesson on Day 4, let the children scramble the "stones" on which the Bible verse is printed. Then they may unscramble the words as they stack the "stones" back in place.

## Extending the Lesson

- Sing the following words to the tune of "B-I-N-G-O." (Consider the abilities of the children in your class when determining procedure: before each stanza you could tell the children the words of the first line and then sing the whole stanza together; or perhaps just the teacher should sing the first line of each stanza with the children singing the repeated parts.)
  1. **I have a friend who loves me so, and Jesus is His name-O. J-E-S-U-S, J-E-S-U-S, J-E-S-U-S. And Jesus is His name-O.**
  2. **I have a friend who died for me ...**
  3. **I have a friend who forgives sins ...**
  4. **I have a friend who lives in heaven ...**
  5. **He'll come again and take me there ...**
  6. **He is your friend and loves you too ...**
- Discuss the fact that people and places may have several names and even nicknames. Give an example of a person the children are familiar with. Point out that the *Promised Land* in our Bible story is sometimes called *Canaan, Judea,* or *Israel.* Also mention that the land God has promised to us has several names: *heaven, paradise, eternal life,* and *everlasting life.*

# Day

## INTRODUCE

Show the children several pictures of famous monuments such as the Washington Monument, Mount Rushmore, the Gateway Arch in St. Louis, or the Lincoln and Jefferson Memorials. (You can find pictures in encyclopedias or library books.) See if the children can identify some of the pictures. Ask, **Do you know why we have monuments?** (As reminders of people and events.) **Yesterday we learned about the people of Israel crossing the Jordan River. But there is more to the story. Let's learn about the people building a monument to remind them of how God had helped them at that place.** Review the story by reading to the children page 11 in the *Moving On* Student Book.

## DEVELOP

To prepare for the children acting out this part of the story, in advance prepare 12 "stones." These can be either bricks or brown

# Entering the Promised Land

*(Joshua 1;3–4)*

At last, the time had come for the people of Israel to go into the Promised Land. God told Joshua, the new leader, "Be strong and brave. Lead My people into the land I have promised to them. I will be with you."

The people were stopped by the Jordan River. The waters were flooding and flowing very fast. God said, "Have the priests carry the ark of the covenant ahead of the people. I will make a path through the river for you."

As soon as the priests stepped into the river, the water stopped flowing. The people walked to the other side. God had Joshua direct 12 men to carry 12 large stones from the dry path and stack them together on the other side. In years to come, whenever someone would ask about the 12 stones, the people would say, "It is a monument to remind us how God helped us in this place."

God is also with you. He will lead you in life wherever you go. He does this because you are His loved, forgiven, and redeemed child.

11

paper bags stuffed with crumpled newspaper. Use a marking pen to write a number and tribe of Judah on one side. (Put *Levi* in parentheses on stone 12. The Levites were priests and temple helpers who lived within all the tribes but did not have a portion of the land for themselves.) On the other side of each stone write a word of today's Bible verse. (Note: See the song below for the names of the tribes of Judah. Include the words *God says* at the beginning of the Bible verse and the reference at the end so that you have 12 portions.)

Act out the Bible story, using the blue paper strips or blue blankets from yesterday. Children will march across the divided river as they sing a song to the tune of "London Bridge Is Falling Down." Assign 12 children to be rock carriers. When their designated number is called they are to place the rock on the Promised Land side, stacking the rocks up to make a monument. (If using paper bags, use tape to hold bags in position.) The children will pretend to be part of each of the tribes, so after each stanza they should line up again on the far side of the river, ready to cross it once more, till all 12 tribes have entered the Promised Land. Sing these stanzas.

(1) Simeon, please go on in, go on in, go on in.
Simeon, please go on in. Trust the Lord.

(2) Benjamin … (3) Ephraim … (4) Zebulun … (5) Issachar … (6) Manasseh … (7) Naphtali … (8 and 9) Dan and Gad …

*(Note: On the remaining stanzas, eliminate the word* please *to fit the rhythm.)*

(10 and 11) Judah, Reuben … (12) (Levi), Asher …

Say, **The monument of 12 stones was a reminder of God's goodness. Whenever someone saw the stones and asked what the monument was for, the people had an opportunity to tell about the Lord.** Look at the stone monument on page 12 of the Student Book. Have children "build" their own monument by writing a word or drawing a picture on each stone to describe a blessing they receive from God. Make a list of shared ideas on the chalkboard so that everyone can readily participate. Include some of the words on the list in a thank-You prayer at worship time.

# Remember

*What are some blessings God has given you?*
*Write a word or draw a picture of these on the stones.*

Words to Remember

*[God says,] "I will never leave you nor forsake you." Joshua 1:5*

12

## Discovery Point

Our loving God uses His power to win victories for His children, sometimes through ordinary people and sometimes in miraculous ways.

## Rahab Helps the Spies

Joshua 2

## Objectives

That by the power of the Holy Spirit working through God's Word, the students will
- grow in trusting faith that God is always on their side;
- know that God sometimes helps them through the efforts of other people;
- rejoice in the victory Jesus has won for them over sin, death, and the power of the devil.

## Day 1 Materials

- Blackline 8-A
- Flashlight
- Costume or headband
- Bag of various items

## Day 2 Materials

- *Moving On* Student Book
- Jenna puppet

# INTRODUCE

At the center of the room place a bright flashlight. Darken the classroom and gather the children together to be seated around the light as if it were a campfire. Pretend that you are Israelite people waiting for word from two spies Joshua sent to investigate the city of Jericho.

Talk about what spies do. (Find out where the enemy is, how many weapons they have, what their weaknesses and strengths are.) Help students get a feel for the excitement and intrigue of the Bible story by using descriptive words and hushed tones. Tell the children to wait quietly as you and a volunteer go out of the room. Put on a costume or wear a sash around your forehead (likewise for the volunteer).

# DEVELOP

Assume the character of the two spies and return to the room. Say something similar to this (but without reading it): **Shh! Quiet everyone! We've just returned from our spying mission. What a story we have to tell! Jericho is a large city with a high wall protecting it. But we know God's power is greater than that wall. We sneaked through the city gate and into the home of a woman named Rahab. Rahab believes in the power and truth of our God. She hid us when soldiers came looking for us.**

**When the soldiers left, Rahab told us that everyone has heard how God parted the Red Sea and defeated all our enemies. She said everyone is afraid of us. She asked us to remember her kindness. We promised to harm no one in her home when we return. She put a red cord in the window so we will know which house is hers.**

**Then she helped us escape. She used a rope to let us climb down the wall to safety. We waited in the woods for three days so the soldiers could not find us. Then we ran here as fast as we could to tell you that God has given the whole land into our hands. Trust the power of the Lord!**

# R E S P O N D

Ask, **Who did God use to help the people in this story?**
(God used the two spies to help the people be courageous; God
used Rahab to protect the spies.) **God gives us helpers today too.**
Let volunteers reach into a bag, grab an object, and tell the class
who might help them with the item. (Examples: math flash
card/teacher; baseball/coach; extinguished matchstick/firefighter;
stop sign/police officer; bandage/nurse, etc.) In a prayer, thank
God for giving you all of these helpers.

Distribute copies of Blackline 8-A. Say, **Let's think about the
helper God sent to help us with our greatest enemies.** Have children cut out the six illustrations. **Our greatest danger comes from
sin and death.** Have children place the words *sin* and *death* side by
side with space between them. **And also from "the power of the
devil."** Have children align those words vertically between the first
two in order to make a cross. Tape the sections of the cross together.

Say, **Jesus won the victory over sin, death, and the power of
the devil. And He gives that victory to us!** Use a crayon to draw
an *X* over each word to show that Jesus defeated those enemies.
**Jesus forgives our sins and makes us strong in faith to live as
His people. He can use us to be helpers too!**

## Jesus Has Won the Victory!

| sin | death |
|-----|-------|
| the | power |
| of the | devil |

## Worship Ideas

- Celebrate the victory we have in the Lord by
singing "My God Is So Great" (*LOSP*, p. 64,
and on CD). Add the actions.
  **My God is so great,** (Cup your hands around
  your mouth.)
  **So strong and so mighty!** (Flex muscles.)
  **There's nothing my God cannot do!** (Hands
  on hips power stance.)
  (Repeat first three lines.)
  **The mountains are His,** (Form peaks with
  hands above your head.)
  **The rivers are His,** (Hands form rippling waves.)
  **The stars are His handiwork too.** (Open and
  close hands quickly to "twinkle.")
  (Repeat first three lines again.)

- Practice these motions to "Praise God, from
Whom All Blessings Flow" (*LOSP*, p. 65). Use
the motions any time you sing this song.
  **Praise God** (Clap on each word.)
  **From whom all blessings flow.** (Extend open
  arms to the sides.)
  **Praise Him** (Clap on each word.)
  **All creatures here below.** (Extend open arms
  downward.)
  **Praise Him** (Clap on each word.)
  **Above, O heavenly host.** (Extend open arms
  upward.)
  **Praise Father,** (Raise right hand to forehead.)
  **Son,** (Lower right hand to heart.)
  **And Holy Ghost.** (Touch each shoulder, com-
  pleting the sign of the cross.)

## Bible Background

Rahab is of special interest not only
because she furthered the cause of the people
of God but also because she became an ancestor of Christ. Rahab had heard of the mighty
works of God. She trusted that He alone could
save her and her family. Hebrews 11:31 speaks
of her faith. This faith she expressed by joining
herself to God's people, even as her neighbors
were fighting against them. And what a blessed
result. After a period of ceremonial preparation
outside the camp, Rahab became fully incorpo-
rated into the chosen nation. She married
Salmon, an ancestor of King David, from the
tribe of Judah. Only much later would God's ultimate plan for Rahab be fulfilled when one of her
descendants would be the Savior of all nations
(Matthew 1:5–16).

## Words to Remember

*I have had God's help to this very day. Acts 26:22*

- Ask children to think of a specific example of how God has blessed them. Let volunteers share their stories. Ask them to begin by saying the words of the Bible verse.
- The most important help we receive is from Jesus, who offers us forgiveness and life eternal through His death and resurrection. This demonstrates God helping us spiritually. He also helps us physically with our wants and needs. Praise God together for His help spiritually and physically.

## Extending the Lesson

- Have children make medallions. On a large circle of colored paper, they are to print the message "✝-is-#-1-2-me" (*Jesus is number 1 to me).* String a length of red cord through a hole at the top of the circle so children can wear them around their necks. **What are you reminded of when you see the red cord?**
- Before class, hide pictures or photos of helpers, such as a pastor, principal, coach, doctor, firefighter, cook, and custodian. The only visible clue should be a red cord (yarn) taped to each picture. Divide the children into "spy" teams to find one (or two) pictures. Gather together and ask each team to tell how God uses people like this in their lives. Later place the pictures on a bulletin board with the red cords reaching to a picture of Jesus at the center. Title the board something like "Jesus, My Helper, Make Me a Helper."

# Day 2

## INTRODUCE

Introduce the lesson using the puppet Jenna, who is hanging her head sadly.

**TEACHER:** Jenna, why do you look so sad? We've been talking this week about all the people God puts into our lives to help us. That should make you very happy.

**JENNA:** I *am* happy God gives me helpers. But that is part of the problem. I need a lot of help because I mess up so much. And I want to help others, but I mess up so much. That's why I'm so sad.

**TEACHER:** But that's why you should be so happy! Talk to God about this. Jesus forgives the times we mess up. And we can ask Him to help us learn and grow and become strong in faith to be a better helper.

**JENNA:** I wish I was like Rahab. It was so cool—the way she helped the spies.

# Rahab
## Helps the Spies

*(Joshua 2)*

God's people were now in the land God promised to them. But wicked people lived there. God told Joshua, "Destroy the wicked city of Jericho."

Joshua sent two spies to find out more about the city's high wall and its army. The spies needed a safe place to stay. A woman named Rahab kept the spies hidden in her home, which was attached to Jericho's wall.

While Rahab hid the spies under grain on her roof, the soldiers pounded on her door. Rahab told them, "The spies have already left. You must hurry to catch them."

When the soldiers left, Rahab told the spies she believed in the great power of God. The spies promised to remember Rahab's kindness. They said, "Hang a red cord out the window. That will be a secret sign so our people will know where you live. No one will hurt you and your family."

Rahab tied a rope to her window. The spies climbed down the rope to safety. They returned to Joshua and told the people, "The Lord has surely given the whole land into our hands."

God blessed the spies through Rahab, their helper. God blesses you with helpers too. Your best help comes from Jesus, who loves and forgives you!

**TEACHER:** But Rahab was also a sinner. She had messed up in a big way. But God forgave her sins and blessed her. She even became the great-great … grandmother of our Savior, Jesus. What a blessing!

**JENNA:** Let's hear Rahab's story again.

## DEVELOP

Review the Bible story, using either page 13 of the *Moving On* Student Book or your own words. Have the children imitate your actions as you tell the story. This will keep them focused. You can tiptoe (in place) to Jericho; place your index finger on your lips (Shh!) as Rahab quietly talks to the spies; crouch low as you tell of Rahab hiding the spies on the roof; hand-over-hand climb down an imaginary rope as the spies escape from Jericho; and run (in place) after hiding in the woods to tell the news to Israel's camp.

## RESPOND

Use page 14 of the Student Book to discuss ways that the children can become helpers. Emphasize that **Whatever you do, whether in word or deed, do it all in the name of the Lord Jesus, giving thanks to God the Father through Him** (Colossians 3:17).

*Option:* Read aloud the Big Book *Jesus Helps Me to Help Others,* available from Concordia Publishing House.

# God
## Bless Us All

*God has blessed us with many helpers. How could you be a helper to these helpers? Draw a red cord (line) to connect pictures with answers in the box. There may be several people you can help wih the same answer.*

Teacher

**Be kind**

**Obey**

Family

Friends

**Cheer up**

**Share**

**Tell others**

Neighbor

Pastor

**Offer to help**

**Say hello**

Jesus

Words to Remember
*I have had God's help to this very day. Acts 26:22*

14

## Discovery Point

Our loving God uses His power to win victories for His children, sometimes through ordinary people and sometimes in miraculous ways.

## The Fall of Jericho

Joshua 6

## Objectives

That by the power of the Holy Spirit working through God's Word, the students will
- grow in confident joy at the great power God continues to use to bless His people;
- know that through Jesus, God gives them the victory over their greatest enemies—sin, death, and the power of the devil;
- praise and thank Jesus that He gives them His victory.

## Day 3 Materials

- Jericho Arch book (Teacher Kit)
- Blackline 8-B
- White mural paper

## Day 4 Materials

- *Moving On* Student Book
- Promised Land poster, Sections 6–8
- Jake puppet
- *Songs Kids Love to Sing*

## INTRODUCE

Say, **Today we are going to talk about the fall of Jericho. But before the wall can come down, we have to build one up.** Children will enjoy helping you prepare the setting. Set out a long strip of white mural paper on the floor or on a table. Have children draw large stones to make the wall. Suggest that each stone be bigger than a computer screen (or person's head). *Option:* Have children stuff paper bags with crumpled newspaper to make the blocks of a wall.

## DEVELOP

Read aloud the story *Jericho's Tumbling Walls.* Then group several chairs together and encircle them with the wall the children made. The teacher can hold the wall in place as she retells the Bible story. The children will be the people of Israel, who move from the camp and around Jericho as the teacher instructs.

Explain that the battle plan was very unusual because God wanted the people to know that **The battle is the Lord's!** Tell the children to circle the city without making a sound and then return to their "camp." Do this a total of six times. Point out how difficult it must have been for the people to say nothing. Also note how frightened the people of Jericho must have been, watching this day after day and wondering when something would happen. Explain the unusual directions for the seventh day. The people marched around the city seven times. The priests blew trumpets made from rams' horns. The people shouted, and the wall of Jericho collapsed. (Act out day 7 and then drop the wall mural.)

**Only one family in Jericho survived the day. Do you know who that was?** (Rahab and her family were saved. After this they lived with the people of Israel.)

## RESPOND

Say, **That day at Jericho was a great victory for the Lord. Jesus won an even greater victory for us. What enemies did Jesus defeat?** (Sin, death, and the power of the devil.) **How did Jesus win the victory?** (By dying on the cross and arising at Easter.) **The best thing about Jesus' victory is that He gives the victory to us! We don't deserve it. We could never do it ourselves. But Jesus loves us, forgives us, and saves us.** Do a victory cheer together.

TEACHER: Give me a V. **Children:** V.
TEACHER: Give me an I. **Children:** I.
(*Continue in the same manner, spelling* victory.)
TEACHER: What does it spell? **Children:** Victory.
TEACHER: Shout it! **Children:** Victory!
TEACHER: Who gives us the victory? **Children:** Jesus.
TEACHER: Shout it! **Children:** Jesus!
All: Yeah!

Distribute copies of Blackline 8-B. Go through the cheer once more, but have the children write the letter they say on one of the stones pictured. Stop after the letter *Y.* Note that one stone remains. **The seven stones remind me of the wall of Jericho. The last stone reminds me of another Bible story in which the victory was even greater. What story and stone do you think it is?** (The stone the angel rolled away at Easter to show that Jesus was alive.) **To remember this great victory, draw a cross on the last stone. This is the victory Jesus gives to us.** (Repeat today's "Words to Remember.")

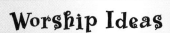

# Worship Ideas

- Dramatically read Psalm 121 to the children. This psalm speaks of the protection and victory we have in the Lord.
- Read Psalm 62:11–12a. Ask what two things the verse tells about God. (He is strong and loving.) Sing the following song, which emphasizes these two characteristics of the Lord. Sing to the tune of "Old MacDonald Had a Farm."

**God is loving; God is strong.**
**I will praise the Lord.**
**He shows love and pow'r to me.**
**I will praise the Lord.**
**With a "Praise God" here and a**
    **"Praise God" there,**
**Here, I'll praise; there, I'll praise;**
**Everywhere, I'll praise, praise.**
**God is loving; God is strong.**
**I will praise the Lord.**

# Bible Background

Modern excavation suggests that the ancient city of Jericho was surrounded by two walls, one 6 feet thick, the other 12 feet. The walls were about 30 feet high. The circumference of the city was approximately one mile. Israel had no experience whatsoever in assaulting a walled fortress. Joshua knew their only hope was in the Lord, who faithfully provided the plan.

The people followed God's plan as they followed the ark of the covenant, reminding them of the presence of the Lord. The sound of the trumpet on the seventh day announces the Lord's coming, and the walls fall down flat. The entire perimeter collapses; Israelite soldiers are able to charge from all angles. God decreed the destruction of the city. The walls of Jericho are to lie in ruins as a permanent reminder of God's judgment.

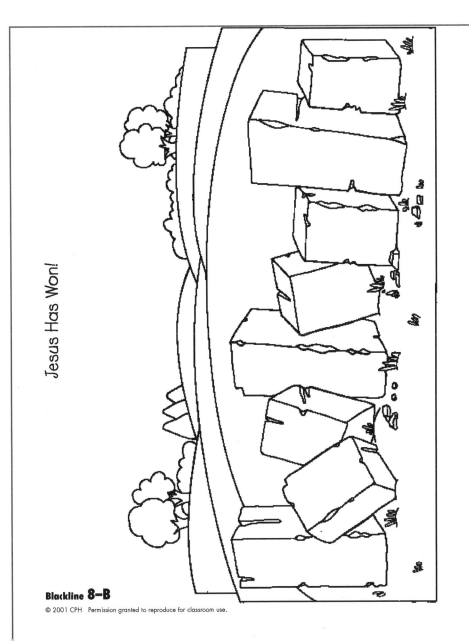

Jesus Has Won!

# Day

## Words to Remember

*Thanks be to God! He gives us the victory through our Lord Jesus Christ. 1 Corinthians 15:57*

Have the children use the Bible words to share a blessing with each other. They will be changing the word *us* to *you* and adding motions.

Each child faces a partner to say the verse. Shake hands on the word *thanks.* Point at your partner on the word *you.* And make the sign of the cross on yourself as you say, "Lord Jesus Christ." Switch partners several times, using this same procedure.

## Extending the Lesson

- Challenge students to spell the word *victory*, using their bodies to form the letters. Talk about the meaning of the word, especially with respect to God's action at Jericho and through Jesus at Calvary.

- Have students figure out the total number of times God's people marched around Jericho. (One time each day for six days. Then, seven times on the seventh day equals 13.)

- Consider how difficult it must have been for hundreds of thousands of Israelites to walk in total silence around the large city of Jericho. Discuss communicating without using your voice. Let the children invent several silent signals to use during the week (such as a signal to indicate it is time to stand up, time for quiet time, or time for recess).

## INTRODUCE

Use the puppet Jake to introduce the lesson.

**JAKE:** Teacher, I just don't get it. Yesterday we talked about the victory we have. We even did a victory cheer. But I don't always win. In fact, my soccer team hasn't won a game yet this year.

**TEACHER:** Jake, we weren't talking about winning games. We were talking about a much more important victory. With Jesus we are all winners. He gives us His love, forgiveness, and salvation.

**JAKE:** You mean I'm a winner even when I'm losing?

**TEACHER:** I guess you could say that. No matter what happens in our day-to-day life, we know God is with us, working to do what is best for us. And because of Jesus, we have the final and ultimate victory—we will live eternally with Jesus in heaven!

**JAKE:** That's even better than the Super Bowl and World Series put together!

## The Fall of Jericho

*(Joshua 6)*

The wicked people living in Jericho were afraid of the people of Israel. They knew God helped His people.

God told Joshua, "Tell the people to march silently around Jericho, once a day for six days. On the seventh day, march around the city seven times. Then the priests will blow their trumpets. The people will shout, and the city walls will fall down."

The people did exactly as God said. When the walls came down, the army of Israel destroyed the city. The two spies remembered their promise to Rahab. They rescued her and her family. Through the power of God, the people of Israel won the victory and were safe.

God has saved us from our worst enemies—sin, death, and the devil. He gives us the victory through Jesus and His miracle of salvation through His death on the cross and resurrection at Easter.

**TEACHER:** You can say that again!

**JAKE:** That's even better than the Super Bowl and World Series put together!

**TEACHER:** Let's hear once more about the victory at Jericho.

## DEVELOP

Without saying a word, motion for all the children to gather around you. Hold up Section 6 of the Promised Land poster. Then hold up seven fingers to indicate it is the seventh day and you will be marching seven times. Silently circle the room seven times with the children following you. Then hold up Section 7 of the poster and make a ta-da trumpet sound and all shout "Hooray!" Then march around the room in a victory celebration singing "I'm in the Lord's Army" (*Songs Kids Love to Sing*, p. 32; this book and CD are available from CPH). When the celebration march is over, have the children be seated and show Section 8 of the poster, which depicts the people of Israel settling into their new homeland. Display all of the Promised Land poster sections on a bulletin board so children can have a close look at each picture.

## RESPOND

When everyone is seated and settled, ask, **What protection did the people of Jericho have?** (A wall.) **What protection did the people of Israel have?** (The Lord.) **Which was the greater protection?** (The Lord.) **We have the same protection against sin and temptation. Jesus forgives our sins and helps us be strong to fight against temptation and follow God's ways.** Read 1 Peter 5:8–9a; Ephesians 6:10; and Psalm 60:12a.

Distribute the *Moving On* Student Book. Use pages 15–16 to review this lesson.

---

# V-I-C-T-O-R-Y!

*(Genesis 1–2)*

|   | ¹J | E | S | U | ²S |   |   | ³J |
|---|---|---|---|---|---|---|---|---|
|   | O |   |   |   | E |   |   | E |
|   | S |   | ⁴S | A | V | I | O | R |
|   | H |   |   |   | E |   |   | I |
|   | U |   | ⁵S | I | N | S |   | C |
|   | A |   |   |   |   |   |   | H |
|   |   |   |   |   |   |   |   | O |

**Down**
1. _____ led the people of Israel.
2. Israel marched around the city on _____ days.
3. God made the walls of _____ fall down.

**Across**
1. _____ is God's Son.
4. Jesus is my _____ .
5. Jesus died to take away my _____ .

Words to Remember

*Thanks be to God!*
*He gives us the victory through our Lord Jesus Christ. 1 Corinthians 1:57*

16

75

# UNIT 3

# Leaders

## Unit Overview

This unit of study and the accompanying Student Book are entitled *Leaders*. As you look at each person in this unit, continue to remind the children that all of these people are sinners, just like you and me. All of them made mistakes and needed the love of God and the salvation won for them and us by Jesus. Though these people are sometimes called "heroes of faith," always point out that the real hero in each person's story is God, demonstrating His grace and power.

Throughout this unit, also look at present-day leaders in home, school, church, city, and nation. Point out that these people, too, are sinners who need a Savior. Teach respect for leaders (Fourth Commandment) and frequently pray for them.

Send home copies of the family letter and Bible verse list for Unit 3 as you begin. (See the Teacher Resource Book.) This will let parents know what their children will be learning during the next few weeks. At the end of the unit, let the children take their *Leaders* Student Book home. Encourage them to show their parents what they have learned. This is the third in a series of nine books that will cover the story of salvation through the Old and New Testaments. Also consider adding some of the following activities to your curriculum to make related connections between God's message of love and all that you do throughout the day.

## Worship Connections

Continue to develop the children's awareness of elements in their church and in worship. Invite three people into your classroom who are leaders in your church: specifically, a pastor, the choir director, and an acolyte. Ask each of them to explain their role in a worship service. Have them wear their robes and explain any of the symbolism. (This will vary from church to church.) Point out that the robes covering the person remind us that who they are is not what is important; the main factor is that the blood of Jesus covers their sins. Jesus is not just a little portion of their lives, for they are now "robed" in Christ and His righteousness. Christ does the same for us. He surrounds us with His love and salvation. (Read Galatians 3:27; Romans 13:14a; and Isaiah 61:10a. Note that the letter *a* following a Bible reference refers to the first portion of the verse; *b* following a reference refers to the latter portion.)

## Community Building

This unit will likely be taught in November—a month that usually begins with elections of leaders. Have a mock election with campaign buttons and posters. Tell the children that you are going to pretend that you want them to elect you to be president of the class. Give a "campaign speech" telling why they should vote for you. Ham it up and say things such as, the new schedule will be one hour of work and five hours of recess per day. Say that you will pay each person $10 to vote for you. Tell them if you see them doing something wrong, you will turn the other way and never say a word about it. Say that they should vote for you because you are taller than they are or went to school longer than they did. Ask, **How many of you would vote for me? Would I be a good leader?** (Point out that good leaders don't make promises they can't keep. Good leaders don't try to bribe or buy your vote. Good leaders don't ignore what is wrong, but try to find a way to change things. What a person looks like, the money she has, or how good an athlete he is does not make a person a better leader.) Discuss what makes a good leader (e.g., points to God as our true leader, points to Jesus as our Savior, follows God's ways as shown in the commandments and the life of Jesus, shows forgiveness and kindness to others). Emphasize that we can do these things only with the Holy Spirit working in our hearts to help us live as children of God.

## Tools for Witness

This unit will probably end near Thanksgiving, a time when we think about some of the early leaders of our country, but we especially think about the many blessings God has poured on us. Make plans for ways to show thankfulness to God by sharing with others so that they have an abundant Thanksgiving Day to celebrate. Have the children make place mats with a thank-You prayer printed on them and a message that emphasizes the greatest blessing God gives—salvation through Jesus Christ. You may want to laminate these and then donate them to a homeless shelter.

## Service Projects

For this Thanksgiving project you will need several adult assistants, the use of a kitchen and oven, timers, and pot holders. Involve the children in baking pumpkin pies for a homeless shelter. (Let the shelter know in advance how many you will be donating.) Either have each child bring a frozen pie from the grocery store or donate money for the purchase of frozen pies. Have the adult assistants instruct the children, in groups of four or five at a time, about the procedures (opening the box, placing the pie on a cookie sheet for easier handling, setting two timers—one for the kitchen and one for the classroom). Note: Children should not have direct contact with the stove. Adults can take the cookie sheet out of the oven and have the children help them carry it over to a cooling rack and place it back in the box when cool. Have the children place a message about the love and forgiveness of Jesus into each pie box.

## Reaching Every Individual

God doesn't choose us to be leaders because of our excellent qualities; He chooses us because of the excellent qualities He has and uses to work *through* us. Help the children to see that God can use each of them to be leaders. Evenly distribute leadership of tasks such as leading the class to chapel or distributing art supplies. It's easy to keep track of this with a simple system. Write each child's name on a separate spring clothespin. Attach the clothespins around the edge of a small box or basket. Each time you need a leader, grab a clothespin, read the name, and place the clothespin inside the box. Children will appreciate the fairness of this system, and they will look forward to a chance to be a leader.

## Integrating the Faith

### Leaders

### Science

Give examples of scientists who were leaders. Note that because we are again dealing with human beings, the possibility for good or evil is always present. Recognize that our ability to think, discover, experiment, and learn is a gift from God. Pray that we may use these abilities to God's glory.

### Mathematics

Leaders often have to deal with the responsibility of budgeting and allocating money. Have the class imagine that they are in charge of a Cub Scout/Brownie banquet (or similar organization). The budget is $100. Plan together how you would use that money and how much you would spend on each item. (Note: Assume that this is a potluck and you do not have to purchase food.) Emphasize wise stewardship of the gifts God gives us.

### Social Studies

As you learn about leaders in our country, continue to pray that God may lead them to govern wisely.

### Language Arts

Ask, **If you were leader of this classroom for one day, what rules and plans would you make?** Have children dictate their ideas and list them on a chart. Decide which ideas are truly useful and God pleasing and mark them with a check. Remind the children that we need God's forgiveness for times we are selfish and unkind. And we need God's blessing to help us live as His people in Christ.

### Fine Arts

Learn several patriotic songs. Pray that God would lead citizens to vote wisely and that God would bless us with good leaders.

### Technology

Technology, just like science and government and any other area of life, is subject to the consequences of sin. Discuss, after praying for God's guidance, proper ways to use new technologies. (For example, using a photocopier to copy pictures or a story without permission is like stealing someone else's work; instead, learn from their ideas and create your own, doing all to the glory of God.)

## Discovery Point

God has a plan for each of us—a plan already complete—to save us from sin through Jesus, His Son. He is a loving God, who cares for His people, sometimes working through other people to bless us.

## Ruth

The Book of Ruth

## Objectives

That by the power of the Holy Spirit working through God's Word, the students will
- recognize God's great love for them through Jesus, their Savior;
- grow in a desire to share God's gifts to them with others;
- know that God will help them love and care for others.

## Day 1 Materials
- World map or globe
- Blindfold
- Large red paper heart, tape
- Blackline 9-A
- Blank paper
- Leaders poster (display and refer to throughout all of Unit 3)

## Day 2 Materials
- World map or globe
- Happy-face stickers
- *Leaders* Student Book

# INTRODUCE

Invite each child to take a turn picking an area on the map or globe while wearing a blindfold. Remove the blindfold to discover the area and ask, **If we went to _____ , would God be there?** Continue, including some lesser known or very small countries. Emphasize how God would be with us any place on the globe or map. His love and care extend to every place they found. Even when we aren't thinking about God, God is thinking about us and is with us. **Today we will hear about a family that moved from place to place and had many changes. But God was always with them.**

# DEVELOP

In advance, prepare a large red construction paper heart. In the first half of the story, three large pieces are torn off the heart. During the second half of the story, the heart pieces are taped back on the heart.

**Long ago there lived a woman named Naomi. Naomi was from a country called Judah. Naomi moved with her husband and sons to a faraway land. There, Naomi and her family started to make a new life. Naomi's sons grew up and married. Things were happy. But then a sad thing happened. Naomi's husband died. Naomi's sons died too. Naomi's heart was broken. That means she felt very sad!** Tear one piece off the large heart.

Continue, **Naomi felt so sad and alone in the faraway land. She decided to move back to her home in Canaan. Naomi told her sons' wives about her plan. "I will go back to Canaan. You, Ruth and Orpah, may go back to your own families." It was hard for Naomi to tell Ruth and Orpah to stay with their families. Naomi knew she would be very lonely. It seemed like Naomi's heart was breaking once again. She felt very sad and very alone.** Tear another piece off the large heart.

**"I'm not staying here!" Ruth said. "I'm going to Canaan with you, Naomi." This news helped Naomi, but she knew things would not be easy.**

**When Ruth and Naomi reached Bethlehem, they had no food. Naomi thought, What will happen to us now? Naomi felt afraid and lonely and sad. Naomi asked, "Where is God? Has He forgotten about me?"** Tear another piece off the heart.

**God had not forgotten Naomi or Ruth. God had a special plan to take good care of Naomi, and He used Ruth as part of His plan.**

**A man named Boaz owned a field of grain. God led Boaz to be kind to Ruth. Boaz said, "Ruth, you may always pick up grain in my fields. You are safe here." Ruth gathered the grain and took it to make bread. Naomi felt happy. She knew there was food to eat.** Tape one torn section back onto the heart.

**God continued to care for Ruth and Naomi. Boaz asked Ruth to marry him and invited Naomi to live with them.** Tape another section onto the heart.

God never forgot about Naomi and Ruth. He kept on taking care of them. Ruth and Boaz had a baby boy and named him Obed. Naomi was so happy! God gave her a whole new family. God takes good care of His people. Tape the final section onto the heart.

God knows that we need His help. God gave us the best help when He sent His Son, Jesus, to earth. How did Jesus show God's love and care for us? (He took the punishment of all our sins. He died for us and rose again.) Draw a cross on the heart.

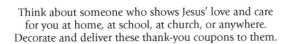

Explain that God always takes good care of us. Even when bad things happen, God can turn them into good. Say, **This story has several main characters. Who is the main person in the story?** Allow for discussion. **We can see that God is the main character in this story. God helped Naomi, Ruth, and Boaz, and He helps us—in the best way of all.**

Because Jesus has cleaned our hearts and made us children of God, we can show love to other people. **Can you tell me ways we can do this?** Encourage a sharing time of ideas. Blackline 9-A provides Caring Coupons for the children to thank those who have cared for them. It also contains coupons indicating that they will show care for others. Provide a time to deliver the notes at school or church. Send the remaining coupons home in a decorated envelope.

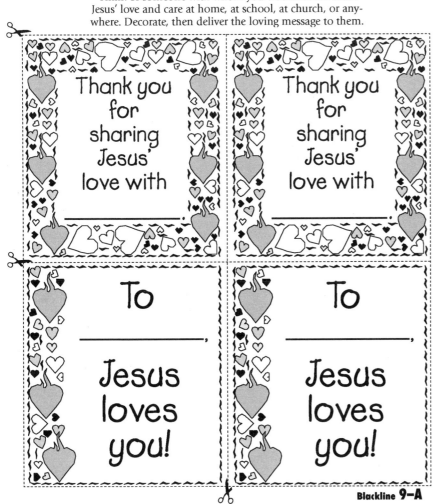

Think about someone who shows Jesus' love and care for you at home, at school, at church, or anywhere. Decorate and deliver these thank-you coupons to them.

Think of someone with whom you would like to share Jesus' love and care at home, at school, at church, or anywhere. Decorate, then deliver the loving message to them.

Thank you for sharing Jesus' love with _____

Thank you for sharing Jesus' love with _____

To _____, Jesus loves you!

To _____, Jesus loves you!

**Blackline 9-A**

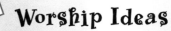

# Worship Ideas

- Respond in song! Sing the response words to the notes F, E, and middle C (F—God's, E—with, C—me) at the asterisk.
  **Teacher:** When I'm at school,
  **Students:** God's with me.
  **Teacher:** When I'm playing with friends,
  When I'm not feeling well.*
  When I'm on vacation with my family.*
  When I'm doing my chores.*
  When I tell my friends about You.*
  No matter where I go.*
  No matter what I do.*
  Thank You, Jesus!* Amen.

- Pray for all the locations you've indicated on the globe. Ask that God's Word and love reach all those living in each area. Pray for missionaries that are serving God in all nations and countries.

# Bible Background

In the Book of Ruth we see that God continues to accomplish His will through chosen individuals. What was so special about Ruth's decision to go to Judah? It was an expression of faith in the true God. She realized that her salvation lay in becoming one of His people. This motivated her tender loyalty to Naomi, even at the prospect of lifelong widowhood in a strange land.

As we look at the faithfulness of Ruth, Naomi, and Boaz, we remember that it was our faithful God who was leading them and blessing them abundantly, even in difficult times. Through them, God makes the next necessary arrangements for the Savior's birth into the world, as Ruth and Boaz become ancestors of Jesus (through their son Obed, father of Jesse and grandfather of King David).

## Words to Remember

*Serve one another in love. Galatians 5:13*

- Sing to the tune of "Bingo":
  **I know a man who said to us
  (Yes, Jesus was His name-O):
    Serve one another in love.
    Serve one another in love.
    Serve one another in love.
      Galatians five:thirteen-O.**
- Play servant charades. Invite each child to think about how they can share Jesus' love and care, and then act out the type of service. As the charade is solved say the Bible verse together.

## Extending the Lesson

- Service projects provide active learning experiences. Perhaps you can involve families, other grades, or the church in these activities. Consider sponsoring one of the following: invite a speaker from a homeless shelter or food kitchen, help a member of the congregation in need, make place mats or cards for a nursing home, have the class deliver greetings and sing a song or two for homebound church members.
- The video *Flying Quilts* is available from Lutheran World Relief. For more information go online at www.lwr.org, or call 1-800-527-3211.

# Day 2

# INTRODUCE

Using the globe or map, review the countries or nations chosen in Day 1. Allow each student to place a happy-face sticker over one of these areas. To protect it, first wrap the globe in plastic food wrap. (If you use a map, laminate it to protect it and reuse it.)

Continue the happy-face theme with the game "Make Me Smile." Choose a volunteer. Everyone else in the class, without tickling or touching, tries to get the person to smile. If time permits, allow several or all of the children to be volunteers. After playing, say, **In our Bible story God turned Ruth's and Naomi's sadness into smiles. Do you think God smiles at us?** Allow time to talk. Emphasize that the love and many blessings God pours down on us are evidence that He is smiling on us. He does so because God is love.

Read Matthew 25:40. Explain that Jesus is talking in this verse. Jesus is happy when we serve others. When we care for others, we are showing our love for the Lord—and that makes Jesus happy.

# Ruth

*(The Book of Ruth)*

When there was not enough food in Canaan, Naomi's family moved to Moab. While there, Naomi's sons married women from Moab. Then a sad thing happened. Her husband and both her sons died.

When Canaan had plenty of food again, Naomi decided to go home. She told her sons' wives, Ruth and Orpah, to stay with their own families in Moab. But Ruth would not leave Naomi. Ruth wanted to take care of her. They went back to the city of Bethlehem. But Naomi was still sad. They were very poor. Naomi thought God was not with her.

Ruth needed to work so they would have food to eat. She went to the farm of a man named Boaz. She picked up all the leftover grain that fell to the ground. She took it home to bake bread. One day, Boaz found out how Ruth was taking care of Naomi. Boaz was very kind to her. Boaz and Ruth got married. Naomi went to live with them. She had a family again. Naomi's family grew when Ruth and Boaz had a baby boy. Naomi was a happy grandmother. She took care of baby Obed.

God cared for Naomi and gave her a new family. God takes care of us too. He gives us people to help and to love us. And He gives us His Son, Jesus.

| | |
|---|---|
| *I'm sad, feeling blue.* | *I'm glad, it is true.* |
| *Who will help me?* | *God, You've helped me.* |
| *Who, who, who?* | *I thank You!* |

1

## D E V E L O P

Use page 1 of the *Leaders* Student Book to review the Bible story. The children are to respond by saying the bold print verses in a sad or happy voice, accordingly. Practice the response words with expression and feeling.

## R E S P O N D

God cared so much for us that He gave His only Son, Jesus, to die on the cross for us so that someday we can go to heaven to be with Him forever.

**We want to show God how much we love Him, but we can't do this without His help. God sends the Holy Spirit to help us live as people of God. He helps us show the love of God to other people.**

*Leaders* Student Book, page 2, is a matching activity. The children match the pieces of broken hearts, drawing lines to connect the pieces of the matching hearts. Help students see that they can care for others at home and at school. They can even care for people who live far away.

Encourage the children to think about and then in one-half of the blank heart draw one person with whom they can share God's love and care. For the other half, the students should think about and then draw or write how they plan to care for that person. Take time to talk about the children's responses. Help the class to catch the vision of caring that begins at home, continues in their away-from-home activities, and can even extend to people in distant places.

Read the Fourth Commandment and its explanation from the catechism (see the Teacher Resource Book). Point out that Ruth lived the spirit of the Law—out of love she honored, served, and cherished her mother-in-law. Discuss the fact that as sinners we break this commandment. But God calls us to repent and forgives us through Jesus. Through the Holy Spirit's power in the Word, He leads us to honor and serve others according to His will.

# Heart Match

*Draw a line to connect the pictures that go together.*
*Show someone helping others.*

**Draw someone who needs your help.**

**Draw how you can help.**

Words to Remember

*Serve one another in love. Galatians 5:13*

2

## Discovery Point

God has a plan for each of us—a plan already complete—to save us from sin through Jesus, His Son. He is a loving God, who cares for His people, sometimes working through other people to bless us.

## Hannah

1 Samuel 1

## Objectives

That by the power of the Holy Spirit working through God's Word, the students will
- desire to turn to God in prayer for guidance from Him;
- know that God calls them to be His own dear children through Jesus Christ so that they may follow His purpose and plan for their lives;
- go to God in prayer and trust that His answer is according to His plan for them.

## Day 3 Materials

- Blackline 9-B
- A scarf and towel

## Day 4 Materials

- *Leaders* Student Book
- Blue, red, and yellow crayons
- Various prayer books and printed prayers

## INTRODUCE

Open with a variety of prayers. Sing a praise prayer such as "Psalm 8" or "Praise Him, Praise Him" (*LOSP*, pp. 50, 68, and on CD).

Invite the children to kneel and pray silently, asking God to forgive their sins.

Sit down as you bow heads and fold hands to pray aloud for others. Begin with, **Heavenly Father, please be with these people we name before You today.** In turn, each child may say a name. Close with, **Please help these people and fill them with Your love. In Jesus' name. Amen.**

Finally, invite the children to stand, raise their arms, and pray a loud thank-You prayer. Shout together, **Thank You, God! Amen.**

Ask, **Those were different ways to pray. I wonder which one God heard the best? Do you think that God heard the sitting prayers more than the standing prayers? How about those short prayers, or did He hear the long prayers better? Did He even hear those silent prayers? Or did He hear those we prayed together better than those we prayed alone? Did God hear the shouting prayer the best? Listen to what God tells us in His Word.** Read 1 John 5:14 and Matthew 7:7. Assure the children that whenever they pray, God is listening. He hears, and He will answer. He may answer in a different way or in a different time than we expect, but He will answer.

## DEVELOP

**A woman named Hannah prayed with her lips moving, but no sound was coming out. She was praying to the Lord with her heart. Would God answer her prayer? Would God show her His plan for her life?** Turn around and place a scarf on your head. Introduce yourself as Hannah. Explain how you have come to the temple at Shiloh to worship and pray.

Replace the scarf with the towel twisted as a turban and introduce yourself as Eli, a priest at the temple at Shiloh. Continue with the following script, changing headpieces for each character.

**HANNAH:** My husband and I have come to Shiloh to worship God. I am sad because I have no children. So, I pray God will give me a son.

**ELI:** One day I was sitting on a chair by the doorpost of the Lord's house. I watched this woman who was praying. Her lips moved, but no sound came out.

**HANNAH:** I was praying with all my heart. I cried. I moved my lips. I asked God not to forget me, and I asked Him to give me a son. I promised God that I would give my son back to Him.

**ELI:** As I watched the woman cry and move her lips, I thought she was drunk. I asked, "How long will you keep on getting drunk?"

**HANNAH:** I told the priest that I was not drunk, but that I was praying. I was pouring my soul out to the Lord.

**ELI:** I told the woman, "Go in peace, and may the God of Israel grant what you have asked Him for."

**HANNAH:** The next day I worshiped the Lord, and then we went home. God did hear my prayer! In time He blessed me with a son. I named him Samuel. When he was old enough I took Samuel to live at the temple and learn from the priest.

**ELI:** This woman brought the boy with her. She reminded me that she prayed and that the Lord gave her what she asked for. Now she was returning Samuel to serve the Lord as she had promised. God had a plan for Samuel. And God has a plan for you.

God has a plan for you and for me. We may not always see that plan. Sometimes it seems like a puzzle. But it is a puzzle God already put together for us when He sent Jesus for our salvation. Print the letters to the following words on cards: POP; SEES; DEED; PUP; BOB. Explain that these words are spelled the same forward and backward. Direct the children to Blackline 9-B. Together, read the directions and work through the puzzles. The clues help to solve the puzzles. Answers: (1) Hannah; (2) eye; (3) dad; (4) mom; (5) noon; (6) wow. In prayer, thank God for His special plan for us to rescue us from sin and its punishment through the death and resurrection of Jesus.

## Forwards and Backwards

Use the clues to help you finish the words that are spelled the same way forward and backward.

1. A woman who prayed for a child.

| H | A | N | N | | | |

2. God gave us two. Each helps us to see.

| | E | | E | | E | |

3. Another name for father.

| | | A | | |

4. Another name for mother.

| | | O | | |

5. One of many times we can pray to God each day.

| | | O | | | N | |

6. What I might say when I am amazed at God's great love for me.

| | | | W | |

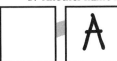

## Worship Ideas

- Make a class prayer book that records the daily prayers of the class for a week or a set amount of time. Place the book on the altar for a set amount of time. During this time the children may use the book to remember the prayers. In time, review the book to find if God has chosen to show us the answer to the prayers. Remember that God will always answer our prayer in the time and way that is best.
- Sing "God, Our Father, Hear Your Children"; "Jesus Listens When I Pray" (*LOSP*, pp. 14, 15, and on CD); "Making Melody in My Heart" (*LOSP*, p. 63).

## Bible Background

For many years Hannah, one of Elkanah's two wives, had no children. For a Hebrew woman, this was particularly painful, as though God were declaring the woman an unfit mother for the Messiah.

Each year Elkanah and his family would travel to Shiloh to offer sacrifices. On one of their trips Hannah pours out her heart to the Lord. She promises God that if He gives her a son, she will dedicate the child to His service (1 Samuel 1:9–17). At first Eli, the high priest, assumes Hannah is intoxicated. But his quick rebuke gives way to a blessing. He sends Hannah to her home with hope that God will answer her prayer. Hannah's outlook on life is instantly transformed (1:18). In the course of time Hannah gives birth to a son, whom she names Samuel. God indeed hears and answers her prayer.

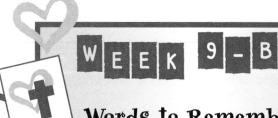

## WEEK 9-B

### Words to Remember

*I call on You, O God, for You will answer me.*
*Psalm 17:6*

- Recite the verse rhythmically, using claps, stomps, or rhythm instruments.
- Recite the Bible verse several times in unison. Start by sitting on the floor and speaking it in a whisper. As you begin to stand increase the volume, so that when you are standing up you are at the loudest voice. Reverse to a whisper as you again are seated.

### Extending the Lesson

- Write new stanzas for the song "Jesus Wants Me for a Helper" (*LOSP*, p. 33) by changing the last line of the first stanza (I can show my love for Jesus ...).
- Make a time line showing the lives of Samuel and David.
- Duplicate helper calendars for each student. Let the children write in dates of the month in small squares on the calendar. In the empty squares they may also write tasks they intend to complete.
- From your Bible read Psalm 127:3. Then use *Where Do Babies Come From?* from the Concordia sex education series to discuss how, according to God's plan, a baby grows from conception.

# Day 4

## INTRODUCE

Display a variety of prayer books. Emphasize that prayers do not have to be written or even spoken. God hears our thoughts too. Encourage volunteers to tell about the times they usually pray to God and what they talk about when they talk to God. It is important that each child know that God is with them at all times and hears and answers their every prayer.

## DEVELOP

Write HANNAH vertically on the board to make an acrostic to reintroduce Hannah.

**H** ad no children.
**A** sked God to give her a son.
**N** ever stopped praying for God's help.
**N** amed her baby son Samuel.
**A** nswer from God made her joyful.
**H** appy to return Samuel to serve the Lord.

# Hannah

*(1 Samuel 1)*

Hannah loved God and served Him. But she was sad because she had no children. One day, Hannah prayed at the temple. She cried, "O Lord, if You will give me a son, I will give him back to You."

Eli, the priest, watched Hannah praying. He saw her lips move, but no sound was coming out. Eli thought that Hannah was drunk, and he asked what was wrong with her.

Hannah said, "I am praying to the Lord because I am very sad."

Eli answered, "Go in peace, and may God give you what you have asked."

Later that year God gave her a baby boy. Hannah said, "I will call him Samuel because I asked the Lord for him."

When Samuel was old enough to live at the temple, Hannah took him to Eli, the priest, and said, "I prayed to the Lord for a baby. He gave me Samuel. Now I will give Samuel back. Samuel will serve the Lord the rest of his life."

God heard and answered the prayer of Hannah. He will hear and answer our prayers, too, in the way and at the time that He knows is best.

*In the story, find Hannah's prayer and underline it in yellow.*

3

As you read page 3 in the *Leaders* Student Book, give the children time to underline the name Hannah with a blue crayon and the name Eli in red crayon. After the story ask the children to find the words Hannah prayed to God, and underline them in yellow. Hint: The words are in apostrophes (talking marks).

Read the following poem. Have the boys stand to act as Eli in the first two verses and the girls stand for Hannah's verses.

**In God's holy house,**
**A priest named Eli served.**
**He watched as Hannah prayed**
**Without a spoken word.**

    **He learned why she was sad,**
    **And as she left he said,**
    **"Do not despair, but go in peace.**
    **God's blessings are ahead."**

**Now Hannah didn't know**
**The things that God had planned.**
**She trusted in the Lord**
**And followed His command.**

    **God answered Hannah's prayer.**
    **She found that she would be**
    **The mother of a special boy.**
    **She praised God joyfully.**

Dear _____,
You are so _____.
I _____ You so much!
Please forgive me for _____
_____.
I ask You to please _____
_____.
Thank You for _____
_____.
In the name of _____
    Amen.

*Draw a picture of yourself praying to God. On the lines write words you might pray.*

Words to Remember
*I call on You, O God, for You will answer me. Psalm 17:6*

4

# R E S P O N D

Make and number five columns on the board to use with the *Leaders* Student Book, page 4. Brainstorm words and phrases to include in the prayers. Print the words in the corresponding columns to help your students write (and pray) several different prayers. Fill in the first column with various names we use to call on God. Next think of a praise word that describes God. Then tell God we love Him and ask God to forgive us. Next, write concerns to bring to the Lord in prayer. End with words of thanksgiving.

Sing this song to the tune of "Oh, My Darlin' Clementine" ("Found a Peanut").

    **Prayed to Jesus, prayed to Jesus,**
    **Prayed to Jesus yesterday.**
    **Yesterday I prayed to Jesus,**
    **Prayed to Jesus yesterday.**

Adapt these words to make additional stanzas for the song: Needed His help; Jesus blessed me; Thanked the good Lord.

Say, **God plans only good things for you. Many times sin and sin's consequences get in the way of the good God has planned. So God sent Jesus to earth to complete His plan for us. Because of Jesus' love and forgiveness, we know God is always with us and can even answer our prayers before we ask.**

## Discovery Point

God has a plan for each of us—a plan already complete—to save us from sin through Jesus, His Son. He also helps us live according to His plan for our lives as His children.

## Samuel

1 Samuel 3

## Objectives

That by the power of the Holy Spirit working through God's Word, the students will

- trust God to guide them in the plan and purpose that He has for their lives as His children;
- know that, as God's children, they can show God's love by serving Him;
- pray that God will give them hearts and minds that listen to Him when He speaks to them through His Word.

## Day 1 Materials

- Audiocassette and player
- Jake and Jenna puppets
- Blackline 10-A
- Soup cans

## Day 2 Materials

- A day planner or calendar
- Styrofoam or paper cups
- *Leaders* Student Book

# INTRODUCE

serve  follow  wait

Invite the children to copy the hand motions as you talk. **Jesus says to us, "Serve the Lord! Follow Me!" But does He say, "Wait until you're 8"?** (Pause for the children's reaction.) **"Don't listen until you're 10"?** (Pause.) **"You're too young to help Me! Don't bother until you are 12"?** (Pause.) **God wants us to listen and follow Him right now! Jesus came to earth as a baby, died on a cross as a man, and came alive again on Easter to rescue us from sin and to help us serve Him no matter how young or old we are. The Bible tells us of children who served God. Let's hear about one of those children today.**

# DEVELOP

Ask several teachers or older students to record the Bible story on an audiocassette. *Leaders* Student Book, page 5, or 1 Samuel 3 provides a guide for the recording. Write these words on a poster for the class to read along with the voice of Samuel: *"Here I am. You called me."* On another poster print, *"Speak, for Your servant is listening."*

Have the class act out the story in the church narthex or the classroom. The person playing as Samuel can follow these actions as the recorded story is played: (1) lie down on the floor or put head on desk, (2) run in place or move feet under the desk (as he runs to Eli), (3) speak the listed words, (4) walk in place (back to bed), (5) sit up and listen (as God speaks).

# RESPOND

Continue with the Jake and Jenna puppets to help the children focus on what a first grader can do as God empowers them.

**JAKE:** *(upset and huffy)* It just doesn't seem fair!

**JENNA:** What doesn't seem fair?

**JAKE:** Well, I really want to be a helper in church, but I can't.

**JENNA:** Why not?

**JAKE:** Because I'm only a first grader. I'm not old enough to be an acolyte at church like my sister. Dad puts away chairs and tables for special events at church, but they're too heavy for me. Mom drives people to church, and it will be a long time before I can drive. I can't even walk to the store by myself yet. And I can't go to another country to tell people about Jesus, like missionaries do. I can't do anything!

**JENNA:** Sounds to me like you have a bad case of the "I can'ts."

**JAKE:** Do you think I have a fever too?

JENNA: No. I think you're looking at things the wrong way.

JAKE: *(turning his head with the words)* What do you mean? I can only look at things one way. Do you mean I have to look at things sideways? Or upside down?

JENNA: *(giggles)* No, Silly. You've been looking at all the "I can'ts" instead of the "I cans." There are lots of things we can't do 'cause we're first graders. But there are lots of things we can do.

JAKE: Like what?

JENNA: *(turning to the class)* I bet our friends can help us think of some. How about it? What are some things that you do to help? *(Allow time for children to answer.)*

JAKE: I never thought about all of those things. Sounds like I'd better get busy. I want to be a helper in church, just like Samuel!

JENNA: Samuel was a young child, too, when he started helping in church. God chose Samuel to be a helper and He chooses us too!

JAKE: Starting right now I'm the "I can" kid. I can do something for the kids in this class—or for you, Teacher. Then after school I can do some helping things for my mom and my dad. I can. I can. I can. *(Jake begins moving away.)*

JENNA: *(shouts)* Jake, wait for me. I'm going to be an "I can" kid too. *(Both puppets start to pick up things on the floor; place pencils on desks; water plants; whisper "Jesus loves you" in a child's ear. Then continue with the blackline activity.)*

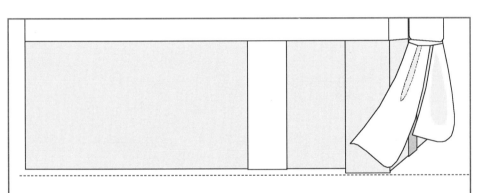

*Directions for a Gift Box Card:*

1. *Color the ribbon yellow.*
2. *Color the gift box light blue.*
3. *Fold on the dotted lines to bring the gift box sides together. These directions will now be on the back of the card.*
4. *God gives us so many gifts. We call these gifts "blessings." Open the card. On the first flap print "From God." Then make a list of some of the blessings God gives you.*
5. *God doesn't need anything from us. But there are some things He wants. He wants our hearts, filled with faith and love for Him. He wants us to serve others. Jesus says when we are kind to others, it is like a gift given to Him. On the last flap inside the card print "From Me." Then make a list of things to do as gifts to serve others.*
6. *God gives us the greatest gift of all. At the top of the center section print "Greatest Gift." Do you know what that gift is? Close the card and look for the yellow clue. Draw a picture of that great gift inside the card. Below it print "Thank You, Jesus."*

**Blackline 10–A**

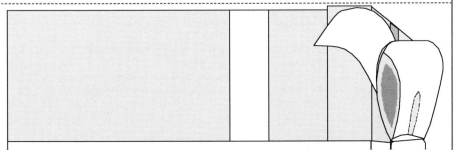

## Worship Ideas

Have the children repeat each line. Say the poem again, inserting the names of the children.

> **"Samuel, Samuel, it's the Lord!**
> **It's the Lord who's so adored!"**

> **"Tell me, Lord, what should I do?**
> **Should I go and work for You?"**

> **"Listen, listen, little one.**
> **Spread My love to everyone."**

> **"Lord, Lord, I'll work today.**
> **I'll do everything You say."**

- Pass an "I can" can around the circle. As the children hold the can they are to share something they can do with the help of Jesus. The class can write an idea every morning and keep it in the can all day. Take time to review those plans at the end of the day.

## Bible Background

Children were often nursed for three years or more in ancient Israel, but as soon as Samuel was weaned, Hannah kept her vow. She brought the little boy to the temple to serve God. Samuel grew up assisting Eli (1 Samuel 1:19–28).

Through his parents and his teacher, Eli, Samuel already knew the Lord as Savior. Until he was about 12 years old, however, God had revealed no specific word to him. In fact, such words or visions of the Lord were rare (3:1). Thus, when God called to Samuel (3:4–8), Samuel thought he heard Eli's voice, not God's. Finally Eli realized the source of the call. He directed Samuel to answer, "Speak, LORD, for Your servant is listening" (3:9). Over the next decades, Samuel would be God's mouthpiece to the people of Israel.

## Words to Remember

*Speak, LORD, for Your servant is listening.*
1 Samuel 3:9

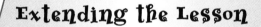

- Emphasize that though we do not hear God's voice as Samuel did, we do hear God's words in the Bible. God's Word is precious to us, because through it He speaks to us, giving us faith and strengthening it. Related to this, you may want to read the explanation of the Third Commandment from the catechism.
- Divide and cut a piece of construction paper into eight pieces. Divide the Bible words onto the eight cards. Have children initial their own set of cards. Pair up to play a form of cooperative concentration. When a match is made, each child will take his or her own card. After all cards are matched students place their cards in the Bible verse order.

## Extending the Lesson

- Ask permission to visit the offices of several church workers. Have the workers share how God empowers them to serve the Lord.
- Have the children make a time line of special days in their lives. (Include birth, birthday, Baptism, first day of first grade, etc.) Send home to involve parents in completion of the project.
- Provide a day planner or calendar page for each student to write a plan to share Jesus' love and care.
- Sing songs of God's plan and our response such as "Go Tell," "Go Tell It on the Mountain," "God's Care," "He's Got the Whole World in His Hands," "I Can Tell," "Love in a Box," "We Love Because God First Loved Us," and "We Pray for Each Other" (*LOSP*, pp. 104, 84, 24, 101, 99, 35, 54, 15, and on Voyages CD).

# Day 2

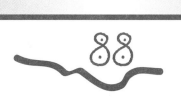

# INTRODUCE

Display a day planner or calendar. Point out that a day planner calendar is used for recording plans for activities, appointments, and special dates for the day, week, or month. When things change, the plans that are written may need to be corrected or crossed out. Say, **God has a plan for us. His plan includes saving us from sin and making us His children. God sent His Son, Jesus, to die for our sins and come alive again to complete His plan. God provides for us in our life here and now on earth and later in heaven. God's plans for us are good. Even when we sin, God's plan for our forgiveness is there. We can trust Him never to leave us or stop loving us.**

# DEVELOP

Have each student make a megaphone/earphone by removing the bottom from a Styrofoam or paper cup. Call each child by name

## Samuel

*(1 Samuel 3)*

NARRATOR: Eli, the priest, was an old man. Samuel was a boy who helped Eli take care of the temple. One night Samuel was asleep. Suddenly he heard a voice calling,
GOD: Samuel! Samuel!
NARRATOR: Samuel thought Eli had called him. He ran to Eli's room.
SAMUEL: Here I am. You called me.
ELI: I didn't call you. Go back to bed, Samuel.
NARRATOR: This happened two more times. Finally Eli understood what was happening.
ELI: It is not I who calls you, but the Lord. Go and lie down. If He calls you again, say, "Speak, LORD, for Your servant is listening."
NARRATOR: Samuel went back to bed and waited. Soon the Lord called.
GOD: Samuel! Samuel!
NARRATOR: This time Samuel did as Eli told him. He sat up and said,
SAMUEL: Speak, LORD, for Your servant is listening.
NARRATOR: God gave Samuel an important message. As Samuel grew up the Lord was always with him. Samuel served God for the rest of his life.

through a cup megaphone. Begin with, **In our story, Samuel finally realized that the voice was God. He said some very special words. How did Samuel answer God?** Permit the children to answer using the megaphones as you use the earphone: "Speak, LORD, for Your servant is listening." **Samuel's answer is called a response. We can also use those same words and talk to God in a responding way. After each sentence I say, you will respond (answer) with Samuel's words.**

- The Lord calls us to hear His Word.
- The Lord calls us to confess our sin and repent.
- The Lord calls us to forgive others.
- The Lord calls us to love each other.
- The Lord calls us to be His servants.

Point out to the children that they were using the name of the Lord to praise and honor Him. Say, **The name of the Lord is special because God Himself is so important. One of the commandments reminds us that how we use God's name shows how we feel about God.** Read the Second Commandment and its explanation from the catechism (see the Teacher Resource Book).

Lead the children in praying: **Dear God, we confess that we have not always used Your name respectfully. Forgive us for Jesus' sake. Help us to grow to live according to Your will. Amen.**

Focus on the positive ways God leads us to use His name, to call upon it in every trouble, pray, praise, and give thanks.

## RESPOND

Divide the class in half to read the Bible story as a choral reading from page 5 of the *Leaders* Student Book. Divide the class into four groups. Each group will read their parts as indicated by color and name. Allow time for each group to practice first.

Direct the children to *Leaders*, page 6. When you finish, reread the plans together in order. God's plan for salvation is as follows: (1) God promised a Savior. (2) The Savior lives and dies. (3) He becomes alive again. (4) Jesus will take God's people to heaven.

# God's Planner
## for _____

*Complete the pictures and fill in the blanks.*

alive    heaven    promised    dies

God _____ a Savior.

The Savior lives and _____.

He becomes _____ again.

Jesus will take God's people to _____.

Words to Remember

*Speak, LORD, for Your servant is listening. 1 Samuel 3:9*

6

89

## Discovery Point

God has a plan for each of us—a plan already complete—to save us from sin through Jesus, His Son. He also helps us live according to His plan for our lives as His children.

## David

1 Samuel 16:1–13

## Objectives

That by the power of the Holy Spirit working through God's Word, the students will
- rejoice that God loves them because they are His own forgiven children, redeemed by Christ Jesus;
- know that God guides and directs their lives to serve the Lord;
- thank and praise God for choosing them to serve Him.

## Day 3 Materials
- Jake and Jenna puppets
- Fabric, small towel, string
- Hair spray
- Blackline 10-B

## Day 4 Materials
- Construction-paper heart in a gift-wrapped box
- *Leaders* Student Book

## INTRODUCE

Select all children that have a common characteristic (long hair, brown eyes, tie shoes, etc.). Have the class determine what one thing is the same about these children. Continue the activity using a variety of common characteristics until all the children are chosen.

Ask the class to stand and come by you. Continue, **All of us are alike in another way. In fact, I'm thinking of the most important way we are alike. The trouble is that we can't see what I'm thinking about. All we can see is the outside of each person. I'm thinking of something on the inside that makes us the same. (Pause.) All believers are alike because we are children of God and God lives in our hearts.**

## DEVELOP

Lead into the Bible presentation. **Listen closely to today's Bible story. Put your hand on your heart when you hear the word *heart*.** Put a Bible times costume on the puppet Jake and use him to tell the Bible story. (Use a strip of fabric to make a headband to cover Jake's hat. Use a small towel and string to make his robe.)

**Hi! I'm David. You'll never believe what happened to me today. I'm just a shepherd boy and the youngest son of Jesse! I was in the fields watching the sheep when I first heard the news. A messenger came out to me and said I must come to my father's house at once. I wondered what was so important that my father would have me leave the sheep. I hurried back home, and when I got there, I saw my father, my brothers, and God's prophet Samuel, waiting for me.**

**I still couldn't understand what was happening. Samuel told me some unbelievable news! Samuel said that God had chosen me to be Israel's next king. Do I look like a king to you? On the outside, I look like a young shepherd. But Samuel says that God looks at the inside, at the heart. I knelt down at Samuel's feet in thankfulness to the Lord. My seven brothers and my father watched as the prophet poured oil on my head. This showed that God chose me to be the next king of Israel. God chose me to do special work for Him! God has a special plan for you too. He wants you to be His own dear child through the forgiveness and salvation Jesus gives!**

## RESPOND

Use the Jake and Jenna puppets to apply today's lesson.
**JENNA:** Jake! Hurry! We're going to be late for school!
**JAKE:** Wait a minute! I have to get my hair just right!
**JENNA:** It looks great to me!
**JAKE:** Jenna, please hand me that hair spray. Maybe that will make my hair perfect.

JENNA: Why do you want to look perfect anyway?

JAKE: Everyone will think that I am important if my hair is perfect.

JENNA: Why, you'd be important to us even if your hair was a mess. Friends don't care if your hair is perfect or not, and I know God always loves you! Remember, through Jesus' love you are His special child.

JAKE: Are you sure? You mean I could just comb my hair any old way and you would still think that I was special?

JENNA: I mean that we think that you are special because we like who you are—the inside you. Jake, what we wear, how we look, or what we own does not make us important to God. Remember what God told Samuel? "The Lord looks at the heart."

JAKE: I guess I was worrying too much about my outside. I forgot that God looks at my heart. He loves me even when I don't feel lovable, right?

JENNA: Right! Now let's get going so we won't be late!

**Jake thought that he was only important or special if he looked perfect on the outside. What was Jake forgetting?** (God looks at the heart.) Help children understand that sometimes we forget and may even judge others by how they look on the outside. Remember, God loves us no matter how we look on the outside.

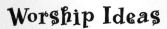

# Worship Ideas

- Sit in a circle to worship. Say to the child on your right, **God chose you, [child's name]. You belong to Him.** The child named repeats those words to the person on the right. Continue around the circle.

- Plan a *What's on the Inside* box. Collect objects that the children might not be familiar with, such as geodes or unusual fruits, vegetables, or nuts. Have the children share other good surprises that come in unusual forms. Recall how Jesus put His love in our hearts. He is not concerned about outward appearances.

- Use a favorite psalm of David for worship. Share that David was not only a shepherd boy but also a writer, musician, soldier, and king. But in one way David was just like you and me. David loved the Lord with all his heart. Use Blackline 10B to make a booklet showing David at various life stages.

# Bible Background

Over time, Israel rejected the direct rule of God. They wanted to have a king, like other nations. Saul, their first king, proved to be unfaithful. God directed Samuel to anoint a son of Jesse to replace Saul as king (1 Samuel 16:1). In choosing David, God looked at the heart, not at outward appearance (16:7).

David remarkably foreshadows the Messiah. He comes from Bethlehem. He is not a tall, handsome warrior like Saul (10:23–24), but a man whose heart is with the Lord. David comes in from tending sheep—a preview of Jesus, the Good Shepherd, who lays down His life for the sheep (John 10:11). From the moment of his anointing, David is filled with the Holy Spirit (compare Acts 10:38). God gave His Old Testament people a glimpse of the salvation that would come through the Messiah, our Savior.

## God's Plan for David

David watches over sheep.

David makes music for the king.

David becomes a soldier.

David becomes the king.

## Words to Remember

[Jesus said,] *"You did not choose Me, but I chose you."* John 15:16

• Play hopscotch using the "Words to Remember" as printed in the illustration. If weather permits, play outside, or tape masking tape on the floor. (Blue painting tape easily peels off.)

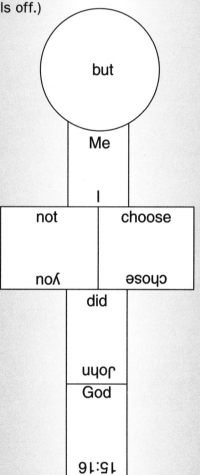

but

Me

I

| not | choose |
|-----|--------|
| you | chose |

did

John

God

15:16

## Extending the Lesson

• Use small boxes (with ovals cut in the lid), or empty tissue boxes to make harps. Stretch rubber bands of different widths around the box and across the opening. Experience the sounds. Do the bands sound the same? Do different size boxes or ovals make different sounds?

• Plan a field trip to a music store that has stringed instruments or invite someone who plays a stringed instrument to class. Ask your guest to talk about the size and the length of the strings and how each affects the pitch.

## INTRODUCE

Before class, write "I love Jesus" on a heart to put inside a box. Then beautifully wrap the box. Place the gift in the worship area.

Exclaim, **Look at this beautiful package! That paper, tied with those ribbons, looks so pretty. Don't you think it looks great?** Admire the box, but do not open it. Rather, continue to talk about the beautiful wrappings. Soon the children will want you to open the package. Resist with words like, **I don't want to open the package. The wrappings are too beautiful. What's inside can't possibly be as wonderful as the outside.** Set the package aside and continue, **This package reminds me of the way we sometimes think about others. We look on the outside and decide things by what we see with our eyes. God does something different. When God looks at us, He doesn't just look at the outside. Where does God look?** (Inside.) Open the package to find the heart. Conclude, **God looks at our hearts. He fills our hearts with love and forgiveness from Jesus, our Savior.**

# David

*(1 Samuel 16:1–13)*

### Scene 1: Shiloh, at the temple

THE LORD: Fill your horn with oil and go to Bethlehem. Find a man named Jesse. I have chosen one of his sons to be the next king.

SAMUEL: King Saul will hear about it. He will kill me.

THE LORD: Take a calf with you for a sacrifice. Invite Jesse to join you. I will show you what to do. You will anoint the one I say.

### Scene 2: Bethlehem

PEOPLE OF BETHLEHEM: Did you come in peace?

SAMUEL: Yes, in peace. I have come to sacrifice to the Lord.

JESSE: I will bring my sons.

ELIAB: I am Jesse's oldest son.

SAMUEL: *(aloud to himself)* Surely this is the new king.

THE LORD: Don't look at how tall and strong he is. People look at the outside. The Lord looks at the heart.

EACH OF JESSE'S OTHER SIX SONS: I am Jesse's [second, third, etc.] son.

SAMUEL: *(aloud to himself)* None of these are chosen. Are there more sons?

JESSE: Just David, the youngest. He is with the sheep.

SAMUEL: Bring him here. *(David arrives.)*

THE LORD: He is the one I have chosen to be king. *(Samuel anoints David with oil.)* I have seen his heart, which trusts the Lord.

7

## DEVELOP

Present the Bible story as a play. The set is the corners of your room. Designate the areas of the room as the town of Bethlehem, another as the hills outside of Bethlehem, a third area as the temple at Shilo. Assign the cast according to age. Line up the children in birth order. The youngest child is David, the oldest child is Samuel, the next oldest is Jesse, the next oldest is Eliab. The rest of the children are the six remaining brothers and the people of Bethlehem. Place David in the hills, Samuel begins in Shilo, and the rest go to the area of Bethlehem.

Have everyone sit in their desks for play practice *(Leaders Student Book, page 7)*. Together, practice reading the Bible story before assigning specific parts. Direct the children where to stand, move, and speak. The children could wear name tags (i.e., I'm from Bethlehem) or simple costumes.

## RESPOND

Tell children to turn to their *Leaders* Student Book, page 8. Explain that each number in the code stands for a letter. Help students complete the activity. The message reads *Jesus loves me.* Ask, **What did Jesus do to show you His great love?** (Jesus died to take away our sins. He came alive again that we may live in heaven one day.)

Continue, **Each of you is very special. Jesus chose you to be God's own child. Jesus lives in your heart. He loves you very much! Jesus promises to always be with you and help you.**

**God lived in David's heart and helped him to be Israel's king. What plans do you think God has for you?** Let the children speculate about work they can do for Jesus—both now and when they are grown. Complete the last two codes on the page. *(Jesus is love. I love Jesus.)*

---

# God Made Me
# Special

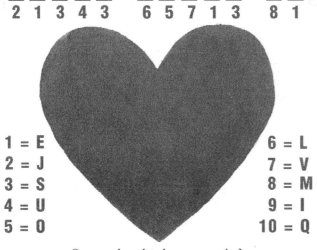

*Can you solve the code to see why you are special? Try it!*

‾‾ ‾‾ ‾‾ ‾‾ ‾‾  ‾‾ ‾‾ ‾‾ ‾‾ ‾‾  ‾‾ ‾‾.
2  1  3  4  3   6  5  7  1  3   8  1

| | |
|---|---|
| 1 = E | 6 = L |
| 2 = J | 7 = V |
| 3 = S | 8 = M |
| 4 = U | 9 = I |
| 5 = O | 10 = Q |

*Can you also solve these two puzzles?*

‾‾ ‾‾ ‾‾ ‾‾ ‾‾  ‾‾ ‾‾  ‾‾ ‾‾ ‾‾ ‾‾.
2  1  3  4  3   9  3   6  5  7  1

‾‾  ‾‾ ‾‾ ‾‾ ‾‾  ‾‾ ‾‾ ‾‾ ‾‾ ‾‾.
9   6  5  7  1   2  1  3  4  3

Words to Remember

*[Jesus said,] "You did not choose Me, but I chose you." John 15:16*

8

## Discovery Point

God gives us what we need most—salvation from sin. In all areas of our life, He works for our good and blesses us with more than we ask.

## Solomon

1 Kings 3:3–15

## Objectives

That by the power of the Holy Spirit working through God's Word, the students will

- grow in their trust in God to guide them in living every day and to eternal life in heaven through Jesus, our Savior;
- know that God blesses them with ability to think, plan, and make decisions in accordance with His will, as they are empowered by the Holy Spirit and His Word;
- do all that they do for the glory of God.

## Day 1 Materials

- Jake and Jenna puppets
- Bible
- Blackline 11-A

## Day 2 Materials

- *Leaders* Student Book

## INTRODUCE

Begin by asking, **If you could have one wish, what would it be?** Let children tell their wishes. **In our Bible story, God asked a man named Solomon what he wanted more than anything else. Let's find out what happened.**

## DEVELOP

Use the Student Book, page 9, and the Bible reference as your guides in telling today's story. Add actions to focus attention on the progression of the story. (You may want children to imitate your actions.) Whenever you speak of Solomon, hold widespread fingers on either side of your head to represent a crown. Tilt your head to one side and rest it on your hands when you talk about Solomon falling asleep and when he woke up. Fold your hands when you speak of Solomon talking to God. Place both hands over your heart when you speak of God talking to Solomon.

## RESPOND

Use the Jenna and Jake puppets to consider the application of this story to our lives. Raise up the puppet that is speaking, or, if you prefer to use just one puppet, combine the puppet parts as one character.

**JENNA AND JAKE:** *(excitedly talking back and forth to each other)* Wow! If I could make a wish, I'd want a swimming pool … or how about a really cool bike … or my own puppet theater … or a jet to take me anywhere … or a kangaroo—I've always wanted a kangaroo!

**TEACHER:** You two certainly have a long wish list.

**JENNA:** This isn't a wish list. It's a prayer list. I'm going to ask God for all of these things.

**JAKE:** Right, just like Solomon did. He asked and *poof!* God gave it to him.

**TEACHER:** That's not exactly what happened, kids. Solomon asked for wisdom so he could help his people—not so he could help himself. His prayer was not selfish or greedy. His request honored the will of God.

**JENNA:** I never thought of that. But God gave him lots of money and fame and power too!

**TEACHER:** But that's not what Solomon asked for. Because God loves us He often gives us more than we ask or need.

**JAKE:** One thing I need right now is forgiveness. I was being selfish. I was putting myself first.

**TEACHER:** Jake, you can be sure that God will give you forgiveness. And through Jesus He gives us so much more.

**JENNA:** I was being greedy too. I'm going to change my prayer list. I want to help others. I want whatever God knows is best for me.

Pray together that God would forgive us and help us to put Jesus first in our lives above everything else. Read aloud Matthew 6:33. Work together on Blackline 11-A to continue this concept. Ask children to look at the letter *I*, which reminds us that too often we selfishly think just of our own wants and wishes. Only God can change our hearts and lives by His grace and the gifts of the Holy Spirit. Tear along the lines to separate the *I* into three pieces. Hold up the top piece to represent number 1, reminding us to put God *first* in our lives. Use the other two pieces to form a cross, reminding us that the kingdom of God is ours through faith in the death and resurrection of Jesus.

*Option:* This lesson can be extended further with study of the Ninth and Tenth Commandments and the explanation in the catechism. Explain that *coveting* is wanting something that is not yours and planning and scheming to get it. *Wanting something* in itself is not wrong, but it can be if it involves greed, selfishness, and discontentment. God blesses us with so much more than we need. Our response to His grace is thankfulness and contentment, especially in the forgiveness and love we have in Christ—that *indescribable* gift!

## Worship Ideas

- Sing the first stanza of "Seek Ye First," which is based on Matthew 6:33.
- Praise Jesus that He is King of kings and Ruler over all by singing "The King of Glory" (*LOSP*, p. 77). Change the words of "Hallelujah! Praise Ye the Lord!" (*LOSP*, p. 58) to sing "Hallelujah! He's King of Kings!"
- Pray this prayer poem together, having the children repeat each line after you:

> **Jesus is God's Son, our King;**
> **Every day His love we sing,**
> **And to Him true hearts we bring,**
> **While in heaven God's praises ring.**
> **Amen.**

## Bible Background

God chose David's son Solomon to follow David as Israel's next king. David prayed for his son to be faithful and obedient. This prayer is fulfilled during the early years of Solomon's reign.

Shortly after assuming the kingship, Solomon declares a period of festival days and sacrifice at Gibeon, the site of the Tent of Meeting and an important place of worship for Israel. There God appears to the new king with a gracious invitation: "Ask for whatever you want Me to give you" (1 Kings 3:5). Solomon responds in faith and humility. Pleased by Solomon's request, God promises not only wisdom but wealth and honor too. By God's blessing, and under Solomon's leadership, Israel rises to new heights of splendor.

## What Is Most Important?

### SEEK FIRST

### THE KINGDOM OF GOD

"Seek first His kingdom and His righteousness,
and all these things will be given to you as well."
Matthew 6:33

**Blackline 11-A**

# WEEK 11-A

## Words to Remember

*Thanks be to God for His indescribable gift!*
2 Corinthians 9:15

- Ask children to *describe* an apple, *describe* your mother, *describe* your favorite baseball player, and so forth. Then explain that the word *indescribable* refers to something that is so wonderful it is hard to find words to describe it. **The indescribable gift God gives to us is Jesus. It is hard to find words that tell of the suffering Jesus willingly took on the cross. It is impossible to find words to describe the gift of heaven that we will have because of Jesus. We have the indescribable gift—Jesus—and so much more.**
- Practice the word *indescribable* by syllables. Also say the word with a rhythmic beat.

## Extending the Lesson

- Divide the class into two teams. Play a "royal" word game. On the board, draw lines to indicate the number of letters in a word. Each team alternates making guesses as to which letters are in the word. Each correct letter guessed gives the team one point; the team that guesses the correct word gets three points. Use words such as *king, queen, princess, prince, palace, majesty, royal.*
- Help children differentiate between *being smart* and *having wisdom*. Explain that wisdom involves using what you know in ways that are helpful, kind, and productive. Make up examples to demonstrate the differences. (Someone may be very smart, knowing the best ways to cook food. But they might not have the wisdom to make healthy choices.) Point out that a person could have one of these gifts, both, or none. Pray together that God would bless the children with wisdom that glorifies God and helps others.
- Display books and pictures of royalty, past and present. You may want to briefly point out why your country does not have a king and in what ways the leaders of your country are different than royalty.

# Day 2

## INTRODUCE

Tell the following short story. **Jill, Sam, and Pete were arguing. Jill said, "Grandma Grayson gives the best gifts. Last year she gave me the best video game, and it wasn't even my birthday. Grandma gives the best.** (Print "Grandma" on the board.)

**Sam said, "No, you're wrong. Uncle Oscar gives the best gifts. Remember when he gave me a new bike when my old one was stolen? I can't tell you how happy I was. Oscar gives the best.** (Directly below the first word print "Oscar.")

**Pete said, "I have to disagree. The best gifts come from Dad. Remember when he gave us tickets to the circus? He gave us a whole day of fun. Dad gives the best gifts."** (Below the other two words print "Dad.")

Then point out that all three children are wrong. **Look at the words for a clue. Can you tell who gives the best gift of all—an indescribable gift?** (Draw a circle that encloses the first letter of each word to reveal the word *GOD*.) **God knows what is best for us and what we need most. We need Jesus, our Savior. God blesses us with more, but nothing as important as this.**

# Solomon

*(1 Kings 3:3–15)*

Solomon was a leader who asked God to lead him. After the time of his father, King David, Solomon became king. One night the Lord spoke to King Solomon in a dream. The Lord said, "Ask for whatever you want Me to give you."

Solomon said, "You showed great kindness to my father, David. Now, Lord, You have made me king. But I don't know how to rule the people. Give me a wise heart so I can know what is right and wrong and help the people in all I do."

God was pleased with Solomon's prayer. The king could have selfishly asked for money or power. But he asked God to help him be a good king. God said, "I will bless you with wisdom. But I will also bless you with riches and honor, even though you did not ask for these things. If you keep Me first in your life, as your father, David, did, I will continue to be with you and bless you."

Solomon woke up from his dream. He worshiped God and celebrated God's love with the people.

God knows and blesses your life too. He gives you the best gift of all—salvation through Jesus Christ. In Jesus He gives you forgiveness and eternal life and makes you children of God!

9

## DEVELOP

Read page 9 of the Student Book. Then review the story by singing this poem to the tune "Are You Sleeping." Have the children repeat each line that you sing, as indicated by an asterisk (*).

Here's a story * Of a king. *
Solomon was his name. * God blessed him. *

He was sleeping, * Late one night. *
In a dream, God asked him, * "What do-you want?" *

He could ask for * Riches, fame. *
But he asked for wisdom * To be-a good king. *

God was happy * That he chose *
To help other people * In the land. *

God gave wisdom * And much more. *
But the very best gift * Is-Christ the Lord. *

## RESPOND

Work together on page 10 of the *Leaders* Student Book. Review the word *indescribable.* Have children connect the dots to draw a cross, which represents the best gift God gives to us. **In Jesus we have forgiveness, peace, joy, heaven, love, kindness, and so much more.** Look at the word *indescribable* and use it as the basis of an acrostic that lists some of the many other gifts God pours into our lives. (I—imagination, interesting sights, invisible angels; N—nose, new toys, nephews, etc.) List the children's ideas on the board and let each person choose one word or phrase to write with each letter listed.

# God Gives His Best...
# and More!

*Directions: Connect the dots to see God's best gift. Use the letters as the beginnings of words that tell other things God gives to us.*

I _____
N _____
D _____
E _____
S _____
C _____
R _____
I _____
B _____
A _____
B _____
L _____
E _____

Words to Remember
*Thanks be to God for His indescribable gift! 2 Corinthians 9:15*

10

97

## Discovery Point

God gives us what we need most—salvation from sin. In all areas of our life, He works for our good and blesses us with more than we ask.

## Jehoshaphat

2 Chronicles 20:1–28

## Objectives

That by the power of the Holy Spirit working through God's Word, the students will
- grow in trust and confidence that God can and will help them at all times;
- recognize that good leaders encourage people to rely on God leading them;
- worship God with songs of praise and thanksgiving.

## Day 3 Materials
- Newspaper
- Blackline 11-B

## Day 4 Materials
- *Leaders* Student Book

# INTRODUCE

Hold up a newspaper as if you are reading it. Then say, **Imagine how people would feel if we heard news that three armies from three countries were coming to attack our city. This is exactly what happened to King Jehoshaphat in today's story. The Bible tells us that he was** *alarmed.* **That means he was upset, worried, and shocked. Let's find out what he did.**

# DEVELOP

On the board, chart paper, or a poster, print five large *P*'s in a column. This will be used to outline today's story. Use the first P to print **Panic.** Point out that the people of Jerusalem knew that their country of Judah was small and so was their army. They had no power against such a large enemy.

But the king and the people knew where to go for help. Use the second P to print **Prayer.** Emphasize that Jehoshaphat was a good leader because, in prayer, he led the people to the Lord, their true leader. From the Bible read the king's words in the last two sentences of 2 Chronicles 20:12. This shows total reliance on God—total trust.

Use the third P to print **Plan.** Explain God's plan for the people—a plan that would show the victory was the Lord's, not theirs. Read aloud verses 15 and 17. God's plan was simply for the people to watch. God would do the rest.

Use the fourth P to print **Power.** God's power was shown as He turned the enemy armies against themselves, ambushing each other, till all were defeated. The victory was so complete it took the people of Judah three days to pick up all the valuables that remained.

Use the fifth P to print **Praise.** Emphasize that the people praised God before and after the victory. Before it, they praised with confidence, trusting in God. After it, they did not forget what the Lord had done, and they continued their praise.

## R E S P O N D

Ask, **How many enemies came to attack the people of Judah?** (Three.) **Did you know that we have three powerful enemies? They are sin, death, and the devil.** (Print the three words on the board.) **We have no power over these enemies. Who alone can help us?** (Jesus.) **The fact is, Jesus has already won the victory! When did that happen?** (At His death and resurrection.) **Now, when sin, death, and the devil try to harm us, we know we can trust Jesus. He has the power to help us!**

**Like the people long ago, let's praise the Lord!** Use Blackline 11-B to identify words that praise God and speak of His greatness. Do the page aloud together so that even emerging readers can be involved. Circle the word in each line that is a word we use to praise God, to honor Him and keep His name holy.

When completed, read the entire list of words that describe God. Say, **"Hallowed be Thy name!"** Ask the children where they've heard those words before. (In the Lord's Prayer.) **We hallow God's name by honoring and keeping His name holy when we praise and thank Him.** You may want to read the First Petition and its explanation from the catechism. (See the Teacher Resource Book.) Then say the Lord's Prayer, asking children to join in saying any of the words they know or pray along silently.

---

### Tell of the Greatness of God!

*Directions: In each line, circle the word that we use to describe the Lord and to praise Him.*

1. blouse     powerful     ocean

2. holy     orange     watch

3. collie     forgiving     lunch

4. homework     paste     caring

5. wagon     awesome     desk

6. mighty     boots     paper

7. kitchen     pencil     wonderful

8. radio     loving     baseball

---

## Worship Ideas

- Sing "I'm in the Lord's Army" (*Songs Kids Love to Sing*, p. 32, and on its accompanying CD, available from CPH). Also read Ephesians 6:10–18 to find out about the weapons and protection God gives us in battling sin and temptation. Emphasize that these battles are individual ones we win through God's power, but the ultimate victory over all has already been won! Read 1 Corinthians 15:57.
- Have a praise parade, singing songs of praise and using rhythm instruments.

## Bible Background

After Solomon's death the kingdom of Israel was divided into two nations, Israel and Judah. Descendants of David continued to rule in Judah. During the reign of one of these kings, Jehoshaphat, invaders threatened Jerusalem. The king prayed to God, humbly admitting the nation's utter helplessness and total dependence on God. He pleaded with God to save the nation from this advancing army.

The faith of the people was not in vain. In the battle that followed, the army did not have to strike a single blow. The Lord so confused the enemy soldiers that they destroyed one another. Jehoshaphat and his people did not forget to thank God. They went immediately to the temple to praise Him.

## Words to Remember

*Give thanks / to the LORD, / for His love endures / forever. 2 Chronicles 20:21*

- Explain that these are some of the words the people of Judah sang as they marched to meet the enemy to see what the Lord had done to deliver them. Explain that the word *endures* means that it lasts. **How long does God's love last?** (Forever!) Emphasize that *forever* means that it will never end.

- Learn the Bible words by phrases. Have the children say the following chant with you:

**Give thanks,**
**Give thanks to the Lord,**
**Give thanks to the Lord, for His love endures,**
**Give thanks to the Lord, for His love endures**
**forever and ever** *(gradually getting softer)* **and ever and ever and ever and ever and ever …**
*(Jump up and loudly shout)* **Hooray!**

- Adjust the melody of "Hallelujah! Praise Ye the Lord!" (*LOSP*, p. 58) to sing the Bible verse as follows.

**Give thanks, give thanks, give thanks to the Lord,**
**For His love endures.**
**Give thanks, give thanks, give thanks to the Lord,**
**For His love endures.**
**Give thanks—forever, forever.**
**Give thanks—forever, forever.**
**Give thanks—forever, forever.**
**Give thanks to God!**

## Extending the Lesson

- Have children use computer and copier technology to make posters and banners. Let them use creative fonts to print individual words that praise God, describing His greatness. Use a copier with an enlarger setting to expand the size of these printed words. Let children add color to the words, background, and borders. Display these in your worship center as a reminder of the many reasons we have for praising God.

- Teach the children the doxology "Praise God, from Whom All Blessings Flow" (*LOSP*, p. 65). Explain the meaning of each phrase. Point out that when they sing this well-known hymn, they are joining the praises of Christians for the past 500 years.

# Day 11

## INTRODUCE

Remind the children that God continues to work His wonders today. Let's keep our eyes open and watch for the deliverance of the Lord! Tell this true story that happened in France during World War II. The enemy Nazis had invaded a small town in France. They parked one of their tanks right next to the home of a family of Christian people. The Sengele [pronounced Sawn-juh-lay] family knew that the American army was nearby, coming to rescue them, but they feared that if the troops destroyed the Nazi tank, their family and their home would also be destroyed. John Sengele, a 10-year-old boy, said, "Let's pray that God will build a wall around us to protect us." The family prayed this prayer. The next morning they saw God's amazing answer. God had, indeed, built a type of wall to protect them. A dense fog covered the whole area. The fog stayed until the tank moved on and the danger was gone. Like Jehoshaphat so long ago, the family praised God! God is with us and continues to bless us in amazing ways!

# Jehoshaphat

*(2 Chronicles 20:1–28)*

Three armies were ready to attack God's people. King Jehoshaphat knew his army was not strong. The people didn't seem to have a chance. Their only hope was in the Lord. The king gathered the people together—the men, women, children, and little ones. He led them in prayer, asking for God's help.

God's plan was that the people should march out with instruments, not weapons, and with choirs, not soldiers. They sang, "Give thanks to the LORD, for His love endures forever."

God told the people to just watch. God would win the day for them. God confused the armies. The enemies fought each other. The people of Israel didn't have to do a thing. The battle is the Lord's! The people were saved.

They returned to Jerusalem, praising God for all that He had done. God protects us too. He has saved us from our worst enemies—sin, death, and the devil. "Thanks be to God! He gives us the victory through our Lord Jesus Christ" (1 Corinthians 15:57).

## DEVELOP

Use the following poem to review the Bible story. After reading it through once, discuss each phrase or sentence.

> Let me introduce to you
> King Jehoshaphat.
> Three armies came (now that's bad news),
> All set to do combat.
>
> "There's nothing we can do to win.
> We're like an old doormat.
> Let's go to God and pray for help.
> He'll win. And that is that."
>
> The people marched, but just to watch.
> God said, "Stand still. Stand pat."
> They trusted God. With His great power,
> No one's a scaredy-cat.
>
> The people sang as they returned
> To Judah's habitat.
> They praised the Lord for all He did.
> They sang "magnificat."

*Option:* Have the children follow your actions as you retell the story, raising arms high in prayer, bowing down to the ground before the Lord at the temple, marching and singing to meet the enemy, applauding the victory God had won, returning and singing praise.

# Praise God for His Power

*Draw a simple picture in each cloud as a reminder of God's power and goodness. Choose from the pictures below or draw your own.*

## Words to Remember

*Give thanks to the LORD, for His love endures forever. 2 Chronicles 20:21*

12

## RESPOND

Ask the children to imagine a scary situation. Have them close their eyes and picture that they are home alone at night. They hear loud booms of thunder. They see lightning flashes. Suddenly they hear a strange sound like something tapping on the window.

Gently begin to sing a song such as "I'm with You" (*LOSP*, p. 32, and on CD). Ask the children to open their eyes and join in singing with you. Point out how the song, reminding us that God is near, is very comforting. Relate this to the singing of Jehoshaphat and his people, who confidently trusted that all was in God's hands as they sang.

Remind the class that Jehoshaphat admitted he was scared of the enemy armies. He was alarmed. Assure the children that when we are afraid, God understands our fears. He loves us and wants to comfort us and give us peace. Read Romans 8:38–39 to the children to emphasize that nothing can separate us from the love of Jesus.

Continue this reassurance by working together on page 12 of the *Leaders* Student Book. Tell the children there are no wrong answers on this page and they may repeat answers if they wish.

*Option.* Refer again to the First Petition of the Lord's Prayer: Hallowed be Thy name. Explain that *hallowed* is a special word in which we pray that God's name be kept holy among us.

Note the relationship between this portion of the Lord's Prayer and the Second Commandment. We are praying for God's help so we may live as His people, using His name in prayer, praise, and thanksgiving.

### Discovery Point

God wants all people to know about His forgiveness and grace. He invites us to share the Good News of Jesus, our Savior.

### Naaman

2 Kings 5:1–19

### Objectives

That by the power of the Holy Spirit working through God's Word, the students will
- realize that God's love is for everyone, even those people who do not look, speak, or act as they do;
- know that God uses all people, even children, to share His love;
- share the message of God's grace with people both near and far.

### Day 1 Materials

- Three apples (one each—red, green, and yellow)
- Knife
- Water and washcloth
- Small paintbrush
- Baking soda
- Blackline 12-A

### Day 2 Materials

- World map
- Removable sticky notes
- *Leaders* Student Book

## INTRODUCE

Display three apples—one red, one green, and one yellow. Ask what the three objects are. Then say, **Of course, they are all apples. They may look different on the outside, and they have different colors, but they all would taste good in an apple pie.** Cut each apple in half and show the inside. **These apples remind me of people. In what ways are people different from one another?** (Hair and skin color, spoken language, manner of dress, abilities.) **How are we all alike?** (Loved by God, need Jesus as Savior.) **God doesn't care where we come from or what we look like. He looks inside us—at our hearts.** (Read 1 Samuel 16:7.) **He wants everyone to know Jesus and be saved. He wants us to learn from Him and share God's message and love with everyone. Today we'll hear about a little girl who told someone from another land about the power of the Lord.**

## DEVELOP

In advance, mix up a paste of baking soda and water. Set out the bowl of this paste, a small paintbrush, a bowl of water, and a washcloth. Tell the children that you are going to tell the story of Naaman by pretending to be him. Instead of wearing a costume, you are going to mimic the very bad disease that he had.

Apply globs of the paste to your face and arms. Explain that Naaman had leprosy. It caused sores on a person's body. There was no cure then, and eventually the people who had leprosy would become weak and die.

Talk about the courage of the little girl who was a servant and actually a prisoner. She could have been angry at the people who captured her; she could have avoided helping people that were not from her own nation. Instead, she knew God's power and that God cares for all people.

Talk about Naaman's anger at speaking only to Elisha's servant and then being told to wash seven times in the Jordan River. **Sometimes God's ways are mysterious. We may not understand. But we can trust that God knows best and will work for our good.**

As you use the cloth to wash off the paste, emphasize that God's power healed Naaman. It was not Elisha or the river that made him well. Naaman recognized this, saying he would worship only the true God. Elisha recognized this and refused to take any gifts for something he had not done. Tell of the great joy in Naaman's changed heart.

## R E S P O N D

Use Blackline 12-A to continue the concept that God loves all people, of all nations, colors, and languages. Children may color the pictures and cut out the two strips of people. By folding back and forth on the dotted lines, the strips of paper will stand upright on the children's desks or your classroom altar. (Point out the child wearing a T-shirt and jeans. This is almost a universal style of clothing for children and many adults today. Despite our many differences, many people are even starting to dress more like each other.) Pray that God will lead us to accept and appreciate the differences that we have, remembering that we are alike in one most important way—Jesus came to be our Savior.

*Option:* Cut out each figure separately. Attach wooden craft sticks to the back of the figures. Stick the craft sticks into a Styrofoam ball that has been covered with blue and green tissue paper to represent the globe. This will be a reminder that Jesus came for the whole world. He loves all people and wants all to be saved.

*Note:* The extra strip is to be sent home to parents to find out the ethnic background of each child. This information will be shared tomorrow.

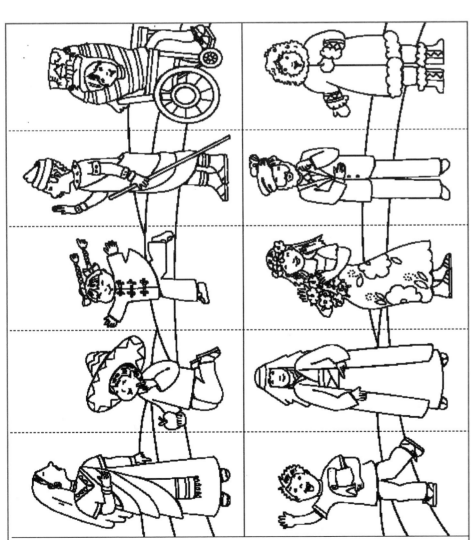

**Parents:** We are learning that God loves people everywhere. Please list where your family ancestors lived before coming to America. Have your child return this note tomorrow. Thank you!

Name:

Origin:

**Blackline 12-A**
Permission granted to reproduce for classroom use. © 2001 CPH

## Worship Ideas

- The theme this week is telling others the Good News message. Ask, **What is the Good News about Jesus?** (He loves us, He died on the cross to take away our sins, He promises us eternal life, through faith in Jesus we live now for Him.) Write down the ideas of the children. Use their words in your worship as a creed—a confession of faith.

- Daily sing "So Go!" (*Songs Kids Love to Sing 2*, p. 50, and on its accompanying CD) or "Go Tell" (*LOSP*, p. 104, and on the Voyages CD). Both are upbeat songs that encourage us to tell others the message of Good News and share the love of Jesus.

- Print *TELL* in large letters on the chalkboard. Instruct the children to shout the word *TELL* each time you point to a letter. Tell them you will say one line of a prayer to go with each letter. Invite them to pray with you in their hearts.

  T—Thank You for sending Jesus to be our Savior.
  E—Every day help us be more like Him.
  L—Loving others just the way they are.
  L—Living to share Your love and message. Amen.

## Bible Background

In this narrative a little girl, perhaps a young teenager, provides a forceful example of one in whom faith in the Lord is alive and well. Taken in captivity, she accepts what has happened to her and shares the hope of healing with her captor.

In the healing of Naaman the Lord Himself shows us what He means by faith. Which is more ridiculous: "Go, wash yourself seven times in the Jordan, and your flesh will be restored" (2 Kings 5:10) or "The blood of Jesus, [God's] Son, purifies us from all sin" (1 John 1:7)? Both require faith. "The foolishness of God is wiser than man's wisdom" (1 Corinthians 1:25). May we unashamedly continue to point to Jesus as God's answer to our needs for time and eternity.

## Words to Remember

*The LORD / is near / to all / who call / on Him. Psalm 145:18*

- Print the Bible verse on the chalkboard. Mark off two-word phrases with slashes. Read each phrase as you point to it. Have the children repeat after you. Do this several times, reading the verse a little faster each time.

- Discuss what it means to *call on* the Lord. We do this in prayer—spoken, sung, written, or in our silent thoughts. God will hear. The prayer can be a simple statement, question, or request. It does not have to be formal, starting with *Dear . . .* and ending with *in Jesus' name. Amen.* Prayers can have that format, but God did not give us rules about prayer styles. He asks only that we pray from the heart, in faith; He listens and answers.

## Extending the Lesson

- Sing the refrain of "Jesus Loves Me" in several languages, including sign language, as indicated at the bottom of pages 42–43 in *Little Ones Sing Praise.* Remind the children that God hears and knows *all* languages. He wants everyone to hear the Gospel message of Jesus, the Savior.

- Make up counting statements or number facts using the number of times Naaman washed in the Jordan River. (For example, after Naaman had washed four times, how many more times did he need to wash?)

- If your class has a rich multicultural heritage, take the opportunity to celebrate the diversity in your room. Plan a special event during which parent volunteers can share information about clothing, customs, songs, dances, and food unique to their heritage. Celebrate the uniquenesses of God's people!

# INTRODUCE

Say, **One special thing about our country is that it is made up of families that came from places all over the world. Some families came to our country long ago. Some are new to our nation. We don't have to go far to find people from all over the world who need to know Jesus as their Savior.** Share the information about family backgrounds on the papers the children return. (If you fear that not many will be returned, you may want to check school records for such information.) Place a removable sticky note on a world map to show where these ancestors came from. (If your classroom is not multicultural, include people you know from other ethnic backgrounds in your neighborhood and church.) Point out that the little girl in today's Bible story didn't even have to leave the room to be able to speak to people from a different national background.

# Naaman

*(2 Kings 5:1–19)*

### Scene 1: A home in Aram

Naaman was an important soldier, a leader of the armies of Aram. But he was sad because he was very sick. The doctors could not help him.

A young girl had been captured from the land of Israel. She worked as a servant to Naaman's wife. The little girl said, "If only my master would visit Elisha, God's prophet in Israel. God could heal him." Naaman and his wife knew they had no other hope. So he traveled to the land of Israel.

### Scene 2: Elisha's house

When Naaman got to the prophet's house, Elisha did not come out to see him. Elisha sent a messenger. This made Naaman angry. The messenger said Naaman should wash himself seven times in the Jordan River. This made Naaman even angrier. He said they had better rivers in his own land.

### Scene 3: The Jordan River

Naaman's servant said, "Why not do what he said? It is not difficult." So Naaman washed seven times in the river. When he came out, he was healed.

### Scene 4: The journey home

Naaman was so happy. He tried to give Elisha a great gift, but Elisha said, "No! I didn't heal you. God did." Naaman said, "From now on I will worship only the true God, who has helped me."

Like the young girl in the Bible, we can tell other people about the love and grace of God. He cares for all people.

13

## DEVELOP

Yesterday you told the story from Naaman's point of view. Today tell it from the viewpoint of four other characters. (The following overviews relate to the four scenarios presented on page 13 in the *Leaders* Student Book. Consider who the real "leader" is in this story. It is not Naaman, the little girl, or Elisha. The ultimate leader and leadership-giver is the Lord.)

First, speak of the events from the little girl's point of view. She was probably very sad to have been taken from her homeland and made to work as a servant. But instead of anger at her master, she was concerned about his poor health. She knew that God alone could help him. So she bravely told the master's wife about the prophet of the Lord.

Next, speak from the viewpoint of Elisha. Elisha did not come out to speak to Naaman, but he sent a messenger with an unusual message. Elisha probably knew that Naaman would be angry about this because he was a powerful leader in a conquering nation. But Elisha wanted Naaman to know that Naaman's forceful commands and Elisha's presence were not essential. Only the power of the Lord could heal Naaman. This is something Naaman needed to learn.

Next, speak from the viewpoint of Naaman's servant. He was a wise man who saw through the pride of Naaman. He pointed out that the plan was so simple, it certainly couldn't do any harm. He must have rejoiced to see his master follow his advice and subsequently be healed.

Comment on Naaman returning, with excitement, to give Elisha gifts of thanks. But Elisha would not take credit for something God had done. Imagine what it must have been like for Naaman's wife to see him return home a changed man. He was changed on the outside because the leprosy was gone. But more important, he was changed on the inside by coming to faith and rejecting all other gods.

## RESPOND

Point out that God wants all people, of all nations, colors, abilities, *and ages,* to come to repentance and faith. And God can use all these people to spread the news of His grace. Emphasize that God used a child to bring an adult to know God. **God can use you to make a difference in the life of a grown-up too!** Read 1 Timothy 4:12 aloud from a Bible. These are important, comforting, and encouraging words that remind children that God values them and what they can do. Use the *Leaders* Student Book, page 14, to continue this concept. Discuss what the child could say in each situation to share the love of God with an adult. (Answers will vary.) Print children's responses on the chalkboard so they can choose the words they want to print in their books.

## What Message of God's Love Can These Children Say?

Words to Remember

*The LORD is near to all who call on Him. Psalm 145:18*

14

# WEEK 12-B

## Discovery Point

God wants all people to know about His for-giveness and grace. He invites us to share the Good News of Jesus, our Savior.

## Jonah

Jonah 1–3

## Objectives

That by the power of the Holy Spirit working through God's Word, the students will
- know that they and all people are sinful and in need of the Savior;
- know that God loves all people and wants all to be saved through Jesus;
- share the love and message of the Gospel with all kinds of people, even those who have been unfriendly in the past.

## Day 3 Materials

- Jake puppet
- Index cards, tape
- Paper plate
- Wooden craft stick
- Blackline 12-B

## Day 4 Materials

- Colored paper
- Plain paper
- *Leaders* Student Book

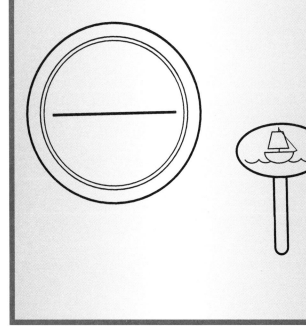

# INTRODUCE

Use the Jake puppet to introduce a lesson concept. Jake "stomps" in angrily.

**TEACHER:** Jake, why are you so angry?

**JAKE:** I'm never going to speak to that dumb old Buster again as long as I live! He is so mean!

**TEACHER:** What happened?

**JAKE:** Buster asked me to bring my new bat and ball to the park to play with him. I thought that would be fun. But then he didn't let me be a captain. He didn't let me be on his team. He didn't even let me play!

**TEACHER:** So you had to sit and watch Buster and his friends play ball? They were mean. That's why you don't want to speak to him. That's how Jonah feels in today's Bible story. He doesn't want to speak to people who had been mean to his country.

Discuss this concept with your class, noting that sometimes people are unkind, and it's difficult to forgive and be loving to someone who has hurt you. But also point out that, **We can be thankful that God is willing to forgive us over and over when we hurt Him by disobeying Him. God calls us to repentance and forgives us. He wants us to change and be more like Him, forgiving even those who are mean to us. This is exactly what God wanted Jonah to do. It's God's will for us too.**

# DEVELOP

In advance, prepare two index cards, printing *Nineveh* on one and *Tarshish* on the other. Tape one card to each of your shoulders. Explain that these are the names of two cities that were very far apart.

Also in advance, prepare a paper plate by drawing a wavy horizontal line and coloring the plate blue below the line. This represents the sea. Cut a slit along this water line to within one inch of both sides of the plate. Cut out a shape similar to the illustration, with a boat on one side and a fish on the other. Tape this to the top of a wooden craft stick.

Begin by explaining that God wanted Jonah to go to Nineveh to tell the people about their sin, their need to repent, and God's desire to forgive them. Jonah did not want to do this because the people of Nineveh were enemies. They had fought against the people of Israel. Push the boat shape through the back of the paper plate as you explain that Jonah went in the opposite direction (toward your Tarshish shoulder). Rock the boat as the storm comes up. Flip the boat to the fish side as you tell about Jonah being tossed overboard and swallowed by a large fish. Continue with the rest of the story, telling about Jonah's repentance, as you move the fish toward your "Nineveh" side. Then describe the repentance of the people of that city.

# R E S P O N D

On the chalkboard print these lines:

**God said, "Yes!"**
**Jonah said, "No!"**

Point out that God said *yes* to saving the people of Nineveh because He loves all people. Jonah said *no* because he didn't like the people. But Jonah found out that you can't stop God's love! Sing "[Oh, You Can't Keep Jesus'] Love in a Box" (*LOSP*, p. 35, and on CD).

**We are all sinners whom God calls to repentance. He forgives us through Jesus Christ.** Distribute copies of Blackline 12-B. Explain that this is not the fish in Jonah's story. This fish is a symbol that reminds people of Jesus. This symbol has been used for almost 2,000 years. As children follow the directions, letters will appear on the fish. Explain that the letters are from the Greek language and stand for the message on the outside border of the fish (Jesus Christ, God's Son, Savior). This is the message God gives us and wants us to share with others, even those people who have not been our friends. God's love is there for everyone.

## Worship Ideas

- God's love is for people in every land. Sing "Jesus Loves the Little Children" (*LOSP*, p. 94, and on CD) to emphasize this.
- Draw a large outline of a fish on a bulletin board or on mural paper. Have children cut out the fish from Blackline 12-B and place them inside the larger fish shape. As they do so, each person can say a prayer, especially for people in other lands or people different from themselves, that these people may learn about the love of Jesus.
- Explain the word *Gospel* as the Good News we have about forgiveness and salvation in Jesus. Ask children to explain more about this Good News (about the cross and resurrection, etc.). Then say this action cheer together.

**We're the Good News** (*thumbs-up sign*) **Kids** (*thumb points to self*)! **We've got Good News** (*clap on "good" and "news"*)! **Jesus died** (*fingers draw a cross in air*) **for you** (*point to someone*)!

## Bible Background

When God calls Jonah to be a missionary to a foreign land, Jonah seeks to limit God's grace to just his own nation. He boards a ship headed for Tarshish, a mining village in faraway Spain. The Lord, however, sends a storm. As the storm rages, repentant Jonah is willing to lose his life in order to save the ship. The sailors throw Jonah overboard, but God uses a great fish to preserve His servant for the mission to Nineveh. Jonah learns that God's grace and compassion extend to his own desperate need and beyond.

In Nineveh Jonah learns that God's Word is indeed powerful (Isaiah 55:10–11). The people of Nineveh believe Jonah's message, repent of their wickedness, fast, and call upon God to be merciful and forgive their sins. The Lord's promise does not fail; it bears abundant fruit by His blessing and purpose. God, in limitless mercy, desires every person to know His love and salvation.

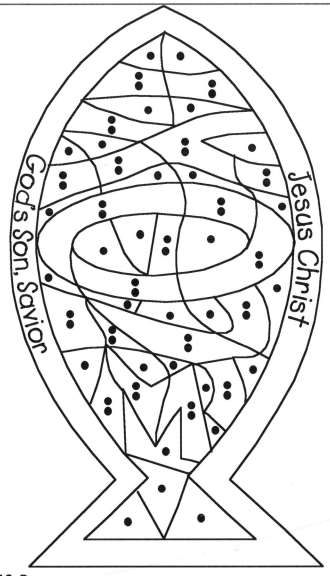

*Directions: Color yellow in every space that has one dot. Color blue in every space that has two dots. Use orange to color the border around the fish.*

God's Son, Savior

Jesus Christ

**Blackline 12-B**
© 2001 CPH   Permission granted to reproduce for classroom use.

## Words to Remember

[Jesus said,] *"Go and make disciples of all nations."* Matthew 28:19

Cut out nine simple fish shapes. Print one word of the Bible verse on each fish. Scatter them on a piece of blue tissue paper or blue cellophane. Let children rearrange the fish in the correct order. (You can number the order on the back of the fish so children can see if they are correct.)

## Extending the Lesson

- Use a soft cloth globe or an inflatable vinyl globe for this activity. Toss the globe to a student. Ask, **Is your right thumb touching land or water?** As you continue this activity, keep a tally to see if more students were touching land or water when they caught it. Discuss mission work around the globe. **How do missionaries travel to other parts of the world to spread the Gospel, God's Good News of salvation through Jesus?** (Fly, drive, walk, take boats, etc.)
- Make "fish" connections throughout the next two days. For example, use fish-shaped crackers as manipulatives when solving math problems. Learn about fish in science, while considering the miracle that Jonah remained alive during those three days in the fish (and digestive juices didn't get him). In art, children can draw fish by making a football shape and adding fins and multicolored scales.

## INTRODUCE

Print each of the following words in large letters on sheets of colored paper: RUN, SLEEP, SPLASH, SWALLOW, SPIT, REPENT. Use these words to review the story. Ask, **Who tried to RUN? Why? How? Why did the sailors wake up Jonah when he wanted to SLEEP? Who made a SPLASH? What happened to the storm? Why? Who SWALLOWed? What was swallowed? Why? Who SPIT? What? Where? Why? Who REPENTed of sin and was forgiven?**

## DEVELOP

Gather the children around and tell them you will make a paper boat and paper fish, two important things in the story. (Depending on their ability, you may let the children follow your directions and make boats and fish too.)

# Jonah

*(Jonah 1–3)*

God told Jonah, "Go to Nineveh. Preach to the people there. Tell them to repent of their sins and change from their evil ways."

Jonah did not want to do God's will. Jonah did not like the people of Nineveh. They were enemies of his people. So Jonah got on a boat going the opposite way. Jonah tried to run away from God. But God is everywhere and knows all things. God sent a big storm. The waves rocked the boat.

Jonah knew the storm was God's message. God did not want Jonah to run away. The sailors were afraid. Jonah told them to throw him overboard. As Jonah fell into the sea, the storm stopped. The sailors saw that God's power is great, and they worshiped Him.

Meanwhile God sent a large fish to swallow Jonah. Jonah prayed to God and asked for forgiveness. God kept Jonah safe inside the fish for three days. Then God had the fish spit Jonah out onto dry land.

Now Jonah was ready to obey. He went to Nineveh and told the people to repent. The people listened. They were sorry for their sins. They asked God to forgive them and help them change their ways. We know that God wants all people to be saved. He calls us to share His message with everyone.

15

1. To make a paper boat, fold a square sheet of paper in half with diagonal corners touching.

2. Fold the bottom corner of this triangle upwards to form a boat and its sail.

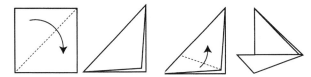

3. Flatten the bottom of the boat by folding under the lower tip.

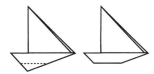

Discuss what the boat had to do with the story of Jonah. Then point out that it can also have something to do with the story of Jesus' death. Draw a simple anchor on the boat (a cross with a curved line under it). Explain that an anchor is another old sign or symbol referring to Jesus because of the cross shape you can see on it.

1. To make a paper fish, make a diagonal crease in the center of a paper square. Fold the two sides to the crease to form a kite shape.

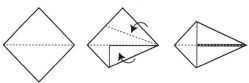

2. Fold down the top tip of the kite. Fold this shape in half lengthwise as shown.

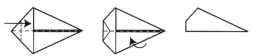

3. Bend the pointed tip up to form a tail. Cut the tip of the tail down the center. Fold the tabs of the tail to the sides to make tail fins.

Discuss what connection the fish has to the story of Jonah. Then explain the connection to Jesus' resurrection at Easter. Jesus compared Himself to Jonah, saying that Jonah was in the fish for three days. Jesus was in the grave for three days, but then He arose to life at Easter, assuring us of eternal life through Him! This message of Christ's death and resurrection is what God wants missionaries (and us!) to share with people in every land.

## RESPOND

Point out that Jonah was a missionary to a city in another country. Today, there are missionaries, like Jonah, who go to other places to tell of God's love and forgiveness. Unlike Jonah, these people do so willingly. Contact your pastor for the names of some missionaries that you can include on your class prayer list. Be sure also to pray for the children who share this mission experience with their parents. Display pictures of missionaries at work. If there are missionaries on leave in your area, invite them to speak about their work to your class. Plan a project to raise money for missions.

Emphasize that we can spread the Gospel Good News right in our own cities and neighborhoods. Look at the rebus on page 16 of the *Leaders* Student Book. Discuss what the children could do and say to Jackie to help her know Jesus and His love. Remind children that Jesus wants us to share His love even with people who seem unlovable.

Poor Jackie

This is a story about Jackie.

___ is always doing what she should ⊘ in 🏫.

She ___ at story ✋.

She ___ the other 👥.

She ___ at others and made them 😠.

She ___ at painting 👉.

Most 👥 did not like 👧.

What could ∪ say to her about 🧔❤️?

How could ∪ forgive and be kind to 👧?

Words to Remember

## Unit Overview

This unit of study and the accompanying Student Book are entitled *Waiting*. This unit is meant to be taught in December, but because of varying schedules from school to school and year to year, you may have to make some adjustments.

Christmas is a time of anticipation, so children understand the concept and difficulty of waiting. Turn their attention, however, to the thousands of years of waiting for the people of the Old Testament. Through all this time God continued to reassure them of His promise of redemption through the Savior. He continued to add more details to the promise as the anticipation heightened.

God waited till the time was right. In all things, we rest on the wisdom of His timing. He knows all things and wants what is best for us. His promises are certain, so we trust and rest assured He knows what is best and when the time is right. In the meantime, we wait on the Lord. Read Psalm 130, especially verses 5 and 7.

Send home copies of the family letter and Bible verse list for Unit 4 as you begin. (See the Teacher Resource Book.) This will let parents know what their children will be learning during the next few weeks. At the end of the unit, let the children take their *Waiting* Student Book home. Encourage them to show their parents what they have learned. This is the fourth in a series of nine books that will cover the story of salvation through the Old and New Testaments. Also consider adding some of the following activities to your curriculum to make related connections between God's message of love and all that you do throughout the day.

## Worship Connections

This would be a good time to discuss the church year and its related colors. Ask the people in charge of the church paraments or your altar guild to demonstrate how and where the church year colors are used in your sanctuary. Point out the pulpit, lectern, altar (using these terms), and any other areas where the colors are placed. Let the children have a close look at the altar cloths, and give them a little history on where the items were made or the cost, pointing out that we want to give our best to the Lord in His house.

Point out that this begins the half of the church year that focuses on the events in the life of Jesus. Advent (blue) is a time of *waiting* for the coming of Jesus (at Christmas and on the Last Day). Christmas (white) lasts for 12 days, including Christmas Day and the days after Christmas. White continues for the season of Epiphany, during which we celebrate events that reveal Jesus as true God (such as the visit of the Wise Men, Jesus' Baptism, the transfiguration). The color purple for repentance and royalty is used during the 40 days of Lent, when we take a closer look at the suffering and death of our Lord. Point out that black is used on Good Friday as a sign of respect for the day on which Jesus died. The following Sunday begins the 40 days of Easter (white), reminding us that Jesus appeared to and taught His followers for more than a month after He arose. Ascension Day always falls on a Thursday but is often celebrated on a Sunday. Ten days after Ascension Day and 50 days after Easter is Pentecost, celebrated with the festival color red. The remainder of the church year uses the color green, signifying growth, as we grow in faith while learning more about God's Word and His love.

## Community Building

Each week during this unit, let the children draw names of a person to whom they will be a "secret friend." Suggest that they do kindnesses, make cards, but not spend money on gifts. Tell them they will have to *wait* till Friday of the week to find out who was their "secret friend." Note that the best way to keep the identity a secret is to be a friend to everyone.

## Tools for Witness

- Provide each child with several removable adhesive notes on which the children are to draw a cross. Tell them to place these on or near Christmas decorations at home that tell about the true meaning of Christmas. **If someone asks why you did this, say, "These decorations remind me what Christmas is all about—Jesus came to this earth to be our Savior from sin."**
- Set out a large laundry bag in which children can put cards, letters, pictures, and other Christmas items they make during this month that they are willing to donate. The bag may remind them of Santa's bag, but it is really meant to be more like a mailbag. Plan on donating the items to rest homes or homebound individuals. Discuss with the children how important this gesture may be to someone who is lonely or sad. Emphasize that these items will spread the Good News of Jesus and share a blessing of kindness and cheer.

## Service Projects

Consider having a special project each week to focus on Christmas giving. Week 1: Gather food for a homeless shelter, especially things that might be enjoyed as part of a Christmas celebration. Week 2: Gather new and used toys to be given to children who have little of their own. Week 3: As you think of baby Jesus, collect baby items to be given to families in need. Week 4: Gather craft supplies and gift-wrap materials so children in need can make a gift to share with family members.

## Reaching Every Individual

As stated before, this is a time of waiting and anticipation. It is probably also a time of restless energy and very little patience. Recognize this as a reality rather than try to combat it. Frequently change the activity the children are working on, provide plenty of movement time, and work in groups, where socialization is inevitable. Contrast these busy times with some quiet restful times: read to the children as they do no more than listen, set aside time for silent reading, and perhaps set out a few extra interest centers for times when individuals can work by themselves.

## Integrating the Faith
## Waiting

### Science

As the children wait for Christmas with anticipation, they will probably see lots of decorations and Christmas cards with snowmen and snowy scenes. Talk about the climate variances at this time of the year in different parts of the country and the world (including Bethlehem). Point out that snow has nothing to do with the meaning of Christmas. Always remember that Jesus came for people everywhere.

### Social Studies

Say, **The birth of Jesus is so important, we even number our years according to when He lived on the earth.** Explain that this year is 20?? because it has been more than 2,000 years since Jesus was born. The years before His birth are labeled B.C., which means "before Christ." **What makes the birth of Jesus truly important for the whole world?** (See John 3:16.)

### Mathematics

Consider the passage of time (waiting) and how it can seem different depending on what you are doing. Have the children sit silently waiting for one minute to pass; have them stand on one foot for one minute; show a video clip, but stop it after one minute; let them have recess for one minute. Talk about how different that minute seemed from one situation to the next.

### Language Arts

Learn to speak and write Merry Christmas in several languages: *Joyeux Noël* (French); *Buon Natale* (Italian); *Fröhliche Weihnachten* (German); *Felíz Navidad* (Spanish).

### Fine Arts

Select a favorite Christmas melody and write words for a new stanza. Work on this together as a group and then sing your new song.

### Technology

As a group, working on computers, design and compose Christmas messages for a card or letter. Send the Christmas message by e-mail to a Christian church or Christian family in another country.

# Day 1

## Discovery Point

God faithfully meets our needs at the time that is best. He forgives our unfaithfulness and enables us to live for Him and to give Him praise through our words and actions.

## Daniel and His Friends

Daniel 1

## Objectives

That by the power of the Holy Spirit working through God's Word, the students will
- be reassured that God is with them, forgiving and blessing them even in hard times;
- realize that when they have difficult choices to make, God's way is always best;
- grow in self-control as they realize that God enables them, as His redeemed children, to live obediently by faith in Christ, their Savior.

## Day 1 Materials
- Chalkboard or paper
- Blackline 13-A
- Colored paper (optional)

## Day 2 Materials
- Seesaw or balance scale
- Weights or blocks
- *Waiting* Student Book

## INTRODUCE

Discuss why waiting is so hard to do. (Use the Jenna and Jake puppets if that will encourage student responses.) Ask the children to give examples of times it is hard to wait (waiting for the weekend to come so you can go to the zoo, waiting till you can open your birthday presents, waiting for the ketchup to come out of the bottle, waiting for your mom to finish shopping because you are bored).

**Today's Bible story is about four young men who had to wait patiently. Waiting can be hard to do. But they trusted that God would help them when the time was right.**

## DEVELOP

Explain that the four young men in today's story were waiting for three important things. (On the chalkboard, list the length of the three waiting periods as you talk about them.) The first thing they were waiting for was to go home. Tell that Daniel, Shadrach, Meshach, and Abednego (probably teenagers at this time) had been captured, along with other people, by the armies of King Nebuchadnezzar. They had to leave their homes in Jerusalem and travel far away to the country of Babylon. It was part of God's plan that the people would not return for about *70 years.* God was with His people and faithful to His promises. When the time was right, even though they had to wait a long time, they would be able to return.

Today's story involves another wait that was much shorter. Explain that the four young men were part of a special group who would be trained to be the king's helpers. They were to be fed food from the king's own table. But the four young men knew this would break God's Law. Some of the king's food was first presented at idol altars. Daniel and his friends did not want to dishonor God by eating something used to honor false gods. Also, God had given rules about how food should be prepared and what should not be eaten. God gave these rules to protect the health of the people. The Babylonian king did not obey God's rules.

Describe the special arrangement with the king's helper. They would have a "food test." Daniel and his friends would eat only vegetables and drink only water. It wasn't easy to speak against the king's plan, but the four young men obeyed God above all else. After *10 days*—a very short wait—everyone could see that Daniel and his friends were healthier and stronger than the men who ate the king's food. Daniel and his friends were faithful to God, and God blessed them. God also made them very wise, and they became good helpers to King Nebuchadnezzar.

The third thing Daniel and his friends were waiting for was the most important of all. They were waiting for the Savior to come. It was not yet the right time. God would have the people wait a long time—about *500 years.* But when the time was right God sent Jesus to be born as our Savior. Daniel and his friends trusted the promises of God. They believed that the Savior would come to take away our sins, to make us right with God, and to be the way to eternal life in heaven. The people had to wait, but they trusted that God always knows what is best and that He would keep His promise.

# R E S P O N D

Ask, **Who is the hero of this Bible story? Is it Nebuchadnezzar, Daniel, Shadrach, Meshach, Abednego, or someone else?** It's not the wicked king. And it's not even the four young men, for they were sinners like you and me and could not obey God's will perfectly on their own. The hero is God. The Holy Spirit, working through God's Word, gave the young men faith to live by. The same is true in our lives—God is our hero. God gives us faith and strengthens us to live according to His will.

Distribute copies of Blackline 13-A. See if anyone can figure out the rebus puzzle. ("Be strong in the Lord.") Say, **In our story today, God gave the four young men strong, healthy bodies. But this Bible verse is talking about a different way that God makes us strong.** Discuss the ways that God alone can make us strong. (Strong in faith in Christ Jesus, strong to obey His will, strong to say no to temptation, strong to trust God even when we have to wait for His answer.) Let children color the pictures if they wish.

the

Ephesians 6:10

# Worship Ideas

- Connect the waiting theme of this unit to the season of Advent. People in the Old Testament times were waiting for the Savior to come. We are waiting for the celebration of the birth of that Savior at Christmas. And we are waiting for His return to take us to heaven on the Last Day. Read aloud Psalm 27:14; Psalm 130:5; and Titus 2:13. All of these are very hopeful and joyful verses because we are not "waiting and wondering" on the Lord. Instead, we are "waiting and trusting" in Him. We are certain He will keep His promises at the time that is best. Sing "I Am Trusting You, Lord Jesus" (*LOSP*, p. 24, and on CD).
- God blessed Daniel and his friends with healthy, strong bodies. Sing an action song such as "I Can Stamp" (*LOSP*, p. 21, and on CD) to thank and praise God for the strong, healthy bodies He has given the children in your class.
- When Daniel and his friends could have been tempted to obey the king rather than God, the Lord made them strong in faith to resist the temptation. We ask God to do the same for us when we pray "and lead us not into temptation" in the Lord's Prayer. Remind the children that the Lord's Prayer was taught to us by Jesus. His words are in the Bible. Ask the children to pray silently as you say the Lord's Prayer and invite them to join you aloud in saying any of the words that they know.

# Bible Background

The Bible story takes place during the time of the Babylonian captivity, a period of 70 years during which the people of Judah were forcibly exiled and the temple in Jerusalem was destroyed. Though this was one of the darkest periods for God's Old Testament people, the Lord kept the spark of faith burning in many hearts. God can work through adversity to strengthen His people.

Daniel and his friends stood firm in their obedience of the ceremonial law, refusing to eat any food from animals declared unclean by God or food prepared in an unclean manner (with blood remaining) or food presented to idols. God had made these rules for the health of the body and soul of His people. God blessed the faithfulness of these young men, also increasing their wisdom, which the king recognized as very great.

# WEEK 13-A

## Words to Remember

*I will call upon the LORD, who is worthy to be praised. Psalm 18:3 NKJV*

Focus on the word *call.* Point out that there are several meanings for the word: (1) to use the telephone, (2) to cry out in a loud voice, (3) to ask someone to come. Consider each definition. **We are definitely not talking about a telephone call to God. Why not?** (We don't need a phone. He hears all our prayers.) **Do we need to call out to God in a loud voice?** (We can use a loud voice to praise God, but we don't have to. He hears everything, even our whispers and our thoughts.) **Are we asking God to come to us?** (We say this as words of comfort, but we also know that God is always near.) Read these other psalm verses that speak of calling on the Lord: Psalm 50:15 and Psalm 145:18.

## Extending the Lesson

• Daniel and his friends grew in health, strength, wisdom, and faith. In prayer, ask the Lord to bless the children in your class to grow in the same manner. Then have each child lie on a large sheet of paper. Have a partner trace around the child and then draw clothing and features. Starting from head to toe, fold each figure accordion-style. Watch it "grow" as you unfold it. On the back of each print "Grow in the Lord and in His Word."

• Children may find the thought of eating just fruit and vegetables unappealing. Interest them in the healthfulness and good taste of the food by preparing a lunch together. Place a variety of vegetables, a can of tomato juice, and seasonings such as garlic powder in a slow cooker to make a vegetable stew or soup. For dessert prepare fruit salad with a fruit-flavored yogurt dressing.

• If time is available, tell the story of the fiery furnace. Point out that Shadrach, Meshach, and Abednego were now grown up and were leaders in the government. Once again, when King Nebuchadnezzar asked them to do something that was against God's will, they stood strong and refused to obey the king. They were willing to remain firm even if God chose to let them die. They trusted not only God's power but also His wisdom to know what would be the best thing to do.

# Day 2

## INTRODUCE

Use a seesaw or balance scale to depict the choices Daniel and his friends were weighing in their minds. Gradually add blocks or weights to the "king's" side, analyzing why they would be tempted to obey him. (They would get to eat food fit for a king; obedience to the king would get them rewards and a good job; if they didn't eat, the king might get angry and kill them.) Then place even more blocks or weights on "God's side" of the seesaw or scale, analyzing the blessings of the Lord. (They knew they could trust God to be with them; they knew God's will was more important than what any person might say; God's power and influence are for eternity; God's faithfulness to them led them to be faithful to God.) The young men could see that in all things God is supreme over any earthly ruler.

# Daniel and His Friends

*(Daniel 1)*

King Nebuchadnezzar captured the city of Jerusalem. He took prisoners. He brought some of the young men to his palace to work in the king's court.

Daniel, Shadrach, Meshach, and Abednego came to study and learn in the king's palace. The king wanted his helpers to be healthy. He gave them rich foods from his own table.

Some of the food had been given to idol gods, and some was not prepared as God's Law said. So Daniel asked the chief official to give them just vegetables and water.

The official was afraid the king would be angry at him if the four young men were not healthy. Daniel said, "Let's test our plan for 10 days." God blessed the four young men. After 10 days they were stronger and healthier than all the other students. God also made them much smarter. The young men were blessed because they obeyed God rather than the king.

## DEVELOP

Have the children imitate your actions (and perhaps your words), as you review the Bible story.

**One day**
> *(Hold up one finger.)*

**King Nebuchadnezzar brought people to his palace.**
> *(Hold open fingers by head to make a crown.)*

**Daniel, Shadrach, Meshach, and Abednego were there.**
> *(Count off four fingers as the men are named.)*

**These four young men**
> *(Wiggle four fingers.)*

**Refused to eat the king's food and disobey God.**
> *(Hold hand up to signal No, stop!)*

**For 10 days**
> *(Show 10 fingers.)*

**Daniel, Shadrach, Meshach, and Abednego**
> *(Count off on four fingers.)*

**Ate only food allowed by God's laws**
> *(Pretend to eat.)*

**And drank only water.**
> *(Pretend to drink.)*

**After 10 days**
> *(Show 10 fingers.)*

---

### Be Strong in the Lord

"Did you ever see such an ugly shirt?"

It's easier to join in
When someone wants to sin.
What could you pray?
Then what could you say?

"Tyrese, please come and help me."

It's easier to do nothing
When you should do something.
What could you pray?
Then what could you say?

It's easier to hit back
When they're on the attack.
What could you pray?
Then what could you say?

"I don't care what Dad said, I want to watch this TV show. He won't find out."

It's easier to disobey
And do it your own way.
What could you pray?
Then what could you say?

**Words to Remember**
I will call upon the LORD, who is worthy to be praised.
Psalm 18:3 NKJV

---

**The four faithful men looked stronger than all the others.**
> *(Flex arm muscles.)*

**God helped Daniel, Shadrach, Meshach, and Abednego obey.**
> *(Point up and then count off four fingers.)*

**God will also help you and me to be strong in faith.**
> *(Point to yourself and the children and hold hands over heart.)*

## RESPOND

Review page 1 in the *Waiting* Student Book and then discuss the scenarios on page 2. Point out that it would have been easier for Daniel and his friends to do what the king said, but God made them strong to follow and obey God's will. Talk about why it is often easier to join in when people sin or to do nothing when you should do something or to hit back when they attack or to disobey and do it your way. (Satan is tricky, making sin look pleasurable and easy. Sin tempts us selfishly to do things we want rather than what God wants.) Say a prayer including all four of the listed temptations, thanking God for His forgiveness through Jesus, our Savior, and asking God to make us strong in faith to resist falling into these sins. (For example: When I'm tempted to join in sinning, make me strong to obey Your will.)

Sing together this little song to the tune "I'm a Little Teapot":

**I'm a growing Christian,**
> *(Stoop low to the floor.)*

**Growing each day,**
> *("Grow up" tall and stretch.)*

**Knowing God loves me**
> *(Hug yourself.)*

**And guides my way.**
> *(Walk in place.)*

**When the devil tempts me**
> *(Act sneaky and mean.)*

**To do wrong,**
> *(Shake a scolding finger.)*

**God gives me faith**
> *(Hold hands over heart.)*

**And makes me strong.**
> *(Flex arm muscles.)*

## WEEK 13-B

### Discovery Point

God faithfully meets our needs at the time that is best. He forgives our unfaithfulness and enables us to live for Him and to give Him praise through our words and actions.

### Daniel and the Lions

Daniel 6

### Objectives

That by the power of the Holy Spirit working through God's Word, the students will
- know that through Jesus, God has forgiven them and made them His children, empowered to live for Him;
- realize that God through His Word strengthens their faith and enables them to face difficulties, confidently assured of God's presence and care;
- do all for the glory of God.

### Day 3 Materials

- Jenna puppet
- Crown (optional)
- Lion half of Blackline 13-B
- Glue sticks
- Brown paper lunch bags

### Day 4 Materials

- *Daniel and the Lions* (Teacher Kit)
- Yarn, Styrofoam cups (optional)
- Angel half of Blackline 13-B
- *Waiting* Student Book

# Day 3

## INTRODUCE

Bring out the Jenna puppet to introduce an initial concept in today's Bible story.

**JENNA:** I am so-o-o-o angry!

**TEACHER:** What's wrong, Jenna?

**JENNA:** Our gymnastics coach made Kenisha the captain of the team. She thinks she is better than the rest of us.

**TEACHER:** Did she say she is better than the rest of you?

**JENNA:** No, but she acts like she is so important.

**TEACHER:** What did she do that makes you think she is proud?

**JENNA:** Nothing. I just don't want her to be the leader.

**TEACHER:** Do you think you might be jealous? Do you dislike Kenisha because *you* wanted to be captain? Are you upset because you know she is good and you are just beginning to learn?

**JENNA:** I think you are right. Being jealous made me be unkind and say things that aren't true. I'm sorry.

**TEACHER:** I know Jesus forgives you. Let's hear a Bible story about some other people who had a problem with jealousy.

## DEVELOP

Narrate today's story as the children pantomime the actions. Choose one person to be King Darius and one to be Daniel. Tell the rest of the children that they will be the "bad guys." In one corner of the room have Daniel pretend to talk to the king, while you are the leader of the "bad guys." Talk in a mean and jealous way about how Daniel was one of the top three rulers in the land. He had done such a good job that the king was going to make Daniel the number 1 ruler over all the others. Pretend to make plans on how to get rid of this "good guy" who makes the rest of them look bad. Since Daniel didn't cause any trouble, the "bad guys" had to make trouble for Daniel.

Take your group of bad guys over to the king to make their plans to trap Daniel. Have Daniel pray on his knees by a window. (Emphasize that Daniel continued to pray as he always did. He did not try to hide his love of God.)

Have the "bad guys" now become lions. (Distribute copies of the lion half of Blackline 13-B. Save the angel portion for tomorrow.) Have the "lions" sit in a circle on the floor with Daniel at the center. The "lions" can hold their lion pictures in front of their faces. Continue telling the story (omitting the part about the "bad guys" later being eaten by the lions because the emphasis should be on God's rescue of Daniel).

# RESPOND

Let the children color the lion faces and use glue sticks to glue the pictures onto brown paper lunch bags (open end on top). Say, **Daniel must have been very afraid of the lions. But He also trusted God. What are some of the things you are afraid of?** As children respond, write their answers on pieces of paper or have them draw a picture of things they fear. **Sometimes when we are afraid we forget to trust God or we do what is wrong. Let's turn our fears over to God and trust Him to do what is best.** Have the children crumple the papers and toss them into their lion bags. Form a prayer circle at your worship center. Circle the lions around your altar. Lead the children in prayer, mentioning things we fear, asking God's forgiveness for our failures, for increasing trust in His care, and that He will make you strong in faith to live as His people.

## Worship Ideas

- Have the children pantomime feelings of sadness, anger, and fear. Say, **Our feelings change. At one time we may feel happy. At other times we may be sad, angry, or afraid. When I feel sad or angry or afraid I like to remember that Jesus never changes.** Read Hebrews 13:8. **Jesus loves us even when we are sad or angry or afraid. His love never changes.** Sing "When I'm Feeling Scared or Sad" (*LOSP*, p. 38).

## Bible Background

When Nebuchadnezzar took the people of Judah into exile in Babylon, it seemed from all appearances that God's people were defeated. Yet 70 years after the first invasion, God raised up Cyrus, king of Persia, to return the nation to its homeland. While in Babylon, a remnant of God's chosen people remained faithful to His Word and prayed daily for restoration. God answered their prayer and opened the door to a new beginning—a return to their homeland and a renewal in faith.

Darius, perhaps another name for Cyrus or the name of the governor of Babylon appointed by Cyrus, led a centralized government directed by satraps of various regions who were accountable to three administrators. Daniel, one of the three administrators, had an impeccable record and was known for his efficiency and honesty. The jealous satraps knew that the only way to discredit Daniel was to focus on his ultimate loyalty to God.

God vindicated Daniel's faithfulness by rescuing His prophet. King Darius gave glory to God. Unfortunately, Darius was a polytheist who saw the Lord God as one god among many gods. While even the heathen recognize God's glory, it was Daniel's trust in the wisdom and power of God that gave the true witness to the Lord.

## Words to Remember

*The Lord is my helper; I will not be afraid.*
*Hebrews 13:6*

- Whisper today's Bible verse. Continue repeating it louder and louder until everyone can say the words in a strong and confident voice. March around the room, clapping hands in rhythm as you chant the verse.
- Have the children say the Bible verse in response to situations in life that you describe:

    *When the thunder crashes and the winds blow, I can remember:* (The Lord is …).

    *When a big kid is mean to me, I can remember:* (The Lord is …).

    *When I'm worried that Mom and Dad are mad at each other, I can remember:* (The Lord is …).

## Extending the Lesson

- Sing about God's helpers, the angels, whom He sends to help us: "Chatter with the Angels," "God Has Sent His Angels Down," and "All Night, All Day" (*LOSP*, pp. 20, 26, and 39).
- Ask a special guest from your congregation to tell of a time when he or she prayed to God during a time of trouble and God answered. It is important for children to hear how God works in the lives of His people today.
- Make a three-column chart labeled *People, Places, Things*. List the children's responses of *people* to pray for, *places* where they can pray, and *things* about which they can pray. Later in the week, use the same chart to list praise statements about God's care.

# Day 4

## INTRODUCE

Tell the children that today they will think about the story of Daniel and the lions from the viewpoint of what several of the characters saw and did. Hold up a folded piece of paper and say, **Here I have what the lions said. What do you think is on this piece of paper?** Listen to responses and then show the blank paper. **The lions said nothing because lions don't talk. And they didn't even roar because the Bible says God's angel had shut their mouths!**

## DEVELOP

Read aloud the book *Daniel and the Lions* (from the Teacher Kit). Ask, **How was Daniel able to be brave and face the lions? Can we learn to be brave like Daniel?** Emphasize that Daniel is not the hero of the story. Daniel did not rely on his own bravery; he relied on God. Daniel trusted that God would know what was best and how and at what time to help. We, too, can have confidence in the Lord.

---

# Daniel and the Lions

*(Daniel 6)*

**Jealous Leaders**

We didn't like Daniel. He was so good and so smart. The king liked him best. We made up a good plan to trap Daniel and have him put to death. But our plan didn't work out. It turned out bad for all of us!

**A Proud King**

I was very happy when the leaders of the land told me how important I was. I liked the idea of everyone praying to me as if I am a god. I made that my law for 30 days. I thought it was a good law. But it turned out to be very foolish. I had to order my best friend and helper to be thrown to the hungry lions. I was too proud, and my law was a bad idea.

**Faithful Daniel**

Bad things happened to me: the other leaders turned against me, the king made a bad law that dishonored God, and I was thrown into a den of wild lions. But I know that God is good. I trusted that God would help me in the way He knew was best. Perhaps God would choose to take me from the problems of this world to my home in heaven. But at this time He decided to help me in an amazing way. He sent His angel to shut the mouths of the lions. The king told everyone how great God is. God turned something bad into something good. Praise the Lord!

3

**God makes us strong in faith through His Word. Listen to what His Word says.** From the Bible read Hebrews 13:6; Ephesians 6:10; Isaiah 41:13; and Psalm 145.

## R E S P O N D

Continue by noting that God not only blesses us through His great power but He also sends His holy angels to protect us. The subject of angels is very popular today, but many people have created angels in their own imaginings. Clarify this subject by teaching the truths we find in Scripture (Psalm 91:11–12; Psalm 103:20–21; Hebrews 1:14).

- People do not become angels when they die; angels are a unique and distinct creation of God.
- We do not pray to angels; we pray alone to God, whom the angels also serve.
- Angels are God's helpers who do what He asks them to do.
- Angels are invisible and powerful.
- Angels can take on a visible form—most of the time this visible form looks like ordinary men, but sometimes angels have appeared with clothing as bright as lightning or with wings or in the sky.
- The appearance of an angel was quite extraordinary because often their first words were "Do not be afraid."

Children may color and cut out the second half of the blackline activity and hang the angels from the ceiling on gold metallic strands. Or hang several angels from the bottom of coat hangers to make mobiles. Students can also tape the angels to large Styrofoam cups to stand on shelves as reminders that we are surrounded by God's angels at all times.

Use page 4 of the Student Book. When the questions are answered correctly, the completed message says that angels are God's *helpers*.

---

## Angels Are God's ___HELPERS___ !

*Directions: Listen as each sentence is read. If the sentence is true, color the first box in the row yellow. If the sentence is false (not true), color the second box in the row. Rewrite the letters you have colored on the line above to finish the sentence.*

| TRUE | FALSE | |
|------|-------|---|
| H | L | Angels are a part of God's creation. |
| T | E | People become angels when they die. |
| M | L | Angels hear our prayers. |
| P | A | Angels are invisible. |
| G | E | All angels have wings. |
| R | F | Angels can take on a shape like a person. |
| S | Q | God commands His holy angels to help us. |

**Words to Remember**
The Lord is my helper; I will
not be afraid.
Hebrews 13:6

4

119

## Discovery Point

We worship the one true God who alone rescues us from sin through the death and resurrection of Christ Jesus. He rebuilds our lives through faith in Him.

## Rebuilding Jerusalem

Nehemiah 4 and 8

## Objectives

That by the power of the Holy Spirit working through God's Word, the students will
- know that God calls them to repentance and offers forgiveness through Jesus;
- recognize that the Holy Spirit works through God's Word to renew and empower their hearts and lives;
- joyfully worship God in all that they do.

## Day 1 Materials

- Brown lunch bags
- Markers
- Roll of paper
- Gold trim
- Box
- Wood blocks

## Day 2 Materials

- Blackline 14-A
- *Waiting* Student Book

## INTRODUCE

Divide the class into four groups and provide materials for four projects. (Allow only 5–10 minutes for this because the projects do not need to be elaborate.) One group is to make several Bible-times homes from brown paper bags by cutting off enough of the top of the bag to have a square shape. Turn that upside down (to make a flat roof) and use markers to draw windows and doors. Another group can use a box to make the temple, adding rolled paper for columns and decorating with gold trim. Another group can build a city wall with wooden blocks. Another group can take a roll of shelf paper to make a scroll, adding Bible words or drawing pictures of biblical events. *Option:* Set out Bible storybooks so children can get ideas from the illustrations.

## DEVELOP

Gather together as a group. Explain that the people of Judah had been captives in Babylon for 70 years. Now God chose to let them return home to Jerusalem. Take your group over to the first project area. Explain that it was winter when the people returned to the city. Everything was in ruins. So the first thing the people did was to build homes.

Move to the next project area. Explain that nearby enemies had many plans to prevent the people from rebuilding their city. But after many stops and starts, the temple was finally rebuilt. The helper God chose to lead this was Zerubbabel.

Go to the next project area. Explain that enemies would come into the city and steal and destroy things because there was no high wall for protection. God chose a man named Nehemiah to lead the people this time. As the people rebuilt the city wall, the enemies would tear down the work they had done. So Nehemiah had half of the workers stand guard with spears and swords. Finally the walls were built.

Move to the next project area. Now the buildings and walls of the city were rebuilt. But much more needed to be done. The hearts and lives of the people were still a mess. God chose a man named Ezra to read the Word of God to the people. When the people heard God's will, they began to cry because they saw that they were sinners. Ezra comforted them with the love and forgiveness God gives and told them to celebrate for "the joy of the LORD is your strength."

# R E S P O N D

When Ezra read to the people from the scroll, it was very much like what we do when we worship in church today. Help children make comparisons. Perhaps do this in your church sanctuary. (Note: The bold words can be read directly from Scripture, starting with Nehemiah 8:4.) **Ezra the scribe** *(much like your pastor)* **stood on a high wooden platform** *(like the pulpit).* **Ezra opened the book. All the people could see him because he was standing above them; and as he opened it, the people all stood up.** *(Similar to rituals and traditions in a church service today.)* **Ezra praised the LORD, the great God; and all the people lifted their hands and responded, "Amen! Amen!" They read from the Book of the Law of God, making it clear and giving the meaning so that the people could understand what was being read. Then Nehemiah the governor said to them all, "This day is sacred to the LORD your God."** *(Refer to the Third Commandment.)* **Then all the people went away to celebrate with great joy, because they now understood the words that had been made known to them.** *(Celebrate joyfully by singing favorite praise songs. Save Blackline 14-A for Day 2.)*

We Receive Forgiveness and Life through Jesus

who comes to us
in God's Word and

The Lord's Supper

Baptism

**Blackline 14-A**

Permission granted to reproduce for classroom use. © 2001 CPH

## Worship Ideas

- Go through a dark hallway or room, leading the way with a flashlight. **We wouldn't be able to see our way if I didn't shine this light.** Compare the flashlight to God's Word, which is like a light showing us God's will and His salvation through Jesus. Read Psalm 119:105.
- Sing "The B-I-B-L-E," "The Best Book of All," and "My Bible Book" (*LOSP,* pp. 48, 49, 54).

## Bible Background

God used the time of the Babylonian captivity to renew His people spiritually. The synagogue movement, with its emphasis on local community worship and study of the Scriptures, began during captivity and continued as a vital part of everyday life from then on.

When Cyrus defeated the Babylonians and consolidated the Persian Empire, he reversed the deportation policy of the previous rulers. He encouraged people to return to their homelands and to worship in their own temples. The Hebrew people rejoiced at this development, but of the approximately two million former inhabitants of Judah living throughout the empire, only about 3 percent returned to Judah. Those who did return were those "whose heart God had moved" (Ezra 1:5). After homes were established, the temple was rebuilt under the leadership of Zerubbabel. The process took many years because of conflict with neighboring enemies and reversals by leaders of the empire.

Almost 80 years later a second wave of people returned. Among these were Nehemiah, who led the reconstruction of Jerusalem's walls, and Ezra, who sought a renewal of the hearts of the people through a study of the Scriptures. The long wait to return home from exile was over, but the people continued to await the fulfillment of the promise that God would send the Savior.

## Words to Remember

*The joy of the LORD is your strength.*
Nehemiah 8:10

In these words Nehemiah reminded the people that their strength was not in thick city walls or the spears and swords of an army. Our strength is in the Lord. And here he specifically refers to the joy of the Lord. Sing songs of joy to celebrate the Lord, our strength.

## Extending the Lesson

- Worship God during your phys ed time. Use balloons and a parachute to demonstrate that worship can take many different forms. Distribute balloons and let the children draw a cross on them with felt-tipped markers. Spread out the parachute on the floor and place the balloons on it. Children are to grab the outside edge of the parachute with their right hand and walk in a circle singing "Rejoice in the Lord Always" (*LOSP,* p. 52, and on CD). Whenever they sing the word *rejoice,* children should raise their arms, causing the balloons to fly up in the air. Later, reverse directions by having the children hold the parachute with their left hand.
- Ezra taught the people God's truth by reading the Scriptures. Set out several Bibles and Bible storybooks. Let children examine these. Remind them that they are continuing what Ezra did so long ago—learning about God from His Word.
- Display pictures of ancient city walls. Note that this defensive practice continued another thousand years, through the changes of empires and through the Middle Ages.

## INTRODUCE

Distribute copies of Blackline 14-A. Let the children complete the picture, tracing over the dotted lines with crayons. Remind them that Ezra read God's Word to the people of Jerusalem so that they could know about God's will and ways. In a similar way today we learn about God's way of salvation, which offers us forgiveness and eternal life through Jesus. We receive these blessings through God's Word, represented by the outline of a Bible, and through the Sacraments of Baptism and the Lord's Supper, which contain God's Word and the promises of forgiveness and eternal life.

## Rebuilding Jerusalem

*(Nehemiah 4 and 8)*

After years of captivity in Babylon, the people's prayers were answered. God blessed them with the chance to return to their homeland and the city of Jerusalem.

The small group of people who returned saw that Jerusalem was in ruins. The city wall was a crumbled mess. It was winter, so the people got busy building homes.

Enemies had secret plans that kept the people from finishing the temple. Finally, Zerubbabel helped the people complete the temple so they could worship there and give glory to God.

The people were not safe till Nehemiah helped them finish the city walls. To keep out enemies, builders and soldiers worked side by side.

The priest Ezra read God's Word to the people. They repented of their sin and rejoiced in God's grace. The homes, temple, walls, and even the hearts of the people were made new again. They thanked God joyfully for His blessings.

5

Review the story of God's people hearing His message as read to them by Ezra from God's Holy Word. Read aloud page 5 of the *Waiting* Student Book as the children follow along, looking at the pictures. Emphasize that the people cried because they knew they were sinners, and they repented. Then they celebrated the joy of the Lord, knowing He gives forgiving grace. The people were happy to hear the Word of God. We rejoice, too, that we have this Word and the blessings it gives in Christ Jesus!

Continue with page 6 of the Student Book. Have children identify some of the places where we can hear God's Word. (Sunday school, individual Bible study, church, home.) Identify people who tell us God's Word. **As we read and hear God's Word, the Holy Spirit helps us grow in faith and in our faith life. He leads us to obey God and His commandments joyfully.** Point out that as we listen and learn God's Word we are obeying particularly the first three commandments: number 1—loving God above all else, number 2—using His name to learn of Him and to worship Him, and number 3—respecting His Word and setting time aside to worship Him. Pray together that God would lead us to grow in faith as we hear His Word.

## Where Do You Hear the Word of the Lord?

What is the most important thing we learn from God's Word?
Draw a picture of it at the center of this page.

**Words to Remember**
The joy of the LORD is your strength.
Nehemiah 8:10

6

123

# WEEK 14-B

## Discovery Point

We worship the one true God who alone rescues us from sin through the death and resurrection of Christ Jesus. He rebuilds our lives through faith in Him.

## John Will Help Get Ready!

Luke 1:5–25, 57–66

## Objectives

That by the power of the Holy Spirit working through God's Word, the students will
- recognize that God's Law shows their sin;
- know that God calls them to repentance through the Savior, who cleanses the sin from their hearts;
- grow in faith, trusting in God's love and forgiveness.

## Day 3 Materials
- Christmas items
- Paper bags
- Blackline 14-B

## Day 4 Materials
- *Waiting* Student Book

# Day 3

## INTRODUCE

In advance, gather several Christmas items (such as a Christmas light, cookie cutter, card, bow). Place one item in each bag and distribute to groups of children. Let each group pantomime the item in their bag and see if the others can guess what it is.

Say, **These items help us get ready for Christmas. How did people get ready for the first Christmas? Let's find out.**

## DEVELOP

Seat students in a circle. Explain, **In our Bible story, God gets the people ready for the very first Christmas—the day Jesus was born. When I do an action during the story, the person on my right will repeat my words and actions to the next person, and so on, all around the circle. Let's practice.** Shake the hand of the person on your right and have him/her pass the action on, until everyone in the circle has participated. Then begin the story.

**Long ago God promised to send a messenger to get people ready for the Savior. Now it was time for the messenger to be born.** Point to your watch and say, "It's time." Let students mimic, passing your action and words around the circle. **God picked Zechariah and Elizabeth to be the parents of this messenger child. There was just one problem.** Hold up your index finger and say, "One problem." **Zechariah and Elizabeth were very old. Most people that old would never have a baby.** Sadly shake your head "No."

**Zechariah was a priest. One day he was alone in the temple. All at once an angel stood beside Zechariah. Zechariah felt very afraid.** Shake, look afraid, and say, "I'm scared." **The angel said, "Don't be afraid. Soon your wife, Elizabeth, will have a baby boy. Name the baby John. He will get people ready for the coming Savior."** Nod head and say, "Get ready."

**Zechariah did not believe the angel.** Wave hand in dismissal and say, "No way." **The angel said, "Because you did not believe, you won't be able to talk until the baby messenger is born."** Pretend to zip lips shut. **The angel left, and Zechariah went outside. He tried to talk to the people, but he couldn't say a word.** Point to closed mouth and shrug shoulders.

**Months later, God's promise came true! Zechariah and Elizabeth had a baby boy. Friends said, "What will you name the baby?" Zechariah wrote the baby's name on a writing pad.** Pretend to write. Say, "His name is John." **Just then, Zechariah was able to talk again. He praised God. He knew baby John would grow up and help people get ready for the Savior of the world.** Raise hands in joy and say, "Get ready for Jesus."

# R E S P O N D

When John grew up to be a man, he preached to the people, "Get ready! The Savior is here! Repent of your sins. Follow Jesus." John helped the people get ready for Jesus on the inside. John pointed to Jesus and said, "Look, the Lamb of God, who takes away the sin of the world!"

Say, **Long ago, people did not get ready for Christmas on the outside the way we do today. They did not have Christmas trees to decorate, presents to buy, or cookies to bake. God sent John to help people get ready on the inside—to get ready in their hearts. God wants us to do the same.**

Distribute copies of Blackline 14-B. Point out that decorating a Christmas tree is a way to get ready for Christmas on the outside. Inside the tree is something that reminds us to get ready on the inside. (A cross.) We get ready by repenting—admitting we are sorry about our sins, receiving God's forgiveness freely through Christ, and changing to live God's way with the help of the Holy Spirit.

**When we celebrate Christmas, we celebrate Jesus' birth, but we also remember *why* Jesus was born. When we see the cross in the Christmas tree, we remember that Jesus' death and resurrection gives all believers the forgiveness of sins and eternal life.**

On the page, have students print the words *For Me.* Say, **Jesus lived, died, and rose again for you and me!**

Christmas Is ...

Directions:
Use a green crayon to color the shapes with one dot.
Use yellow to color the shapes with two dots.

Blackline **14-B**
© 2001 CPH   Permission granted to reproduce for classroom use.

## Worship Ideas

- Explain the purpose of the Advent wreath. Note that the circle shape reminds us of God's continual and unending love. The candles remind us that Jesus is the Light of the world. Sing "Light One Candle" (*LOSP*, p. 78).
- Have children stand in a circle to form a living Advent wreath. Choose four students to stand inside the "wreath" to represent candles, with arms raised above their heads and fingertips touching to represent flames. Sing the "Advent Wreath Song" (*LOSP*, p. 80).
- Add actions to the song "The King of Glory" (*LOSP*, p. 77). The King of Glory comes (*place imaginary crown on head*), the whole world rejoices (*wave hands over head*); Open the gates before Him (*arms together in front of you, then spread them apart*), lift up your voices (*cup hands at sides of mouth*). Say, **Jesus is King over all! He came to take away our sins so we can live with Him in glory in heaven.**

## Bible Background

At the close of the Old Testament, the prophet Malachi announces that the Lord is coming to His people. "I will send My messenger, who will prepare the way before Me" (Malachi 3:1). John is that messenger, born as a prelude to the Savior's birth. But more important, John will grow up to prepare the way for the Savior's ministry by calling people to repent of their sins and receive the forgiveness and grace offered by the Lamb of God.

John is like Elijah, a prophet whose manner of life reflects the priority and urgency of God's mission to the world. His clothing is unpretentious, and his diet is austere. A simple thought dominates his preaching: Christ is at hand. And John properly recognizes his secondary role, saying, "One more powerful" comes afterward, and John is lower than a servant before Him, unworthy to untie the Messiah's sandals (see Luke 3:16–18). In humility, John points to the Savior of us all.

125

## WEEK 14-B

### Words to Remember

*Look, the Lamb of God, who takes away the sin of the world! John 1:29*

Read the entire verse from the Bible so the children hear the context of the situation. John verbally and physically pointed to the Savior. Have the children point to a cross or picture of Jesus as they say the Bible words.

### Extending the Lesson

- While the children are eagerly waiting for Christmas, explore calendars in math class. How is an Advent calendar different from a December calendar? Count how many days till Christmas; find what day of the week is Christmas Eve; count how many days of vacation you have, and so forth. Note that the calendar year is marked approximately from the birth of the Savior. So it has been more than 2,000 years since the first Christmas.
- In language arts, make a list of items that help us celebrate Christmas (such as bell, tree, snow, star). Have children develop an accompanying list of rhyming words. **Can you use these words to make up your own Christmas poem?**
- Make Christmas wreath treats. Follow the recipe shown on a box of crispy rice cereal. Add green food coloring to the melted marshmallow mixture. Children may form wreath shapes from spoonfuls of the mix. (First apply a cooking oil spray to fingertips so mixture doesn't stick to fingers.) Add red hot candies for holly berries. Make extras to give to families or shut-ins, along with a homemade Christmas card that tells the true meaning of Christmas.

# Day

## INTRODUCE

Ask the children to demonstrate how they might look if they were waiting, afraid, or excited. **These feelings are all part of the story of John.**

## DEVELOP

Use those rehearsed expressions to review the Bible story. Once again have the children demonstrate someone who is waiting. Say, **God's people were waiting. They had been waiting a long time. For what were they waiting?** (For the Savior to come.) **Why did they and why do we need a Savior?** (Because we are all sinners who cannot help ourselves out of the problem of sin. Only Jesus, who is holy and true God, could do that.)

Have the children demonstrate being afraid. **Why was Zechariah frightened when he went into the temple?** (An angel appeared to

### John Will Help Get Ready!

*(Luke 1:5–25, 57–66)*

The people had been waiting for years for the coming of the promised Savior. Now the right time had come. God said He would send a messenger to prepare the way for the Savior. That messenger would be born as a baby to old Zechariah and Elizabeth. God sent an angel to announce this to Zechariah when he was in the temple. Zechariah would not believe it, so the angel said Zechariah would not be able to speak until the baby was born.

Zechariah and Elizabeth were happy on the day the baby was born. Friends asked if they would name him after his father. Zechariah wrote "His name is John" on a tablet and spoke the words aloud. The greatest reason for joy was that John would help people get ready for the Savior.

When John grew up he told people, "The Savior is here!" He told them to get their hearts ready as he said, "Repent! Confess your sins and be baptized. Turn from your sinful ways and follow God's ways." The message John spoke is still important for us today. Repent and be forgiven in the name of Jesus!

7

him.) **Why didn't Zechariah believe the angel's news?** (He didn't trust that God would give a baby to such old people.)

Have the children demonstrate being excited. **Why was everyone so excited when John was born?** (God had kept His promise to Zechariah; Zechariah could talk once again; and most important, the birth of John meant that soon the Savior would come.)

## R E S P O N D

Have the children act like they are waiting again. Say, **Zechariah and Elizabeth had to wait months before John was born and months before Jesus was born. We don't have to wait. We know all about Jesus and what He did.** Have the children act excited. **The most exciting thing Jesus did was to save us. How did He do that?** (Through His death on the cross and resurrection at Easter.) **Now that's something really exciting! That's why we celebrate Jesus' birthday!**

Continue by discussing the picture on page 8 of the *Waiting* Student Book. The picture shows people getting ready for Christmas on the outside and on the inside (in their hearts).

Say, **The Miller family is busy getting ready for Christmas. Grandma Miller and the cousins are here too. Let's look to see how this family gets ready for Christmas. Maybe we can get some ideas of ways we can get ready—both outside and inside.**

## Getting Ready for Christmas?
### On the Outside? On the Inside?

**Words to Remember**

Look! the Lamb of God, who takes away the sin of the world. John 1:29

We sometimes decorate trees to get ready for Christmas. Mark is hanging a cross on the Christmas tree. He's thinking about why Jesus was born. **Is Mark getting ready for Christmas on the outside?** Yes, he's decorating the tree. **Is Mark getting ready on the inside?** Yes, he's remembering that Jesus came to be our Savior from sin. **Draw a heart beside Mark to show that he's getting ready on the inside for Christmas.**

The cousins are helping Mark decorate the tree. Both cousins want to put the star on the top of the tree. **Are they getting ready for Christmas on the outside?** Yes, they are decorating the tree. **Are they getting ready for Christmas on the inside?** No. **Can God help them?** Yes. God can show them their sin, forgive them, and help them share. **Make a heart near the cousins.**

Continue, **Dad is hanging the green garland. Green is the color for life. Dad knows that because of Jesus, we have eternal life. Is Dad getting ready for Christmas on the outside?** Yes, he's hanging the garland. **Is Dad getting ready on the inside?** Yes, he's remembering that God gives us eternal life through Jesus, His Son. Have students make a heart near Dad.

Ask, **Can you find Steve? He's angry because he can't go play with the neighbors. Is Steve getting ready for Christmas on the outside?** No. Be sure children know that outward preparation is not mandatory. Outward preparations (trees, gifts, cookies) serve as reminders of God's love for us in Jesus. **Is Steve getting ready on the inside?** No. His anger is getting in the way. **Can God help Steve get ready on the inside?** Yes, God can forgive Steve and give him true joy. **Make a heart beside Steve.**

Direct the students' attention to Grandma and Mom. Have students brainstorm ways their outward actions might help them get ready for Christmas on the inside. (E.g., Grandma can remember God gave us the gift of Jesus—the best Gift of all. Cookie-cutter shapes may remind Mom of Jesus and His love.) Tell students to make a heart near Mom and Grandma.

Let students tell how their family gets ready for Christmas on the outside. Ask, **How might God use these outward things to get us ready for Christmas on the inside?** Accept reasonable answers.

### Discovery Point

God kept His promise. He sent His Son, Jesus, into this world as a baby so He could save us from our sins.

### Jesus Is Born

Luke 2:1–7

### Objectives

That by the power of the Holy Spirit working through God's Word, the students will
- know that Jesus was born as a baby to grow up to suffer and die for the sins of all people and to rise from the dead;
- praise God in song and prayer for sending Jesus to be their Savior;
- tell others about Jesus, the Savior of the world.

### Day 1 Materials

- Newspaper
- Manger bulletin board
- Yellow paper word strips
- Blackline 15-A

### Day 2 Materials

- Jake and Jenna puppets
- *Waiting* Student Book
- Holy Land poster

## INTRODUCE

Hold up a newspaper and say, **It would be big news in the papers and on TV if a new king was born in a far-off land. What do you think the bed of a baby king would be like? What kind of clothes would he wear? What kind of home would a baby king live in? Who or what would surround the baby in his room?** Point out that Jesus was born from King David's royal family. Even more important, as the Son of God, Jesus was born King of kings, King of heaven and earth. Yet He was not born in a palace with soft pillows and fancy clothes and servants around Him. That's because Jesus came to be one of us, one of the humblest of people, so that He could take our place and take the guilt of our sins. **What an amazing story of not just a baby, but a story of God and His love!**

## DEVELOP

In advance prepare a bulletin board or poster by drawing a large manger. Note that the legs of the manger must be removable rectangles, used later in the lesson for another message. Also prepare 16 strips of yellow paper with words printed on them. Distribute these to the chil-

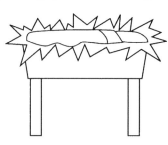

dren. (Children not receiving a strip can look forward to doing something similar later in the week.) Call numbers one at a time; have the child with that number bring the strip up so you (or he) can read the word; then the child may attach the yellow strip to the manger bed as you use that word to tell part of the Christmas story. The word list follows.

Expand on some of the extra comments as you tell the story.
1. **time** (The waiting was over; it was time for the Savior to be born.)
2. **Roman** (Caesar Augustus, the Roman emperor, made a law.)
3. **census** (Everyone had to go to their hometown to be counted for taxing purposes.)
4. **Joseph** (Promised to be the husband of Mary.)
5. **Mary** (Expecting a baby soon.)
6. **Nazareth** (Traveled from Nazareth in Galilee.)
7. **Bethlehem** (The little town where their ancestors had lived.)
8. **David's family** (They were from King David's royal family.)
9. **baby** (Our great God became a little baby.)
10. **firstborn** (Mary's first child.)
11. **Son** (Jesus is the Son of God, true God and true man.)
12. **Jesus** (Means "He will save us from our sins.")
13. **Immanuel** (Means "God with us.")
14. **wrapped** (Jesus was wrapped in simple strips of cloth.)
15. **manger** (Straw in an animal food tray was His bed.)
16. **no room** (The crowded village had no room for this tiny, but greatest guest.)

# R E S P O N D

Say, **When we think of Christmas we like to think of the beautiful story and the cute baby. We don't like to think so much about sin and death. But that is exactly why that little baby was born at Christmas. Jesus came to take away our sins by His death on the cross.** (Remove the legs of the manger and use them to form the shape of a cross above the manger.) In prayer and song, thank Jesus for coming to this earth as a humble baby for the purpose of obtaining forgiveness and eternal life for us.

Distribute the blackline activity. After the children have followed the directions say, **Jesus is the Son of God who came to this earth.** (Remove the child's slip and move the *Jesus* slip of paper to the earth.) **Jesus did this so you could become a child of God.** (Have children write "Child of God" on the second blank line.) **Jesus came to earth so that one day we can go to heaven.** (Insert the child's slip into place above the word *heaven*.) Read 2 Corinthians 8:9 and either read or sing stanza 3 of the Christmas carol "Let Us All with Gladsome Voice."

## Worship Ideas

• Use this finger play frequently throughout the week till it becomes familiar to the children.

> **Here is the stable on Christmas Day.**
> **Here is the manger where Jesus lay.**
> **Angels sang songs of peace on earth.**
> **So let's celebrate our Savior's birth.**
> —CSB

Add these actions for line 1: To represent the stable, position hands as if folded but then pulled apart just enough so thumbnails overlap.

Line 2: Turn hands over (fingers still interlaced), palms up, and rock the baby.

Line 3: With interlaced fingers pointing up and spread widely, wiggle the fingers to represent winged-angels flying.

Line 4: Clap your hands, with fingertips pointing up.

• Celebrate that the Son of God came to earth to make you a child of God by singing "Child of God" (*LOSP*, p. 98) and reading 1 John 3:1.

## Bible Background

The virgin birth of Christ defies scientific verification since it is a one-time, unrepeatable event. But it is both true and essential. Had Jesus been conceived in the ordinary way, with human mother *and* father, He could not have been the Son of God, but only a man. His death on the cross could not have been sufficient sacrifice for the sins of the world. Jesus could not have been the Savior from sin, for He would have been guilty of it Himself. His death could not have merited forgiveness for us, because it would only have been the punishment He Himself deserved. Wonderfully, as the virgin-born Son of Mary, Jesus is indeed Immanuel, God with us. This is a double assurance, telling us not only that God is present with us but also that Jesus is nothing less than God Himself.

At the right time, God's chosen time, He sent His Son as the Messiah. In retrospect we can see the wisdom of God in choosing that particular time so that eventually the message of salvation through the death and resurrection of Jesus would travel swiftly and widely throughout the world. The Roman Empire, in its world domination, had established a time of peace. The good system of Roman roads and travel, the Roman postal system efficiently carrying letters (epistles), and the common language used throughout the empire were used by Jesus' followers to spread the Gospel message to countries and cultures throughout the world.

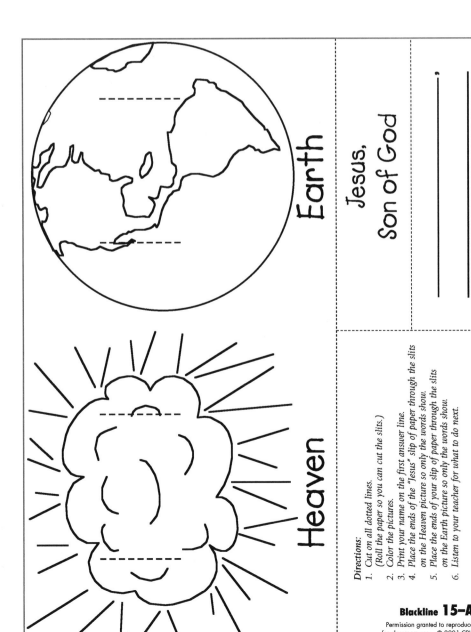

**Earth**

**Jesus, Son of God**

**Heaven**

*Directions:*
1. Cut on all dotted lines.
   (Roll the paper so you can cut the slits.)
2. Color the pictures.
3. Print your name on the first answer line.
4. Place the ends of the "Jesus" slip of paper through the slits on the Heaven picture so only the words show.
5. Place the ends of your slip of paper through the slits on the Earth picture so only the words show.
6. Listen to your teacher for what to do next.

**Blackline 15–A**

## WEEK 15-A

### Words to Remember

*Give Him the name Jesus, / because He will save His people / from their sins.*

Matthew 1:21

- Divide the class into three groups and have each group learn one of the three phrases indicated in the Bible verse. Explain the significance of each phrase. Then say the phrases in order, first whispering, then gradually getting louder each time, until you shout the words in celebration.
- Write the words of the Bible verse on paper Christmas ornaments. Mix them up and ask the children to place them in the right order. Hang these ornaments from a green garland.

### Extending the Lesson

- Tape Christmas cards to large sheets of paper. Have the children dictate sentences that you can print below the pictures. Compile these in a special Christmas book to share.
- Use the Big Book *The Savior Is Here! Listen and Cheer!* (available from CPH). Use it as a choral reading. Children say the words on the left, and the teacher reads the dialog on the right of each portion of the story. Involve emerging readers by having them manipulate the cutout figures from the back of the book.
- Use a calendar to list all of the children's birthdays. Whose birthday is closest to the day we celebrate Jesus' birthday? Count how many days to Jesus' birthday or to your own birthday.
- Ask a mother with a new baby to come and tell about things she does to make sure her baby stays healthy. If possible, ask the mother to bring the baby in each month (or bring in several babies, each a month or two apart in age). What differences do your students see? What new things can the baby do as he or she grows? Praise God that Jesus understands us so well because He did so many of the things we do—learn to walk and talk, laugh and play, eat and sleep. Praise Him that He became one of us so that He could take our place—suffering the punishment of our sin—so that we can go to "His place" in heaven.

# Day 2

## INTRODUCE

Bring out the Jake and Jenna puppets, one rushing in from the right and the other from the left. Lift or extend the puppet that is supposed to be talking. They are both excited because they have good news to tell. Each wants to be the first to speak. Listen to Jake's news (*Jesus loves us*). Jenna says that is her news too. Then say, **That is such good news. We can hear it over and over again. The two of you remind me of Jesus' disciples. When someone told them to stop talking about Jesus, they said, "We can't help it. We just have to tell everyone what we have seen and heard about the love of Jesus."** Read their words from Acts 4:20. Then sing the refrain from "Go Tell It on the Mountain" (*LOSP*, p. 84).

### Jesus Is Born!

*(Luke 2:1–7)*

The waiting was over! It was time for the Savior to be born. Mary and ___**Joseph**___ left their town of ___**Nazareth**___ because the Roman ___**emperor**___ had made a law that everyone should be counted and taxed. They had to go to their family's hometown. So Mary and Joseph traveled about 80 miles to the city of David called ___**Bethlehem**___.

The little town was filled with ___**visitors**___, so there was no room for Mary and Joseph in the ___**inn**___. The only place where they could rest was a stable, a barn for ___**animals**___. That night the baby Jesus was born. Mary wrapped baby Jesus in ___**swaddling**___ cloths. She placed Him in a manger. Baby Jesus' first bed was a box filled with hay for animals to ___**eat**___. Jesus is true God, born on earth for you and me. Jesus came to take away our sins. ___**No one else/Only Jesus**___ could do that for us.

## DEVELOP

Tell the Christmas story using the Student Book *Waiting*, page 9. Tell the children to raise their hands every time they hear you make a mistake in this well-known story and to give you the correct answer. Explain each correct answer and then continue. As you read the story, insert these errors into the blanks: *Jonah, Chicago, elephant, Boston, fish, palace, apples, diaper, sleep on, Only 10 other people.* Next, distribute the books to the children and together print the correct answers in the blanks. (List words on the chalkboard to avoid stress about spelling: *Joseph, Nazareth, ruler, Bethlehem, people, inn, animals, swaddling, eat, Only Jesus.*) Read aloud the story from Luke 2:1–7.

## RESPOND

Page 10 of the Student Book extends the concept initiated in Day 1: Christ became poor so that we may become rich. Emphasize that this is not rich in money. There are better ways to be rich, ways that last forever. Have the children use crayons to trace over the dotted letters. Point out that being rich in these things means that God gives them abundantly to us. These are things that make us truly blessed and truly happy. These are things that He gives us now and will continue eternally in heaven. **Jesus was born in a manger and wrapped in swaddling cloths so that He could give us the crown of life—eternal life in the kingdom of heaven.**

Have the Holy Land poster available for use in units 4–8 whenever you feel it is appropriate. The pictures of Bethlehem, the Sea of Galilee, the Garden of Gethsemane, and the city of Jerusalem will help the children understand the setting of many new Testament Bible sories.

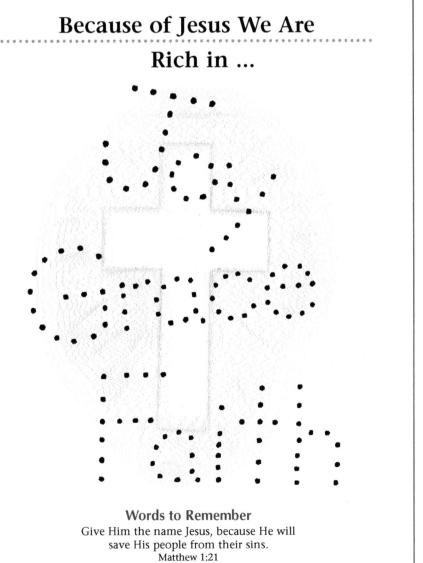

# Because of Jesus We Are
# Rich in ...

**Words to Remember**
Give Him the name Jesus, because He will
save His people from their sins.
Matthew 1:21

10

## Discovery Point

God kept His promise. He sent His Son, Jesus, into this world as a baby so He could save us from our sins.

## Shepherds See the Savior

Luke 2:8–20

## Objectives

That by the power of the Holy Spirit working through God's Word, the students will
- recognize humankind's need for a Savior;
- rejoice that the Savior, Jesus, has come;
- share the salvation story with others.

## Day 3 Materials

- A printed invitation
- Phone
- Bells, drums, cymbals
- Blackline 15-B

## Day 4 Materials

- Christmas *Fold 'n' Tell* (in Teacher Kit)
- Manger scene from Day 1
- New yellow word strips
- Black, white, brown, yellow, red, blue paper
- Stapler or tape

# INTRODUCE

Ask, **If you were going to have a birthday party, how would you invite people to come?** If someone says they would send out invitations, hold up an invitation card. If someone says they would call people on the phone, hold up a cordless or toy telephone. If these ways are not suggested, hold the items up as clues or suggest them yourself. Then say, **God sent a fantastic birthday invitation when Jesus was born—angels filled the sky, announcing the Savior's birth and singing praises to God. Let's celebrate this part of the Christmas story in special ways.**

# DEVELOP

Divide the class into three groups, giving each group a set of rhythm instruments—bells, drums, or cymbals. Explain: **You will provide some sound effects as I tell the Bible story. When Group 1 hears me say "angel" or "angels," they will ring their bells** (or clap hands). **When Group 2 hears me say "shepherds," they will sound the drums** (or stomp feet). **When I mention baby Jesus, Group 3 will clang the cymbals** (or say "Happy birthday"). Practice, so students know what to do. Raise your hand to signal stop.

**It was nighttime.** *Shepherds* **were watching their sheep in the fields outside Bethlehem. Suddenly a bright light shone all around the** *shepherds.* **They saw an** *angel* **in the light. The** *shepherds* **were afraid! The** *angel* **said, "Don't be afraid. I have good news for you and for all people. Tonight** *baby Jesus* **was born in Bethlehem. You'll find** *baby Jesus* **lying in a manger."**

**Then the sky was filled with many, many** *angels.* **They praised God and sang, "Glory to God on high, and peace, good will to men." Then the** *angels* **went back to heaven. The sky was quiet and dark again. The** *shepherds* **said, "Let's go to Bethlehem. Let's find** *baby Jesus."*

**So the** *shepherds* **hurried to Bethlehem. They found Mary, Joseph, and** *baby Jesus* **just as the** *angel* **said. On the way back to their fields, the** *shepherds* **told everyone, "Good news! Tonight** *baby Jesus,* **the Savior, was born!"**

Let students use their instruments to answer these Bible story review riddles: **We were sent by God to tell shepherds the Good News. Who are we?** (Angels.) **We ran to Bethlehem. Who are we?** (Shepherds.) **Mary and Joseph were My parents. Who am I?** (Jesus.) **I will grow up and die on a cross to forgive sins. Who am I?** (Jesus.)

# RESPOND

Say, **If you need a Savior, sound your instrument.** Remind the children that everyone needs Jesus as a Savior because we are all sinners who do wrong things. Only Jesus can help us because He is true God. Through Jesus our sins are forgiven. God promises us eternal life in heaven, and He helps us grow in faith and in our Christian life today.

**If you can tell someone about God's Good News of salvation, sound your instrument.** Like the shepherds, we can tell others the good news of Jesus. Distribute Blackline 15-B, which children can use to tell others about our Savior. Children are to color the six sections and then cut them out. Sing this little counting song, using the tune "Ten Little Indians." Arrange the corresponding piece of the scene in place to complete a Christmas picture.

**One—here is the little stable.**
**Two—see Joseph and see Mary,**
**Three—the manger, hay, and baby,**
**All on Christmas night.**

**Four—the shepherds came to praise Him.**
**Five—the stars were shining brightly.**
**Six—the angels sang of glory,**
**All on Christmas night.**

—CSB

One—here is the little stable.
Two—see Joseph and see Mary,
Three—the manger, hay, and baby,
All on Christmas night.

Four—the shepherds came to praise Him.
Five—the stars were shining brightly.
Six—the angels sang of glory,
All on Christmas night. -CSB

**Blackline 15-B**

## Worship Ideas

- Pray for all people who do not know Jesus as their Savior or believe in Him. Ask God to use you as His messengers in some way to share the faith that you have.
- Using a clear piece of plastic, trace over the picture on page 11 of the Student Book. Use the overhead projector to enlarge this picture. Shine the image on a large sheet of mural paper and trace over the lines. Cut holes where the faces appear. Let children stand behind the Christmas scene and look through the openings, becoming part of the Christmas story as you read aloud Luke 2:1–20. Since most children will want to participate, do this several times throughout this week and the next.

## Bible Background

When the angel appeared to the shepherds, and "the glory of the Lord shone around them," God's most profound revelation of His glory, the birth of His Son as Savior, was publicly announced. The angel was joined by a "great company of the heavenly host," a term that has connotations of a vast army. Here, however, the army announces peace, for the Savior has come to reconcile God and humankind. This peace makes possible a relationship rooted in God's forgiveness, through Christ Jesus. The angels sang of glory in the highest and peace on earth. This brings to mind the words of Philippians 2:10, that "at the name of Jesus every knee should bow, in heaven and on earth."

 **Day**

## Words to Remember

*I bring you good news of great joy that will be for all the people. Luke 2:10*

- The "Words to Remember" are part of the rebus (the second sentence) on page 12 of the *Waiting* Student Book. After doing the activity, have children identify these "Words to Remember" by underlining them with a red crayon.
- Point out that the angel was the first to share the good news of the Savior's birth. Later, the shepherds told this good news to everyone they saw. Jesus asks us to carry on, sharing this joyful news. Jesus says, "Go and make disciples of all nations" (Matthew 28:19).
- After the angel shared this good news, the angel chorus broke into songs of gloria. Say the Bible words together and then burst into song, singing the refrain of "Angels We Have Heard on High." Repeat the Bible verse and then joyfully sing the refrain of "Hark! The Herald Angels Sing."

## Extending the Lesson

- God used angels and shepherds to tell the message of the Savior's birth on the first Christmas. Brainstorm ways that this message is spread throughout our world today. The faithful witness of a believer will always be important, but God can enable us to use methods such as TV, radio, CDs, and e-mail to share the Gospel.
- Encourage students to bring favorite Christmas books to school. Read and evaluate the books. How many tell the true story of Christmas? Brainstorm ways that some stories might be adapted to include the real meaning of Christmas.
- Work together to compute the following: Suppose each person in your classroom told just one person about the real meaning of Christmas each day from now until Christmas (or for one week). How many people would hear the Good News of Jesus? (Remind children that we can share this Good News with people who know and love Jesus too. We are not limited to sharing the news with people who don't know Jesus. The fellowship of believers is important too.)

## INTRODUCE

Use the Christmas *Fold 'n' Tell* from the Teacher Kit to introduce your continuing discussion of the Christmas story. Practice the folds in advance (directions are printed on the back of the story card). Scenes will show Jesus' birth, shepherds in the field, shepherds and the angel, shepherds and many angels, the angels going away (the favorite part of the story card for most children), and the shepherds worshiping the Savior.

Multiple copies of *Fold 'n' Tell* are available from CPH. Consider placing several in an activity center. (Children are often better at manipulating the folds than adults!) Or, consider ordering more for Christmas gifts for your class so they can share the true story of Christmas with others.

# Shepherds See the Savior

*(Luke 2:8–20)*

The night when Jesus was born, there were shepherds out in the fields, watching over their flocks of sheep. Suddenly there was a bright light shining all around them. An angel of the Lord appeared. The shepherds were terrified until they heard the good news. The angel told them that the Savior was born in Bethlehem.

Suddenly the sky was filled with angels praising God and saying, "Glory to God in the highest, and on earth peace." When the angels left, the shepherds hurried to Bethlehem to see what had happened. They found Mary and Joseph. Baby Jesus was in a manger, just like the angel had told them.

As the shepherds returned home, they told everyone the wonderful news that they had heard and seen. The people were amazed. The shepherds praised God. And Mary treasured all these things in her heart.

11

## DEVELOP

To review the Bible story, add yellow word strips to the manger scene as you did on Day 1 of this week. The 15 new words and phrases you will use to tell this portion of the Bible story are (1) shepherds; (2) fields; (3) flocks; (4) angel; (5) afraid; (6) great joy; (7) all people; (8) sign; (9) heavenly host; (10) glory to God; (11) on earth peace; (12) Bethlehem; (13) hurried; (14) spread the word; (15) amazed.

Now retell Jesus' story with a variety of colors of strips of paper. Either distribute the colored strips or pass around colored paper and let the children cut off their own strips. Explain what the colors stand for: black—the darkness of the night; white—the bright angel; brown—the stable; yellow—the straw on which baby Jesus was sleeping in the manger; red—the blood of Jesus shed on the cross to forgive our sins, which is the reason He came to earth; blue—heaven, where we will live one day because Jesus has saved us.

These strips can now be placed one on top of another and stapled together at one end to make a shaker or looped to make a paper-chain necklace. Suggest that the children use these to tell others about Jesus. The children can be messengers, sharing the message of the angel.

## RESPOND

Look at page 12 of the Student Book to hear again the angel's message (here in rebus form):

*Do not be afraid. I bring you good news of great joy that will be for all the people. Today in the city of David, a Savior has been born to you. He is Christ the Lord.*

Discuss further our role as messengers, telling the Good News of the Savior. Say, **In science, you learn about sound vibrations, and about echoes. Have you ever heard an echo? Where? What did it sound like?** Then point out that a good place to hear an echo is on a mountain. **If you shout something on a mountain, your message echoes back and forth, and many people can hear your message. Perhaps this is why we sing "go tell it on the mountain." We want the message of the Gospel to echo, repeating over and over so many people will hear of the Savior.** With that thought in mind, sing the song together (*LOSP*, p. 84, and on CD).

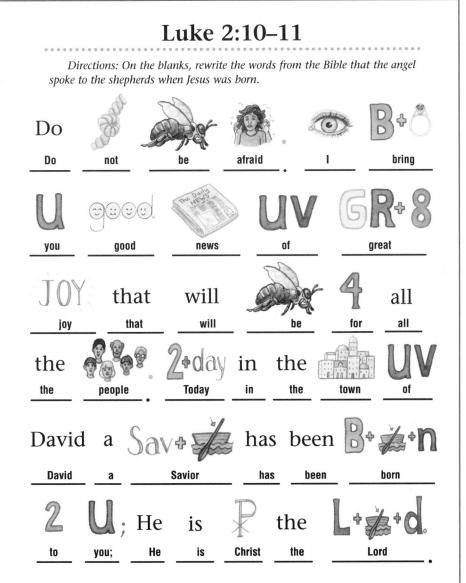

# Luke 2:10–11

*Directions: On the blanks, rewrite the words from the Bible that the angel spoke to the shepherds when Jesus was born.*

Do \_\_\_\_\_ \_\_\_\_\_ \_\_\_\_\_ . \_\_\_\_\_ \_\_\_\_\_
Do / not / be / afraid / I / bring

\_\_\_\_\_ \_\_\_\_\_ \_\_\_\_\_ \_\_\_\_\_ \_\_\_\_\_
you / good / news / of / great

\_\_\_\_\_ that will \_\_\_\_\_ \_\_\_\_\_ all
joy / that / will / be / for / all

the \_\_\_\_\_ . \_\_\_\_\_ in the \_\_\_\_\_ \_\_\_\_\_
the / people / Today / in / the / town / of

David a \_\_\_\_\_ has been \_\_\_\_\_
David / a / Savior / has / been / born

\_\_\_\_\_ \_\_\_\_\_ ; He is \_\_\_\_\_ the \_\_\_\_\_ .
to / you; / He / is / Christ / the / Lord

12

## Discovery Point

Jesus came to the earth to save all people from their sins. He came for people of all ages and all places.

## The Wait Is Over for Simeon and Anna

Luke 2:22–40

## Objectives

That by the power of the Holy Spirit working through God's Word, the students will
- know that God kept His promise to send a Savior, to bring forgiveness and salvation;
- trust that Jesus came for people of all generations and all lands and all times;
- praise God for Jesus, who brings light to this sin-darkened world.

## Day 1 Materials
- Flannelgraph materials (in Teacher Kit)
- Blackline 16-A

## Day 2 Materials
- Family photos
- Elderly man and woman visitors
- Baby doll
- Bells
- *Waiting* Student Book

## INTRODUCE

Tell the children, **We've been talking about the birth of Jesus. God sent a host of angels to announce that the Savior is born. They filled the skies with songs.** Now switch your voice to a soft whisper and say, **But sometimes God uses a still, soft voice. God the Holy Spirit told a very old man named Simeon that he would see the Savior. Let's learn about that special day.**

## DEVELOP

Display figures from the flannelgraph set in the Teacher Kit to represent Mary, Joseph, Simeon, Anna, and baby Jesus, with temple pillars for a background. (It is not necessary to cut every detail of the figures. Leaving a simple white border around the figures is easier and gives a nice accent to the shapes.) Use the following narration as a guide, adding to or adapting it as you choose.

Tell the children, **Baby Jesus was just a little over a month old when His family took Him to the temple in Jerusalem. Let's imagine what the people were thinking on that special day.**

JOSEPH: It is such a special day to be in God's house with our whole family. We have brought special offering gifts to thank God for blessing us with the birth of baby Jesus. I was so amazed when we met Simeon. He is a very old man who has been faithful to God all these years. Simeon recognized baby Jesus as the promised Savior. He held the baby in his arms and thanked God that he was able to see this day and the salvation God gives to all people through Jesus.

SIMEON: Dear Lord, You have kept Your Word. My eyes have seen Your salvation in Christ, my Lord. He is the Light of the whole world. I am ready now to leave in peace.

MARY: How did Simeon know that this tiny baby is the Savior? Simeon's words remind me of the promise God gave to Abraham thousands of years ago—the Savior will be a blessing for all people. And now we are joined by Anna, another person of the older generation. She comes to the temple night and day, serving God.

ANNA: Praise God that I have lived to see the day that the Savior has come. God will do mighty things through this little baby. I must tell everyone I see that our Savior is here. God's promise is fulfilled.

## RESPOND

Point out, **The four adults in our Bible story were very blessed on that special day. When they went to church that day, they all saw and praised God for Jesus, our Savior. You and I are blessed, too, when we go to church, to God's house. We are especially blessed to "see the whole picture." We know what Jesus did to save**

**us.** Discuss and ask questions about how Jesus grew up to one day die on the cross to take away our sins. The story does not end there. Jesus rose from the dead at Easter and promises to take us to eternal life in heaven. **You and I have seen God's plan of salvation through Jesus. When we look at a cross, we remember all that Jesus did to redeem the world.**

Distribute copies of Blackline 16-A. **Jesus, His parents, Simeon, and Anna went to the temple church. I go to (name) church. This is a picture of a church that has a problem.** Point out that when they decorated this church, they forgot something very important. (A cross.) **Jesus' death on the cross is most important for us, because without Him we would have no chance of forgiveness of our sins or eternal life in heaven. Praise God that we have this through Jesus!** Tell children to decorate the church with crosses wherever they think it could use one. Then look at the sentence at the bottom of the page. Help the children write the name of their church on the first answer line and the times for services on the second line. Suggest that children give this to a family member, neighbor, or friend to invite them to come to church to learn of Jesus and to worship Him.

You are invited to come to church.

Where? _____

When? _____

# Worship Ideas

- Darken the room and turn on some Christmas lights. **Christmas lights can remind us that Jesus is the Light of the world. In our Bible story, Simeon called Jesus a light. Because of the darkness of sin we would not be able to see the way to heaven. But Jesus is the Light and shows us the way.** Sing "This Little Gospel Light of Mine" (*LOSP*, p. 103).

- Point out that many of the children in your class may have been a baby, like Jesus, the first time they went to church. For many of them, that first time may have been at their Baptism. Talk about what happens in Baptism—the water and the words that the pastor says. Note that it is the action of the Holy Spirit that brings the special blessings of faith in Jesus and forgiveness to the heart of the baptized person. Emphasize that it is the Word of God that has the power. Water by itself cannot do this. Also reassure unbaptized children that they, too, have the blessings of forgiveness and faith as the Holy Spirit works through the Word of God that they hear. And they can look forward to the day when they will be baptized too. Sing "Child of God" (*LOSP*, p. 98).

# Bible Background

Luke 2:21–22 records the circumcision and presentation of Jesus. As the holy, sinless Son of God, Jesus was not obliged, as all human beings are obliged, to submit to the Law of God. Yet the heavenly Father sent His Son to be "born of a woman, born under law, to redeem those under law" (Galatians 4:4–5). In His perfect obedience to God, Jesus did what every person is unable to do: He fulfilled the Law and earned salvation by His life, death, and resurrection.

The presentation of a child occurred 40 days after birth and very much involved both parents. The mother was to present the priest two animals (lamb and dove) for a sin offering and burnt offering. This was a time of rededication to God after the ceremonial purification time required after the birth of a child.

Every firstborn male was to be consecrated to the Lord (Exodus 13:1). Fathers redeemed their sons, buying them back with an offering of five shekels of silver (Numbers 18:16). The greater redemption was to come when Jesus offered up His body and blood on the cross to redeem all people from sin and death.

# WEEK 16-A

## Words to Remember

*My eyes have seen Your salvation. Luke 2:30*

- Point out that these are the words of Simeon. He saw the face of the Savior. We see how Jesus saved us by His death and resurrection. We see the cross of Christ that gives us salvation.
- "I see" can mean "I see with my eyes" or it can mean "I understand." Right now we "see" with understanding. But the Bible tells us that one day, in heaven, we will see Jesus face-to-face. We will see Him as He is! Praise God for our Savior Jesus!
- Listen to a recording of the Nunc Dimittis—Simeon's words of praise set to music. Ask children to raise their hands when they hear the "Words to Remember" they have learned.

## Extending the Lesson

- Display baby pictures of each child in the class. Keep the identities a secret and see if children can guess who each one is. Discuss how much the children have grown since the pictures were taken. Read Luke 2:40, which tells about Jesus growing. Besides growing older, what other ways do children grow? How do we grow in faith? (By the power of the Holy Spirit, working through God's Word.)
- To grow as God wants us to grow, we need to keep our bodies healthy. Talk about nutrition and the food pyramid. Chart what the children eat each day for a week. Be sensitive to children who may be from other cultures. If some children come from families that cannot afford enough nutritional food, talk with your principal, pastor, or school nurse to see how the needs of these children can be met.
- Make a time capsule to help children become aware of how they have grown during the school year. Have each child trace around one foot and write their name on it. Place these tracings, along with samples of art, handwriting, spelling, and math from each child, in a box. Open the box at the end of the school year and let the children compare their foot size, handwriting, and skills then with now. Thank God in prayer that He helps us to grow in many ways.

## Day 2

# INTRODUCE

Show several of your family photos with young children, adults, and elderly family members. Explain that the photos show several *generations*, people at different ages and stages of life. Have children look at the picture on page 13 of the *Waiting* Student Book. Have them identify the different generations pictured there. Say, **Jesus loves people of all generations. He came to save people of all ages. Jesus loves babies and grandparents and everyone in-between.** Read Mary's words from Luke 1:50: "His mercy [forgiving love] extends to those who fear [honor] Him, from generation to generation." **As we retell the story of Simeon and Anna, think of all the generations of people God loves.**

# The Wait Is Over for Simeon and Anna

(Luke 2:22–40)

When baby Jesus was about 40 days old, Mary and Joseph took Him to the temple-church in Jerusalem. This was the custom in those days. They brought a thank-You gift to God for Jesus.

In the temple was an old man named Simeon. Simeon held baby Jesus in his arms. He knew that Jesus was the promised Savior. Simeon said, "Oh, Lord, Your promise is true. I have seen the Savior of all people. I am ready now to depart in peace." Simeon was very happy. He had waited a long time for this day.

There was a woman in the temple named Anna. She was more than 80 years old. She served in the temple day and night because she loved God. She praised God when she saw Jesus. Then she told everyone that the Savior has come! He will rescue us from sin and its punishment. He will give us eternal life.

In the days to come, Jesus grew strong and was filled with wisdom. God watched over Him and loved Him. God watches over you, too, because He loves you!

13

## DEVELOP

Review the Bible story, acting it out in a special way. Invite an elderly man and woman to take the parts of Simeon and Anna. Take your class to the church sanctuary and stand in a semicircle at the front of the church. Have "Simeon" stand near one side of the altar with a Bible and have "Anna" stand near the other side of the altar. Have two children carrying a doll (or, better yet, parents with their infant) walk from the back of the church to the altar, while the teacher reads Luke 2:22–27. When "Mary, Joseph, and Jesus" are standing near the altar, have "Simeon" read Luke 2:28–35 and "Anna" read Luke 2:36–38. Then "Mary and Joseph," holding "Jesus," can walk out as the teacher reads Luke 2:39–40.

Close by praying together for the children in your class, their parents, grandparents, and people of all generations, thanking God for His love and asking Him to bring more people to know and believe in Jesus as their Savior.

## RESPOND

Celebrate God's love with bell ringing. Say, **We hear lots of bells at Christmastime when we celebrate that Christ is born. We also hear bells every time we go to church to worship the Lord.** Either give each child a small bell to ring or rotate a few bells between groups of children. Sing this song to the tune "Are You Sleeping." Repeat each line at the asterisk (*).

> **Ring the bells, *
> Loud and soft. *
> Ring to all the world, *
> Christ is born! ***

Sing again, changing the last line to "Christ is here" or "Jesus saves" or choose your own words.

Together look at page 14 of the Student Book. Point out that churches today come in all sorts of shapes and sizes. In the center of the page, have the children draw the church they go to. Ask them to draw a picture of themselves going to church with people of other generations. Praise God for His great love for all people!

---

## Come, Worship the Lord at His House!

**Words to Remember**
My eyes have seen Your salvation.   Luke 2:30

14

## Discovery Point

Jesus came to the earth to save all people from their sins. He came for people of all ages and all places.

## Wise Men See the Time Has Come

Matthew 2:1–12

## Objectives

That by the power of the Holy Spirit working through God's Word, the students will
- know that all people need Jesus as Savior because all people are sinners;
- rejoice in God's unconditional love for all;
- witness to their faith in Jesus, their Savior, by sharing the Gospel's good news.

## Day 3 Materials

- Yellow paper star
- Three foil-wrapped stars
- Flashlight
- Blackline 16-B
- Wooden craft sticks

## Day 4 Materials

- *Waiting* Student Book
- Paper star

## INTRODUCE

In advance, cut out a large yellow star. Tape the star to your forehead or cheek so students will be sure to notice it. When children comment about the star say, **My star caught your attention, didn't it? In today's Bible story, God used a star to get some people's attention too. It worked. Let's learn more about it.**

## DEVELOP

Before class begins, make three star shapes. Wrap the stars with aluminum foil. Display the stars near the ceiling on three different walls in your classroom.

Darken the room as much as possible. You will shine the flashlight on the different stars in the room as you tell the story.

Point the flashlight on the first star. Say, **Wise Men lived in a land far away from Bethlehem. One night they saw a bright, new star in the sky. The Wise Men said, "The time has come. The new King has been born. Let's go see Him."**

Point the flashlight on the second star. Say, **The Wise Men traveled for many, many days. Finally they came to Jerusalem. The Wise Men asked, "Where is the baby who will be the new King?"**

**The Bible teachers said the baby was to be born in Bethlehem. But King Herod thought to himself, I am the king. I will not let anyone take my place. I will kill this baby.**

**Then Herod told the Wise Men to let him know where the baby was so he could worship the new king too. This was a lie. King Herod really planned to kill Jesus.**

Point the flashlight on the third star. **The Wise Men followed the star to Bethlehem. It led them to the house where Jesus lived. The Wise Men gave Him gold and other wonderful gifts. They praised and worshiped Jesus. That night God told the Wise Men, "Do not go back to Herod." So the Wise Men went back to their own country another way.**

## RESPOND

Discuss: **We know that the shepherds told many people about the Savior after they saw Him. Do you think the Wise Men did the same thing?** (They didn't tell King Herod, but it is likely that they took the news to their distant homeland. The Wise Men probably were the very first foreign missionaries. After such a long and exciting journey, they would certainly tell friends and neighbors about what they had come to know of the Savior of the world!) Ask, **Can first graders witness, telling what they know about Jesus? Yes, you can! We can share Jesus' love with others through our loving words and actions. We can start right here in our classroom.** Help students realize that sometimes our sins get in the way of sharing the Good

News. Sometimes jealousy, selfishness, or bossiness stands in the way of our witness. God's Law shows us our sin. But the Gospel shows us our Savior. God calls us to repentance. He gives forgiveness and new life as the Holy Spirit works in our heart to strengthen our faith and life as God's child. Ask, **Can first graders witness to people living far away in other countries?** Yes, through special offerings, prayers, food/clothing drives, and letters of encouragement to missionaries.

Direct the students' attention to the blackline activity. Point out that sometimes it's hard to share Jesus' love with people different from ourselves. Sometimes we let the differences stand in the way of our witness. Talk about the differences (age, skin color, type of speech or dress, physical abilities) that sometimes separate people. God's love brings people together because God loves everyone the same.

Ask, **Does Jesus love people with handicaps?** Yes. **Can Jesus help you love people with handicaps too?** Yes, God's love is stronger than our prejudices. He can help us share the Gospel message with all people. Have students draw a heart near the physically handicapped person. Continue in the same way for each illustration. Children may then color and cut out the pictures, attach them to wooden craft sticks, and use them as puppets to role-play situations in which people can talk to each other about God's love and share kindness.

God Loves Everyone

**Blackline 16–B**
© 2001 CPH  Permission granted to reproduce for classroom use.

# Worship Ideas

- Seat students in a circle. Say, **Today we're going to give Jesus a special birthday gift. Let's see ... how much wrapping paper will we need?** Begin to unroll a short length of the gift wrap as you stand in the middle of the circle. Build interest by unrolling the paper until it completely fills the middle of the circle. Say, **What can we give to Jesus? What do you think Jesus wants for His birthday? The Bible gives us a clue. It says, "Love the Lord with all your heart, with all your soul, with all your mind, and love your friends and neighbors too." Let's give Jesus ourselves. Let's ask Him to help us love our friends and neighbors too.** Invite all students to sit on the gift wrap and sing "Christmas Is a Time of Joys" (*LOSP*, p. 107) or another favorite Christmas song.

- Before worship, place a jingle bell inside your pocket. Jingle it as you ask, **Can you guess what I have in my pocket?** Let children guess. **You knew it was a bell because you can hear it jingling. You've heard jingle bells jingle before. Once you've heard something, you can usually tell someone else about it. It's a little like sharing the real meaning of Christmas. Because you've heard about Jesus, you can tell others the Good News.** If you have rhythm bells, let students use them as you sing "Ring the Bells" (*LOSP*, p. 108).

# Bible Background

We know very little about the Wise Men, not even their number (though we do know about the three gifts). This lack of information reminds us that Jesus, not the Magi, is the center of this story. Jesus' love is for all people, rich or poor, from near or far, of any nation, culture, or language.

Note that though nativity scenes conveniently place the Wise Men at the stable at Christmastime, the Bible tells us that they came to the *house* where the family was living. The gifts they brought may have symbolized the person and work of Jesus: gold, befitting a king; frankincense, burned in worship and reminding us that Jesus is true God; and myrrh, used to prepare bodies for burial, a preview of His redeeming death.

# WEEK 16-B

## Words to Remember

*Arise, shine, for your light has come. Isaiah 60:1*

- The star and this verse can remind us that Jesus is the Light of the world. Point out that the darkness of the world refers to sin and the troubles it causes. Jesus is called the Light because He shows us the way to forgiveness and to heaven. Jesus changes the picture of a world darkened by the sadness of sin to a world bright with hope and promise through our Savior. Sing "This Little Gospel Light of Mine" (*LOSP*, p. 103).
- Celebrate the fact that the time of waiting is over. "Your light has come!" The Savior has come and has won salvation for us. Now we wait for that day when we will enter life in heaven with Him.

## Extending the Lesson

- In language arts classes this week, challenge students to see how many new words they can make from letters found in the words *Merry Christmas*. Do this as a group. Select words from your list to add to your spelling words.
- Teach students how to draw a five-pointed star in art class. If some students already know how, let them teach a friend. (It may help to think of a person standing with arms and legs stretched out. Draw a line from toe to head, to other toe, to opposite hand, to other hand, and back to beginning toe.) Also demonstrate how to make a six-pointed star from overlapping two triangle shapes.
- Use a star-shaped cookie cutter to cut cheese slices. Place a cheese star on top of a toasted English muffin for a starry treat! Read and discuss Philippians 2:15b–16: "Shine like stars in the universe as you hold out the word of life."
- In science class, check out various star constellations. (Your librarian may have helpful references, charts, etc.) Make your favorite constellation, using gummed stars on black construction paper. Use white chalk to connect the stars to form a recognizable image. Can you use your imagination to create a brand new constellation?

# Day

## INTRODUCE

Invite children to play follow the leader. Say, **We'll play the game a bit differently today. We won't have a leader. Ready? Go.** Begin walking aimlessly. After a short while say, **This is silly. We can't play the game this way. We need a leader. We need someone to show us the way. That's why God put the special star in the sky—to show the Wise Men the way to the Savior, Jesus. And that is why Jesus came to the earth. He not only shows the way, He is the way to heaven!**

## Wise Men See the Time Has Come

*(Matthew 2:1–12)*

Mary, Joseph, and baby Jesus were now living in a house in Bethlehem. Wise Men from a country faraway came to see the Savior. They had seen and followed God's special star, which led them in their travels.

First, they had stopped in Jerusalem because they thought the king would be born in a palace. They asked, "Where is the one who has been born king of the Jews? We saw His star in the east and have come to worship Him."

King Herod, a cruel man, was worried that someone was trying to take away his kingdom. He asked the teachers what the Bible said about where the Savior would be born. He asked the Wise Men about the star. He lied and said he wanted to worship the Savior too.

The star led the Wise Men to Bethlehem and stopped over the place where Jesus lived. The Wise Men worshiped and praised God that the Savior had come at last. They gave Him gifts of gold, frankincense, and myrrh. Then they returned home by a different way because God had warned them in a dream not to go back to King Herod.

In this story we see that God loves all people from all nations. Jesus came to save the whole world. He calls us to repent of our sins and believe in Him. He wants us to tell everyone the Good News of salvation in Jesus.

## D E V E L O P

Read the Bible story on page 15 of the *Waiting* Student Book. Then say, **It was not just a star that led the Wise Men to Jesus. What else helped lead the way? Hint: It is something that still leads us to know Jesus today.** (The Bible.) Point out that the Scriptures told the Wise Men the Savior would be born in Bethlehem. **What else do we learn about Jesus from Scripture?** (Answers will vary, but be sure to mention Christ's death and resurrection if no one else does.) **In what ways does the Bible lead us today?** (Leads us to know Jesus, leads us to repentance, leads us to live a godly life, leads us to learn about faith and eternal life—all through the power of the Holy Spirit, working through God's Word.)

## R E S P O N D

Point out that Jesus is the Light of the world, and He says to us, "Let your light shine" (Matthew 5:16). This happens with Jesus leading the way and the Holy Spirit empowering us. Look at page 16 in the *Waiting* Student Book. **While we are waiting to see Jesus face-to-face, we live each day for Him. With God's help, shine for Jesus!** Read the Bible verses to the children, and let them draw and then discuss pictures of ways we shine in our actions, following Jesus by being forgiving and kind and by sharing His love and His message.

Conclude with a praise parade. Lead the children around the room as you sing "Go Tell" or "Go Tell It on the Mountain" (*LOSP*, pp. 104, 84, and on CD). As you lead the line of marching children, hold high a Bible on which you have attached a star to remind children that God leads us today through His Word in the Scriptures.

# Shine for Jesus

*Directions: Read the Bible verses. Draw pictures to show ways we can shine for Jesus in what we do and say.*

Be kind ... forgiving each other just as in Christ God forgave you. Ephesians 4:32

May our Lord Jesus Christ ... strengthen you in every good deed and word. 2 Thessalonians 2:16–17

Since God so loved us, we also ought to love one another. 1 John 4:11

**Words to Remember**
Arise, shine, for your light has come.
Isaiah 60:1

16

# UNIT 5
# Listen

## Unit Overview

This unit of Bible study and the accompanying Student Book are entitled *Listen*. We begin now to study Jesus' ministry, and for that reason *listen* is a key word. We want to hear what Jesus did and what He said. His words and deeds bring us eternal life. We could ask for nothing more. He asks us to listen and then tell, sharing His message of love and salvation with others. So let's listen with our ears and our hearts, learning His Word and also living it!

Send home copies of the family letter and Bible verse list for Unit 5 as you begin. (See the Teacher Resource Book.) This will let parents know what their children will be learning during the next few weeks. At the end of the unit, let the children take their *Listen* Student Book home. Encourage them to show their parents what they have learned. This is the fifth in a series of nine books that will cover the story of salvation through the Old and New Testaments. Also consider adding some of the following activities to your curriculum to make related connections between God's message of love and all that you do throughout the day.

## Worship Connections

Remind the children again and again that "listen" is this unit's theme. Take the class to the church sanctuary. Point out two places where we listen to the Word of God. Say, **This is the lectern. God's Word in the Bible is read here. This is the pulpit. The pastor explains God's Word to us here.**

Ask the children to point out other places in the sanctuary where they can hear God's Word. (In Baptism at the baptismal font, at the altar in the Lord's Supper, many hymns say God's Word in the form of poetry, many sung and spoken parts of the liturgy are quotations directly from Scripture.) Demonstrate how the pastor looks at the congregation when he is speaking the Word of God to us. When we are responding in prayer, praise, and offerings, the pastor will usually face the altar as a reminder that we are directing this to the Lord. (Note that in discussions like this you are helping children to become more aware of the form of the worship service and its vocabulary.)

While our focus is on listening with our ears, we can also learn about God by looking with our eyes. Give children paper and pencils. Let them walk around the sanctuary, drawing pictures and writing words of things they see that remind us of the truths of God. Gather after about 10 minutes and share ideas.

## Community Building

This unit has several lessons about Jesus choosing His team of disciples. Sometimes choosing teams can be a traumatic experience for children, especially if they are chosen last or chosen with scornful looks. To alleviate this problem to some extent, try this plan about once each month. Pair up all the children as team captains. Give each pair a class list to work on together, cutting apart the names, selecting teams, and gluing the lists of names to another sheet of paper to make two team lists. Suggest that captains put their own names at the top of their list, but then mix up the remaining names so no one can tell who was chosen first or last. Gather the lists and use them throughout the month. This will save the embarrassment of waiting and waiting to be chosen (and it will also save you time over the course of the month). Speak about the purpose of this activity and encourage children to be sensitive to the feelings of others.

## Tools for Witness

Several stories in this unit have a strong evangelism emphasis. Help children to see that they don't need to wait to grow up to tell about Jesus; they don't need to travel to far places to tell about Jesus. Sharing the love of Jesus is a *right now, right here* thing.

Ask the children to think about their neighbors. **Think about this—do your neighbors know that you are a Christian? Have you talked to them about what this means to you? Can they see evidence of your Christian beliefs?** Together make plans to develop ways to give a Christian message in your neighborhood. Send a letter home to enlist parent involvement.

- As a family, make a large banner to place over your front door. The banner can say something like "Jesus Loves You and Me."
- If you play music outdoors on the deck or by the pool, consider playing Christian praise songs. If your music is being "shared with the neighborhood" anyway, share music that has an important message.
- Give neighbors a written invitation. (Perhaps leave it at their front door.) Say that your family will be going to church this Sunday. Suggest that, if they would like to join you, they meet at your house at a certain time. Take a caravan of cars to church!

## Service Projects

Especially during Week 18, develop plans to have a fish fry. Involve parents in the food preparation and publicity. Involve the children in setting and cleaning tables. Make fish-shaped place mats, design under-the-sea centerpieces, and hang giant paper fish hooks (covered with aluminum foil) from the lights. Ask for a freewill donation (suggesting a minimum to cover costs). Emphasize that all proceeds will be used to help spread the Gospel.

Title publicity posters "Help Us 'Fish' by Eating Fish!" Point out that Jesus calls us to be fishers of men, catching people for His kingdom. So, to help catch people for Christ, you will give the proceeds to a missionary or Bible translator project.

## Reaching Every Individual

As people of God, we want to hear and learn His Word. As we share His message, it is also important to recognize that children have varying abilities, attention spans, and background experiences. Be cautious that any memorization or Bible-related activity the children are involved in does not give anyone the feeling that their faith is inadequate and that they are a spiritual failure. Our only failure is sin, and Jesus has resolved that through His death and resurrection. Emphasize that our relationship with Jesus is based solely on His loving grace, not on anything we can or can't do. As together you study God's Word, children should have a safe environment of support, compassion, and acceptance—the same environment in which our loving and forgiving Savior enfolds us.

## Science

Fish, literally and symbolically, play an important role in this unit. Consider related "fish" activities in science. Set up an aquarium; learn about fresh-water and salt-water species; place paper over a fresh, whole fish and make inked rubbings that show the scales on the fish; have a "fish" treat—Gummi fish floating in blue Jell-O.

## Social Studies

This unit lends itself well to a simple map study. The towns of Nazareth, Jericho, and Jerusalem are settings for some of the Bible stories. The areas of Galilee, Samaria, and Judea will be mentioned. Water formations such as the Sea of Galilee and the Jordan River will also play an important part.

## Mathematics

As you study Jesus' calling and sending out of the disciples, use manipulatives to explore how many 12s (dozens) there are in 72 (6).

## Integrating the Faith

## Listen

## Language Arts

Language Arts obviously play a significant role in a unit on *listening*. Study various forms of communication—recorded, printed, braille, sign language, and so forth. Practice sharing a Gospel message, using a variety of these forms of communication. Display Bibles printed in various languages, emphasizing that the message is the same in each—the message of salvation through Christ Jesus.

## Technology

As you encourage children to witness to one another and to their families in simple, everyday language, provide an activity that will help them become aware of opportunities to speak about God. Prepare an audiotape with a single repeated message such as "God is good!" Each evening send the tape and an audio-cassette player home with a different child. He or she can watch for times when a Christian response would be appropriate and then play the taped response. Have the child count the number of times the phrase was played. The recorder should be returned the next day so another child can take it home.

## Fine Arts

Acting out Bible stories is fun, but it also reviews facts and reinforces concepts. Involve the children in their own costuming. Ask each child to bring a two-yard length of fabric and some string. (The fabric could be part of an old bedsheet or beach towel.) It should be simple and plain, with no design other than stripes. Cut a slit at the center of the fabric through which a child can stick his or her head. Let the fabric drape over the clothes at the front and back, and tie the robe together at the waist with the string. You are now ready for a crowd scene. (Individual robes can be folded and stored in gallon-size ziplock bags.)

## Discovery Point

The Holy Spirit calls us to faith in Jesus as our Savior and continues to enlighten and guide us through God's Word.

## Jesus in the Temple

Luke 2:41–52

## Objectives

That by the power of the Holy Spirit working through God's Word, the students will

- believe that God speaks to them through His Word today, in places such as the church;
- grow in their desire to show God their love and devotion through worship;
- joyfully worship God in His house.

## Day 1 Materials

- Photos of houses and a church
- Flannelgraph materials
- Blackline 17-A
- Yarn or ribbon
- Paper punch

## Day 2 Materials

- *Listen* Student Book

# INTRODUCE

Show the children several photos of houses and let them guess who lives there. (Show a photo of your house, photos of homes of several of the children, or famous homes such as the White House.) Conclude by showing a photo of a church. Ask, **Whose house is this?** (God's house.) Explain that a church building is dedicated to God so we call it God's house. Read today's "Words to Remember" (Psalm 122:1). Then say, **Those are the words of King David. Today we'll hear the story of another person who was glad to go to God's house.**

# DEVELOP

Use the flannelgraph materials in the Teacher Kit to tell the story. Place half of the temple scene on the right side of your flannelgraph board. Over this place an entire countryside scene. Roll the country scene back to reveal the temple at appropriate times in the story. There is quite a bit of movement in the story: walking to Jerusalem, going to the temple, Mary and Joseph walking a day's distance from Jerusalem and then hurrying the day's distance back, Jesus in the temple with the teachers, and the whole family returning to Nazareth.

As you tell the story, include some of the following ideas. Nazareth was quite a distance from Jerusalem, so people in Nazareth, like Mary, Joseph, and Jesus, would worship each week in their local synagogue and worship at least once a year in the beautiful temple-church in Jerusalem. Even though it took several days to get there, they tried to be in Jerusalem for the special celebration of Passover. Usually people walked in large groups on this pilgrimage. They did it for safety reasons, and it provided an opportunity to socialize. Children often walked together as a group with their friends. That's why Mary and Joseph didn't notice Jesus was missing until late in the day. They thought He was with the other children or relatives.

# R E S P O N D

Ask, **What did I say is another name for a church?** (God's house.) **What did Jesus call the temple-church?** (His Father's house.) **God is our Father in heaven. He is the best Father of all. He never makes mistakes; He is always kind; He never forgets; there is nothing He can't do. We can always feel safe and happy and loved when we are in God's house. God never changes. He is always good and forgiving. He is the perfect Father.**

Ask, **What do you think Jesus and the temple teachers talked about?** (The Scriptures—God's Word.) Distribute Blackline 17-A. Read the Scripture verses aloud to the children. Tell them they will vote on their favorite of these verses, and from that vote, they will determine a class favorite. Children vote by marking an *X* in one of the bottom boxes. After reading and voting, let the children cut on the dotted lines and color each section to make a bookmark. Punch a hole in the bottom box of each one and string yarn or ribbon through the hole to add a decorative fringe. *Option:* Laminate the bookmarks before adding ribbon. The heat of the laminator melts the crayon and gives an interesting effect. Suggest that children give some of the bookmarks to family and friends.

## Worship Ideas

- Throughout the week use several portions of your church liturgy that are sung. Choose short portions or refrains so that children can quickly learn them. Encourage them to listen for these songs during worship at church and join in praising God with the whole congregation.

- Teach the children this little prayer. Suggest that they pray words like these before worship, asking God to help them grow in faith and in their faith life through His Word. Note: This prayer may be sung to the tune of "Who Made the Sky So Bright and Blue" (*LOSP*, p. 74).

      **Lord Jesus bless the spoken Word**
      **And bless my hearing too,**
      **That after all is said and heard,**
      **I may believe and do.**

## Bible Background

When a Jewish boy was still very young, his parents began teaching him simple prayers and Bible passages. At age 6 a child was traditionally sent to the synagogue school, where he learned God's Word and basic reading and writing skills. At age 12 he—along with all adult males—was obligated to travel to Jerusalem to attend the Passover and other festivals.

Women and children often accompanied their husbands and parents, and it was customary for extended families to travel together for fellowship, support, and security.

The incident in Luke 2 shows the perfect obedience of Jesus—a sharp contrast with the way we live as disobedient children. Jesus' obedience to His heavenly Father goes all the way to the cross. Through His obedience we receive salvation and the power to obey those God has placed over us.

**Blackline 17-A**

## Words to Remember

*I was glad when they said to me, "Let us go into the house of the LORD." Psalm 122:1 NKJV*

- Visit God's house. Stand in the various areas of the church and tell the children the name we use for that location, such as the nave, the chancel, the choir loft, the balcony, the narthex, the aisle. Perhaps the pastor could lead this little excursion through the church and church vocabulary.

- Emphasize that the church is more than just a building. The church is the group of believers who gather to learn and worship, to pray and praise. **God lives with His people; so anywhere God's people are they can say, "We are the church!"** Sing "We Are the Church" (*LOSP*, p. 106).

## Extending the Lesson

- Let each child make a Scripture scroll. Make copies of the Bible verses learned in the first four units of lessons. (Copy the lists in the letters to parents in the Teacher Resource Book.) Let children use glue sticks to attach these lists to rolls of white shelf paper. Let each child roll up the scroll and look at the Scripture verses they have been learning. Perhaps they can read these verses to their families.

- Do a praise cheer that involves counting by even and by odd numbers:

  **Two, four, six, eight;**
  **Jesus, You are really great.**
  **One, three, five, seven;**
  **He will take us home to heaven.**

- Display a variety of Bibles (such as children's Bibles, pocket Bibles, large-print and braille editions). If possible display a Bible printed in another language. Emphasize that God's Word is for everyone! God wants all people to come to know the truth about Jesus and be saved.

# Day 2

# INTRODUCE

(Use the following line of questioning to help children understand Jesus' response to his parents at the temple.) Ask, **If your family went to a big store and your mom was looking for you, where could she expect to find you?** (Responses may include the toy department.) **If your family went to the ball game and your dad was looking for you, where could he expect to find you?** (Answers might include talking to the coach or getting a soda.) **When Mary and Joseph were looking for Jesus, where did He say they could have expected to find Him?** (In His Father's house.)

## Jesus in the Temple

*(Luke 2:41–52)*

The Bible tells us Jesus grew bigger, smarter, and stronger every day. He had friends who liked Him, and He was dearly loved by God.

When Jesus was 12 years old, He went with His family to Jerusalem to celebrate the Passover. They walked and talked with other families along the way. They worshiped and prayed in God's temple.

After several days, when the celebration ended, everyone started walking home. That evening Mary and Joseph looked for Jesus. They thought He was with friends. But they couldn't find Him anywhere.

They hurried back to Jerusalem. On the third day, they found Jesus in the temple. He was listening to the teachers and asking them questions.

Mary said, "We were so worried. We searched everywhere for You."

Jesus said, "Didn't you expect that this is where I'd be—in My Father's house?" Then the family returned to Nazareth. There Jesus grew and obeyed His parents in all things.

God speaks to you today through His Word. God blesses you in many ways as you grow each day.

1

## DEVELOP

Review the Bible story by doing a little "traveling" in your classroom. Have the children stand in the back of the room. Tell them to take one step forward every time you read a statement that is true. If you read a false statement, they should remain in place. **Jesus was 12 years old.** (True.) **Jesus, Mary, and Joseph went on a trip in their new car.** (False.) **The family walked all the way from Nazareth to Jerusalem.** (True.) **The family celebrated Passover with many other people.** (True.) **When it was time to go home, Jesus ran ahead of the crowd.** (False.) **When Mary and Joseph could not find Jesus, they hurried back to Bethlehem.** (False.) **Jesus did not obey His parents.** (False.) **Jesus wanted to learn more about God, His heavenly Father.** (True.) **We read and hear God's Word and go to God's house because we want to learn more about our heavenly Father and worship Him.** (True.)

## RESPOND

Introduce several concepts to the children about the Scriptures. Show them how much of the Bible is the Old Testament, which was written before Jesus was born and looked to the fulfillment of God's promises in Him. Show the New Testament and explain that it tells about the life of Jesus in four books called the Gospels, and then it tells what happened in the early years of the Christian church as Jesus' followers spread the news of the Savior. Point out that the Bible is a book of many books, 66 in all. Emphasize that God inspired the words of Scripture, so we can be certain that it is true!

Discuss the Third Commandment and its explanation in the catechism. Point out that in Old Testament times people went to worship in God's house on Saturday, the Sabbath Day. In the New Testament times and continuing to today, we worship on Sunday to honor Easter Sunday, the day Jesus rose from the dead. That is our special Sabbath Day, but any day and every day is a good day to worship the Lord!

Today the children begin to use a new Student Book, titled *Listen.* This is exactly what Jesus was doing in God's house. He also listened to His parents and obeyed them. Luke 2:52 tells about Jesus as He continued to grow. Read this verse with the children as printed on page 2 of their books. Then discuss each picture of Jesus growing in various ways. Answer the questions in a class discussion and then pray that God would lead each of you to follow Jesus and to grow in the ways that He did, through the blessings and power of almighty God. (Answers will vary, except for the third question. How much does God love you? Eternally, endlessly, so much that He sent Jesus to save you.)

---

## Growing in the Lord

Jesus grew in wisdom and stature, and in favor with God and men.
Luke 2:52

What do you like to study and learn? _____

How tall are you?

Who are your good friends?

How much does God love you? **He saved us through Jesus; His love is endless.**

### Words to Remember
I was glad when they said to me, "Let us go into the house of the LORD."
Psalm 122:1 NKJV

2

## Discovery Point

The Holy Spirit calls us to faith in Jesus as our Savior and continues to enlighten and guide us through God's Word.

## Jesus Is Baptized

Matthew 3:13–17

## Objectives

That by the power of the Holy Spirit working through God's Word, the students will
- grow in their joy of knowing that through Jesus they have become God's own dear children;
- talk about the blessings they receive through Baptism: faith, forgiveness, the power to live as God's children, and the promise of heaven;
- thank and praise God for calling them into His family through His Word.

## Day 3 Materials

- Artifacts from your Baptism Day
- Flannelgraph materials
- Felt fabric
- Jake and Jenna puppets
- Blackline 17-B

## Day 4 Materials

- Cake pan holding mud
- Pitcher of water
- Towel
- *Listen* Student Book
- Pastor interview

## INTRODUCE

Show artifacts of your own Baptism (such as a Baptism candle, certificate, clothing you wore, photos taken, the names of sponsors or godparents). Discuss what your Baptism means to you. **Let's learn about the day Jesus was baptized.**

## DEVELOP

Use flannelgraph figures to tell the Bible story. Use pieces of felt fabric to make simple additions to the set in the Teacher Kit. For example, use white felt to make a dove, yellow felt to make rays indicating God's voice from heaven, and blue felt to indicate the Jordan River. Cut a slit in the blue felt so that you can partially insert John and Jesus into the water.

## RESPOND

Use the Jake and Jenna puppets to bring up three important questions about Baptism.

**JENNA:** Why do Christian people want to be baptized?

**JAKE:** Because Baptism is a special gift from God!

**JENNA:** And you never turn down a gift.

**JAKE:** You're right. Baptism is a special way God blesses us with faith, forgiveness, and a future in heaven.

**TEACHER:** And Baptism is God's will for us. God's Word says, "Get up, be baptized and wash your sins away" (Acts 22:16). And also, "Repent and be baptized, every one of you, in the name of Jesus Christ for the forgiveness of your sins. And you will receive the gift of the Holy Spirit. The promise is for you and your children" (Acts 2:38–39).

**JENNA:** Why did Jesus get baptized?

**JAKE:** I don't know. Jesus never sinned. He is true God Himself. He didn't need to be baptized. I'm puzzled!

**TEACHER:** Maybe I can answer that for you. Jesus did not need to be forgiven or baptized. But He wanted to lead a perfect life in our place and fulfill all things for us. Jesus is a perfect example for us, showing us how God wants us to live.

**JENNA:** Well, I've got one more question. My cousin Julian believes in Jesus. But he hasn't been baptized. What will happen to him?

**TEACHER:** It is by the power of God's Word working in Baptism and the power of God's Word working in your heart that the Holy Spirit brings you to faith in Jesus. Julian has forgiveness by faith in Jesus.

**JAKE:** And he can look forward to the day when he, too, will be baptized. Julian is a Christian now. And someday he will be able to call himself a *baptized* Christian!

Use Blackline 17-B to emphasize that Baptism is not just water; it is water connected with God's Word. Provide materials that children can use to decorate the picture such as gold pens for the edges of the Bible, red felt to glue over the bookmark, and crayons to color the water drops light blue and to trace over the dotted letters. After cutting out the water drops, children can use glue sticks to adhere them onto the picture of the Bible.

Explain that a *sacrament* is a sacred act
- instituted (given) by God,
- in which God joins His Word of promise to a visible element (something you can see),
- and by which He offers the forgiveness of sins earned by Christ (see Luther's catechism).

Point out that the three water drops remind us that we are baptized in the name of the Father, Son, and Holy Spirit. The words on the drops remind us of blessings we receive by God's grace: He *calls* us to repentance and to be His own dear children, He *forgives* us in Christ, and He *empowers* us through the Holy Spirit to live a Christian life.

# Worship Ideas

- If possible, show a video of a recent Baptism. Encourage children to say words of the creed and Lord's Prayer that they know along with the congregation.
- Plan to celebrate Baptism birthdays throughout the year. Sing a song such as "Child of God" (*LOSP*, p. 98). Give a special card or sticker to the celebrant. Recognition of these days will help children think about the continuing importance of Baptism in their lives. Always be sensitive to children who have not been baptized, encouraging them to talk to their parents about Baptism and to look forward to the day when they will be baptized.

# Bible Background

Why would Jesus want to be baptized? After all, John was baptizing for the forgiveness of sins, and Jesus had no sin to be washed away. Jesus' explanation, that His Baptism was "to fulfill all righteousness" (Matthew 3:15), suggests three reasons.

First, Jesus' Baptism was a public seal of approval of Jesus as the Messiah. He was anointed with the Holy Spirit, and the heavenly Father announced that He was His Son. Second, the anointing of the Holy Spirit strengthened Jesus for the work ahead. With this strength He showed His power over Satan, who tempted Him in the wilderness shortly thereafter. Third, by being baptized, Jesus put Himself in the place of all those who did need Baptism for the forgiveness of their sins—the whole human race.

Though He had no sin, Jesus became sin so we could receive His righteousness. (See 2 Corinthians 5:21.) When Jesus sacrificed Himself on the cross, the payment would be credited to all people.

*Directions: Cut on this line. Cut out the water drops. Glue the drops onto the picture of the Bible.*

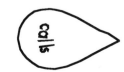

**Blackline 17-B**

## WEEK 17-B

### Words to Remember

*[God says,]* "I have called you by your name; you are Mine." Isaiah 43:1 NKJV

- This verse reminds us of our personal relationship with the Lord. Because of Jesus we can call God *Father*, and together we are *brothers and sisters* in Christ. Let children go around the room, shaking each other's hands, and calling each other Brother _____ or Sister _____ , by name.
- Pronounce a personal blessing for each child as you place your hand on each child's head, in turn, and say the Bible verse, including the individual's name in the verse. Children can also sign their names to the printed verse in the Student Book.

### Extending the Lesson

- In math class, graph the number of birthdays and Baptism birthdays per month. Which month has the most celebrations? Which has the fewest? Did you include Jesus? Though we don't know the exact dates, we celebrate Jesus' birthday in December and His Baptism in January.
- Plan a unit on water. Display a bulletin board entitled "Uses for Water." Include Baptism.
- Have children "paint" on sidewalks with water; discuss why the paintings eventually disappear. Discuss the water cycle, emphasizing that God continues to send the clouds, the rain, and the sunshine. His love for us is constant.
- Observe *changes* in water as it is heated or frozen; talk about how God *changes* our lives through His forgiving grace; emphasize that God's love is *changeless*.

### INTRODUCE

Before class, set out a flat cake pan with some mud in it. Also fill a large pitcher with water and set it beside a towel. Gather the children around as you take a handful of mud and squeeze it between your fingers. Say, **I'm making a mess with this mud. This reminds me that sin makes a mess of our lives.** Now pour the water over your hands to clean them. Dry with a towel and say, **Washing my hands to get them clean reminds me of Baptism. Baptism washes away my sins through Jesus. Baptism has water, but it is the Word of God *with* the water that washes me clean of the guilt of sin.** Point out that you wash your hands several times each day to be clean. **But we don't need to be baptized several times. Baptism is a special gift of God; salvation from Jesus is complete.**

## Jesus Is Baptized

*(Matthew 3:13–17)*

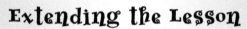

*This is My beloved Son.*

Jesus was 30 years old. It was time for Him to begin His ministry to the people. Jesus went to the Jordan River, where John was preaching. John was getting the people ready to meet the Savior. John said, "Repent of your sins and be baptized." John told the people that the promised Savior was coming.

Jesus asked John to baptize Him in the Jordan River. At first John didn't want to, because He knew Jesus is the Son of God. But Jesus said, "Let it be so. I want to fulfill all things." So John obeyed.

As Jesus was baptized, the heavens opened up. The Holy Spirit came down to Him in the shape of a dove, and the Father's voice from heaven said, "This is My Son, whom I love; with Him I am well pleased."

John pointed to Jesus and said, "Look, the Lamb of God, who takes away the sin of the world!"

At the end of His ministry Jesus said, "Go and make disciples of all nations, baptizing them in the name of the Father and of the Son and of the Holy Spirit" (Matthew 28:19). Jesus wants all people to be saved, to learn the truth about Him, and to be baptized.

## DEVELOP

Use the *Listen* Student Book, page 3, to review the story of Jesus' Baptism. Spend most of your time on Baptism as it is celebrated today. Ask your pastor to visit the class to speak about the Sacrament, or meet him in church at the baptismal font, where he can try to answer the children's questions. Or watch a videotaped interview in which you have asked the pastor questions about the Baptism celebration. Emphasize that Baptism is not merely something that happened to you long ago; it is significant every day of your life. Daily we are forgiven, and daily we live in God's grace as His people.

## RESPOND

Continue with page 4 of the Student Book. Read the story of Raul's Baptism. Discuss the elements of the chart that compare Jesus' Baptism to Raul's. Point out that different churches may have slightly different customs about Baptism. God doesn't give us a set of rules about procedures. What He has told us is that Baptism is water with the Word; we are to baptize in the name of the Father, Son, and Holy Spirit; we receive the gift of forgiveness through Jesus and faith in Him through the power of the Holy Spirit. The amount of water, the number of sponsors, the time and place are not prescribed by God, but are based on the practices of the church. Conclude by singing praise to God and by reading the catechism's selection of Bible verses related to Baptism (see the Teacher Resource Book).

## A Very Special Day

This was a special day for Raul. He listened to Pastor Gomez talk about the blessings we have through Jesus. He said, "In Baptism, through water and the Word, God makes you His child and washes away your sin."

Raul looked at his sponsors, Mr. and Mrs. Hernandez. They were the ones who first told his family about Jesus, our Savior. As Raul's sponsors, they promised to pray for him and help him learn about Jesus and His love.

Pastor Gomez made the sign of the cross over Raul's forehead and over his heart. Jesus died on the cross for me, thought Raul. Then Pastor Gomez poured water on Raul's head three times and said, "I baptize you in the name of the Father and of the Son and of the Holy Spirit."

Raul said, "I am now a *baptized* Christian. I will remember this day every day! I know Jesus forgives me and will always be with me."

|  | Jesus' Baptism | Raul's Baptism |
|---|---|---|
| Age | 30 years | 7 years |
| Why wanted? | To fulfill all things | To receive forgiveness and new life in Christ |
| How done? | Went into the river | Water poured three times |
| God is here | In Jesus, the Son; the Father's voice; the Spirit as a dove | "Baptizing in the name of the Father, Son, and Holy Spirit." |

### Words to Remember

[God says,] "I have called you by your name; you are Mine."
Isaiah 43:1 NKJV

4

## Discovery Point

Jesus wants each of us to come to know Him as Friend and Savior. He invites all people to follow Him and empowers believers to share the Good News with others.

## Jesus Chooses Disciples

John 1:35–51

## Objectives

That by the power of the Holy Spirit working through God's Word, the students will

- rejoice that Jesus has called them to be His own;
- know that God wants them to tell of His saving grace and that He empowers and enables them to do so;
- serve God in all that they do.

## Day 1 Materials

- Blackline 18-A

## Day 2 Materials

- Blackline 18-A
- Teacher Resource Book or *Songs Kids Love to Sing 2* CD
- *Listen* Student Book

## INTRODUCE

Distribute Blackline 18-A. Have the children cut on the solid lines and fold on the dotted lines. Point out the words at the center (A Dozen Disciples). That will be the theme for today's lesson. Place the activity sheet facedown as you learn about the disciples Jesus chose.

## DEVELOP

Have the children fold the first disciple, Andrew, so that he is standing up. Explain that Andrew had been following John the Baptist to learn more about the Savior that was coming. One day John pointed to Jesus and called Him the Lamb of God. Immediately, Andrew followed Jesus. He listened to Jesus all day. The very next thing he did was run to tell the good news that the promised Savior was here. He ran to tell his brother Simon Peter. (Fold up the Peter illustration.)

Point out that Andrew and Peter were fishermen who worked with their friends James and John. Soon they became disciples too. (Fold them up.) Andrew was the first disciple. Peter, James, and John were Jesus' closest friends.

Continue by telling the story of Philip. Jesus said to him, "Follow Me," and he did just that. (Fold Philip up to a standing position.) Philip also went to get a friend—Bartholomew (also known as Nathanael). Bartholomew didn't think that someone as important as the Savior would come from an unimportant little town like Nazareth. But when Jesus spoke to him, Bartholomew knew that Jesus is the Son of God. (Note that Bartholomew is at the end of the illustrations.)

As you fold up the remaining illustrations, comment that we know about some of the disciples, such as Thomas and Matthew, the tax collector. But some we know very little about. Some disciples had more than one name to distinguish them from disciples with similar names. There were two disciples named James. One was the son of Zebedee, and the other was the son of Alphaeus. (Sometimes the second one is called James the Less, not because he was unimportant, but perhaps because he was younger or shorter.) Jude was also called Thaddeus, perhaps to distinguish him from Judas Iscariot, who betrayed Jesus. And Simon (not Simon Peter) was known also as the Zealot because of his political connections.

# R E S P O N D

Emphasize that Jesus' words "Follow Me" meant more than merely walking wherever He went. **Jesus called the disciples to faith, to listen and learn, to speak of His love, to be a helper, to be a friend, and to be forgiven.** List these phrases on the board, noting that this isn't a complete list.

Jesus calls us to be disciples too. Just like the disciples, we can't follow perfectly. But God is there always with His forgiveness and empowering grace to help us grow as His people. Say each child's name (individually or by groups) as "disciple Kim" or "disciple Jeff," and then read through the list on the board, saying, **Jesus calls you to faith, to …**

## Worship Ideas

- The lesson theme (Jesus chooses us to be His disciples who share His message of love and salvation) is emphasized in many songs from *Little Ones Sing Praise*, such as "God Chose Me" (p. 107), "Jesus Wants Me for a Helper" (p. 33), "Go Tell" (p. 104), "Go Tell Your Brother" (p. 107), "This Little Gospel Light of Mine" (p. 103), "I Can Tell" (p. 99), and "Jesus Is My Special Friend" (p. 43). Many of these are also on the Voyages CD.
- Sing "God Is So Good" (*LOSP*, p. 57, and on CD). Let the children make new stanzas for the song to tell about the lesson theme. (Point out that the new phrases will need to have four counts or syllables.) Repeat the new phrase three times and close with "God is good to me." Possible phrases: He calls me friend; I'll follow Him; Let's tell His news; I am forgiven.

## Bible Background

The fact that Christ calls people to be His disciples—rather than people initiating the relationship themselves—has at least two implications for our lives. First, since Christ calls us, we know we are His own, not by our own goodness or decision, but purely by His grace. In Baptism Christ marks us for lifelong, committed service to His kingdom. By God's grace we will introduce family and friends to Jesus, come and see more of Him in His Word, and, by the Spirit's power, follow Him wherever He asks us to go.

Second, we need never doubt that we are indeed disciples, though we may feel inadequate to carry out such an honored calling. Jesus has come to us, has invited us to walk and work with Him. In Baptism and His Word Jesus assures us that He has forgiven our sins and given us life with Him forever. He will enable us to do the things He asks of disciples.

## A Dozen Disciples

Bartholomew

Judas

Simon

Thaddeus

James, son of Alphaeus

Matthew

Simon Peter

Andrew

James

brother John

Philip

Thomas

*Directions: Cut on the solid straight lines between each man's picture. Fold on the dotted lines.*

**Blackline 18-A**
Permission granted to reproduce for classroom use. © 2001 CPH

## Words to Remember

*[Jesus said,] "I have called you friends."*
John 15:15

- Say this Bible verse. When you get to the word *friends* shake hands with a boy and a girl and bring them to the front of the room. Say the verse again, and at the word *friends*, the boy shakes hands with someone and brings that person forward. The girl does likewise. Next time you say the verse, all four children shake hands with people and bring them forward. (If you notice a child who is being ignored, step in and shake hands.) **Jesus calls us His friends; He wants us to share His loving friendship with all people.**

- Walk around the classroom as you say the Bible verse aloud. When you say the last word of the verse, choose as the new leader the child sitting nearest to where you stopped. Continue this pattern of saying the verse and choosing a new leader till everyone has a chance.

## Extending the Lesson

- In math class, provide manipulatives so that children can make sets of a dozen and a half dozen. **Jesus started with a dozen disciples. With disciples like you and me, Jesus now has millions of disciples who follow Him in love!**

- Play follow the leader. Lead the children around the room and to other areas of the school. Make the game interesting by adding arm and leg motions. Point out that when Jesus says "Follow Me," He is talking not about footsteps, but about faith and living each day. Jesus is our guide in all that we do, at home, at school, at work, at play. He even gives us the faith and forgiveness needed to be His followers!

## INTRODUCE

Use the blackline activity from yesterday to learn a new song, "There Were Twelve Disciples." (See the Teacher Resource Book. The song is also on the *Songs Kids Love to Sing 2* CD, available from CPH. Note that the melody is similar to "Bringing in the Sheaves.") The disciples' names are printed on the blackline activity in the same order as listed in the song.

## DEVELOP

Have the children follow your words and actions in this echo pantomime.
**John the Baptist pointed Andrew and his friend to Jesus.**
*(Point to the distance.)*
**Andrew and his friend hurried to follow Jesus.**
*(Walk in place quickly.)*

### Jesus Chooses Disciples

*(John 1:35–51)*

Andrew and his friend wanted to know about the promised Savior. They listened to John the Baptist tell about the Messiah. One day, Jesus walked by. John pointed to Jesus and said, "Look, the Lamb of God, who takes away the sin of the world!" Andrew and his friend rushed to see Jesus. They listened to Jesus all day. Then Andrew rushed to his brother, Simon Peter. Andrew said, "We have found the Savior!" Andrew took Peter to see Jesus.

The next day Jesus met Philip. Jesus said, "Follow Me." Philip was so glad to follow Jesus. He wanted his friend Bartholomew to know Jesus too. He said, "God's promise has come true. I have seen the Savior. He is Jesus.

He is from Nazareth."

Bartholomew was not sure about this. He said, "Can anything good come out of the small town of Nazareth?"

Philip said, "Come and see."

When Bartholomew heard Jesus, he believed that Jesus is the Son of God. He followed Jesus too.

Jesus chose many helpers. We call them *disciples*. The disciples lived, worked, and laughed with Jesus. In Matthew 28, Jesus says, "Go and make disciples of all nations." Jesus calls us to be His disciples too. By the grace and forgiveness of Jesus, we are His friends and helpers too.

5

They listened to Jesus all day.
*(Put a hand behind your ear.)*
**Then Andrew rushed to find his brother.**
*(Run in place.)*
**He said, "Peter, come and see Jesus."**
*(Wave to call someone to come.)*
**Jesus had two new friends.**
*(Hug or shake hands with a friend.)*
**Jesus said to Philip, "Follow Me."**
*(Wave to call someone to come.)*
**Philip was so excited. He ran to find his friend Bartholomew.**
*(Run in place.)*
**Bartholomew was not sure that Jesus was the Savior.**
*(Frown and cross arms stubbornly.)*
**When Jesus talked to him, Bartholomew believed.**
*(Cross hands over heart.)*
**Now Jesus had four new friends.**
*(Count off on four fingers.)*
**Soon Jesus had a dozen disciples. The number grew and grew. His followers numbered 72, then 500, then 3,000, then 5,000, and more and more!**
*(Open and close your fingers to indicate large numbers.)*
**I am a follower of Jesus, and so are you!**
*(Point to yourself and then to the others in the room.)*

## RESPOND

List the following words on the board: *rich, smart, wise, humble, faithful.* Check off each word on the list as you ask, **When Jesus chose His disciples, do you think He picked them because they were rich?** (No, many were poor fishermen.) **Because they were smart?** (No, many were Galileans, who were considered less educated than Judeans.) **Because they were wise?** (No, time and again we see examples where a disciple did or said the wrong thing or just didn't understand.) **Because they were so humble?** (No, we see Peter boasting and all the disciples arguing about who was the greatest.) **Because they were faithful?** (No, they were all sinners, who later deserted Jesus when He was captured in the Garden of Gethsemane.) **Jesus didn't choose them or us because of who they were or because of who we are. Jesus chooses us because of who *He* is—He is God and God is love. We are His disciples not because of what we do, but because of what He does in us and because of the righteousness He gives to us!**

Turn to page 6 in the *Listen* Student Book. The activity reminds us of life in Jesus. When the correct answers are filled in, they will form a cross, which reminds us how we are able to live in Christ. He died to take away our sins.

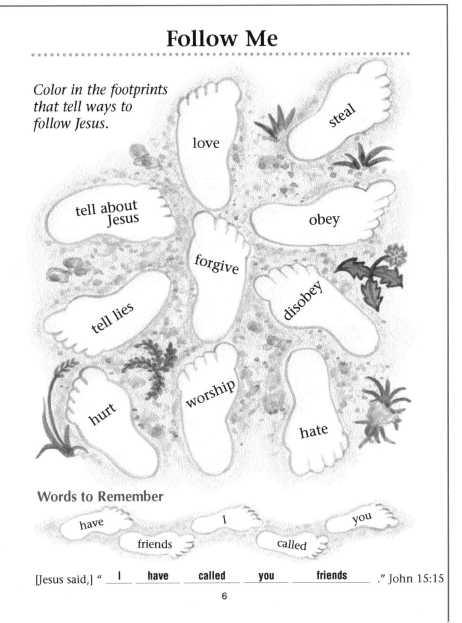

## Follow Me

*Color in the footprints that tell ways to follow Jesus.*

love

steal

tell about Jesus

obey

forgive

tell lies

disobey

hurt

worship

hate

**Words to Remember**

have    I    you

friends    called

[Jesus said,] " __I__ __have__ __called__ __you__ __friends__ ." John 15:15

6

# WEEK 18-B

# Day 3

## Discovery Point

Jesus wants each of us to come to know Him as Friend and Savior. He invites all people to follow Him and empowers believers to share the Good News with others.

## The Big Catch of Fish

Luke 5:1–11

## Objectives

That by the power of the Holy Spirit working through God's Word, the students will
• rejoice that God has brought them to faith in Jesus and made them His own children;
• know that the Holy Spirit will empower them to share the Good News of the Gospel;
• joyfully share Jesus with others, in words as well as in acts of love.

## Day 3 Materials

• Fishing pole
• Flannelgraph materials
• Blackline 18-B
• Glue sticks

## Day 4 Materials

• Jake and Jenna puppets
• *Listen* Student Book

## INTRODUCE

Capture the children's attention by showing them a fishing pole (even if it is simply a stick with a string tied to it). Let the children tell about their personal fishing experiences. Then say, **Some of us fish for fun. Some people have a job to catch fish and sell them. If they want to catch a lot of fish, they use a big net instead of a pole. Our Bible story today is about friends of Jesus who were fishermen. Jesus taught His friends about a *new* kind of fishing. Listen carefully to see if you can do this too.**

## DEVELOP

Use flannelgraph figures to tell the Bible story. Use the shoreline scene, Jesus, a crowd of people, disciples and their fishing boat. Use the Bible reference and the Student Book narrative as your guide in telling the story. (Note: Point out that the word *men* refers to *people, humankind.* God wants all people—men and women, boys and girls—to belong to Him.)

Point out that this is an important Bible story because it shows the power of Jesus as true God. But perhaps even more important is the message Jesus gives—He wants to catch people! He wants to bring all people to faith in His salvation.

# R E S P O N D

Distribute copies of Blackline 18-B for the children to color. The top shows fish in a net in the blue sea. The other section reminds us that Jesus is interested in catching *people.* He doesn't use a net; He uses God's Word to catch us and bring us to faith. That is why it is so important to share the Word of God with others. Have children cut out the illustration, fold on the dotted line, and use glue sticks to attach the two shapes back-to-back. This reminds us of the two kinds of fishing in the story. Ask, **What is the new kind of fishing Jesus spoke of?** (Catching people.)

Rejoice that you have been caught by Jesus by singing this song to the tune of "I Am Jesus' Little Lamb." Discuss the last line, which tells what it is like to be caught by faith. We are forgiven by Jesus, and then He sets us free to live as people of God. (See Galatians 5:1, 22–23.)

> **I am Jesus' little fish.**
> **This is more than just a wish.**
> **I am certain Jesus caught me!**
> **I know He will always love me.**
> **"You are Mine," He says to me.**
> **"You're forgiven and set free!"**
>
> —CSB

**Blackline 18-B**
© 2001 CPH  Permission granted to reproduce for classroom use.

## Worship Ideas

- Make a fishing pole from a stick and string with a magnet attached (as the "hook"). Use colored paper to make fish shapes. Write each child's name on a fish. Attach a metal brad or magnetic tape to each fish. Have children be "fishers of men" by using the pole to catch a fish shape. (If a child catches his or her own name, toss it back in and try again.) When all fish have been caught, allow time for children to pray silently for the classmate named on their fish.

- Read aloud 1 Timothy 2:3–4. (Remind children again that the word *men* refers to people in general.) Say, **This verse tells us that God wants everyone to be saved. He wants all people to repent and to come to faith in Jesus. Jesus came for all people of all nations, all races, all languages, all ages, rich and poor, far and near, men and women, boys and girls.** Thank God by singing "God Loves Me Dearly" (*LOSP*, p. 85, and on CD). If children do not know all the stanzas, they can listen to the message and then join in singing the refrain.

- Sing songs from the "Witness" section of *Little Ones Sing Praise,* especially "Go Tell" (p. 104 and on CD). Point out that to be fishers of men, to witness, and to tell about Jesus, which all mean the same thing, is God's will for us.

## Bible Background

After the miraculous catch of fish, Simon Peter recognized that he stood in the presence of God's Messiah, the Lord of the universe. Peter, who knew he was unworthy, said, "Go away from me, Lord; I am a sinful man!" (Luke 5:8). Peter was overcome by the strength of Jesus' grace and righteousness in sharp contrast to his own weakness and failures.

Jesus, in turn, extended His word of comfort and pardon. "Don't be afraid" is His greeting to His anxious people. Jesus is the Son of God, the almighty Lord who reveals mercy and salvation to sinful human beings. He calls men and women from the empty waters, gathering them for eternal life in His righteousness. He also equips His followers to join in the work. As we today carry out our work of sharing Jesus, we, too, are conscious of our unworthiness and sin, but we look to the Savior's love and mercy in all circumstances.

## WEEK 18-B

### Words to Remember

*"Come, follow Me," Jesus said, "and I will make you fishers of men." Matthew 4:19*

- Display the Bible words on fish-shaped papers in a scrambled arrangement. Let children put them in the right order and then say the words together.
- Let individuals say the Bible verse. After a child finishes, give that child a "fish handshake" (quickly and lightly flip-flap your open palm against the child's open palm).

### Extending the Lesson

- As a group, make an under-the-sea mural with lots of shapes and colors and patterns of fish. Point out that just as there are all kinds of fish in the sea, there are all kinds of people in the kingdom of God. **Jesus loves people of all nations and languages. He loves them short and tall, big and small, no matter what they look like or what they own. Jesus wants all people to be saved!**
- Invite professional church workers to speak to the class about their full-time job of sharing the Gospel with others. Invite people who are not professional church workers to speak to the class about how they have opportunities to tell others about Jesus, to share His love, and to live as Christian people in whatever they do. Jesus says to all of His people, "Follow Me. I will make you fishers of men."

# Day

## INTRODUCE

Use the puppets to introduce the lesson.

**JAKE:** *(chasing Jenna)* I'm gonna catch you! I'm gonna catch you!

**JENNA:** It's not recess. It's not time to play. Why are you trying to catch me?

**JAKE:** Well, in our Bible story, Jesus said to catch people.

**JENNA:** Jesus didn't mean you should chase after people. When Jesus said "from now on you will catch men" He is giving us a job to do. He wants us to bring people to hear God's Word. He wants us to tell about His forgiveness and salvation.

**JAKE:** So I can catch people after all. With the Bible as bait, I can tell about the love of Jesus. And the Holy Spirit works like a net, gathering the people in faith and making them people of God. Let's go. Let's get to work. Let's go fishing!

## The Big Catch of Fish

*(Luke 5:1–11)*

One day Jesus was near a lake, talking to a large group of people about the love of God. The people crowded around Jesus, trying to see and hear Him. Jesus got into Peter's boat and asked Peter to push the boat a little way from shore. Jesus taught the people on shore as He sat in the boat.

When He finished teaching, Jesus asked Peter to take the boat out onto the lake to catch some fish. Peter said, "We fished all night and didn't catch anything. But because You ask us to do this, we will."

Peter and Andrew went out into the deep water and let down their fishing nets. Many fish began to fill the nets. There were so many fish, the nets began to break. Peter and Andrew called to

their friends James and John to bring their boat over to help. Soon both boats were so full they began to sink.

Peter and his friends were amazed. They could see that Jesus is truly God's Son, our Savior. Jesus said to the men, "Come, follow Me, and I will make you fishers of men." Jesus meant that they had a new job, telling people about Jesus and salvation and gathering people into God's kingdom.

So Peter and his friends left their boats and their nets and went with Jesus. From now on they would live for Jesus. He asks us to do the same—to tell others about salvation through Jesus and to live for Him.

7

## DEVELOP

Review the Bible story by singing this song to the tune of "Mary Had a Little Lamb." Encourage the children to join in singing the repetitive parts in each stanza. Note: Repeat the bold words twice.

Peter was a **fisherman** ...
Peter was a fisherman and couldn't catch a fish!

Jesus taught the **crowd on shore** ...
Jesus taught the crowd on shore from Peter's fishing boat.

Fish appeared from **everywhere** ...
Fish appeared from everywhere. The nets began to break.

James and John! Come **here to help** ...
James and John! Come here to help with this big catch of fish.

Jesus said, "Come, **follow Me**" ...
Jesus said, "Come, follow Me. From now on you'll catch men."

## RESPOND

Together look at pages 7 and 8 of the *Listen* Student Book. The activity on page 8 leads children to discover what a "fisher of men" does. As children follow the directions, they will fill in the spaces

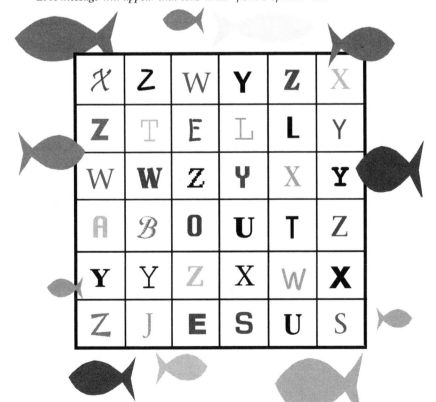

# Don't Hide the Message!

*To reveal the message, color over any box that has the letters W, X, Y, or Z. A message will appear that tells what "fishers of men" do.*

| | | | | | |
|---|---|---|---|---|---|
| X | Z | W | Y | Z | X |
| Z | T | E | L | L | Y |
| W | W | Z | Y | X | Y |
| A | B | O | U | T | Z |
| Y | Y | Z | X | W | X |
| Z | J | E | S | U | S |

### Words to Remember
*Look back at the Bible story. Find Jesus' words at the end of the story.*
*Write the missing words on the blank lines.*

"Come, ___follow___ ___Me___ ," Jesus said, "and I will make you
___fishers___ of ___men___ ." Matthew 4:19

8

marked by the letters *W, X, Y, Z.* After they have discovered the answer *(tell about Jesus)* read aloud Psalm 96:2. Ask, **Can you tell me which word in the Bible verse means to "tell about Jesus."** (Proclaim.) **The word *proclaim* sounds stronger than the word *tell.* Proclaim means to announce it, to shout it out with excitement. Our love of God leads us to be proud of what God has done and to proudly tell others about Jesus so they can know the Good News too!** Sing a song that proudly proclaims what God has done such as "Thank the Lord and Sing His Praise" (see the Teacher Resource Book or the Post-Communion Canticle in several forms of liturgy). Another possibility is "My God Is So Great" (*LOSP,* p. 64, and on CD).

*Option:* Make beautiful fish-shaped booklets. Give each child three different colors of paper. Ask them to move the papers so that about one inch can be seen of the right edge of the bottom two sheets of paper. (See Figure 1.)

Figure 1

Take the left side of the group of papers and fold them over far enough so that at least one inch of all edges of paper can be seen. (See Figure 2.)

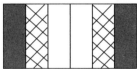
Figure 2

This will give you a booklet of six sheets of paper with pages gradually increasing in size. (Note that the middle two pages will be the same color.) Staple the booklet on the fold.

The booklet is ready to use as is, but with a few snips of the scissors, you can cut the book into the shape of a fish. Lightly draw a football shape with a triangular tail over the pages. (See Figure 3.)

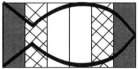
Figure 3

Cut off the edges, and your book is ready. Children can retell the Bible story on the pages of the book. Or they can write sentences or draw pictures about Jesus that they can tell others.

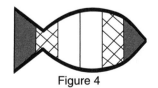
Figure 4

161

## Discovery Point

Jesus loves us unconditionally and calls us to repentance and faith in Him, our dear Friend.

## Jesus Calls Matthew

Luke 5:27–32

## Objectives

That by the power of the Holy Spirit working through God's Word, the students will

- grow in confident faith, realizing that Jesus loves them even though they are sinners;
- know that Jesus calls them to repentance and takes away their sins through His death and resurrection;
- joyfully share the Gospel message of salvation with others.

## Day 1 Materials

- Jake and Jenna puppets
- Blackline 19-A

## Day 2 Materials

- Yellow or gold paper circles
- Brown bag
- *Listen* Student Book
- Paper towels
- Clothesline and clothespins

## INTRODUCE

Use the Jenna and Jake puppets to introduce concepts in today's lesson. Raise up the puppet that is speaking.

**JENNA:** Jake, did you hear that Coach is putting Freddy Farnsworth on our soccer team?

**JAKE:** Oh, no! I don't want to play with Freddy. Keep him away from me.

**JENNA:** That's what I said. Freddy's big brother, Frank, is so mean. I bet Freddy is mean too.

**JAKE:** He probably is mean. And remember, last year he sure couldn't run very fast. I hope he ends up just sitting on the bench.

**JENNA:** What was Coach thinking? We don't need Freddy on our team!

Set the puppets aside and say, **This conversation reminds me of people in today's Bible story. Jenna didn't give Freddy a chance because she thought he would be mean like his brother. The people in the Bible story didn't like the tax collector named Matthew because they thought he would be a cheater like the other tax collectors were. Jake didn't like Freddy because of what Freddy was like long ago. Jake didn't realize that maybe Freddy had changed during the past year. The people in the Bible story were angry because Jesus was eating with Matthew and other tax collectors. They didn't realize the possibility that Jesus had changed their lives. Let's learn more about Matthew.**

## DEVELOP

Begin by saying that Jesus came to a town where Matthew was sitting at his table or booth collecting taxes from the people who passed by. When Jesus said "Follow Me," Matthew got up, left everything, and went with Jesus.

Matthew gave a great banquet for Jesus. He invited friends and other tax collectors. The Pharisees, leaders in the church, criticized Jesus for eating with such sinful people.

Make two large squares on the chalkboard (or use poster paper). In the first one print these words:

**The Pharisees did not like Matthew because …**

**1. He worked for the Roman government.**

**2. Many tax collectors cheated and lied.**

**3. They had to pay him money.**

In the second box print these words: **Jesus loved Matthew …** Leave the rest of the box blank. Point out that Jesus didn't love Matthew because of something Matthew did or didn't do. Jesus' love is *unconditional.* His love for us isn't based on reasons. **He just loves us because He loves us. Jesus is God, and God is love! Jesus doesn't say, "I'll love you if you do this or that." His love is unconditional. Nothing we do can make Him love us more, and nothing we do can make Him love us less!**

# R E S P O N D

Celebrate God's unconditional love by singing songs the children suggest. Also try this song to the tune of "B-I-N-G-O."

**I have a friend who loves me so,
And Jesus is His name-O.
J-E-SUS, J-E-SUS, J-E-SUS,
And Jesus is His name-O.**

Use Blackline 19-A. Have children cut out and arrange the puzzle pieces into the shape of a heart to find the answer to the question "Why Does God Love You?" Point out that there are extra pieces that will not be used in the puzzle. The extra pieces are incorrect answers. (God does not love us because we do good things—we could never do enough good to earn His love. God does not love us because we go to church. He doesn't need a reason to love us. God loves all people. The only reason some people do not know the love of God is because they have turned away from Him or have not heard about Him and do not have faith in Him.)

**With Jesus in our hearts, we are not the same people we were before. Jesus has washed away our sin. He makes us able to share God's love with others.** Because of Jesus, Matthew was a changed person; you and I are too. Read 2 Corinthians 5:17.

## Worship Ideas

- Continue to use Blackline 18-A and the song "There Were Twelve Disciples" as the children learn about Jesus' disciples and being one of His disciples.
- Point out that Matthew was the writer of one of the four Gospels—the books of the Bible that tell about the life, death, and resurrection of Jesus. Read a portion of the Book of Matthew (5:3–9). Explain that these are the words of Jesus. Matthew heard the words and was inspired by the Holy Spirit to write them down so that we can hear God's Word today.
- Sing "Amigos de Cristo" (*LOSP*, p. 23, and on CD). Explain that the title is Spanish for "Friends of Christ." **It is so amazing! Jesus has picked us to be His friends!** Read John 15:14a. Discuss what Jesus did for us that is the ultimate in friendship. (See John 15:13.) Teach the children portions of the hymn "What a Friend We Have in Jesus" or ask an older class to come in and sing it for your group.

## Bible Background

In the call of Matthew we see God's grace in choosing His followers. Matthew was unworthy—particularly so in Jewish eyes. Tax collectors were always viewed by the Jews as evil because they collaborated with the Romans in taking money from their own countrymen. Often tax collectors were dishonest, for the Roman system allowed them great freedom to assess whatever taxes they could. Matthew was a tax collector of the worst kind—a customs house official. He had opportunity for greater cheating than most tax collectors.

Yet Jesus calls Matthew to repent and believe the Good News of salvation. Jesus had come to save sinners, just as a doctor heals the sick (Matthew 9:12). In response, repentant sinners are led to serve God faithfully by demonstrating kindness to others in need (9:13).

## Why Does God Love You?

*Directions: Cut out the puzzle pieces that answer this question correctly. Put those pieces together to make a heart.*

God is love.

I'm cute.

I am a good person.

I go to church.

Because of Jesus.

I always obey

I'm never wrong.

His love is unconditional.

I deserve it.

**Blackline 19–A**

# Day 2

## Words to Remember

*[Jesus said,] "I have … come to call … sinners to repentance." Luke 5:32*

Explain the word *repentance:* Jesus calls us to repentance, leading us to recognize our sins, to be sorry about the bad things we do, to turn away from our sins knowing we are forgiven, and to show love instead.

## Extending the Lesson

- Review the Jenna/Jake conversation at the beginning of Day 1. Point out that they were breaking the Eighth Commandment. **We do the same when we say bad things about other people, whether the bad things are true or not.** The catechism explains that we live according to God's will when we limit our speech to *speaking well of others*. Discuss scenarios such as, **What kind thing could you say about someone who is grumpy?** ("Perhaps she does not feel well.") **What kind thing could you say about someone who almost hits your dad's car?** ("We all make mistakes; let's forgive him.") **What kind thing could you say about someone who loses in a spelling bee?** ("Don't worry. I know that you do lots of other things well like drawing pictures and doing math.")
- As you talk about Jesus, our truest friend, print the word *FRIEND* on the board vertically to begin an acrostic. Have the children use each letter in the word to identify other words that tell about Jesus and the ways He demonstrates His friendship to us. (Examples: F—orgiving, R—edeemer, I—ncredibly kind, E—verlasting life, N—ever-ending love, D—aily blessings.)
- In math class, learn about the appearance and value of various coins. Set up a play store, where children can "purchase" items (empty cereal boxes, etc.). Determine a cost of each item and the amount of tax per dollar.
- Set out a variety of coins. Let the children use drawing paper to make rubbings of the designs on the coins.

## INTRODUCE

Introduce today's lesson concept with this little story. Show a picture of a sad child or draw a frowning face on the board. Explain, **This is Bobby. He is very sad. Bobby went to the doctor, but the doctor's office had a sign that said, "No sick people allowed here."** **So Bobby went to a fast-food restaurant, but on the door was a sign that said, "Hungry people—do not enter!" So Bobby went to a toy store, but the sign outside the toy store said, "No children can come in."** Point out that this is just as silly as the Pharisees who complained when Jesus talked to sinners. Jesus is the only hope for sinners. They need Him. He would never turn them away. Read Luke 5:31–32.

---

### Jesus Calls Matthew

*(Luke 5:27–32)*

"I don't like Matthew. My dad says he cheats others to make himself rich. I think he is a terrible sinner."

"I'm not going to cheat anymore. I'm going to follow Jesus. I will help Jesus tell others that God's forgiveness is for all people. After all, God forgives me. Jesus said so!"

"I know Matthew. He's a greedy tax collector. I think he cheated me by making me pay more money than I should. I bet he kept the extra money for himself."

"I know all about Matthew's sins. But I love Matthew anyway. I want to forgive him. I want Matthew to follow Me and be My disciple."

*Look at the pictures. Draw a line to the words you think each person said. Circle the picture of the person who shows unconditional love. Draw a box around the person who repented.*

9

## D E V E L O P

In advance, cut yellow or gold paper circles to represent coins. Print one of each of the following sentences on a coin. Place the coins in a money bag (brown paper sack). Let children draw a "coin" from the bag. As you state the numbers in order, from 1 to 14, the children should read or give you the corresponding sentence.

*(1) Matthew collected tax money at his tax table. (2) Jesus walked by and said, "Follow Me." (3) Matthew got up and left everything behind. (4) He went to be with Jesus. (5) Matthew had a great dinner for Jesus. (6) He invited other tax collectors. (7) The Pharisees complained. (8) They didn't think Jesus should be with sinners. (9) They forgot that they were sinners too. (10) Jesus said, "I have ... come to call ... sinners to repentance." (11) Jesus wants sinners to repent and be sorry about the bad things they do. (12) Jesus wants us to turn away from our sins. (13) Jesus wants to help us live as people of God. (14) This happens only with the help of God.*

*Option:* Read the following poem to further review the Bible story. First, though, point out that Matthew is also known by the name Levi.

Matthew sat down in his office one day.
As the people came by with their taxes to pay,
They grumbled and scowled and frowned in disgust.
They said, "Matthew Levi, you're charging too much!"

But Matthew just smiled as he counted his gold.
He thought, I'll be rich before I am old.
Matthew's big grin didn't last very long,
For deep in his heart he knew he was wrong.

The Lord Jesus walked past that office one day.
Matthew couldn't believe what he heard Jesus say,
Just two little words, "Follow Me." That was all.
And Matthew obeyed the Lord Jesus' call.

The Savior asked others to follow Him too,
Forgiving their sins and making them new.
"Follow Me," the Lord Jesus invites us today.
"Dear Jesus, please help us to follow," we pray.

Adapted from *Fingers Tell the Story*, © 1989, CPH.

## R E S P O N D

Continue with pages 9 and 10 in the *Listen* Student Book. The activity page reminds us that Jesus calls us to repentance, which includes turning things around from sin to serving God.

Work together on a special class project. Give each child a paper towel that is at least 10 inches long. Children are to draw a simple shape of a person, cut it out, draw a cross, and print their own name over the heart. Display these people shapes by clipping them with clothespins from the shoulders to a clothesline. Add a sign to the clothesline that says, "Jesus Washed Our Sins Away." Emphasize that Jesus did this by dying on the cross for us. This changes our hearts and also our lives.

---

## Repent—Turn Around

To repent means to turn away from sin and turn to doing God's will. We can do this only through the forgiveness and grace we have through Jesus. Look at each picture. Then draw what can happen as the person lives in repentance, turning away from sinful actions and living as people of God.

I don't want to clean up my room!

Play with your own toys, crybaby.

### Words to Remember
[Jesus said,] "I have ... come to call ... sinners to repentance."
Luke 5:32

10

## Discovery Point

Jesus loves us unconditionally and calls us to repentance and faith in Him, our dear Friend.

## Jesus Sends Out Many Helpers

Luke 10:1–24

## Objectives

That by the power of the Holy Spirit working through God's Word, the students will

- rejoice that in His great love God sent Jesus to save all people from sin and death;
- desire to love others by telling them the Good News of God's love and salvation in Jesus;
- discover that they can share God's love with others in what they say and do, anywhere and anytime.

## Day 3 Materials

- Drawing paper
- Blackline 19-B
- Straws or pencils
- Tape or glue

## Day 4 Materials

- Teacher Resource Book
- *Listen* Student Book

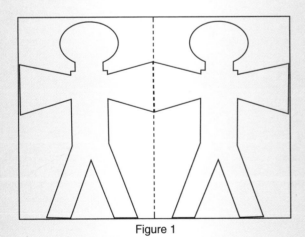

Figure 1

## INTRODUCE

Teach the children this little song to the tune of "The Farmer in the Dell."

**Please, come and be my buddy.**
**Together we will study**
**Of Jesus' love and care for us.**
**You'll be my Bible buddy.**

Tell them each time they sing the song you will say one or more letters of the alphabet (randomly). Anyone whose first name begins with the letter called is to choose a partner and come and sit near you. Repeat the process till everyone is gathered around you. (You may need to start the process by choosing someone yourself if you have an uneven number of children.)

When everyone has gathered, ask, **Why is it often good to have a partner?** (Partners can help; it's fun to share and do things together; you can encourage others if there is a problem.) **Jesus knew how important a friend can be. One day when He had a big job for some people to do, He had them work with partners.**

## DEVELOP

Use the Bible story printed on page 11 of the *Listen* Student Book as your guide in telling the Bible narrative. Then ask, **What was the important job Jesus gave to the 72 people?** (They went to many towns, telling people to repent and get ready because Jesus, the promised Savior, was near.)

Review the story by having each child make a set of paper partners by folding a paper in half and drawing a simple person shape that has one arm extending to the fold. (See Figure 1.) Cut out the doubled paper and open to reveal the partners. In order to make 72 people (36 pairs) some children will need to make two sets of partners. (For example, in a class of 18 children, each child would need to make two sets of partners.)

Have the children march around the room, waving the 72 partner people they made as you sing the following song to the tune of "When Johnny Comes Marchin' Home Again" ("The Ants Go Marching"):

**God's children marching two by two—Hurrah! Hurrah!**
**God's children marching two by two—Hurrah! Hurrah!**
**God's children marching two by two,**
**They stop to tell others, "God loves you!"**
**And they all go marching,**
**Out—in twos—to share—God's love.**

After singing the song several times, have the children display their paper people on a bulletin board that has a picture of Jesus at the center. Children may write their names and the names of friends and family members on the partner people.

# RESPOND

The theme of this lesson is "telling about Jesus." We can equip children by giving them tools that catch their interest and help them explain God's love to others. This is the purpose of Blackline 19-B (and of many of the activities suggested throughout the curriculum). Children are to cut on the dotted lines of the first activity. (Suggest that children can cut the inside of the heart by first rolling the paper and cutting a slit at the center. Then they can insert a scissors blade into the slit and cut out the section.) When the directions are followed, an important message is revealed. **Our hearts are full of sin. Jesus changes us by washing away our sin. Now we are children of God.** Let the children practice showing and telling this message with a partner.

In the second activity, color and cut out the two rectangles (showing Jesus and the world). Tape the top of a straw or pencil to the bottom (back side) of one picture to make a handle. Tape or glue the other picture to the back of this. Place the straw between your hands and rotate the handle back and forth rapidly. This will create an optical illusion in which the picture of Jesus seems to be combined with the picture of the world. **This reminds us that Jesus is with us and loves all the people of the world.** Sing "He's Got the Whole World in His Hands" (*LOSP*, p. 101, and on CD). Encourage the children to share this message with others.

*Directions: Cut on the dotted lines. Place the heart over the other section. When the two pieces line up at the top, you see a heart messed up by sin. When the two pieces line up at the bottom, you see a heart cleansed by faith in Jesus..*

*Directions: Cut out these two little squares. Use tape to attach them back to back at the top of a drinking straw. Place the straw between your hands. Move it quickly back and forth. The two pictures will seem to combine. That reminds us that Jesus is with us in this world.*

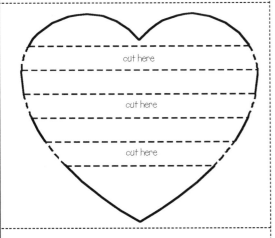

cut here

cut here

cut here

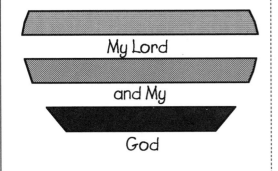

My Lord

and My

God

# Worship Ideas

- Have children sit with partners to do "buddy songs." Sing "Hallelujah! Praise Ye the Lord!" (*LOSP*, p. 58, and on CD). One partner sings "Hallelujah," and the other sings "Praise ye the Lord." Sing it again, switching roles. Use the same process with partners echoing repeated phrases in the song "This Is the Day" (*LOSP*, p. 53, and on CD).
- Use partners to each say half of the wonderful words Jesus said to the 72 people who returned from telling His message. Jesus said, **"Rejoice that your names / are written in heaven"** (Luke 10:20)
- Lead the children in praying, **Heavenly Father, we ask You to open the hearts of people in our families, neighborhoods, town, country, and the world. Lead them to hear of Your salvation and to trust in You by faith. Please give us courage and power to speak of You to people who already know You and also to people who do not know You as their Savior. We pray in Jesus' name. Amen.**

# Bible Background

Did Jesus send out 70 or 72 disciples? The number is unclear from manuscripts used by Bible translators. This difference, however, should not detract us from the message of the text: *The kingdom of God is supremely important, and there is an urgency about preaching the Gospel.*

God offers His kingdom to all, and the Gospel has phenomenal power (Luke 10:18–19). However, God does not force people into the kingdom. Some will reject the Gospel—to their judgment (10:10–16). We, the messengers, may grow discouraged by such rejection, which is primarily a rejection of Jesus and His Father (10:16). God calls us to move on and bring the Good News to others, rejoicing that our names are written in heaven (10:20).

# Day 4

## Words to Remember

*Go home to your family and tell them how much the Lord has done for you. Mark 5:19*

What a powerful message this is for children. Even if they don't know someone who is not a child of God, they can still witness every day to their family members. God wants us to encourage each other in the faith. (See Galatians 6:10.) Ask children what the Lord has done for them today or this week (helping them to identify specific blessings). Have them suggest motions to do as they say the Bible verse.

## Extending the Lesson

- Just as Jesus sent out the 72, He also asks us to be His messengers. Point out that one way we can share this message is in song. Plan to have the class sing at a Sunday worship service. Encourage the children to really *proclaim* the words so that the message, not just the melody, is heard.
- Have each child bring 72 of something to class (such as 72 beans, chips, or buttons). Suggest that they each bring their collections in ziplock plastic bags. Display the collections together. Observe how the number grows when each set of 72 combines with others. **We also want the church of God to grow and grow in numbers throughout the world.**

## INTRODUCE

Call two children by name to stand by you. Then sing one stanza of "Go Tell" (*LOSP*, p. 104, and on CD). Then have each of those children choose two people and bring them forward. Sing another stanza. Then the new people each choose two and so on till everyone is chosen. Point out how quickly the Good News can spread and how quickly God's family gets bigger when we each tell just two more people.

### Jesus Sends Out Many Helpers

*(Luke 10:1–24)*

Jesus wants all people to know God's great love for them. One day Jesus told 72 helpers to go to the towns where He would soon visit.

Jesus said, "There is much to do and not many workers. I am sending you. Don't take anything that will slow you down or keep you from doing your job.

"If you enter a town and people welcome you, stay with them. Tell them about Me and that I am coming. If people do not welcome you, go somewhere else. People who listen to you, listen to Me. People who don't listen to you will not listen to Me. They will not believe the heavenly Father who sent Me."

The 72 helpers went out and did just as Jesus had told them. When they came back, they were excited and amazed at all that happened.

Jesus said, "I have given you power to speak God's Word. And remember what is truly most important—rejoice that your names are written in heaven!"

Jesus is our Savior too. He wants us to be His helpers who tell others about His love and salvation. He will help us and bless us.

11

## D E V E L O P

Review the story of Jesus sending out 72 people, two by two, as you read this poem. You may want to have the children echo your words in each line to keep them focused on the meaning.

**Jesus appointed 72**
**And told them just what they should do.**
**"The job is big, the workers few.**
**So, go! I send you two by two.**

**"Don't take a lot of things, I say.**
**Don't stop to chat along the way.**
**Go to one place and there you'll stay,**
**Until it's time to go away."**

**They told each one who stopped to hear,**
**"God's kingdom now is very near.**
**We have Good News, so have no fear!**
**Our Lord forgives! Let's give a cheer."**

**It's our job too—the work's not done.**
**Go tell your friends, tell everyone,**
**That God has given His own Son!**
**Christ's victory for us is won!**

## R E S P O N D

Emphasize the words *tell everyone what He has done* as you practice and then sing "Thank the Lord and Sing His Praise." The song and two versions of the melody are in the Teacher Resource Book.

Use the activity on page 12 of the *Listen* Student Book to give children more practice in speaking conversationally about the Lord and His blessings. Use the page to guide a class discussion about possible things a person could say in response to the printed words. It is not necessary to fill in the blank speech bubbles, but if the children are capable and time permits, list possible responses on the board so children can copy them in the speech bubbles.

*Option.* Have each child draw a large cross shape on colored paper. Then glue rice or beans to cover the cross. Say, **Your mosaic crosses remind me that Jesus died on the cross to save the world. The many seeds on the cross remind me of the many people in the world that Jesus loves.** (You may want to read Jesus' words in Luke 10:2. Here He compares the people of the world to a harvest field, with seeds that need to be gathered. He wants us to be workers gathering people to Jesus.)

---

## What Can You Say?

*What words could you say to these people*
*to remind them of God's love?*

### Words to Remember
Go home to your family and tell them how much
the Lord has done for you.    Mark 5:19

## Discovery Point

God, in His great love for us, forgives all our sins through Jesus' death and resurrection and empowers us to live according to His will.

## The Parable of Two Sons

Matthew 21:28–32

## Objectives

That by the power of the Holy Spirit working through God's Word, the students will

- know that God wants them to obey His will and that He offers them forgiveness through Jesus when they fail;
- grow in love for God and in their willingness to obey Him as He leads and guides them;
- pray that God will give them cheerful hearts to obey His will and to show loving-kindness to others.

## Day 1 Materials

- Stack of papers and books
- Jake and Jenna puppets
- Parable poster
- Blackline 20-A

## Day 2 Materials

- Blackline 20-A
- Colored paper
- Glue sticks
- *Listen* Student Book

# INTRODUCE

Place a pile of papers and a pile of books on the floor or a table near you. Use the Jenna and Jake puppets to introduce the story. (To emphasize when a puppet is speaking, raise the puppet high or place the puppet in front of your face.) Bring out the Jake puppet, who bounces along, humming a tune.

**TEACHER:** Hi, Jake. You seem happy today. Would you help me for just a minute? Please pick up that pile of papers.

**JAKE:** Oh, Teacher, I don't want to do that. I'm in a hurry to go to the park to play. You'll have to find someone else to help.

*(Move the puppet on his way. Then have him come back slowly, look at the papers, look at the teacher, scratch his head, hang his head, and then have him go over to the papers and pick them up. Remove the Jake puppet and bring out the Jenna puppet.)*

**TEACHER:** Hi, Jenna! You seem happy today. Would you help me for just a minute? Please pick up that pile of books.

**JENNA:** I would be glad to! You know you can always count on me to do what I should do!

*(Have Jenna put her hands to her mouth as if she is giggling, turn around, and leave in the opposite direction of the books as she bounces on her way. Take off the puppet.)*

Ask, **Which puppet did what I asked?** (Jake.) **Jenna used the right words, but Jake's actions obeyed. Jesus once told a story very much like this. Jesus liked to use stories to teach a lesson. We call these stories "parables."**

# DEVELOP

In advance cut apart the six sections of the Parable poster. Show the pictures one at a time to the children and display them on a bulletin board as you tell the Bible story.

First, show the title section—*The Son Who Did.* Use the first two pictures to tell about the first son. Point out that he gave a disrespectful and disobedient answer. But he repented—he was sorry. He changed his ways and did his father's will.

Show the next two pictures, telling about the second son. Point out that he said the right words, but his words were empty. His words were a lie. God wants our words to be followed by actions of obedience.

Continue with the most important part of the lesson. Show the picture of Jesus on the cross. Place it in the center, slightly overlapping the other four pictures. Point out that the title actually fits best with this picture—Jesus is the Son who truly did His Father's will. Jesus forgives the things we say and do that are wrong. Jesus calls us to repentance and gives us power through the Holy Spirit to live changed lives, obeying God's will. This happens only through Him.

Suggestion: Use removable tape to change the poster title from *Did* to *Died.* Squeeze in the letter *e* as a reminder that we are brought to repentance and forgiveness through Jesus, who died for us.

## RESPOND

Refer to a term used earlier—*God's will.* Explain that God's will is what God wants. The Ten Commandments tell us what God wants for our lives. Briefly review them, using Blackline 20-A. (Note: The blackline will be used again tomorrow, so collect them after your discussion.) Continue by saying, **Because we are sinners, our will is often not like God's will. We cannot fully obey God's will, no matter how hard we try. God knows this. But His will also is that people will be saved for eternal life in heaven. So God sent His Son, Jesus, to live and die and arise for us. We pray that, as His forgiven people, God will lead us and enable us to live according to His will.**

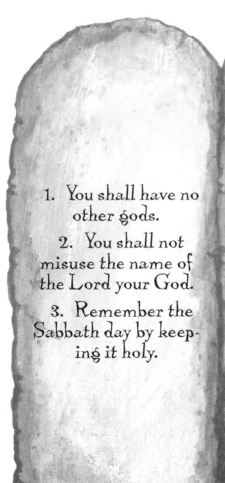

1. You shall have no other gods.

2. You shall not misuse the name of the Lord your God.

3. Remember the Sabbath day by keeping it holy.

4. Honor your father and your mother.

5. You shall not murder.

6. You shall not commit adultery.

7. You shall not steal.

8. You shall not give false testimony against your neighbor.

9. You shall not covet your neighbor's house.

10. You shall not covet your neighbor's wife, or his manservant or maidservant, his ox or donkey, or anything that belongs to your neighbor.

**Blackline 20-A**

## Worship Ideas

- Have a "sandwich prayer." Two children stand a few feet apart. They will repeat the beginning and the ending of prayers. One person will always begin, saying, *We pray to You, dear Lord!* The other person will always end, saying, *In Jesus' name. Amen.* Have volunteers (one per prayer) stand between the "two slices of the sandwich." The middle person speaks the prayer request or praise statement (the "filling" of the sandwich).

- Use, adapt, or add to this responsive prayer.

**TEACHER:** Jesus, You tell us to follow You.

**CHILDREN:** Help us, Lord, to do this.

**TEACHER:** You tell us to obey our parents.

**CHILDREN:** Help us, Lord, to do this.

**TEACHER:** You ask us to love and be kind to each other.

**CHILDREN:** Help us, Lord, to do this.

**TEACHER:** Give us hearts that gladly do what you ask.

**CHILDREN:** Help us, Lord, to do this.

**TEACHER:** We pray in the name of Jesus, who forgives us and leads us to follow Your will as children of God. Amen.

## Bible Background

Jesus spoke this parable to the chief priests and elders of the people (Matthew 21:23). In their positions of leadership, they had said yes to the responsibility of bringing God's message of hope in the promised Messiah to the people. However, they were proclaiming a contrary message of reliance on good works. Jesus now places repentant tax collectors and prostitutes ahead of them (21:31–32).

This parable guides us today to be faithful in carrying out God's work, and not sit by idly or proclaim a contrary message. He also urges us to bring His message to today's "tax collectors and prostitutes," those who may seem unworthy of membership in God's kingdom. Remember—God offers forgiveness and salvation to *all!*

## WEEK 20-A

### Words to Remember

*My Father's will is / that everyone who looks to the Son / and believes in Him / shall have eternal life. John 6:40*

- Let children say the verse in quartets, with each of the four people saying one phrase as indicated above.
- There are 19 words in the Bible verse. Form a chain of 19 children, assigning, in order, one word of the verse. (Assign one word to two children or two words to one child to adjust for the number in your class.) Go through the verse, having children say the word assigned to them.

    Break the chain into the four phrase groups. Say the verse again. Now mix up the order in which the children are standing in each phrase group, but ask them to still say their words in the proper order. Then mix up where everyone is standing, but still have children say the words in the proper order.

### Extending the Lesson

- Make a concentration game with an interesting variation. On index cards draw pictures of things that are opposites (salt shaker/pepper shaker; boy in swimsuit/boy in snowsuit; tall woman/short woman; rainy day/sunny day). Children start with cards facedown. A player turns over two cards when it is his or her turn. If the cards match as opposites, the player keeps the cards. The person who collects the most cards wins. **We have opposites in our Bible story: one boy says no, the other says yes; one boy works, the other doesn't.**

## INTRODUCE

Distribute Blackline 20-A again. Review by saying that the Ten Commandments show us God's will for our lives. **It is God's will that we love the Lord above all; it is also God's will that we show loving-kindness to each other.** Then begin to tear your copy of the blackline, pointing out that we sinners often fail. We lie; we have temper fits; we try to get what does not belong to us … As you say these things, continue to tear the page into little pieces. Ask the children to do the same.

Then pass out sheets of colored paper. Either have the children draw a large block cross on the page or have the shape already reproduced for them. (See TRB.) Have the children use glue sticks to glue the broken pieces of the commandments onto the cross. Say, **We break God's Law. We disobey His will. But Jesus took our brokenness and our sins to the cross. Jesus took the punishment for our wrongs. Because of Jesus, we are now blameless in God's eyes, and we can live according to His will.** Read or say together the lesson's "Words to Remember."

## The Parable of Two Sons

*(Matthew 21:28–32)*

This is the story of the son who obeyed and the son who didn't.

Jesus often used stories to teach people about God's love and God's will. One day He told this story:

A man had two sons. The father went to his older son and said, "Son, go and work in the vineyard today."

The son answered, "I will not!" But later he changed his mind. He was sorry about what he had said. So he went to the vineyard and worked as his father had asked.

A short time later the father went to his younger son and said, "Son, go and work in the vineyard today."

The younger son said, "Yes, I will go, Sir." But the younger son did not go. He did not work in the vineyard that day.

When Jesus finished telling the story, He asked, "Which son did what his father wanted?"

The people answered, "The first one."

It is God's will that we obey. It is also God's will that our sins be forgiven through Jesus. It is God's will that we live with hearts changed by faith.

172

## DEVELOP

Review the story of two sons, one who obeyed his father's will and the other who did not. Act out the story. Half of the children act as one brother, and the other half act as the other brother. The teacher is the father and narrator.

## RESPOND

Print the word *obey* on the board. Ask what the word means. Ask, **In our story, what did the son who said yes do?** (Nothing.) **What did the son who said no do?** (He did obey.) **This reminds us that sometimes our actions can be even more important than our words. Saying it is one thing, but doing it is more.**

**Besides your parents, who does God want you to obey?** (Anyone in authority.) **What is one time when you should disobey?** (When you are told to go against God's will. God's ways must come first, even before what parents say.)

Play a brief game of "Who Am I?" to discover who some of those authorities are that we should obey. Note that there can usually be more than one answer. Talk about how the children can honor and show love to each person.

- **I drive young people to an important place almost every day. Later I drive them home. Who am I?** (Bus driver, parent, car-pool driver.)
- **I work in a school to help you learn and grow in many ways. Who am I?** (Teacher, TA, principal, coach.)
- **When your mom and dad are gone, I am in charge. Who am I?** (Baby-sitter, grandparent, day-care worker.)
- **I work all around your town to help keep you safe. Who am I?** (Mayor, firefighters, police officers.)

Work together on page 14 of the *Listen* Student Book as you identify people to honor. Explain that *honor* means to show respect and kindness to people in order to show that they are important to you. Pray together that God will help all of you to do this not just in words, but also in actions. Recognize that this happens as we, God's forgiven people, are empowered by Him to live according to His will. **In the Lord's Prayer we say, "Thy will be done." We are asking God that we may see, live, and love His will for us. We pray that our will can become like God's will—that the two will be the same.** Say together the Lord's Prayer while seated. Stand during the Third Petition: *Thy will be done on earth as it is in heaven.* Then continue while seated.

*Option.* Direct the class to form a circle around one child, who serves as the leader. Children walk around the circle singing this song to the tune of "Did You Ever See a Lassie."

> **Did you ever see me helping**
> **And helping and helping?**
> **Did you ever see me helping,**
> **Do this and do that?**

Children stop, the leader pantomimes a helping action, and the other children imitate the action while singing:

> **For the Lord God gives me His love,**
> **Yes, His love, yes, His love.**
> **Then the Lord helps me to show love,**
> **To show love to you.**

Then the leader chooses a new leader. Play until everyone has a chance to lead. Afterwards, as children rest, read 1 John 4:10–11. **This is God's will for us.**

---

## Lord, Help Me Obey Your Will

*Directions: When you are led by God to do His will, who can you honor and obey? Draw their pictures in the circles. Write their names on the lines.*

( )      ( )

_____    _____

( )      ( )

_____    _____

### Words to Remember
My Father's will is that everyone who looks to the Son and believes in Him shall have eternal life.
John 6:40

14

## Discovery Point

God, in His great love for us, forgives all our sins through Jesus' death and resurrection and empowers us to live according to His will.

## The Parable of the Good Samaritan

Luke 10:30–37

## Objectives

That by the power of the Holy Spirit working through God's Word, the students will
- know that since God has saved them from sin, they can respond to His grace by loving others;
- grow in their awareness of the needs of other people and in their willingness to do God's will for them;
- show kindness to others, even those who do not love them.

## Day 3 Materials

- Flannelgraph materials
- Blackline 20-B
- Tape or stickers

## Day 4 Materials

- Colored paper
- *Listen* Student Book

## INTRODUCE

Say, **Today I would like you to tell me a little about your neighbors. Who is your neighbor? What does your neighbor do?** Listen to the children's responses, then say, **Once someone asked Jesus, "Who is my neighbor?" Jesus answered the man by telling a story. Let's listen to the story Jesus told.**

## DEVELOP

Place the flannelgraph figures you will need in your Bible, open to Luke 10. Set up the desert or hillside background. As you tell or read the story, hold up the flannelgraph characters as they appear in the story and add them to the background scene. When the story is finished, ask, **Who is your neighbor?** (Anyone who needs help.)

Consider also using the Hear Me Read Big Book *Who Will Help?* (available from Concordia Publishing House). Note that if this is purchased as a classroom set (order no. 56-1920), you will receive a Teachers Guide with additional activities and ideas for teaching this Bible story.

## RESPOND

Ask, **If you were one of the people in Jesus' story, who do you think you would be?** Point out that though the Good Samaritan is the "hero" of the story, very often we are like the "other guys." Like the priest and Levite, we may be so busy with what we want to do that we don't stop to help someone else. (For example, ignoring Mom's need for help or telling a brother "do it yourself" because you want to play or watch TV.) Even worse, sometimes we laugh at someone who needs help. (For example, pointing and laughing at someone who spills something rather than helping them clean up the mess.) We also might see ourselves as the one waiting for help rather than the one giving help.

Say, **To be strong to do God's will we first need His forgiveness for the things we do wrong. We pray that God will help us live by faith, with strength from Him to do His will. The Good Samaritan and you and I can do good, but only through Jesus.**

Give each child several copies of Blackline 20-B so that they can make several Happy Grams. Children are to cut out the shape, sign their names, complete the sentence (or leave it as is), fold on the lines, and seal at the center with tape or a sticker. Talk about people to whom they can give a Happy Gram and what they can do to help others.

# Worship Ideas

- Continue to emphasize that we show love to others because Jesus first loved us. He originates the love that is in our hearts. Sing of God's love: "Father, I Adore You" (*LOSP*, p. 13), "Say to the Lord, I Love You" (p. 18), "Love, Love, Love" (p. 30), "Love in a Box" (p. 35), "We Love" (p. 54). All of these songs are on the Voyages CD.
- Together create a contemporary story similar to the parable, in which a child needs help on the playground. Act it out together.

# Bible Background

An expert in the law had asked Jesus, "Who is my neighbor?" Jesus answers this question in the parable. Then He asks the lawyer, "Which of these three ... was a neighbor?" Jesus made this hated Samaritan a model for true neighborliness. God's Law demands that we love the neighbor, whoever the neighbor may be, that we support and show compassion to all people.

By nature, we cannot keep God's command. On our own we cannot be a "good Samaritan." Jesus, the true "Good Samaritan," has fulfilled the Law's demand in our place. His atoning sacrifice is our hope of forgiveness and the source of strength to love both God and our neighbor as He has loved us.

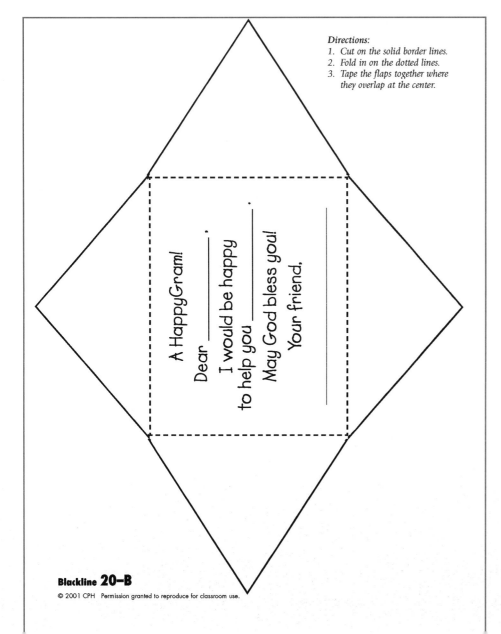

*Directions:*
1. *Cut on the solid border lines.*
2. *Fold in on the dotted lines.*
3. *Tape the flaps together where they overlap at the center.*

A HappyGram!

Dear _____,

I would be happy to help you _____.

May God bless you!

Your friend,

_____

**Blackline 20-B**
© 2001 CPH  Permission granted to reproduce for classroom use.

## Day 4

### Words to Remember

*[Jesus said,] "Love each other as I have loved you." John 15:12*

Print the Bible verse on various colors of paper. Cut out each sheet to make five or six puzzle pieces. Mix the pieces together. Children are to sort out puzzle pieces of the same color and put them together to reveal the Bible verse.

### Extending the Lesson

- Plan several class projects to involve the children in helping others. Find out about the needs of a local homeless shelter. Write a letter to parents and involve them in collecting needed items, fund-raising, and distribution. Plan collections of food, toys, clothes, blankets, personal care items, and so on. Set out a different box for each type of item. Let children decorate the boxes to indicate what type of item goes in each one.

- Point out the significance in Jesus' story that only a Samaritan stopped to help. The Jewish people thought of the Samaritans as ungodly enemies. Jesus wanted to remind us that He loves all people and wants us to do the same. Discuss prejudices today—people disliking someone just because of where they come from, what their religion or skin color is, or because they are poor. Point out that it is important to learn about other cultures, seeing their uniqueness and value. It is God's will that we show loving-kindness to everyone in the name of Jesus, our loving and kind Savior.

### INTRODUCE

On four sheets of colored paper print one of each letter in the word *HELP*. Hold up the letter *H* and say, **I am thinking of some parts of our bodies that begin with the letter *H*. What could they be? How can we use these to help someone?** (Hands, head. Responses will vary.) Hold up the letter *E* and follow the same process. (Possibilities are ears and eyes.)

Hold up the letter *L* and say, **I am thinking of another way to describe the actions we do to help someone.** (Loving.) **We do helping, loving actions because of what Jesus has done for us. How is helping a way of showing love?**

Hold up the letter *P* and say, **I'm thinking of something we can do to help people anywhere at anytime. We don't even have to be near them to help in this way. What is it?** (Pray.) **Let's pray now: Dear Lord, please give us helping, loving hearts. Bless our families and friends. In Jesus' name. Amen.** Continue by reviewing the story of a helper, the Good Samaritan.

---

## The Parable of the Good Samaritan

*(Luke 10:30–37)*

One day a man asked Jesus, "Who is my neighbor?" Jesus answered the man's question by telling this story:

A man was traveling from Jerusalem to Jericho. Suddenly some robbers attacked him. They took his money and beat him until he was almost dead.

A short time later, a priest came walking down the same road. When the priest saw the hurt man, he crossed to the other side of the road and went on his way.

Soon, a Levite, another worker in the temple, came by. He, too, saw the man but hurried on his way.

Then a Samaritan man came by. People from Jerusalem did not like people from Samaria. But the Samaritan man thought only about the man who was hurt and needed help, not whether they were friends. The Samaritan man stopped to help. He bandaged the man's wounds and put him on his own donkey. The Samaritan man took him to an inn and cared for him.

The next day the Samaritan gave the innkeeper some money and said, "Take care of this man until he is well. When I return, I will pay you what I owe."

Jesus asked, "Which of the three men was a good neighbor to the man who was hurt?"

His listener answered, "The Samaritan who helped him."

Jesus said, "Go and do as he did."

Jesus asks us these questions. And then He empowers us to live as people of God.

Who is *your* neighbor? How can *you* be a neighbor to others?

15

# DEVELOP

Use the following action narrative to review the story. Have the children imitate your actions.

**Step, step, step. A man was walking to Jericho.** *(Walk in place.)*

**Jump, jump, jump. Robbers jumped out from behind a rock.** *(Jump three times.)*

**Punch, punch, punch. They hurt the man and stole everything he had.** *(Punching actions.)*

**Run, run, run. Then they ran away.** *(Run in place.)*

**Oh, oh, oh. The poor hurt man felt very bad.** *(Hold your head in pain.)*

**Look, look, look. Along came a priest. Surely he would help.** *(Hand to forehead to look to the distance.)*

**Step, step, step. But he just walked right on by.** *(Tiptoe in place.)*

**Look, look, look. Another man who worked in the temple-church was coming. Would he help?** *(Hand to forehead again.)*

**Run, run, run. But he hurried right on by.** *(Run in place.)*

**Please, please, please. A third man was coming. Please, please help!** *(Fold hands as if pleading.)*

**Hooray! Hooray! He stopped. He bandaged the wounds. Hooray!** *(Shout hooray.)*

**Clip, clip, clop. This good Samaritan man carried the hurt man away on his donkey.** *(Walk in place as if leading a donkey.)*

**Dear Lord, help us to be helpers, in Jesus' name. Amen.** *(Fold hands; make the sign of the cross at the end of the prayer.)*

Adapted from *Fingers Tell the Story,* © 1989, CPH.

# RESPOND

Work together on page 16 in the *Listen* Student Book to review lesson information and concepts. Then again display four colored sheets of paper, this time with the letters of the word *PRAY* printed on them. Hold up one letter at a time to introduce each statement of your closing prayer.

**P—Please bless our friends and families.**

**R—Remember our sins no more because of Jesus.**

**A—Always, You are near and hear our prayers.**

**Y—You are the almighty God, Savior of the nations! Amen.**

---

## Share God's Loving-Kindness

**Down**

1. God promises to give us what we **NEED** .

3. Something we can do to help others at any time and any place. **PRAY**

**Across**

2. The good Samaritan stopped to **HELP** the hurt man.

4. God gave us rules that He wants us to **OBEY** .

**Words to Remember**

[Jesus said,] ♥ ▲ **V** ●

each other as I have ♥ ▲ **V** ● ★ you.

John 15:12

16

# UNIT 6

# Changes

## Unit Overview

This unit of study and the accompanying Student Book are entitled *Changes*. This unit reminds us again of the changes God makes in our lives. Jesus begins by calling us to repentance and taking away our sins. The changes continue as the Holy Spirit leads us through God's Word to grow in faith and to live by faith. Daily our lives are changed by the many blessings God pours on us, spiritually and physically.

Send home copies of the family letter and Bible verse list for Unit 6 as you begin. (See the Teacher Resource Book.) This will let parents know what their children will be learning during the next few weeks. At the end of the unit, let the children take home their *Changes* Student Book. Encourage them to show their parents what they have learned. This is the sixth in a series of nine books that will cover the story of salvation through the Old and New Testaments. Also consider adding some of the following activities to your curriculum to make related connections between God's message of love and all that you do throughout the day.

### Worship Connections

Help children to become more involved in worship services by making them aware of familiar elements that regularly occur. Though some children may have the feeling that church is mostly for grown-ups, help them identify things that they can recognize throughout the service. Have them help you make a list of things they listen to or understand in church. The Church Checklist Blackline in the Supplemental Activities section of the Teacher Resource Book can guide this discussion. Children may color over or put an *X* on the sections discussed. Also, consider providing copies of this blackline for use on a Sunday morning to help children be aware of what is going on. (Note: Do not make this an assignment.)

Familiar elements include bells (before and at the end of the service); greeting ("Good morning"; "We begin in the name of the Father, Son, and Holy Spirit"); Bible readings; prayers; hymns (joining in familiar refrains or humming along with the melody); choirs; music (piano, organ, keyboard); special instruments (trumpet, flute, etc.); children's talk; offering; Lord's Prayer; Baptism; Lord's Supper. Talk about times in the worship service when they use their ears to listen; in what ways they use their eyes and what they see; in what ways they use their voices. Estimate how many times they stand, noting that it is respectful to stand and also gives

people a chance to move around and stretch.

Help children understand that they, too, are members of God's family and of the church. God's house is a place for them. Help them to feel comfortable and at home in their Father's house and to be involved in worshiping Him.

### Community Building

*Thankfulness* is a recurring theme in many lessons in this unit. Play a thankful game. Have the children sit in a circle. One person mentions something for which she is thankful. The next person mentions something for which he is thankful and also repeats the thing mentioned by the first person. The third person gives a new item and repeats the previous ones. Continue this pattern until someone cannot repeat all the previous items. This person, then, starts a new game, and the process continues. Say, **God blesses us repeatedly, over and over again. He blesses us so much we often can't remember all the things for which to give thanks.**

### Tools for Witness

Have children make this tool, which can witness to their families about the significance of praying together. Provide materials so children can decorate boxes or jars in overlapping mosaic patterns of torn tissue paper, gold braid, and other materials applied with white glue. Tell the children to take these home and suggest that whenever a need occurs family members write prayer requests on small slips of paper and drop them into the jar. Then plan a family prayer time, perhaps at the end of the meal on Sunday evening, to bring the requests to God in prayer. (If a request has been answered in the meantime, suggest that a prayer of thanks be given.)

### Service Projects

An important way to serve others is to pray for them, for God can help in ways we never can. Obtain a prayer list from your pastor. Pray for individuals and have children work together to make cards and print this message on them: "The _____ graders at _____ School prayed for you this week. May God bless you!" These cards and letters will serve as an encouragement and a witness to those who receive them.

## Reaching Every Individual

In this unit, as you study about God's healing and blessing, it is good to recognize God's hand even in the midst of difficulties. Rather than look at any disabilities negatively, focus on the positive. What are ways God blesses those with impairments? (Glasses, wheelchairs, hearing aids, etc., may not cure a problem, but are indeed a blessing in living with one.) God blesses us with helpers such as doctors, therapists, teachers, and friends who help people cope with and rise above difficulties. Encourage children to look at someone's problem not as something unusual, but as an opportunity to reach out with kindness and friendship.

## Social Studies

Money plays a significant role in two of the unit's Bible stories (Zacchaeus; the widow's offering). Talk about coins used in ancient times. Point out that the people in Israel probably used Roman coins because the Romans had conquered their land. Discuss metals used in coins then and now. Then share the words of the explanation of the Second Article of the Apostles' Creed that tell how we were bought back from slavery to sin. It says that Jesus has "purchased and won me from all sins, from death, and from the power of the devil; *not with gold or silver*, but with His holy, precious blood and with His innocent suffering and death."

## Science

As you discuss the changes God makes in the earth through erosion, volcanic eruption, and various weather conditions, you may also note the changes God makes in the hearts and lives of His people. **God's hand is all around us, changing, creating, and preserving.**.

## Mathematics

As you discuss the story of the widow's offering, have the children determine how much of an offering they would collect if each child in the class brought two pennies; if they brought two pennies each day for a week; if everyone in the school brought two pennies each day for a week. Consider planning such a school-wide offering. **Remember that God can do a lot with a little. But also remember that the widow didn't really give a little—she gave her best. She gave her all!**

## Integrating the Faith

## Changes

## Language Arts

Use several of the unit's stories to make comparisons between *a lot* and *a little*. For example, the woman who poured oil on Jesus spent *a lot* on her gift, while the widow's gift may have seemed like *a little*. But Jesus was grateful for both because He looked at the heart of the giver, not the gift. Compare the stories of Zacchaeus and the 10 men with leprosy. Zacchaeus had *a lot* of money; the group of 10 could only beg. Zacchaeus and the one healed man both showed *a lot* of thankfulness.

## Fine Arts

In this Bible unit we see people desperate for healing, desperate for forgiveness and salvation. Jesus was their only hope. Have children make a mosaic of an anchor, which is the symbol for hope, based on Hebrews 6:19. Emphasize that the anchor shape is made up of a cross with a smile below it. That reminds us of the joy we have in Jesus. At the bottom of the pictures print "Hope in the LORD" (Psalm 130:7).

## Technology

Use computers to design and make banners that celebrate and give thanks for the changes and blessings Jesus brings to our lives. Make several copies of each banner so they can be displayed in the hallways and shared with other classes.

## WEEK 21-A

### Discovery Point

We are sinners, undeserving of God's grace. But He calls us to repentance and faith in Christ Jesus, forgiving our sins and enabling us to respond with thankful hearts and in service to others.

### A Woman Anoints Jesus

Luke 7:36–50

### Objectives

That by the power of the Holy Spirit working through God's Word, the students will

- rejoice in the loving grace of God, who brings them to faith in Jesus;
- know that through the Word of God and the blessing of saving faith in Jesus, the Holy Spirit empowers them to do loving deeds for others;
- grow in service to God as they show love and care for others.

### Day 1 Materials

- Variety of invitations
- Blackline 21-A
- Story props

### Day 2 Materials

- Newspaper front page
- Story cube (Teacher Resource Book)
- Jake and Jenna puppets
- *Changes* Student Book
- Puppet People poster

# Day 1

## INTRODUCE

Display and discuss different kinds of invitations. **Have you, or someone you know, ever received an invitation? To what were you invited?** Let the children discuss the events and how they felt when invited. **Did you feel happy? excited to attend? special because you were included? Jesus received an invitation too. He was invited to a dinner at Simon's house.**

## DEVELOP

Prepare the class to pantomime the story. Assign the parts of Jesus, Simon, invited guests, the sinful woman, servants, and a messenger. Distribute props such as a perfume bottle, cushions or pillows, a tablecloth or blanket as the table, towels for headpieces, costumes, a broom, baskets, and cups colored to appear as if made of clay.

As you read the following, pause at the asterisks to allow time for children to act out the narration. Begin with a servant sweeping the floor.

**This is the house of a rich and important man named Simon. He is planning to invite guests to dinner. \* Simon sends out his messenger to invite friends. \* The messenger makes a special invitation to Jesus.**

**Simon gathers his servants around him. \* He tells the servants what to do to get ready for the special meal. \* Some servants prepare the food. \* Some servants set the table. \* Some place the cushions where the people will relax. \***

**As the invited guests arrive at the door, they remove their shoes. \* Simon motions for them to sit at the table. \* The guests talk and begin to eat. \* An uninvited woman comes in and stands near Jesus. \* She has a jar of perfume in one hand. \* She is crying, and her tears land on Jesus' feet. She bends and dries the tears with her hair. \* As a thank-You gift to Jesus, she pours the perfumed oil on His feet. \***

**Simon was upset when he saw the woman. She was a sinner. He would never let someone like her in his house. He would never let her come near his guests. \***

**Jesus knew what Simon was thinking. Jesus said to him, "Simon, when I came to your house, you did not honor Me. You did not have water to wash the dust off My feet. But this woman has honored Me by washing My feet with her tears and anointing Me with perfume."**

**Jesus turned to the woman and said, "It is true that she has sinned much. But she is sorry, and I forgive her. See how thankful she is." \***

**The other guests talked to each other, wondering about what Jesus had said and done. Jesus blessed the woman and said, "Your faith has saved you; go in peace." \* The woman left, knowing that her whole life had changed.**

Conclude, **This story is about a woman who gave Jesus a gift. But more than that, it is about the gift Jesus gave to her. It is the gift of faith in His forgiveness and salvation. God gives us the same gift. Jesus died on the cross and came alive again so that our sins are forgiven, and by faith we will live with Him in heaven. It's amazing! We receive the invitation, and we also receive the gift!**

## RESPOND

Continue, **God loves everyone and wants all people to be saved.** Ask the children to stand when they hear their Bible story character's name (words in italic). Note: When the person who played Simon is called, Jesus will hold His hand; next Simon will hold the hand of the woman, and so on. ***Jesus*** **died for the sins of** ***Simon*,** **for the sins of the** ***woman*,** **for the sins of the** ***messenger*** **and** ***servants*** **of Simon, for the sins of the** ***guests*** **at the dinner, and for the sins of** ***you*** **and** ***me!*** **Jesus loves us so much and wants all people to be saved. He invites us to speak His invitation to others.** Lead a discussion on ways to share God's invitation. Help the children understand how they can do this with words and also with actions. Distribute and discuss Blackline 21-A.

Write a story or draw a picture of how you could invite a person to know how much Jesus loves them. Color the frame.

Celebrate!

Who: You are invited

Where: To the kingdom of God

How: By the Gospel of Jesus' love, through faith in Him

Why: To receive forgiveness, a new life in Christ, and eternal life in heaven.

## Worship Ideas

- Have the class sit on a rug or blanket. As a reminder of the woman in the Bible story, pour lotion on your hands, rub them together, and then pray, **Dear Jesus, we love You so much. Help us to show our love by loving other people.** One at a time, pour lotion onto the hands of each child and have the child add a petition to the prayer. Close the prayer: **Thank You for letting us show our love for You by showing love to other people. In Your name we pray. Amen.**

- Remind the children that God is so forgiving toward us. And He asks us to be forgiving of others. In the Lord's Prayer, we pray that He will help us to follow His example. The prayer, in the Fifth Petition, says, **And forgive us our trespasses as we forgive those who trespass against us.** Say the prayer together, standing to shout the words of the Fifth Petition.

## Bible Background

In this event we see Jesus calling a sinful woman to repentance and to the forgiveness He offers her. We also see Jesus reaching out to Simon the Pharisee. Jesus tells a parable to teach Simon about God's forgiving nature and the need for all people (including Simon) to rely on this grace. Jesus' parable calls Simon to see his own sin and need for a Savior and to reflect to others the forgiveness the Lord offers to him.

This anointing, as does a later one in Bethany a week before Christ's crucifixion, calls to mind His goal, which is to die for the sins of the world. This anointing looks to the Lord's final battle and ultimate victory over sin, death, and the devil.

## Words to Remember

*[Jesus said,] "Your faith has saved you; go in peace." Luke 7:50*

Emphasize that the saving faith we have is not something that we choose or do—it is a gift of God. It is faith relying on Christ alone that receives the gifts of forgiveness and eternal life He offers. Read aloud Ephesians 2:8–9.

Display three gift-wrapped boxes, one inside the other. Print on the outer one in large letters the word *Faith*. **Faith is a gift from God. By faith in Jesus, we receive the gift of forgiveness from Him.** Open up the *Faith* box and take out a box labeled *Forgiveness*. **Because we have the gift of forgiveness, our sins are gone. We are holy in God's eyes, and He invites us to receive the gift of eternal life.** Open the *Forgiveness* box and take out the *Eternal Life* box. *Option:* You may choose to include another box labeled *Joy* inside the *Eternal Life* box.

## Extending the Lesson

- Plan a class trip to the offices of a local newspaper. Later, talk about the greatest news we have—the Good News, the Gospel.
- Encourage everyone to wear sandals one day. Talk about Bible times facts, noting that bare feet or sandals were the common footwear of the day. Most people traveled by walking, and the paths were usually made of dirt or sand. Cleanliness was important, and foot washing was a courtesy offered by a host and usually performed by a servant.
- Help children understand the cultural significance of anointing with oils. In the Mideastern culture of those times, an honored guest was made comfortable by foot washing and anointing with oil. The oil was soothing, healing, and often fragrant—all of which was appealing in a dry, dusty region. Oil might be placed on one's head, hands, or feet. Special anointing with oil was used at the appointment of a new king, and oils were also used as part of the burial ritual for the dead. Both of these had implications for Christ, King of kings, who would die, be buried, and rise again for our salvation.

## INTRODUCE

Hold up and scan a newspaper as you talk about looking for good news stories. As you talk, you will be tearing the four corner sections from the paper, leaving the shape of a cross.

Say, **When we read the newspaper, we learn what is happening in our town, state, nation, and the world. We call this the news. I enjoy reading good news, especially stories about people helping other people. Sometimes, though, there isn't much good news in the paper.** Scan the newspaper page. **Hmm. Here's some bad news. A bank robber took money that didn't belong to him.** Tear one corner section from the paper. Crumple the bad news and toss it aside. Continue, **Uh-oh. Here's more bad news. A woman lied to the government and was put in jail.** Tear off another corner section. Pretend to read more. **Oh, dear! More bad news! Some people started fighting and were badly hurt. They had to go to the hospital!** Tear off another corner of the page and toss it aside. Continue, **What's this? More bad news. Some kids took a computer game from a store**

---

## A Woman Anoints Jesus

*(Luke 7:36–50)*

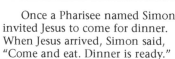

Once a Pharisee named Simon invited Jesus to come for dinner. When Jesus arrived, Simon said, "Come and eat. Dinner is ready."

While Jesus ate with Simon and the other guests, a woman came into the house. She was crying because she felt sorry for all the bad things she had done. She knew that Jesus would forgive her many sins.

Then the woman knelt down beside Jesus and began wiping the tears that had fallen on His feet with her hair. She poured perfumed oil on Jesus' feet to honor Him.

Simon saw the woman. He became angry. Simon thought, Jesus should know how sinful this woman is. He should not talk to her. He should send her away.

Jesus knew what Simon was thinking. Jesus said, "Simon, when I came to your house, you did not wash My feet. You did not honor Me. But this woman has honored Me by washing My feet with her tears and anointing Me with perfumed oil."

To the woman Jesus said, "Your sins are forgiven. Your faith has saved you. Go in peace."

Jesus knows we are sinners too. He wants us to be sorry about the wrong things we do. He wants to forgive us because He loves us. He gives us the peace in our hearts that only He can give.

1

**without paying for it. They were shoplifting.** Tear the final corner section from the paper.

Say, **What a lot of bad news! But wait!** Hold up the remaining portion of the page so that students can see the newsprint cross shape. **Now I can see good news! The good news is that even when we sin, Jesus still loves us. He wants the bank robber, the woman who lied, the people who were fighting, and the shoplifters to learn about God's mercy and repent of their sins. Jesus wants them all to be changed into His forgiven friends. And that's not all! Jesus loves and forgives us too. That's good news!** Tape the cross near the altar.

# DEVELOP

Reproduce the story-cube pictures from the Supplemental Activities section of the Teacher Resource Book. Attach one on each side of a cube-shaped tissue box or duplicate the pages and have each child make a story cube for review. Display this visual as you tell the Bible story, using the narrative in the *Changes* Student Book, page 1, as your guide.

Review the story, having children number the pictures in their book in the correct order.

---

## Jesus Makes the Difference

*Directions: In each pair of pictures read what one person says. Then decide how the other person could respond in a way that shows Christ-led kindness. Jesus helps us in what we say and do through His saving grace.*

Hey, Ricki. I'm going to borrow your bat.

Okay. You can use my baseball too.

You aren't praying for Jill, are you? She is so mean to you.

Yes, I did. I think Jesus is the only One who can make us friends again.

No one's looking. Let's tip these bikes over.

Think how those kids will feel. I wouldn't want someone to do that to me.

---

**Words to Remember**
[Jesus said,] "Your faith has saved you; go in peace."
Luke 7:50

2

# RESPOND

Use the Jake and Jenna puppets to continue with concepts from the Bible story. Hold up the puppet that is speaking to help children focus on the character.

**JENNA:** That woman in the Bible story was really lucky. I wish I could be like her.

**JAKE:** Why do you say that? Simon was angry at her for crashing his party. That doesn't sound good to me.

**JENNA:** But she was able to do something special for Jesus. I wish I could do something for Jesus, just once.

**JAKE:** But, Jenna, you can! And you can do it every day!

**JENNA:** How? I'm just a little kid. And I've never seen Jesus.

**JAKE:** Jesus tells us in the Bible that whenever we help someone else, we are also helping Jesus! Matthew 25:40 says, "Whatever you did for one of the least of these … you did for Me."

**JENNA:** You mean that if I read a book to my little sister, it would be like reading it to Jesus?

**JAKE:** That's what He means! We also serve Jesus when we are kind to others.

**JENNA:** So if I'm nice to my brother and let him use my baseball bat, it's like letting Jesus use it?

**JAKE:** Now you've got the idea.

**JENNA:** Wow, this changes everything! I could make a peanut butter and jelly sandwich for my cousin when he visits. It would be like …

**JAKE:** Like making a sandwich for Jesus!

**JENNA:** And I could clean up my toys so my mom doesn't have to, and that would be like …

**JAKE:** Like helping Jesus.

**JENNA:** *(walking away, talking to herself)* And I could say hi to Grandma on the phone, and I could help Dad pick up leaves, and I could be friendly to our neighbors, and I could be kind to their puppy, and …

**JAKE:** *(looking at the kids)* What kindness can you do, knowing it is also a kindness to Jesus?

Throughout this unit and the ones to follow, use the Unit 6 Puppet People poster in role-play situations. Cut out the figures and attach them to wooden craft sticks. Have children use them to demonstrate situations where people are showing kindness to each other.

Conclude with the activity on page 2 of the Student Book.

## Discovery Point

We are sinners, undeserving of God's grace. But He calls us to repentance and faith in Christ Jesus, forgiving our sins and enabling us to respond with thankful hearts and in service to others.

## Zacchaeus Has a Friend

Luke 19:1–10

## Objectives

That by the power of the Holy Spirit working through God's Word, the students will

- grow in joy as they recognize that God loves them and forgives them for Jesus' sake;
- know that as sinners made saints in Christ, they are chosen by God to be His own dear children;
- praise God for His forgiveness and the power to live as His chosen children by faith in Christ Jesus.

## Day 3 Materials

- Zacchaeus Fold 'n' Tell (Teacher Kit)
- Blackline 21-B
- Paper letters

## Day 4 Materials

- Counters (three per child)
- Wooden craft stick
- Play dough
- Green glove
- Flannelgraph materials
- *Changes* Student Book

## INTRODUCE

Sing "Zacchaeus" (*LOSP*, p. 55, and on CD). Say, **Lots of people like the story of Zacchaeus because of the cute song about the short man. But Zacchaeus had a serious problem. He was a tax collector, and most people didn't like tax collectors. A tax man was not very welcome, even in church. There were at least two reasons tax collectors were disliked: (1) the money they collected was used to help their enemies, the Romans, who had conquered their land; (2) tax collectors often charged extra high rates and kept the extra money for themselves. That made them traitors and robbers. There they sat by every city gate, getting richer and richer. Let's hear how the life of Zacchaeus was changed one special day.**

## DEVELOP

Tell the story using the Fold 'n' Tell "Jesus Is a Friend to Zacchaeus," which is in the Teacher Kit. The directions are printed on the back of the illustrated page. Practice in advance so you can show the movement in the story fluidly. After telling the story, you may allow students to use the Fold 'n' Tell to retell it. (These story folders are available from CPH in class quantities.) Sing the Zacchaeus song again.

## RESPOND

Point out that Zacchaeus *confessed* he was a sinner. **Confession includes two things: (1) admitting you are wrong; (2) being sorry about what you did.** Ask the children to listen to two stories and then tell you what part of confession is missing in each story.

Elana was playing with her favorite doll. Her sister had one just like it, except the clothes were a different color. Elana wasn't careful; she accidentally pulled the arm off her doll. She was about ready to cry, but then she had an idea. Her sister was at soccer practice, so Elana secretly changed the clothes of the two dolls. When her sister got home she noticed her doll was broken. She asked Elena what had happened. Elana lied, saying, "Don't ask me. I've been busy taking care of my own doll all afternoon. You need to be more careful with your toys." (Elana did not admit she was wrong.)

Matt was running through the crowded mall. He wanted to catch up with a friend he had spotted. Matt said, "Excuse me," as he pushed a little girl out of the way. Matt said, "Excuse me," as he jumped over a woman's shopping bag, ripping off the handle. Matt said, "Excuse me," as he annoyingly shouted out his friend's name. Matt said, "Excuse me," as he rushed past the security guard, who was trying to slow him down. (Matt was not really sorry about the things he was doing that upset others.)

Jesus calls us to repentance. He calls us to confess our sins and then, being truly sorry about them, to change our ways. We can't do this on our own. That's why the Holy Spirit comes to us through God's Word to lead us in faith and in our faith life. Use Blackline 21-B to discuss what our life is like as we are led by the Lord to follow Jesus, our forgiving Savior.

---

### Jesus Leads! Let's Follow!

Look to Jesus to see what life as a Christian is like.
He sends the Holy Spirit to our hearts as we hear God's
Word. The Holy Spitit gives us faith to believe in Jesus
and receive His good gifts. The Holy Spirit helps us to live as people of God.
Look at the list—see what Jesus does. Then draw a picture
or write words to show what you do as the Lord
leads you to live as His child. Jesus says, "Follow Me!"

| Jesus Shared ... | I Follow Jesus ... |
|---|---|
| Love |  |
| Forgiveness |  |
| Peace |  |

# Worship Ideas

- Point out that most worship services begin with a confession, which is a starting point where we recognize our need for the Savior. This is followed by absolution, where we hear that God forgives us for Jesus' sake. Read one of the confessional prayers at the beginning of one of the forms of liturgy. Ask the children to pray along silently. Assure them of the love and forgiveness that is theirs from Jesus.

- Say this responsive prayer. After each of your statements the children will say and motion these phrases:

**For you!** *(Hold up four fingers; then point to someone.)*

**For me!** *(Hold up four fingers; then point to yourself.)*

**For all!** *(Hold up four fingers; then point around the whole group.)*

The lead-in statements for the teacher are as follows:

- **God's love is …**
- **God's forgiveness is …**
- **God's care is …**
- **God's peace is …**

# Bible Background

Like Matthew, Zacchaeus was a tax collector, a person many in Palestine would have considered unworthy of membership in God's church. The truth is, by nature *none* of us is worthy. Rather, by nature we are spiritually dead, enslaved to sin and the power of the devil. Jesus, however, sets people free. His death and resurrection mark the decisive victory that redeems and renews humankind. By faith we share His triumph. We are delivered from our enemies and restored—partially in this life and fully in the life to come—to the image of our Creator and Savior God. As Jesus welcomed Zacchaeus, so Jesus gladly welcomes us and gives us new life in Him.

# WEEK 21-B

## Words to Remember

*The Son of Man came to seek and to save what was lost. Luke 19:10*

- In advance, cut out the letters *L-O-S-T* from colored paper. Place the letters around the room in unconventional and partially hidden spots. Tell the children that they will be looking for four paper letters. When they see one, they are not to point to it or give anyone clues as to where it is, but just say, "I spy!" When a child has spied all four letters, the child should be seated. When everyone is seated, take the letters and arrange them in the correct order.

  Ask, **In today's Bible words, what was lost?** (People who are sinners, including you and me.) **Jesus came looking for us. He came to the earth to save us. He comes to our hearts through God's Word and the power of the Holy Spirit, bringing us to faith. Because of Jesus, we are not lost. We are found! We are not losers. We are winners.** Read aloud 1 Corinthians 15:57.

## Extending the Lesson

- In your classroom, display a tree branch that is held upright in a container (such as a coffee can filled with sand). During the next few weeks hang objects on the tree that recall the eight stories in this unit. For example, symbols representing this week's stories could be a perfume bottle and a bag of coins. Ask the children how the object relates to the story. At the end of the unit, have the children review the stories as they refer to the various objects displayed.
- Set out a variety of coins—these could be coins used daily, foreign coins, or play money. Encourage children to demonstrate how Zacchaeus performed his job before and then after he met Jesus. *Option:* Provide paper, which children can place over coins to make crayon or pencil rubbings that reveal the coins' patterns and imprints.

# Day 4

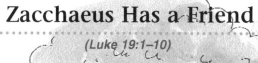

Distribute three game counters to each student. Explain that you will give them five tasks to do. Anytime they fail to follow the directions, they must give up a counter. To win the game you must end up with at least one counter. The prize will be an extra 10 minutes of recess. Here are the tasks:

- **In three seconds tell me the sum of 9,687 and 943.**
- **Spell antidisestablishmentarianism.**
- **Tell me what you were doing 10 days, 14 hours, and 6 minutes ago.**
- **Tell me the name of your great-great-grandfather's uncle.**
- **Tell me the phone number for the state capitol.**

Stop when all the counters have been collected. Discuss what happened. (The tasks were too difficult, if not impossible.) Say, **This game reminds me of the Ten Commandments. They are tasks that are impossible to do perfectly. No matter how hard we try, we cannot be perfect. We fail because we are sinful.**

## Zacchaeus Has a Friend

*(Luke 19:1–10)*

A large crowd of people gathered in the city of Jericho. They heard that Jesus was coming. People said, "I want to see Him." They pushed and shoved to get to the front of the crowd.

At the back of the crowd stood a small man. His name was Zacchaeus. He was a tax collector. He cheated people and kept their money for himself. Zacchaeus did not have many friends. Zacchaeus wanted to see Jesus too. He pushed and shoved to get to the front of the crowd, but no one would let him through.

Suddenly Zacchaeus ran ahead of the crowd. He climbed up a tree. He saw Jesus coming along the road. Jesus stopped right under the tree where Zacchaeus sat. Jesus looked up and said, "Zacchaeus, hurry and come down. I want to go to your house today."

Zacchaeus was so surprised! He hurried down the tree with a big smile on his face and a heart full of joy. The people grumbled, "Why is Jesus going to the home of such a terrible sinner?"

But Jesus forgave Zacchaeus. Jesus changed Zacchaeus' heart. Zacchaeus said, "Lord, I will give half of everything I have to the poor. If I have cheated anyone, I will give back four times as much as I took."

Jesus said to Zacchaeus, "Today salvation has come to this house. I, the Son of Man, have come to look for and save those who are lost." These blessings of forgiveness and salvation are also for you and me. Thank You, Jesus!

3

So God sent Jesus into the world, and Jesus obeyed every one of God's laws. Jesus was perfect for you and for me! We do not deserve God's forgiveness or eternal life in heaven. But God gives that to us through the perfect righteousness of Jesus. Because of sin, we lose. But then Jesus gives us His victory. That's even better than losing a game and still getting 10 extra minutes of recess anyway. (Plan to give the children extra recess later to express the joy of an undeserved gift.) **Today we'll review the story of a man who was a real loser, until he met Jesus. Jesus changed his life.**

## DEVELOP

To review the story, attach a wooden craft stick to a flannelgraph figure of Jesus. Insert the end of the stick into a circle of play dough so that it will stand. Use your arm as a puppet stage—as the sycamore tree. Either wear something that has long brown sleeves or make a paper sleeve from construction paper. This will stand for the trunk of the tree. Wear a green glove to stand for the leafy part of the tree. Put your elbow on a table, with your arm vertical and fingers outstretched. Place a flannelgraph man (Zacchaeus) onto one of your green fingers (tree branches), and gather the children around you to retell the story.

## For God So Loved the World

· · · · · · · · · · · · · · · · · · · · · · · · · · · · · · · · · · · · · · · · · · · · · · · · · · · · · · · ·

*You can be certain Jesus loves you. Our Lord loves all people, and He wants all people to be saved. As a child of God, you receive His love, which He asks you to share with others. Read the poem and then draw a picture of the variety of people Jesus loves.*

Jesus loves the sick, the well,
The very old, the little ones.
Jesus loves the rich, the poor.
How about you?

Jesus loves the one who's hurt,
The crying one, the hungry one.
Jesus loves them, tall or small.
How about you?

Jesus loves the muddy ones,
The ragged ones, the clean ones too.
Jesus loves them, smart or not.
How about you?

Jesus loves them, near or far,
Dark or light, in-between.
Jesus loves the fat and thin.
How about you?

### Words to Remember
The Son of Man came to seek and to save what was lost.
Luke 19:10

4

## RESPOND

Point out that people thought Zacchaeus was so sinful—a hopeless loser. But Jesus came to save people who were lost in sin (including you and me). **Jesus takes away our sins. We are not losers—we are winners! He gives us His victory over sin, death, and the devil. Through Jesus, we have won eternal life in heaven.** Then invite the children to come together for an echo pantomime.

**Zacchaeus was a little man, as small as he could be.** *(Stoop down low.)*
**When Jesus came to teach the crowd, Zacchaeus couldn't see.** *(Make a sad face.)*
**He stood up on his tippy toes and stretched his neck way out.** *(Stand on tiptoes and stretch neck.)*
**He jumped and jumped to get up high until his tongue hung out.** *(Jump around, then pant.)*
**At last he cried, "I've got a plan!" And climbed right up a tree.** *(Pretend to climb a tree.)*
**And from the branches way up high Zacchaeus then could see.** *(Lean over and look down.)*
**Then Jesus saw him and called out, "Zacchaeus, come down here!"** *(Pretend to climb down tree.)*
**Salvation came into his house. Zacchaeus gave a cheer!** *(Make happy face.)*

Adapted from *Fingers Tell the Story*, © 1989 CPH.

Conclude with pages 3 and 4 of the *Changes* Student Book.

## WEEK 22-A

### Discovery Point

Because Jesus has made us forgiven and redeemed children of God, we can go to our heavenly Father in prayer.

### A Woman Prays for Her Daughter

Matthew 15:21–28

### Objectives

That by the power of the Holy Spirit working through God's Word, the students will
- know that Jesus wants to hear our prayers;
- confidently pray, knowing their heavenly Father will answer in the way and time that is best;
- bring petitions for others to the Lord in prayer.

### Day 1 Materials
- Flannelgraph materials
- Wooden craft stick
- Blackline 22-A

### Day 2 Materials
- *Changes* Student Book
- Jake and Jenna puppets

## INTRODUCE

Write *911* on the chalkboard in large numbers. Ask if anyone knows why those numbers are important. Emphasize that 911 is a phone number to be used only in an emergency—when someone is in trouble. Discuss situations when 911 should be used. Explain how 911 connects the caller with people who can help.

**There is someone else we can call on anytime. This person does not use a telephone. The Bible tells us who this person is.** Read Psalm 50:15 aloud. Ask, **Who can we call to?** (God.) **What kinds of trouble might you have?** (Answers will vary.) **What does God say to do when we have trouble?** (Call to Him.) **Why?** (God loves us and promises to help us.)

**Everyone has troubles. No matter what the trouble is, calling to God is always right. When we tell Jesus about our troubles, He listens. He answers our prayers in the way and at the time that is best. He loves us and wants to help.**

## DEVELOP

In advance, attach a wooden craft stick to the back of a female flannelgraph character. Use this as a stick puppet to tell today's Bible story.

**I want to introduce you to a woman from Canaan. We don't even know her name. We only know where she lived, that her daughter was sick, and that she had faith that Jesus could help her. Here is her story.**

**My people came from a country that was called Canaan. I am a Canaanite woman. Jesus and His people were Jews. Often, Jewish and Canaanite people did not like each other. In fact, we rarely spoke to them, and they didn't speak to us either.**

**But I didn't care who came from where. I needed help. And I knew that Jesus was the only person who could help me. You see, my little girl was very sick, and there was no one else who could help her. We had all heard how Jesus could heal sick people. I believed that Jesus had the power to heal my daughter too.**

**When I saw Jesus walking along the road, I called out to Him. I begged Him to heal my daughter. At first He did not answer me, so I asked again. His disciples told Him to send me away. It seemed at first that Jesus would not help me. But I would not give up. I kept asking Him to help. Finally He said, "Woman, you have great faith! Your request is granted." That very hour my daughter was healed. When I got home she was well!**

**Jesus hears your prayers too. He wants you to ask Him for what you need. Talk to Jesus. He will answer at the time that is best and in the best way. He knows when and how to help.**

## R E S P O N D

The woman in the story was persistent. That means she didn't give up. She prayed again and again. She trusted the kindness of the Lord. Explain that you will read some statements about prayer. If you say something true, the students should stand up. If what you say is not true, the students should sit down. This is not a right or wrong game. It is a learning game. Talk about the statements when needed.

1. **Prayer is a way to talk to God.** *(True.)*
2. **When I pray I must be in church.** *(False.)*
3. **I can pray with my mouth closed.** *(True.)*
4. **I must have my hands folded when I pray.** *(False.)*
5. **We can pray anytime of day or night.** *(True.)*
6. **Jesus listens when we pray for someone else.** *(True.)*
7. **Jesus always answers right away.** *(False.)*
8. **Jesus answers prayer in the way that is best.** *(True.)*

Use Blackline 22-A to make a prayer book today. Add a prayer each day of the week. As you look at the word *PRAY* and the four types of prayer, explain to the children: *P* is for praise, saying good things about God and what He has done for you; *R* is for repent, saying we are sorry for our sins and asking for forgiveness; *A* is for ask, but not for yourself (that is the last prayer), as you pray for other people and their needs; *Y* is for yourself, because Jesus wants to hear about your concerns and needs.

## Worship Ideas

- Sit in a circle for a passing prayer. Thread a large wooden bead onto a length of twine. Extend the twine around the circle so each child can hold onto it with both hands. Tie the ends together. Demonstrate by beginning the prayer as you hold the bead between your hands. Say a prayer, and then slide the bead to the next person. (This helps identify whose turn it is to pray. Children may feel free to pass it on without praying aloud.) Close the prayer by thanking God for hearing and answering the prayers and adding, **In Jesus' name we pray. Amen.**

- Begin praying with hands pressed together, palms and fingers touching. Model the motions as you pray.
  *(Hold thumbs close to your heart.)* **I pray for people close to me: neighbors, friends, and family.**
  *(Tap pointer fingers together.)* **I pray for those who haven't heard the news of Jesus and His Word.**
  *(Tap tall fingers together.)* **I pray for leaders to be strong and follow Your Word all day long.**
  *(Tap ring fingers together.)* **For weak and sick ones pray a prayer, "Dear Jesus, keep them in Your care."**
  *(Tap little fingers.)* **And last of all my prayer will be, a little prayer that's just for me. Amen.**

## Bible Background

This is the only known occasion during Jesus' ministry that He went outside the boundaries of Palestine. Probably the woman was a Gentile who descended from the Canaanites that inhabited Syria and Palestine before the conquest by Joshua. Jesus may have gone to the region to avoid a premature clash with hostile Jews and to secure some privacy with His disciples. His undertaking of a brief ministry to Gentiles also foreshadows the universal nature of the Gospel.

Again and again during Jesus' ministry He brought the Good News of salvation to people thought to be unworthy—tax collectors, prostitutes, Samaritans, lowly fishermen, zealots, and many more. He would say to us, "The children you teach are worthy. I make them worthy because I have redeemed them. They are children of God!"

## Words to Remember

*Call to Me / and I will answer you.* Jeremiah 33:3

- Divide the class into two groups. The first group is to "call" out the first three words. The other group is to "call" out the last five words. Do this several times. Then switch group responses, and finally say the whole verse together.

- Say this litany, with children responding at the asterisk with the Bible "Words to Remember."

When I am frightened, God says * .

When I feel alone, God says * .

When my feelings are hurt, God says * .

When I am sick, God says * .

When my work is hard, God says * .

When I need forgiveness, God says * .

Conclude with, **Father, thank You that we can talk to You anytime, anywhere, about anything. In Jesus' name. Amen.**

## Extending the Lesson

- When we pray, God hears and responds. We are communicating. Explore praying with different forms of communication (spoken and written words, telephone messages, e-mail, audiocassette recorders, and videotape cameras).

- Pair up students to follow the actions in this prayer.

**Thank You, God, for hands to shake my partner's hands.**

**Thank You, God, for feet to walk around my partner.**

**Thank You, God, for arms to wave at my partner.**

**Thank You, God, for eyes to see my partner's eyes.**

**Thank You, God, for a voice to say "Hi" to my partner.**

**Thank You, God, for feet to tiptoe around my partner.**

**Thank You, God, for knees to bend up and down with my partner.**

**Thank You, God, for legs to walk to my chair and sit down.**

# Day 2

## INTRODUCE

Use the Jenna puppet to discuss the "right time" to pray.

**JENNA:** I wish it was lunch time.

**TEACHER:** Goodness, Jenna! You just ate breakfast!

**JENNA:** Well, then I wish I could go to bed.

**TEACHER:** But the day is just beginning. Why do you wish it was a different time?

**JENNA:** I need to talk to Jesus.

**TEACHER:** Jenna, Jesus listens to our prayers all the time—not just at mealtime and bedtime!

**JENNA:** Really?

**Teacher:** Yes, really! God tells us in the Bible that He hears us whenever we pray to Him. *(Read Isaiah 65:24.)*

**JENNA:** Wow! God hears and answers me anytime. Thank you for telling me this good news.

**TEACHER:** Would you like to learn a song about prayer? (Sing stanza

## A Woman Prays for Her Daughter

*(Matthew 15:21–28)*

**DISCIPLES:** One day as we walked along, a woman called out to Jesus.

**WOMAN:** Lord, help me. My daughter is very sick.

**DISCIPLES:** Send her away, Jesus. She isn't one of our people.

**WOMAN:** Help me! Please, Jesus!

**DISCIPLES:** Jesus isn't answering her. But she still keeps on asking Him for help.

**WOMAN:** Jesus, help my little girl! Please!

**DISCIPLES:** Send her away, Jesus. She is too loud.

**WOMAN:** I know You can make my little girl well. No one else can help me!

**JESUS:** You have very strong faith. Go home now. Your daughter is well.

*You, too, can be sure that Jesus loves you and will answer your prayers when you talk to Him.*

5

3 of "Won't You Come and Sit with Me" [*LOSP*, p. 37]. Add the following stanza about prayer.)

**Jesus hears us when we pray,**
**When we pray, when we pray.**
**Jesus hears us when we pray.**
**Pray to Jesus now.**

TEACHER: *(as Jenna hurries away)* Jenna, where are you going?

JENNA: I'm going to do what the song says. I'm going to pray to Jesus right *now!*

## DEVELOP

Read together the short play on page 5 of the *Changes* Student Book. Choose a child to read the words of Jesus. Invite the boys to read the words of the disciples and the girls to read the words of the woman. Practice the story with Jesus speaking calmly, the disciples sounding annoyed, and the woman loudly calling out in a pleading voice.

Use this Bible story to note that God does much more than "give us gifts." He indeed provides clothing and shoes, food and drink, house and home, as stated in the explanation of the First Article of the Apostles' Creed (see the catechism in the Teacher Resource Book). God also *preserves* and *protects* us. He does not leave us alone—He takes care of us, guarding, healing, and restoring us.

## Call Upon the Lord

Look at these people who need help. What can you do for them? Here is a clue: What letters do the shapes look like? What do these letters spell?

Do you know where these people live? Do you know what they need most from Jesus? Here is a clue: What letters do the shapes look like? What do these letters spell?

> **Words to Remember**
> Call to Me and I will answer.
> Jeremiah 33:3

6

And why does God do this? As stated in the First Article explanation, "All this He does only out of fatherly, divine goodness and mercy, without any merit or worthiness in me." And what is our response? "For all this it is my duty to thank and praise, serve and obey Him. This is most certainly true." Discuss with the children some of the ways God preserves and protects us. (Through His miracles in our lives, through other people like parents and doctors, through the care of His angels.)

## RESPOND

Use the Jake and Jenna puppets to learn more about prayer.

JENNA: I just don't understand. Why didn't Jesus heal the little girl right away when her mother asked?

JAKE: I think Jesus wanted to teach the mother to keep on praying. You know, Jesus doesn't always give us what we want right away.

JENNA: Sometimes He does. Once when I got lost, I prayed, and just at that minute, my mom found me!

JAKE: Yes, sometimes Jesus does answer right away. But sometimes we have to keep on praying—like when you had pneumonia and didn't come to school for a long time. Our class prayed for you every day until you got better.

JENNA: Well, I've been praying for a cat for a long, long time. And so far, God hasn't given me one.

JAKE: But isn't your mom allergic to cats? If God answered your prayer like you wanted, it would hurt your mom. I think God knows what is best.

JENNA: God is really wise, isn't He? You know, I think Jesus waited to answer the mother so that He could also teach the disciples a lesson.

JAKE: You're right. I think Jesus wanted them to know that He loves all people. He came to be the Savior for the whole world.

JENNA: I'm so glad we can talk to the Lord in prayer.

JAKE: And He promises to listen and do what is best for us.

Direct the students' attention to page 6 of the *Changes* Student Book. Have the children describe the concern pictured in each situation in the first row. Point out that the shapes of the pictures are similar to shapes of letters. **What word do the letter shapes spell?** *(PRAY.)* **God wants to hear our prayers.**

Then see if the children can identify the country or continent the people come from in the second row. *(South America, Africa, Northern Europe, Asia.)* Again look at the picture shapes. **What word do the letter shapes spell?** *(LOVE.)* **God loves people of all races and all nations.**

## Discovery Point

Because Jesus has made us forgiven and redeemed children of God, we can go to our heavenly Father in prayer.

## Ten Men with Leprosy

Luke 17:11–19

## Objectives

That by the power of the Holy Spirit working through God's Word, the students will
- confidently approach their heavenly Father for all their needs;
- understand that Jesus can save us—both physically and spiritually;
- thank and praise God for His goodness and love.

## Day 3 Materials

- Chain of paper people
- Blackline 22-B
- Jake puppet

## Day 4 Materials

- Cookie or candy treat
- 10 Lepers Fold 'n' Tell (Teacher Kit)
- *Changes* Student Book

## INTRODUCE

Write these words on the board: *merci beaucoup, danke schön, grazie, gracias.* See if anyone knows what the words say. Then explain that the words say "thank you" in French, German, Italian, and Spanish. Tell the class that even though we may have a hard time saying some of these words, God understands each word perfectly. Ask why "thank you" is important in any language. **Today's lesson is about people who did and didn't remember to say thank you.**

## DEVELOP

In advance, cut out a paper chain of 10 people. (Suggestion: Drawing two people on a paper that has been accordion folded into five sections is easier to cut than trying to cut out a single shape through 10 folds.)

**Outside a village lived 10 men who had a bad sickness called leprosy. Leprosy was a very bad skin disease that made sores all over a person's body.** Use a pencil to draw several dots on the 10 paper people. Do not use a felt-tipped pen because the ink will soak through. **In those days there was no medicine that could cure leprosy. People with leprosy were not allowed to live with healthy people. Instead, they had to live by themselves, outside of town, away from their family and friends.**

**One day the 10 men saw Jesus walking along the road. They began to call out, "Jesus! Master! Help us!"** Lift the paper chain up each time you loudly call. **The 10 sick men believed that Jesus could make them well, just as He had healed others.**

**Jesus saw the 10 sick men and heard their call for help. Jesus did not make the sick men better right away. Instead He said, "Go and show yourselves to the priests."** This was the rule in that land: if you were healed, you first had to be checked over and approved by the priests before you could return to your home and family.

**The 10 men trusted Jesus' words. They obeyed Him and ran on their way to see the priests.** Move the paper chain as if running away. **As the 10 men hurried along, the sores on their skin healed. Their sickness had been cured! They were well!** Turn the paper chain over to the unmarked side. Then move it up and down as if jumping for joy. **Now the men could return to their families and friends. The leprosy was gone. Jesus had made them well!**

Tear off one man from the paper chain. Set the others down, and bring the one man forward. **One man was so happy to be healed that he ran right back to thank Jesus. "You did it! You made me well, Jesus! Thank You! Thank You!"**

**Jesus asked, "Didn't I help 10 of you? Where are the other nine men?" Then Jesus looked at the thankful man and smiled. "Go home to your family and friends," Jesus said. "Your faith has made you well."** Move the man as if he is happily skipping on his way.

Continue, Jesus gives us many things—even without our asking for them. When Jesus answers our prayers, we can tell Him thank You. We can thank Him that He forgives our sins, gives us eternal life, and blesses us every day.

## R E S P O N D

Read the following Bible verses aloud and have the children raise their hands (or stand) every time they hear the word *help*.

- **Acts 26:22—I have had God's help to this very day.**
- **Psalm 121:1—I lift up my eyes to the hills—where does my help come from? My help comes from the LORD, the Maker of heaven and earth.**
- **Psalm 115:9—Trust in the LORD—He is [your] help and shield.**

When we think about everything God has done for us, we want to say thank You. Blackline 22-B provides an opportunity to express this. Children may add extra drawings to the background, if they wish. They are to color the page with crayons. *Option:* To give a stained-glass look, continue by placing pictures on newsprint, brush pictures with baby oil, dry, and staple a black paper frame to the edges.

## Worship Ideas

- Sing songs to the Lord. Select favorites from *LOSP* or the Voyages CD that specifically use the word *thank*.
- For each child, provide an enlarged version of a paper person similar to the paper-chain people you used in the story presentation. The children are to write on the shape the name of someone for whom they would like to thank God. As you gather for worship the children are to place the paper people on the altar. Have a silent prayer time so each child can thank God for that person. Close with **We thank You, God, for the gifts of these people and for Jesus, the best blessing. In His name we pray. Amen.**

## Bible Background

Leprosy was a term used to cover a variety of skin diseases. Persons with leprosy were obligated by law to separate themselves and cry "Unclean! Unclean!" as a warning to others of their condition (Leviticus 13:45–46). Not until a priest had pronounced them clean and the prescribed offering had been made could lepers be readmitted to society (14:1–32).

The story of the 10 men with leprosy is closely related to the previous sections of Luke 17. As faith manifests itself in love and forgiveness (verses 1–4) and in service to the Lord (verses 5–10), so also faith responds in grateful praise to God (verses 11–19). "Made you well" (verse 19) refers to wholeness and wellness in the fullest sense—salvation. This Samaritan received forgiveness of sins and a place among God's children.

**Blackline 22-B**

# WEEK 22-B

## Words to Remember

*Give thanks to the LORD, for He is good.*
Psalm 136:1

- Pair up children to shout the "Words to Remember" to each other by half verse. Take the class to the gym or outside. Stand the members of each pair about 10 feet apart. Have them cup their hands around their mouths to call out the memory verse. Recall the lepers calling out to Jesus.
- Throughout the day, ring a bell or give a signal. At the signal, the children will stand, raise their arms in praise, and say in unison, "Give thanks to the LORD, for He is good."

## Extending the Lesson

- There are many people homebound or in hospitals and nursing homes who would be thankful for a gift of cheer. Ask for ideas from the class. Be prepared to add suggestions, such as making craft-stick frames and adding a Bible verse instead of a picture. Vote and plan to make someone happy.
- Discuss attitudes toward people who have disfigurements, are crippled, or have a debilitating disease. Sometimes people shy away from or stare at those people. (Compare this to the separation and isolation the men with leprosy must have felt.) Point out that people with such conditions are often the ones who most need our support, cheer, and touch. Discuss ways to welcome and befriend people in need. (This discussion may help prepare children to respond warmly in similar life situations.)

## INTRODUCE

In advance, practice this scenario with a child. To introduce the lesson, you will say, **Oh, (child's name), come here. I have a special treat for you today.** Give the child a cookie or candy bar. The child grabs it and runs out the door. Act surprised and hurt. Ask, **Did (child's name) forget something?** (The child forgot to say thanks.) **Our Bible story is about nine people who forgot to say thank You to Jesus.** At this point the child should stick his/her head through the doorway and say thank you. Say, **And thank you for being a good actor.** Applaud as the child takes his/her seat.

## Ten Men with Leprosy

*(Luke 17:11–19)*

 had leprosy. No  could make them .

Then they  . They called out in a loud voice,

"  , help us!"  was the only  who could

help. When  the 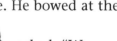, He said, "Go show

yourselves to the priests." As the 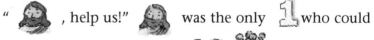 ran, they

 that they were .  came back to .

He praised God in a loud voice. He bowed at the  of

 and thanked Him.  asked, "Were not all 10

made ? Where are the other 9 ?" Then He said

to the 1 , "Rise and go; your faith has made

you ."

Jesus also helps you and me. Saving us by dying on the cross is one of many great things Jesus has done for us. Let's thank Him for blessing us!

7

## D E V E L O P

Use the Fold 'n' Tell card from the Teacher Kit to retell the events of the Bible story. (Practice in advance, using the instructions and illustrations on the back as a guide. Point out the parallel between the posture of the thankful man and the posture of the children thanking Jesus.)

Then students can read the rebus story from the *Changes* Student Book, page 7. Have half of the class read the words and the other half "read" the pictures. Switch parts halfway through the story.

## R E S P O N D

Point out that sometimes we are like the nine forgetful men. **Sometimes we might forget to tell our good and loving Lord thank You. When that happens, God leads us to be sorry and repent. God forgives our unthankfulness for Jesus' sake. And even when we forget, God never forgets us. He continues to bless us with many, many good things.**

Direct the children's attention to the *Changes* Student Book, page 8. Explain that many blessings from God are shown on this page. Help the children understand that all good gifts come from God. God often blesses us through other people. To their parents, God gives health and abilities to work at a job so that they can buy food, clothing, and many things for the family. It would be best to work on the activity together so that no one becomes confused or frustrated. Say a prayer in which you thank God for each thing pictured (or assign a picture to each of 11 prayer volunteers).

## Hidden Message Picture

God has given us many, many blessings. Some of these good gifts are shown here. Draw yourself and a friend in box 8. Then circle the first letter under each picture. Write these letters above the matching numbered answer blanks.

9. Good food   4. Nice clothes   6. Your Son   2. Home

3. Animals   8. Us   7. Other people

10. Our family   1. Toys   5. Kindness   11. Days of life

T H A N K   Y O U ,   G O D
1  2  3  4  5   6  7  8   9  10  11

### Words to Remember
Give thanks to the LORD, for He is good.
Psalm 136:1

8

195

## Discovery Point

All people are sinners and do not deserve God's love. But God is merciful. He calls us to repent, and He offers forgiveness and new life in Christ.

## Two Men Pray

Luke 18:9–14

## Objectives

That by the power of the Holy Spirit working through God's Word, the students will

- recognize their need for a Savior who forgives their sins;
- go to God in prayer with repentant hearts, trusting in His grace;
- rejoice in Christ's love and in the change He makes in their lives.

## Day 1 Materials

- Jake and Jenna puppets
- Styrofoam cups
- Blackline 23-A

## Day 2 Materials

- *Changes* Student Book

# Day 1

# INTRODUCE

Use the Jake and Jenna puppets to help introduce an important Bible story concept.

**JENNA:** *(in a singsong voice)* Teacher likes me more than you.

**JAKE:** Why do you say that?

**JENNA:** *(smugly)* Because I don't get into trouble like you do.

**TEACHER:** *(hugging both puppets)* Wait a minute! I love you both the same.

**JENNA:** *(holding head high)* But you really like me better because I'm always good. Right?

**TEACHER:** Well, Jenna, I really do love both of you the same. I've learned about love from God. You see, God never stops loving us. He does not like the bad things we do, but He leads us to be sorry when we do wrong. And He gladly forgives us. He showed His great love for all people by sending Jesus to be our Savior.

**JENNA:** I think that I need to say I'm sorry to Jake. *(To Jake)* I said some mean things earlier. I acted proud, as if I was better than you. I'm sorry, Jake.

**JAKE:** I forgive you, Jenna. And I'm glad God and Teacher love both of us, aren't you?

# DEVELOP

In advance prepare two puppets from Blackline 23-A. Be sure to draw the tax collector's closed eyes and sad mouth in pencil so you can later erase them and change them to indicate the change God made in his life.

Say, **Jesus knew that some people thought they were perfect. They believed obeying lots of rules would get them into heaven. But Jesus wanted everyone to know that we are all sinners and that He is the only way to heaven, so He told this story.**

Hold up the Pharisee puppet. **Many Pharisees thought they were very good and very important. They were so busy keeping their rules that they sometimes forgot God's will. They did not show love to others. This Pharisee was very proud. He could see what other people did wrong. Compared to them, he thought he was perfect.**

Hold up the tax collector puppet. **Tax collectors were not well liked. Many people thought they cheated and broke the rules. This tax collector knew he had done wrong. He was sorry.**

Hold up the Pharisee and the tax collector puppets. **Jesus told a story about these two men who went to the temple to pray.**

Pharisee puppet, raised high. **The Pharisee stood up in front of everyone and prayed about himself. In a proud, loud voice he said, "God, I thank You that I am not like other men. I am generous and good, and I obey the rules." This man thought God would like all the things he did. He didn't think he needed a Savior, because he didn't think he was a sinner.**

Hold the tax collector puppet low. **The tax collector stood off in a corner. With eyes down and head bowed he prayed, "God, have mercy on me, a sinner." Jesus said, "I tell you that this man, rather than the other, went home forgiven by the love of God."**

Erase the tax collector's eyes and mouth and change his expression to a happy one. **God forgave the tax collector. God had changed his heart so he could live a new life as a child of God. The tax collector knew God loved him. How joyful he must have been!**

## RESPOND

Have each child make puppets similar to the ones you used. To review the story, have them lift up the puppet you describe. The answers are listed in parentheses as *PH* for Pharisee and *TC* for tax collector.

*Who am I?* I was proud (PH); I prayed about myself (PH); I prayed for help (TC); I thought I was better than other people (PH); I admitted I was a sinner (TC); I am thankful I'm not a bad person like others nearby (PH); I said I'm sorry (TC); I asked for mercy (TC); I bragged about the good things I do (PH); I was humble (TC); I think God loves me because I'm so good (PH); I don't think God's love is for everyone (PH); I trust God will forgive me (TC); I'm happy (TC).

*Directions for making puppets:*
1. Color the clothing of each man.
2. Draw closed eyes and a sad mouth on the tax collector in pencil.
3. Cut out each shape.
4. Use tape rolls to attach each man to an upside-down Styrofoam cup.

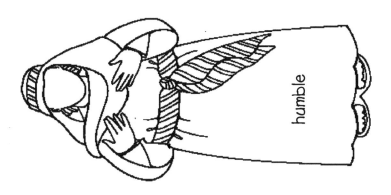

humble

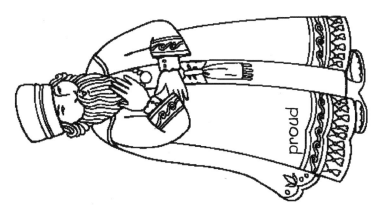

proud

# Worship Ideas

- Demonstrate this finger play as you read the poem. Children may imitate your actions. Hold your palms parallel and tap together the fingers of your right and left hand as they are mentioned. Fold your hands on the last line.

**Ten little fingers were arguing one day.**
**Who was most important? Who should get his way?**
**The thumbs weren't talking; the pointers didn't care;**
**The tall ones felt important; the ring men wouldn't share.**
**The pinkies, though so little, said, "Let's pray to God above. Let's tell Him that we're sorry and ask Him for His love."**
**Ten little fingers stopped arguing that day.**
**They gave a big "I'm sorry" hug and then began to pray.**
  Close with prayer:
**Thank You, Lord, for Your dear Son.**
**My forgiveness He has won.**
**He redeemed and set me free.**
**Now I'll live eternally. Amen.**

- Lead the children with this prayer: **Dear Lord, we know we are sinners. Every day we do wrong things. We are sorry, and we need Your forgiveness. We trust that You forgive us because of Jesus. Together we pray the prayer of the tax collector: God, be merciful to me, a sinner. Amen.**

# Bible Background

In the First Commandment God says, "You shall have no other gods." Our sinful nature resists that command. We find it easy to find ways we are better than others, and we claim to have merit on our own. It seems distasteful to be "poor in spirit" (Matthew 5:3), to find nothing about ourselves that merits God's favor, to be humble.

So Jesus exalts humility (Luke 18:14). Of course, humility does not save us. Rather, humility admits the futility of trying to save ourselves. With that barrier removed, the Gospel works to create and strengthen faith. Through faith in Jesus as our Savior, we travel life's pathway justified before God.

# Day 2

## Words to Remember

*God, have mercy on me, a sinner. Luke 18:13*

- Explain several key words to the children. The word *mercy* refers to undeserved kindness. The word *humble* is the opposite of proud. **The tax collector said these words with a humble attitude, seeing God as far greater than he. He prayed for God's forgiving mercy, even though he knew he did not deserve it. He based his prayer totally on the love of God.**

## Extending the Lesson

- Frequently call a one-minute "drop everything and pray" time throughout the week. Provide a moment for quiet prayer or a few joyful moments to sing. Consider using a signal (Autoharp chord, bell, recording) to begin and end each time period.
- Sing "Father, I Adore You" (*LOSP*, p. 13, and on CD). Change the second line to "lay my sins before You."

## INTRODUCE

Ask the children to help you make a list of sinful wrong things that children sometimes do. (For example, sometimes I am selfish with my toys, sometimes I am not a friend to my friends, sometimes I act like I'm better than people who seem different.) Then go through the list together, saying one item at a time, followed by the tax collector's prayer: **God, have mercy on me, a sinner.** Erase the item and go on to the next one, continuing this pattern until all sins are erased. Say, **This is a good way to begin the day, knowing that Jesus has forgiven our sins. When God looks at us, it's just as if He erased our wrongs; it's just as if we had never sinned at all! Now we can go on through the day with happy hearts, living as children of God.**

## Two Men Pray

*(Luke 18:9–14)*

Jesus often told stories called parables to help people understand God's love for them. Jesus knew that some people listening to Him did not understand how much they needed a Savior. Jesus said, **"Two men went to the temple to pray. One was a Pharisee. The other was a tax collector."**

God, I thank You that I am better than other people. I do not steal. I do not lie. I thank You that I am so good and not like that sinful tax man standing over there.

Pharisee

God, have mercy on me, a sinner.

Tax collector

When the tax collector went home he was happy because he was forgiven. He understood God's great love and the gift of salvation we have through Jesus.

Jesus

## DEVELOP

Review the Bible story. Ask the children to imitate your actions. Tell them that everyone will be playing the parts of both men in the Bible story. To contrast the two characters, step to one side to be the Pharisee and take a step or two in the other direction to be the tax collector.

Walk in place. **Jesus told this story, "One day two men went to the temple to pray."** Both men needed God's love. Both men needed God's forgiveness.

Fold your arms over your chest and hold your nose up in the air. **The first man was a Pharisee, a rich man who was a leader in the church. He looked proud of himself and held his head high.**

Bow your head and fold your hands. **The second man was a tax collector who knew he had done wrong. He humbly came to pray.**

Act proudly again. **The Pharisee said, "O Lord, I have done many good things."**

Bow head humbly. **The tax collector said, "O Lord, I admit I have sinned."**

Act proudly. **The Pharisee said, "I am better than other people. I do not steal. I do not lie. I'm not like that awful man standing over there. He doesn't belong here with people like me."**

Bow head. **The tax collector said, "God, be merciful to me, a sinner." He trusted God's forgiveness. He wanted God to change his life.**

Show a stern, suspicious look while walking in place. **The Pharisee went home. But he was not happy inside because he didn't understand that he needed God's forgiveness. He only saw what others did wrong. He did not see his own sins and his need for the Savior.**

Have a smiling, happy face while walking in place. **The tax collector went home happy. He understood that God loves all people. He knew that God forgave his sins. We, too, can be happy, knowing that because of Jesus we are forgiven children of God!**

## RESPOND

After reading the story on page 9 of the *Changes* Student Book, work on page 10 together. As the children give their answers, add some of the following thoughts to your discussion.

1. God loved each one of us so much that He sent His only Son, Jesus, to earth. Since we can't be perfect, Jesus was perfect for us. Jesus never did anything wrong. Yet He took everyone's punishment for sin—the punishment that we deserved—when He died on the cross.

2. Everyone sins. No one is "good enough" to deserve heaven. So Jesus became our substitute. He was perfect for us. Everyone needs the Savior, Jesus. He won the victory for us. We will go to heaven because of Jesus' goodness. The good things we may do happen because Jesus has changed our hearts so we can now live for Him.

3. God does not like the wrong things we do, but God always loves us. We are not perfect people, but God has perfect love. He calls us to repentance and wants to forgive us.

4. Nothing we do can make God love us more, and nothing we do will cause God to love us less. God is love.

5. God not only forgives our sins for Jesus' sake, but He also sends the Holy Spirit into our hearts, empowering us as He works through the Word of God to live joyfully for our Lord.

As you look at the illustration, ask the children to fill in the blanks—first with a name for God, then with their own name. Finally the children can draw a self-portrait in the blank shape.

---

## Yes or No?

Read the words. If you agree, write *Yes* on the line. If not, write *No*.

1. <u>Yes</u> Jesus died, taking the punishment for my sins.

2. <u>No</u> If I am really good, I will go to heaven.

3. <u>No</u> If I sin, God won't love me.

4. <u>Yes</u> God forgives me and always loves me.

5. <u>Yes</u> The Holy Spirit will help me obey God joyfully.

God, have mercy on me, a sinner.

" _____ , have mercy on _____ , a sinner."

**Words to Remember**
God, have mercy on me, a sinner.
Luke 18:13

10

## Discovery Point

All people are sinners and do not deserve God's love. But God is merciful. He calls us to repent and offers forgiveness and new life in Christ.

## The Lord's Prayer

Luke 11:1–10

## Objectives

That by the power of the Holy Spirit working through God's Word, the students will

- be assured that God listens to all prayers and answers them in the way He knows is best for us;
- praise God that He takes care of our physical and spiritual needs;
- grow in appreciation of the words the Lord taught us to pray.

## Day 3 Materials

- Telephone (*optional:* computer, fax, express mail envelope)
- Flannelgraph materials
- Blackline 23-B

## Day 4 Materials

- Jake and Jenna puppets
- Paper bags
- Noisy objects
- *Changes* Student Book

# Day

## INTRODUCE

Ask, **If I needed to give a message to someone who lived in** *(a state far away)*, **how could I get the information to her immediately?** Explain several communication possibilities such as a telephone, fax machine, computer e-mail, or express mail.

Continue, **Sometimes even these things can't help. Maybe the other person is out of town or isn't paying attention or just doesn't want to listen. There is someone, though, who is always ready to listen. Who is that?** (Jesus.) **You don't need a phone or fax machine, e-mail, or the post office to talk to Jesus. How do we talk to Him?** (In prayer.) **Remember, Jesus is always near, and Jesus will always hear! Let's learn what Jesus taught about prayer.**

## DEVELOP

Display flannelgraph materials showing Jesus and His disciples on a hillside and say, **Sometimes Jesus went off to a quiet place. There He would pray to His heavenly Father. One day His disciples asked Jesus, "Lord, teach us to pray." Jesus replied with the words we call the Lord's Prayer. This prayer taught the disciples special words to use when we talk to God. People around the world have been using these words for about 2,000 years!**

## RESPOND

Distribute copies of Blackline 23-B, which the children can cut apart and use in your discussion of the Lord's Prayer. Enlarge one copy of the blackline to use as a teaching aid.

(Symbol: a small child's hand in a father's large hand.) *Our Father who art in heaven.* **We all have a loving Father in God. He always wants what is best for us. He cares for us and guides us.**

(Symbol: children with raised arms.) *Hallowed be Thy name.* **God's name is holy and special. When we hallow God's name, we praise and worship Him. We want to use God's name in the best way.**

(Symbol: crown.) *Thy kingdom come.* **God's kingdom includes all who believe in Jesus, here on earth and in heaven. We pray that more people will hear God's Word and be brought to faith in Jesus and come into His kingdom.**

(Symbol: heart and world.) *Thy will be done on earth as it is in heaven.* **What do you think God wills or wants for the world? It is God's will to show His love to all people through our Savior, Jesus. It is God's will that we love Him and also show love to the people of the world. It is God's will that we share the Good News about Jesus with others.**

(Symbol: bread.) *Give us this day our daily bread.* **We are not asking just for bread, but for everything we need to live on earth.**

Martin Luther writes, "Daily bread includes everything that has to do with the support and needs of the body, such as food, drink, clothing, shoes, house, home, land, animals, money, goods, a devout husband or wife, devout children, devout workers, devout and faithful rulers, good government, good weather, peace, health, self-control, good reputation, good friends, faithful neighbors, and the like."

(Symbol: handshake.) *And forgive us our trespasses as we forgive those who trespass against us.* We are asking God to forgive us for the wrong we do. We are also telling God that we want His help so that we will forgive others who have hurt us.

(Symbol: mean face.) *And lead us not into temptation.* Temptations are things that encourage us to do wrong. We pray that God will lead us away from doing bad things. With His help we can say no to temptation. We ask God to help us follow where He leads us.

(Symbol: happy face.) *But deliver us from evil.* We ask God to protect us from all evil. God can protect us and keep us safe because God is stronger than sin, death, and the devil. This makes us happy.

(Symbol: a cheer "Hooray!") *For Thine is the kingdom and the power and the glory forever and ever. Amen.* These words are filled with praise and honor for our God. We know that someday God will take His children to be with Him in heaven forever.

# Worship Ideas

- Use a class concept map (web) to write the children's words to describe what a good father does. (Takes care of his children, gives them what they need, guides them in the right way, helps them in trouble, and always loves them.) **Earthly parents are not always good parents because they are sinners just like everyone else. Some parents are not as kind as others. Some parents may not even be around to see their children. But we all have a perfect parent, a perfect Father, in God. He will always love us and will always do what is best for us. He has made the perfect home for us in heaven and given us Jesus, who saved us. Someday our Father will take us to our heavenly home.** Show sensitivity to situations where a father may not be considered "good" or is absent. Hold up the Lord as the true Father and perfect example of fatherly love.

- Hand out wooden tongue depressors. Give directions for children to write their name on one side. Decorate the other side with paint, markers, glitter, or stickers. Put the dry sticks in a can. Pull out sticks to pair up prayer partners or to select small prayer groups.

- Sing songs about prayer from *Little Ones Sing Praise* (pp. 13–15).

# Bible Background

The Lord's Prayer is the model, or standard, for the disciples and for us. Before Jesus speaks it, though, He gives basic principles for authentic prayer. Let prayer be personal, private, and communal, but never for public display. Offer prayer sincerely, reverently, faithfully, but without pretense of senseless repetition. Our Father in heaven, Jesus assures His disciples, knows, understands, and hears the prayers of His children.

Hearing our prayers, our Father answers with His good gifts. He loves us with true fatherly devotion, sending His own Son to die for our forgiveness and life. Because of Jesus we have the confidence to approach the living God, assured of His mercy and goodness.

### Words to Remember

*Lord, teach us to pray. Luke 11:1*

- Considering the abilities of the children, you may choose to learn the Lord's Prayer. Some students in the class may already know the Lord's Prayer; others may be ready to learn it. Some children may have difficulty learning the entire prayer. Rather than reciting it individually, practice the prayer as a group. Learning the following actions may also be helpful.

**Our Father who art in heaven.** *(Hold up one hand as if reaching for your heavenly Father's hand.)*

**Hallowed be Thy name.** *(Hold both hands up to praise God's name.)*

**Thy kingdom come**. *(Extend arms out and around as if welcoming all people to know Jesus.)*

**Thy will be done on earth as it is in heaven.** *(Hands over heart, knowing that love is God's will.)*

**Give us this day our daily bread.** *(Reach palms out to receive blessings.)*

**And forgive us our trespasses as we forgive those who trespass against us.** *(Handshake.)*

**And lead us not into temptation.** *(Cross arms over chest as if God has helped us say no to temptation.)*

**But deliver us from evil**. *(Hands folded and touching face, in earnest prayer.)*

**For Thine is the kingdom and the power and the glory forever and ever. Amen.** *(Raise both arms in praise.)*

### Extending the Lesson

- Use a copy of Blackline 23-B to review the Lord's Prayer. Adhere self-stick magnetic strips on the back of each symbol. Place the symbols on a magnet board or cookie sheet. Mix them up and then let children put them in the correct sequence.

## Day

## INTRODUCE

Write the following words on colored paper: *Padre, Dad, Pop, Papa, Daddy, Pa.* Read the words to the children and ask, **Do you know how all these words are alike?** (They are all names for Father.) **What do we call God in the Lord's Prayer?** (Father.) **Why do we call Him Father?** (He loves us, takes care of us, and gives us what we need. He is a perfect Father.) **Why *can* we call Him Father?** (Because of Jesus, who has made us children of God by taking away our sins. You may want to refer to the explanation of the Second Article of the Apostles' Creed, which reviews what Christ has done for us to restore this relationship.) **Listen again to how Jesus taught His friends to talk to God, their Father.**

## DEVELOP

Invite the class to teach the Lord's Prayer to Jake and Jenna.
**CLASS:** Our Father who art in heaven.

### The Lord's Prayer

*(Luke 11:1–10)*

Father
name
come
will
Give
forgive
not
evil
power
glory

Our _____ who art in heaven,

Hallowed be Thy _____ ,

Thy kingdom _____ ,

Thy _____ be done on earth as it is in heaven.

_____ us this day our daily bread;

And _____ us our trespasses as we forgive those who trespass against us;

And lead us _____ into temptation,

But deliver us from _____ .

For Thine is the kingdom and the _____ and the _____ forever and ever. Amen.

11

**JENNA:** I like to call God "Father." I hardly ever see my earthly dad. Sometimes I need to talk to someone, but no one is there. So I remember that God loves me very much and will listen to me and help me.

**CLASS:** Hallowed be Thy name.

**JAKE:** I forgot what *hallowed* means.

**TEACHER:** Can anyone help Jake? (It means to make God's name holy, sacred, or very important to us.) We praise God's name in a special way.

**JENNA:** We want to use His name in the best way.

**CLASS:** Thy kingdom come.

**JENNA:** Now what is God's kingdom again?

**TEACHER:** *(to class)* Do you know? (God's kingdom includes everyone who believes in Jesus.) We pray to be in His kingdom and for the kingdom of believers to grow.

**CLASS:** Thy will be done on earth as it is in heaven.

**JAKE:** Oh, I remember what God's will is—that means what God wants. We pray for help to do what He wants and to live as His people.

**CLASS:** Give us this day our daily bread.

**JENNA:** And I remember that daily bread means everything we need.

**CLASS:** And forgive us our trespasses as we forgive those who trespass against us.

**JAKE:** When I say this part, I think about the wrong things I do. And

I think about how God forgives me because Jesus died on the cross for my sins.

**JENNA:** We can also think of people who have hurt us and ask that Jesus will help us forgive them too.

**CLASS:** And lead us not into temptation.

**JAKE:** Would God lead us into temptation?

**TEACHER:** *(wait for answers from class)* No, we're really praying that God leads us *away* from temptation and that He keeps us from wanting to do bad things. Only God can help us say no to doing what's wrong.

**CLASS:** But deliver us from evil.

**JENNA:** I know evil means "bad or dangerous things." But what does deliver mean?

**TEACHER:** We are asking God to guard and keep us, or protect us, from evil. God has power to deliver us from all evil, even from the evils of sin, death, and the devil.

**JENNA:** I like the last part of the prayer the best! It's like a big, loud cheer for God!

**JAKE:** Let's say it together!

**CLASS:** For Thine is the kingdom and the power and the glory forever and ever. Amen.

## R E S P O N D

In advance, gather objects such as bells, rocks, and metal spoons. When the objects are placed in separate paper bags, they must make distinct sounds when they are shaken. Say, **I have some mystery objects inside these bags. Listen carefully and see if you can identify what is inside them.** Allow children to respond, and then show the objects to confirm guesses.

Say, **You had to listen very carefully, didn't you? Listening is important. It is especially important to know that God listens to us when we pray. He cares when we feel sad or glad. He cares when we are worried, hurt, or afraid. He also loves to hear about our joys and good times too. God cares and listens because He loves us so much.**

**But God does more than just listen. What else does He do?** (He answers our prayers; He even gives us things we haven't asked for; He gave us His very best—His own Son to be our Savior.) **God knows what is best for us and when is the right time to help. God is a wonderful, loving Father!**

Continue with pages 11 and 12 of the *Changes* Student Book. Point out that four items on page 12 will need to be outlined with a circle *and* a square. (The things that bless us eternally are also important in our daily lives right now.)

---

### Now and Forever

Our Father in heaven gives us what we need. Put a ☐ around what we need to live now. Put a ◯ around what blesses us eternally.

**Words to Remember**
Lord, teach us to pray.
Luke 11:1

12

## WEEK 24-A

### Discovery Point

Sin leads us to be selfish and self-concerned. God forgives us for Jesus' sake and enables us to give generously from the heart.

### Zebedee's Sons and Jesus

Mark 10:35–45

### Objectives

That by the power of the Holy Spirit working through God's Word, the students will

- confess that sometimes they are selfish and self-centered and will ask for forgiveness;
- have confidence that they are forgiven by God for Jesus' sake and are empowered by Him to serve;
- follow Jesus' example by doing things for others in love, always to the glory of God.

### Day 1 Materials

- Jake and Jenna puppets
- Flannelgraph materials
- Blackline 24-A

### Day 2 Materials

- Colored paper
- *Changes* Student Book

# Day 1

## INTRODUCE

Use the Jake and Jenna puppets to introduce the lesson.

**JENNA:** Hey, Jake! Don't forget we're riding home with my mom today.

**JAKE:** Okay. But I get the front seat!

**JENNA:** *(angrily)* But it's *my* car, and *my* mom is driving!

**JAKE:** *(angrily)* But you sat in front last time!

*(Move the puppets apart to show anger and unresolved conflict.)*

**TEACHER:** *(to the class)* Have you ever heard arguments like this?

More than one person wants the biggest, or best, or first place. Jesus' disciples had that problem. Jesus taught them to think less about themselves and more about serving others. Let's listen to the story and see what happened.

## DEVELOP

Use flannelgraph figures of Jesus, James, John, and the other disciples to tell the Bible story.

Place the Jesus figure on the flannelgraph board and explain that Jesus had power to do great things. Add the group of disciples. **For a while Jesus' disciples thought He would be an earthly king. They did not understand that Jesus came to suffer and die for the sins of all people.** Move the group of disciples to the background. Place two figures, for James and John, outside of the group. **James and John were brothers. They were the sons of a man named Zebedee. James and John were disciples of Jesus. They watched Jesus make sick people better and blind people see. They heard Jesus preach about God's love to everyone.**

Move James next to Jesus. **One day James came to Jesus and said, "Teacher, we want You to do for us whatever we ask."**

Move John next to Jesus. **John asked, "When You are King in glory, let me sit on one side of Your throne and my brother at the other side." James and John wanted to be important. They wanted to be the greatest of the disciples.**

Move the group of disciples closer. **Jesus' other disciples listened to what James and John said. They became angry. "Why should James and John sit in places of honor? Who do they think they are! Do they think they are better than us? We are important too!"**

Point to the figure of Jesus. **Jesus was sad to see that His disciples still didn't understand. Perhaps everyone else wants to be best, be first, have the most, be on top, or be the leader, but Jesus wants us to be different. He says we become great by putting others first, thinking of them the most, helping them to be the best. Jesus said, "Do not try so hard to look important. Instead, try hard to help others." Then Jesus explained, "Even I did not come to earth to be served and honored. I came to serve others."**

# RESPOND

Help the students understand their own personal selfishness through these questions. Direct them to answer these questions silently in their hearts. **Do you want to be last in line? Do you offer to take the smallest treat? Are you happy when you have to wait for a turn?** Ask other questions appropriate for your class.

Continue, **Most of the time we want just the opposite, don't we? We are like James and John. We want to be first. We want the biggest and best for ourselves. We don't always think about the feelings of others when we are selfish. We like others to serve and honor us.**

**Through God's Word, the Holy Spirit helps us see our sin. He helps us be sorry for not serving others and for thinking only about ourselves. When we tell God we are sorry for our sin, what can we be certain of?** (He forgives us for Jesus' sake and gives us the desire to serve others. God also gives us opportunities to serve.)

Encourage children to observe servant behavior in each other. Distribute copies of Blackline 24-A to the children. They are to sign their names after the word *From*, color the design, and cut apart the notes. Today, whenever they see someone showing humility, courtesy, and service, they can give that person one of the notes. People receiving notes can write their names on the top line. At the end of the day, ask children to place all the exchanged notes on the classroom altar, not taking credit personally, but giving God the glory because it is He who changes us and enables us to live for Him.

## Serving with the Savior's Love

# Worship Ideas

- Sing this song to the tune of "Row, Row, Row Your Boat":

**Serve, serve, serve the Lord.**
**Serve Him every day.**
**Share His love with everyone.**
**Share in every way.**
**Love, love, love the Lord.**
**Love Him every day.**
**Share His love in all you do**
**Share in all you say.**

- Sing this helper song to the tune of "Alouette":

**Alleluia, singing alleluia.**
**Alleluia, singing allelu.**
**Is there something we can do?**
**We can help you, _____ and _____ .** (Two students' names.)
**_____ and _____, we can help.**
**We can help, _____ and _____ . Oh—**
**Alleluia, singing alleluia.**
**Alleluia, singing allelu.**

- Point out that James and John and the other disciples did not understand about Jesus being King until after His death and resurrection. Like many other people at the time, they thought Jesus would be an earthly king who would live in Jerusalem and drive out the Romans. Instead, Jesus is a heavenly King. He lives in our hearts and drives out sin, death, and the devil. Say the Lord's Prayer, asking children to stand and shout the phrase "Thy kingdom come" when they come to that part of the prayer. Explain that we are asking in this prayer that the church on earth will grow and that together with all believers we look forward to life in heaven. Sing songs of praise that refer to Jesus as King.

# Bible Background

This incident immediately follows an account of Jesus' predicting His death (Mark 10:32–34). Obviously failing to understand what Jesus had told them, James and John seek places of honor in His kingdom, a request in sharp contrast to Jesus' call for His followers to serve and not to be served.

Later, after Jesus' resurrection and the outpouring of the Holy Spirit, James, John, and the other disciples did understand. Faithful unto death, they received the crown of life.

## Words to Remember

*Serve one another in love. Galatians 5:13*

- Pantomime different serving actions (hold out one hand for sharing; walk in place for running an errand; stand still for waiting your turn; pretend to dust; kneel to pull weeds). Let the children guess.
- Sing the Bible verse to the tune of "The Farmer in the Dell":

**Serve one another in love.**
**Serve one another in love.**
**Galatians chapter five, thirteen.**
**Serve one another in love.**

- Toss a beanbag to one child, who must say the first word of the Bible verse. That person tosses the beanbag to another child, who will say the next word, and so on, until the verse is complete. Allow all to have a turn. Encourage children to speed up the pace as they learn the verse.

## Extending the Lesson

- Have children make "serving acrostics." Each child is to write his or her name vertically and then use these letters to begin words or phrases that describe ways to serve others.

  **M** akes friends
  **A** lways shares
  **R** eads to others
  **K** ind.

- Use a dictionary to discuss the meaning of *serve* and words for which it is the root word (such as *service, serving, servant*.)

# Day 2

## INTRODUCE

In advance, prepare a pair of yellow rubber gloves (or other bright gloves). Use tape to attach eyes and a mouth to give the gloves the look of a frowning face.

Hold up your gloved hands and say to the class, **I'd like to introduce you to these mad-looking guys. Let's call them "Pushy Hands."** Share examples of Pushy Hands' actions, such as pushing their way to the front of the line, wanting their own way, and shoving to get what they want. Use your hands to demonstrate these actions.

Hide your hands behind your back and bring them out again as you say, **Or perhaps these hands are actually "Proud Hands."** Use your hands to proudly pull out the lapels of your jacket and pat yourself on the back. Discuss how Proud Hands point to how important they think they are, thinking they are better than others, or wanting the first and best.

Direct everyone to look at their own hands and ask, **Have your hands ever been pushy or proud? Sometimes we want to be first. We like to feel important. We want to have the biggest and best for**

### Zebedee's Sons and Jesus

*(Mark 10:35–45)*

Zebedee's sons, James and John, were disciples of Jesus. One day they asked Jesus, "Please give us whatever we ask. Please let us sit in a place of honor beside Your throne in Your kingdom."

The other disciples heard what James and John asked the Lord. The other disciples became angry. "Do James and John think they are better than us? We are important too!"

Jesus felt sad when He saw His disciples arguing. Jesus said, "Do not try so hard to be important. Instead, try hard to serve others."

Then Jesus explained, "I did not come to earth to be served and honored. I came to serve others."

Why do we say that Jesus is the greatest Servant of all? What did Jesus do for others? Hint: Connect the dots around the words.

```
        · S ·
        · A ·
· S E R V A N T
        · I ·
        · O ·
        · R ·
```

13

ourselves. We do not think about other people's feelings. When we think and act this way, we sin. Jesus helps us when we are pushy and underhanded. He leads us to be sorry for our selfishness, and He forgives us. Jesus is so good to us.

**Jesus changes us. He gives us helping hands.** Pull the frown off each glove and turn it around to make a smiling face. Introduce "Helping Hands" as hands that share, are kind, and like to make other people happy. **As we review today's story, remember that James and John came to Jesus with pushy and proud hands and hearts. Jesus taught them to be humble and to help.**

## DEVELOP

In advance, in large letters, print the word *FIRST* on sheets of paper, one per child (minus one) in the class. The child who plays the part of Jesus should get a paper that says *LAST*.

Have the child playing Jesus stand on one side of the room with his paper behind his back. All the other children are to be in a group on the other side of the room. You will narrate the story. Choose two children to play James and John. Have them walk over and stand on either side of Jesus as you tell about the questions they asked. Have them wave their signs high.

Then focus on the other disciples and their anger and jealousy. Have them angrily wave their signs high as they show they want to be first and best.

Then have "Jesus" motion for them to sit quietly as he shows his paper. Explain the difference that Jesus makes. He came to serve, not be served. In His kingdom the greatest are those who are willing servants to others. Share how Jesus served all people through His suffering, death, and resurrection. In Jesus, we have forgiveness of sins, eternal life, and the power and love to serve others.

## RESPOND

Ask the students to imitate you, saying, **I want you to do what I do.** Have them copy various actions (stand up, place hands on hips, raise both arms and lower them, stomp both feet).

Say, **You imitated me very well. Imitate means "to do the same thing." Sometimes it's pretty easy to imitate. Other times it's hard. Listen to what God says to us in His Word, the Bible.** Read Ephesians 5:1–2. Ask, **Whom are we to imitate?** (God.) **How do we imitate Him?** (By living a life of love.) **Whom does the verse mention as living a life of love?** (Jesus.) **How did Jesus show His love for us and for all people?** (He suffered, died, and rose again for us.)

Continue, **It's hard to imitate God. In fact, we can't do it without His help. He gives us power to live a life of love.** Pray together that God would lead you to truly imitate Him in all you do. Then work together on the activity in the *Changes* Student Book, page 14.

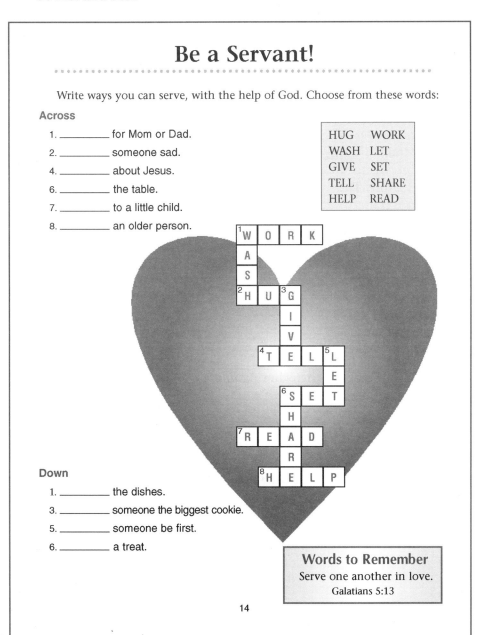

## Be a Servant!

Write ways you can serve, with the help of God. Choose from these words:

**Across**

1. _____ for Mom or Dad.
2. _____ someone sad.
4. _____ about Jesus.
6. _____ the table.
7. _____ to a little child.
8. _____ an older person.

| HUG | WORK |
|-----|------|
| WASH | LET |
| GIVE | SET |
| TELL | SHARE |
| HELP | READ |

**Down**

1. _____ the dishes.
3. _____ someone the biggest cookie.
5. _____ someone be first.
6. _____ a treat.

**Words to Remember**
Serve one another in love.
Galatians 5:13

14

## Discovery Point

Sin leads us to be selfish and self-concerned. God forgives us for Jesus' sake and enables us to give generously from the heart.

## The Widow's Offering

Mark 12:41–44

## Objectives

That by the power of the Holy Spirit working through God's Word, the students will

- know that Jesus calls them to repent of selfishness, as He leads them to have a generous heart through the power of the Holy Spirit and His Word;
- desire willingly and cheerfully to share God's blessings with others;
- plan ways to offer their love to God by giving Him gifts of time, praise, money, and talents.

## Day 3 Materials

- Penny, $1 bill
- Rhythm instruments
- Offering plate or basket
- Clock
- Hymnal
- Money
- Blackline 24-B

## Day 4 Materials

- Large and miniature candy bars
- Two $1 bills
- *Changes* Student Book
- Jake and Jenna puppets

# Day 3

# INTRODUCE

Show a penny and a dollar bill. **If I gave you a choice, would you rather have a penny or a dollar? Why? How would you use the money?**

Hold up the penny and dollar bill again and ask, **Which offering would make God happier? The amount is not important to God. What is important is the heart of the giver. God knows if someone is glad to give to Him. He knows if people are cheerful givers who want to help others and if they are unselfish in what they give. Listen to the story and see what Jesus said about two offerings.**

# DEVELOP

Say, **Today we will learn about a woman's offering and why it was so special to Jesus.** Provide loud rhythm instruments so all children can be involved in the sound effects. (Cymbals and tambourines work well.) Explain that whenever you point to the large group, they are all to play the instruments till you give the signal to stop. Say, **The noise stands for the large number of coins being placed in the offering.** One girl should be separated from the group. When you point to her she should make two soft sounds, hitting the triangle (or two soft rings with a small bell). This will be the symbol for the poor widow. Practice using cues at the appropriate time in the story.

**Jesus was teaching at the temple. He watched the people bringing their offerings.** (Group sound.) **Some rich people put much money into the jar.** (Group sound.) **Soon other people came into the temple. They walked up to the offering jar and put in money too.** (Group sound.)

**Then Jesus saw a poor lady coming to give her offering. She didn't have much money. She had only two little copper coins. But she put them both into the offering jar.** (Widow's sound.) **She was glad she could bring an offering to the Lord.**

**Jesus knew the lady's offering was all she had. He said, "This woman has given more than anyone else." The disciples were surprised to hear Jesus' words. They knew the woman had placed only two small coins into the offering jar.** (Widow's sound.) **They wondered what Jesus meant.**

**Jesus explained, "The other people gave only a little part of their money.** (Group sound.) **They have a lot of money left.** (Group sound.) **But this woman gave all her money to the Lord.** (Widow's sound.) **She doesn't have any money left."** (Silence.) **She trusted that God would take care of her.**

**God has given us so many things. All that we have belongs to Him. He even gave us His only Son, Jesus, to be our Savior. Jesus gave His whole life for us. Now we can give God our praise, our time, our money, our thanks, and most of all, our love.**

## RESPOND

Before class, bring a church offering plate or basket to your worship area. Place the following items inside the offering plate: a clock, Christian songbook or hymnal, and money.

Show the offering basket as you ask, **Can you tell me where you usually see this basket/plate? How do we use it?**

Show the money that is inside the offering basket. Say, **This is what we usually see inside the offering basket. We give our money to the Lord as an offering to show our love for God.**

Continue with, **I wonder why a clock is inside the basket?** Lead the discussion toward the gift of time. **The clock reminds us that we can give our time to Jesus. When we take time to go to church and Sunday school, read the Bible, or have family devotions, we are also offering our time.** Ask children to mention times when we take time to help others. Say, **Jesus helps us to give the gift of time for the good of others.**

Return attention to the basket/plate. **Why do you think a songbook would be inside the offering basket? Let's offer a song of praise to Jesus now.** Use the rhythm instruments and sing a praise song such as "We Love" (*LOSP*, p. 54, and on CD).

Review lesson concepts by using Blackline 24-B.

## Worship Ideas

- Give each child two pennies as a reminder of the widow woman in the Bible story. Pass around an "offering jar." Ask children to drop the pennies in the jar. As they do so, thank God for His many blessings and pray that He will bless the offerings they give to help other people come to know Jesus as their Savior.
- Pray the following prayer:
  **Thank You, God, for all Your gifts.**
  **Accept my gift to You.**
  **Use it for Your work on earth**
  **So others love You too. Amen.**

## Bible Background

Some see in this story merely a moral lesson: Jesus is satisfied with nothing less than total commitment. Indeed, He does desire absolute surrender and total trust in Him. However, such high-level sanctification must proceed from free forgiveness. Commitment is not something we can create; it is a response to God's forgiving love in Christ.

Jesus showed that the value of a gift is determined by the spirit in which it is given. All of us must feel humiliated by the widow's two coins. Only He who commended her, who gave Himself as the perfect sacrifice for all people, can and does forgive our miserly stewardship.

Who's Who?

I gave two small coins. I know God would take care of me.

We were rich. We gave money, but we had lots of money left.

I love all people. I died to take away sins.

I gladly give to Jesus. I know He will take care of me.

*Directions: Draw yourself in the blank box. Then draw a line from each riddle to the correct picture.*

**Blackline 24-B**

## Words to Remember

*God loves a cheerful giver. 2 Corinthians 9:7*

Have each child write the Bible "Words to Remember," using a block of paraffin on a large piece of white paper. Then have them read the words aloud as they paint a paint wash (paint diluted with water) over the page to make the words appear.

## Extending the Lesson

• At an activity center, place various coins in individual envelopes. The children can feel the envelopes and determine the coin, and then make a rubbing on the envelope to check if their determination is correct.

• Let the children clean pennies with water and one of the following: salt, baking soda, baking powder, or flour. Have them first predict which white powder will clean the best. You may want to provide plastic gloves to keep the mess to a minimum.

• Put a penny into each of five small containers. Fill each container with one of the following: oil, water, saltwater, sugar water, and vinegar. At the end of the week check and discuss what has happened.

• Invite people who are involved with the offerings at church (ushers, counters, treasurer) to visit the class and discuss how the money is used to spread the Gospel message and the love of God to other people in the world.

# Day

# INTRODUCE

Practice this scenario in advance with two children. Give the first child an oversized candy bar (like those sold at movie theaters or video stores) and give the other child a miniature inch-long candy bar.

Ask the children if they would give you some of their candy. The first child is to break off one-fourth of the large bar and give it to you. The second child should give you the entire miniature bar. Ask the class, **Who gave me more?** Listen to responses. Then point out that though the first person may have given you a large piece of candy, she still had more than that left for herself. The second person gave you all he had. There was nothing left for himself. **Perhaps he didn't give more candy, but he did give more kindness.** Point out that this relates to the story of the widow's offering. Jesus was looking at her heart, not at her gift.

## The Widow's Offering

*(Mark 12:41–44)*

Jesus was teaching at the temple. He sat down near the place where people placed their offering money. Jesus watched as many people gave their offerings to the Lord. He saw many rich people give large amounts of money to God.

Soon Jesus saw a woman enter the temple court. The woman's husband had died. She was very poor. Jesus watched the woman. She put two very small copper coins into the offering. Then she walked away.

Jesus said to His friends, "This poor widow has given more than all the other people." The disciples were surprised to hear Jesus' words. They had seen the two small coins and wondered what Jesus meant. Jesus explained, "The other people gave only a little part of their money. They have lots of money left. But this woman gave all her money to God. She trusts that God will take care of her."

Jesus gave the greatest gift of all. He gave Himself to die on the cross so that we have the gifts of forgiveness and eternal life. We give our offering gifts in thanks to Him for His great gifts to us.

15

## DEVELOP

Review the Bible story, inviting the children to repeat your actions throughout the story.

Say, **Jesus was teaching at the temple.** (Stand up.) **He sat down near the offering jar, where people brought their gifts of money to the temple and to God.** (Sit down.) **Jesus watched the people as they put their offering money into the jar.** (Pretend to put coins in a container.) **Some rich people were proud to give a lot of money.** (Stand proudly with your chest out and pretend to offer handfuls of money.)

**Then a poor widow** (bow your head humbly) **came and put in two** (hold up two fingers) **very small coins.** (Pretend to put coins in container.)

**Jesus called His disciples to Him.** (Beckon with your hands.) **Jesus said, "I tell you the truth, this poor widow** (point outward) **has given more than all the other people."** (Point to indicate the whole group.)

**The disciples wondered what Jesus meant.** (Scratch your head; look puzzled.) **Jesus explained, "The other people gave only a little part of their money. They have lots more money left. But she gave all her money to God."** (Open your arms wide.) **She trusted God completely to provide for her needs.** (Place hands over heart.)

### Offering Gifts of Thankfulness

*Follow the directions.*

1. Draw a happy face on the child.
2. Draw money in the small envelope.
3. Draw a line from the envelope to the offering basket.
4. Draw a line from the offering basket to the ways the money is used.

> **Words to Remember**
> God loves a cheerful giver.
> 2 Corinthians 9:7

16

## RESPOND

Use the Jake and Jenna puppets to continue the lesson. Jenna is busy picking up a dollar bill, setting it down, picking up another dollar bill, setting it down, and holding her head as if she doesn't know what to do.

**JAKE:** Hi, Jenna. You look very confused. What's the trouble?

**JENNA:** I have a big problem—I have too little money. I want to buy my mom a birthday present. I want to give a thank-You offering to Jesus. But if I give one dollar to Jesus, I'll only have one dollar for Mom's gift. I know my big brother is spending at least twice as much.

**JAKE:** Your problem isn't that you have too little money, Jenna. Your problem is that you don't understand gifts. Your mom doesn't care how much money you have or how much you spend. She is happy to know you love her.

**JENNA:** You are right, Jake. Mom always says that it's the thought that counts.

**JAKE:** It's the same with giving to Jesus. He knows our heart. He knows if we are being selfish or just giving leftovers. He is happy when we give out of thankfulness and love.

**JENNA:** You are right again, Jake. The Bible says that "God loves a cheerful giver!"

Continue by looking at the *Changes* Student Book together. Guide the class through page 16. Say, **What is missing on the boy?** (A smile.) **This boy is named David. He feels so happy. He is thinking about all the good gifts God has given to him. The boy is glad that God has given him parents, clothes, toys, a home, school, and church. Most of all, David is glad that God sent Jesus to be his Savior. When David thinks about all God has done for him, he feels very happy. He wants to tell God thank You. One way to say thanks to God is by giving an offering.** Have students draw a smiling face on the boy. Students can also draw money inside the envelope. During the discussion, they should draw a line from the envelope to the offering basket.

Take a few minutes to look at the church scene pictured. Help students understand where their offering money is spent. Salaries for church workers are paid by the offerings. Missionary supplies (Bibles, books, housing, etc.) are also supported through congregational donations. Offerings help pay for maintenance on the church and school property (heat, lights, telephone, repairs, etc.). **We support churches, schools, and missions because Jesus wants everyone in the world to know and believe in Him as Savior and Redeemer.** Tell the children to draw a line from the offering basket to the ways money is used in this church.

# UNIT 7
# Salvation

## Unit Overview

This unit of study and the accompanying Student Book are entitled *Salvation*. Explain that this is a big word that means about the same as a smaller word that starts with the same two letters—*save*. God's plan of *salvation* was to send Jesus to *save* us.

This unit takes us up to and through most of Holy Week. We see that Jesus cares about individuals—women and men, children and grown-ups. We see happy and sad times, as we remember that Jesus did all things for us and that God is with us in all things. Jesus teaches us to believe, to serve, to pray, and to give ourselves completely to Him, even unto death, for He died to save us.

Send home copies of the family letter and Bible verse list for Unit 7 as you begin. (See the Teacher Resource Book.) This will let parents know what their children will be learning during the next few weeks. At the end of the unit, let the children take home their *Salvation* Student Book. Encourage them to show their parents what they have learned. This is the seventh in a series of nine books that will cover the story of salvation through the Old and New Testaments. Also consider adding some of the following activities to your curriculum to make related connections between God's message of love and all that you do throughout the day.

## Worship Connections

Point out to the children that all the special words used in church might make it hard to understand what is going on. So make a special visit or field trip to the church to learn about some of the words that describe the building itself. **Church buildings often have many rooms for meetings, classes, and other things. But the special place where we go to worship God is called the *sanctuary*.** Go to the sanctuary and explain its three main parts, going from the back to the front. The *narthex* is the back area, where some of the "business" of the service is conducted (by ushers, greeters, offering collectors, etc.). Next is the *nave*, where the congregation sits in chairs or benches (pews), responding to God's Good News. The *chancel* is the area where the Word of God is spoken to the people.

Point to the area of the chancel where the Word of God is read at the *lectern*, explained from the *pulpit*, and is an essential part of the Sacrament of Baptism at the *font* (fountain) and at the *altar* (table) in the Sacrament of the Lord's Supper. (Depending on the ability of your class, you may also want to explain terms such as *candelabra, rail, choir loft, balcony*.)

Gather the children together and give each child a card on which you have printed one of the terms they have learned that day. You may want to say the word as you hand it to the child, to avoid confusion or embarrassment. At your signal, children are to walk and stand near the part of the sanctuary listed. Do this several times to review the terms.

Ask children to stand next to their favorite part of the sanctuary. Use a Polaroid camera to take a picture of each child in that area. Back in the classroom, use the pictures to review terms. Ask each child why he or she particularly likes that part of the sanctuary.

## Community Building

Have children be seated in an open area. Set a large number of inflated balloons in the center. Say, **Jesus came to earth to stomp out sin. These balloons can stand for the sins around us. Jesus used two things to destroy the power of sin—His death on the cross and His resurrection at Easter.** Tell the children that, at your signal, they are to use their two feet to stomp out the balloons. Anyone who chooses not to may stand on the sidelines and cheer on the others. After all balloons are popped, have children throw away the pieces. **This can remind us that Jesus got rid of our sin and its punishment. He has cleared our hearts and made us blameless and guiltless. In God's eyes we are pure and innocent because of Jesus.**

## Tools for Witness

Provide materials so children can trace around a cross pattern onto white contact paper. Then have them color the cross in various patterns and designs with multiethnic crayons (such as peach, beige, brown, black—available at most teachers stores). Then children may cut out their crosses, peel off the backing, and wear the cross stickers they have made. **The many skin colors shown on your crosses remind us that Jesus loves all people, of all colors, and He wants them all to be saved. When someone asks about the cross you are wearing, be sure to explain its special message.**

## Service Projects

Recognize the importance of a simple personal witness that children can share in their daily lives. But also recognize that they can have a far-reaching effect in spreading God's Good News. Try this idea: Plan a fund-raiser to raise money to buy an ad in the newspaper or a radio spot to tell people about the love of Jesus. Have it be a straightforward message of Jesus and salvation (not an ad for a church event).

## Reaching Every Individual

Role play is a good way to encourage children to verbalize what they know and believe. But some children are unsure of themselves or unsure of what to say. Using the figures on the Puppet People poster can be helpful, as children project their thoughts onto the puppets. (The puppet figures can be laminated for durability. You can attach a wooden craft stick to the bottom of each figure to use as a handle. Or consider attaching a section of a cardboard tube to the back so that the puppet figure can stand alone.) If you have a child that is hearing-impaired, be sure that the child has a clear view to see your lips and facial expressions. If a child has verbal difficulties, work as partners, allowing the child to pantomime your words.

## Social Studies

Briefly discuss what the land of Israel is like geographically so that children have an idea of the setting of the Holy Week stories. Use the Holy Land poster, perhaps cutting the pictures apart and matting them to add individual emphasis. Ask, **Do any of these pictures remind you of someplace you have been?** (Children might note a resemblance to areas of the Southwest. This comparison may help them visualize the settings.)

## Science

When you study plant life, include examples of plants indigenous to the land of Israel. Study olive trees and the importance olive oil has been to that region. Compare pictures of a variety of types of palm trees. Sample dates, pomegranates, and olives.

## Mathematics

One of the main reasons we use math frequently in our daily lives relates to money. Discuss how we can use our money to honor God and to serve others.

## Integrating the Faith
## Salvation

## Language Arts

Discuss the importance of names. (We don't like it when someone teases or misuses our name because it reflects on us personally. God even gave a commandment to protect His name.) Read aloud the statement of the thief on the cross in Luke 23:42. We don't know the man's name, but we can be certain that God does. Read the last line of "I Am Jesus' Little Lamb," stanza 1, which says that Jesus "even calls me by my name." Then sing the entire song. Also see Isaiah 43:1. Praise God that by faith in the complete forgiveness we have in Jesus, we are also known by the names "saint" and "Christian."

## Fine Arts

Note that the love of Jesus changes the ugliness of death on a cross into something beautiful that gives us salvation and eternal life. Give each child a pile of colored gratings (made earlier by rubbing crayons over a vegetable grater). Have children mix the colors together on a piece of waxed paper and move the gratings into the shape of a cross. One at a time, children may take their crosses to an adult assistant, who will place the waxed paper on top of several newspapers, place another sheet of waxed paper over the gratings, and cover this with more newspaper. Then the adult will use a warm to moderately hot iron on this "sandwich" to melt the crayons. When this has cooled, with the crayons holding the sheets of waxed paper together, children may trim the excess paper from their beautiful cross and hang it in a window.

## Technology

Use a paper shredder as an analogy when talking about salvation. Place a picture of a cross on the shredder's container. On several sheets of paper, either print the word *sin* in large letters or have the children write down sinful things people do. Run the papers through the shredder. Then say, **This reminds me that Jesus gets rid of the guilt and punishment of our sins. He changes us as by faith we are new people who live for Him.** Pick up and then drop some of the shreds back into the container. Say, **Jesus gives us *complete* salvation. He takes away our sin. It is gone!** Throw the shreds into the trash. Hold up the empty shredder container and say, **When God looks at us now, He sees no sin. Through Him we can now live lives of faith, obedience, kindness, and joy.**

# WEEK 25-A

## Discovery Point

Jesus calls all people, women and men, boys and girls, to repentance and faith in the salvation He offers.

## Jesus Visits Mary and Martha

Luke 10:38–42

## Objectives

That by the power of the Holy Spirit working through God's Word, the students will
- realize that God speaks to them in His Word, offering salvation in Christ;
- desire to learn more about God through His Word, putting Him first in their lives;
- know that they can hear God's Word and learn about Jesus in school or at home as well as in church.

## Day 1 Materials
- Colored paper

## Day 2 Materials
- Blackline 25-A
- Jake and Jenna puppets
- Toys or boxes
- *Salvation* Student Book

# Day 1

## INTRODUCE

Ask, **If you knew that Jesus was coming to visit your house later today, what would you do to get ready?** Listen to responses. **What would you plan to do once Jesus arrived?** After hearing their responses, say, **In today's Bible story, Jesus went to visit the home of two sisters named Mary and Martha. Listen carefully to see what the sisters did.**

## DEVELOP

As you tell the story in the following manner, stand and act like you're working when you speak of Martha, and sit quietly when you speak of Mary.

**Mary and Martha were so happy to have Jesus come to their home.**

**Martha swept the floor and shook the dust from the rugs, while Mary sat and listened.**

**Martha cleaned and cut the vegetables, while Mary sat and listened.**

**Martha set the table with plates and cups, while Mary sat and listened.**

**Martha mixed ingredients and baked the bread, while Mary sat and listened.**

**Martha stopped. She was angry. She said to Jesus, "I need help. I have worked and worked and worked, while Mary sat and listened."**

**Jesus said, "Martha, Martha, you have been busy with many things. But Mary has chosen the one thing needed."**

Ask children what that "one thing needed" is and why it is so important. Point out that cooking and cleaning, watching TV and playing games, eating lunch and washing your hands are things people do each day. There is nothing wrong with doing that. But none of those things last. Tomorrow comes, and you do them all over again. **The one thing we truly need, the one thing that lasts forever, is the love of Jesus. And because He "loved us to death" (His death on the cross), He has taken away our sin. He gives us life in heaven that will never end. Now that is something truly important and lasting!**

*Option:* To review the story read it from the Bible in Luke 10:38–42. Then read it from the Hear Me Read Big Book *Sit Down* (available from Concordia Publishing House). Note: If you purchase the classroom set, a Teachers Guide pamphlet with extra ideas and activities for teaching this story is included.

## R E S P O N D

Ask, **How did Martha try to serve Jesus?** (By cooking and cleaning.) **Was it wrong to cook and clean?** (No.) **Was it the wrong *time* to cook and clean? Why?** (Yes. God wants to be number 1 in our hearts—the first and most important thing in our lives.) **How did Mary serve Jesus?** (By listening to His words.) **How can we listen to Jesus today?** (We hear God's Word whenever the Bible is read or explained.) **Where can we hear God's words?** (In church; as you are doing right now in school; at home as Mary did.) **Can you tell me about times you and your family hear or tell about God and His Word in your own home?** Listen to responses.

Encourage the children to pray *for* their families and to also pray *with* their families. As a class plan and write together a prayer for families. Print their words on the chalkboard. Provide colored paper so children can copy the prayer and decorate it. Suggest that they place it on a family bulletin board or message center (refrigerator door) and then read it together at mealtime or prayer time. **Encourage your family to put God first, above all other things, in your home!**

*Note:* The blackline activity will not be used till Day 2.

---

**Directions:** *The beginnings and endings of these sentences do not make sense. Cut on the dotted lines to separate and split the sentences. Rearrange the pieces to retell the Bible story correctly.*

| | | | | | | | |
|---|---|---|---|---|---|---|---|
| getting the food ready. | Word] is needed." | Mary did not help. | how Jesus died to save us. | listened to Jesus. | "Do not be upset." | Mary and Martha. | "Tell Mary to help me." |
| 1. Jesus visited His friends | 2. Martha worked hard | 3. Mary sat and | 4. Martha was upset because | 5. Martha said to Jesus, | 6. Jesus told Martha, | 7. "Only one thing [God's | 8. God's Word tells us |

**Blackline 25–A**

---

## Worship Ideas

- In your worship time, focus on the First Commandment and its explanation from the catechism. (See the Teacher Resource Book.) This is God's will for us—that He is the main priority in our lives, now and eternally. Explain that the "other gods" in our lives are anything that becomes more important to us than God Himself. Too often one of those "other gods" is our own sinful self—seeing what we want for ourselves as most important, the first priority, in our lives. We need God's forgiveness. We need God's help to live as His people.

- Sing "Jesus, Name Above All Names" (*All God's People Sing* 145, available from Concordia Publishing House). Emphasize the first line: *Jesus, name above all names.* This reminds us that Jesus wants to be first in our lives. Read Acts 4:12 aloud and find out why Jesus is so important. (He is the only One who can bring us salvation.) Listen to the song again and make a list of the many different names for Jesus. **Whatever name we use, we know that Jesus has saved us from sin, death, and the devil. He has won for us eternal life!**

## Bible Background

The Gospel of Luke includes a major "travel narrative" (9:51–19:27), an extensive report on the final part of Jesus' public ministry before His arrival in Jerusalem to suffer and die for us. During their travels, Jesus and the disciples were often guests in the home of people who believed His message and supported His mission. On one occasion they stayed in Bethany, where Martha and Mary welcomed the Lord with genuine hospitality. (For a second example of Mary and Martha's love and gratitude toward Jesus, see John 12:1–8.)

In the Luke account Jesus directs His followers—in the midst of numerous daily obligations—to the one critical, urgent need: to hear His Word. There Jesus offers His words of life and forgiveness. As Peter stated to Jesus in John 6:68–69, "Lord, to whom shall we go? You have the words of eternal life. We believe and know that You are the Holy One of God."

## WEEK 25-A

### Words to Remember

*Let the word of Christ dwell in you richly.*
Colossians 3:16

- At the beginning and closing of each school day this week say these Bible words to the children as a blessing. Explain that the word *dwell* means to "live" in you. Point out that the word *richly* is not talking about money; it's like saying that you want God's Word to overflow in your heart. Say that this is your prayer for the children, that Jesus would live in their hearts abundantly.

- Hebrews 4:12 says, "The word of God is living and active." 1 Thessalonians 2:13 says, "The word of God … is at work in you who believe." God's Word is not just something told thousands of years ago. It has power today to change hearts and lives. It is God the Holy Spirit working through the Word who brings us to repentance and faith. The Word is the means through which the Holy Spirit works; that is why we call God's Word a means of grace. (You may want to point out that the Sacraments of Baptism and the Lord's Supper are also means of grace. The Sacraments are not things we do; the Holy Spirit is at work through them, giving, building, and strengthening our faith in Christ Jesus. The Sacraments are means of grace because they contain God's Word.)

### Extending the Lesson

- Have the children help you prepare a meal similar to what Martha might have prepared for Jesus. Set out grapes and cubed pomegranate; bake bread and serve it with cheese or honey; mix a salad with olive oil dressing.

- Point out that in Bible times they had no electricity for vacuum cleaners and no brooms like the ones they have at home. When Martha cleaned the house, she probably used a broom made by her brother. Set out materials so children can make their own little hand brooms from bunches of straw (available at craft stores). Use string to tie the straw to a stick.

## INTRODUCE

On the chalkboard draw three long rectangles. Print "To Do" at the top of each. Say, **Let's make a Kid's "To Do" list. What are things you do each day?** List their responses. (Eat, play, watch TV, go to school, etc.) In the second rectangle print Martha's "To Do" list on the day Jesus visited. (Cook, clean, set the table, etc.) Change the shape of the third rectangle, making it a short box. Say, **Mary's "To Do" list that day was very short. There was only one thing on it. Jesus called it the one thing needed. What is that?** (Hearing God's Word.) Read aloud John 3:16, pointing out that this is the one thing we need to hear above all things—that Jesus is our Savior, who gives eternal life. Draw arrows from the third list to the top of the two other lists to indicate that Jesus wants this to be at the top of our lists too.

### Jesus Visits Mary and Martha
*(Luke 10:38–42)*

One day Jesus came to see His friends Mary and Martha. The sisters were very happy to see Jesus. Martha worked hard, getting everything clean and ready. She was fixing a good dinner for Jesus to eat. But Mary did not help.

Mary sat down beside Jesus so that she could listen to His words. Martha became upset. She said to Jesus, "Tell Mary to help me!"

"Martha, Martha," Jesus said, "do not worry and be upset. I want Mary to listen to My words. I want you to listen too. There is one thing that is most important. The one thing needed is God's message of love and salvation."

We can hear Jesus speak to us, too, in God's Word. We can hear God's Word when we worship in church. We can hear God's Word like you are doing right now in school. And just like Mary, you can hear God's Word in your own home. When do you talk about Jesus in your home?

1

## D E V E L O P

Review the Bible story with a matching game. In advance, prepare one copy of Blackline 25-A. Cut the sentences and phrases apart on the lines. Mix up the phrases. Give a half sentence to each of the children. Give them a signal (such as a bell tone) at which time they move around the room, looking for the other half of their sentence. Give a signal to stop and have the partners stand or sit together. Children who do not have a word strip are to attach themselves to other partners and become the readers for that group. Call off numbers and have the sentences read in order to retell the story. Give children copies of Blackline 25-A, which they can later cut out, mix up, and put together like a puzzle.

*Option:* Learn a little more about Mary and Martha's family. Find their town of Bethany on a map. Note that it was close to Jerusalem, where Jesus was headed, knowing it was time for Him to die on the cross. Point out that they lived with their brother Lazarus, who died but was brought back to life by Jesus—to the great joy of the sisters. You may also note that the family may have been wealthy, considering that Mary anointed Jesus with an oil that cost as much as a year's wages.

## R E S P O N D

Use the Jenna and Jake puppets to introduce a concept. Have Jenna move boxes or pick up toys as you bring out Jake.

**JAKE:** Jenna, are you going to church with us? My family's in the car out front, ready to go.

**JENNA:** I'm not going to church. I have to clean my room, otherwise I can't go out to play this afternoon. It's going to be a busy morning for me.

**JAKE:** Jenna, Jenna. You are just like Martha. She was too busy cleaning to listen to Jesus.

**JENNA:** This is different. I don't want to clean. But my mom says I have to.

**JAKE:** No, it is not different. You are doing this because you want to play outside this afternoon. What is most important to you? Is *playing* the one thing you need the most?

**JENNA:** Wow! I never thought of it that way. I do want Jesus to come first, above other things.

**JAKE:** I'll tell you what. You come with us. Afterward, I'll help you clean your room. And then we can play outside together this afternoon.

**JENNA:** Jake, you are a good friend. I'm going to go to church with you. But church isn't the only place to hear God's Word. You just shared it with me right here!

Use the new Student Book *Salvation* (page 2) to reinforce the concept that we can hear God's Word in many places and situations. Explain that salvation is God's plan to save us through Jesus' death and resurrection. Jesus saves us by taking away our sins, giving us new lives as children of God, and preparing a place for us in heaven. **This book will tell us about salvation in Christ Jesus, the one thing that we truly need above everything else!**

---

### God's Word Comes to Me

We can hear God's Word in many places. Look at the pictures. Then write **home, church,** or **school** to tell where God's Word is being heard.

home

school

school

church

home

church

### Words to Remember

Let the word of Christ dwell in you richly.

Colossians 3:16

## Discovery Point

Jesus calls all people, women and men, boys and girls, to repentance and faith in the salvation He offers.

## Jesus Blesses the Children

Mark 10:13–16

## Objectives

That by the power of the Holy Spirit working through God's Word, the students will
- feel confident joy in knowing Jesus loves them at all times;
- know that the Savior Jesus welcomes all children to Himself, forgiving their sins and blessing them;
- praise and thank Jesus for His love.

## Day 3 Materials

- Jake puppet

## Day 4 Materials

- Blackline 25-B
- Bright gloves
- *Salvation* Student Book
- Polaroid camera (optional)

## INTRODUCE

Use the Jake puppet to introduce the lesson. Bring him out slowly, with his head hanging down.

**TEACHER:** Jake, you sure don't look very happy. What's wrong?

**JAKE:** I'm either too little or too big.

**TEACHER:** What do you mean?

**JAKE:** Well, my brother just got his driver's license. Dad lets him drive everywhere. I'm still too little for that. But at the same time I'm too big.

**TEACHER:** You're too big for the car?

**JAKE:** No, I'm too big for some of my favorite clothes. Mom packed up my favorite Mongo Congo sweatshirt and my favorite Hi-Speed tennis shoes and gave them away because I'm too big to wear them anymore.

**TEACHER:** *(thinking)* Hmmmmm. Too little and too big. I know one thing where you are just the right size—always! You are just the right size for Jesus.

**JAKE:** *(doubtfully)* I am?

**TEACHER:** You are!

**JAKE:** *(hopefully)* I am?

**TEACHER:** You are. You are inright, outright, upright, downright, just right for Jesus. Because of Jesus, God has forgiven your sins and made you His child. You can always be sure He loves you.

**JAKE:** *(happily)* I can be sure! I am just right for Jesus.

*Option:* Read 1 John 3:1 and sing "Happy All the Time" (*LOSP*, p. 59, and on CD).

## DEVELOP

Today's Bible story reminds us of Jesus' great love for children. Role-play the story by dividing the children into three groups—parents, children, and disciples. Plan to play the part of Jesus as you narrate the story and direct the movement of the groups. Use page 3 of the *Salvation* Student Book as your script for telling the story. Then review the story using the following action poem.

**Many people crowded near.** *(Scrunch up as if crowded.)*
**Jesus spoke so they could hear.** *(Cup hand behind ear.)*
**Suddenly, they heard a noise.** *(Look startled.)*
**Here came parents, girls, and boys,** *(Hand above eyes to look.)*
**Looking to see Christ, their friend.** *(Wave.)*
**But His helpers said, "Dead end!** *(Hands up to stop.)*
**Stop! He's busy. Go away!** *(Scold while shaking index finger.)*
**Try again some other day."** *(Shoo away with both hands.)*

**Jesus shouted, "Wait! Don't go!** *(Hand raised high.)*
**I love children, too, you know.** *(Hands over heart.)*
**Bring them here for Me to bless.** *(Beckoning, welcoming motion.)*
**May God bring you happiness."** *(Repeat, touching the heads of children.)*

Adapted from *Fingers Tell the Story*, © 1989 CPH.

## RESPOND

Continue, **The disciples hurt others by the unkind words they said. When have you been hurt by what someone said?** Let children share. **When have you hurt someone by words you said?** After several scenarios have been related, say, **Jesus loves us even when others don't. And when we are unkind to others, He calls us to repent. He wants to forgive us. He wants to help us change and be more loving like He is.** Help children understand that while Jesus does not like the wrong things we do, He always keeps on loving us. He wants to forgive us and help us grow in faith and in our faith life. Jesus' love will never end. Have each person give themselves a hug as a reminder that the love of Jesus surrounds them. (Note: The blackline activity will be used on Day 4.)

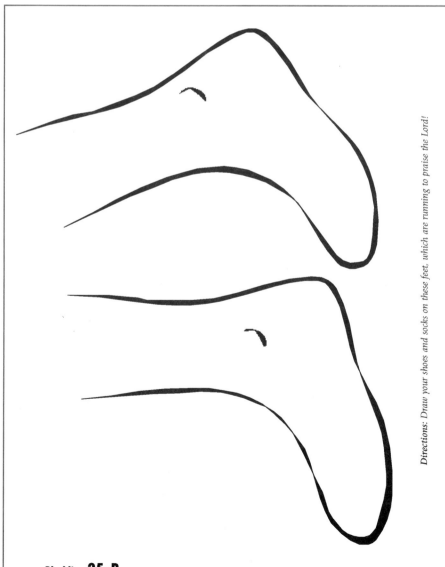

*Directions: Draw your shoes and socks on these feet, which are running to praise the Lord!*

## Worship Ideas

Children love to be active. Praise God with your whole self. Read Isaiah 40:31 as the children act out the movements (soar with arms, run and walk in place). Act out these praise poems and close with prayer.

**I will stand and raise each arm.**
**Jesus keeps me from all harm.**

**Then I think I'll wink and say,**
**"Jesus helps me when I play."**

**I will shout and say, "Hooray!"**
**Jesus loves me every day.**

**I will hop with dancing feet.**
**Jesus' love is really neat.**

**Now it's time to sit again,**
**Fold our hands and pray to Him.**

## Bible Background

During Jesus' public ministry He preached the Good News of salvation and taught God's Word. He healed the sick, cast out demons, and demonstrated His divine power. Jesus even revealed His glory to three followers when He was transfigured on a mountain. Such an important person, the disciples reasoned, should be shielded from the frolic and fracas of young boys and girls.

But Jesus has a different view. Children belong to God. Children are a model illustration of trust in the Father's love. God comes into our lives not by our preparations, knowledge, or effort, but through His tender mercy. As the Holy Spirit comes to us in Baptism and God's Word, Jesus calls, embraces, and welcomes us into His eternal kingdom. We are His children, whatever age we may be!

## Words to Remember

[Jesus said,] "Let the little children come to Me." Mark 10:14

Personalize these words by walking around the room, placing your hand on a child's head. Say the Bible verse, inserting the child's name in place of the words *the little children*. Continue in this manner with each child.

## Extending the Lesson

- Have students demonstrate ways the children may have come to Jesus. For example, some may have come skipping, running, hopping, and even crawling (infants).
- Sing songs that refer to children such as "Child of God" (*LOSP*, p. 98) and "Jesus Loves the Little Children" (*LOSP*, p. 94, and on CD).
- Discuss what life must have been like for children in Bible times. Point out that there was no TV, no computer games, no baseball. **Children probably made up their own games and made their own toys.** Provide natural materials and suggest that children invent ways to use them in a game or to make a toy (such as acorns used as markers in a throwing contest, rags wrapped to make a ball, or leather scraps to make a doll). Point out that Israel has a Mediterranean climate that would be warm and sunny much of the year like Southern California, so children probably played outdoors a lot. Choose a game to play outdoors that involves no playground equipment.

# Day

## INTRODUCE

Prepare a bulletin board with the title "We Run to Jesus, Our Friend." Place a picture of Jesus at the center. Distribute copies of Blackline 25-B. Children may draw and color shoes on the feet, print their first name on one and last name on the other, and cut them out. Praise God with your feet by having children run up to the bulletin board as you call individual names. They will place their paper feet on the board as if running to Jesus from all directions. Then sing the action song "Say to the Lord, I Love You" (*LOSP*, p. 18, and on CD).

## DEVELOP

Say, **We just used our feet to praise God. Now I'm going to use my hands to retell the Bible story, because hands play an important part in it.** Place yellow rubber gloves or some other type of bright gloves on your hands to focus attention on them.

## Jesus Blesses the Children

### (Mark 10:13–16)

One day some grown-ups heard that Jesus was teaching nearby. "Let's take our children to see Jesus. We want them to hear Him talk about God's love. We know Jesus loves children."

Some parents carried their little children. Other children skipped alongside the grown-ups on their way to see Jesus. They were excited and happy!

Soon they saw a large crowd of people listening to Jesus. When Jesus' disciples heard the children and saw them coming, they said, "Stop! Don't bother Jesus now. He is too busy. He does not have time to talk to children."

The parents and children were sad. They turned to go away. But Jesus said, "Wait! Let the children come to Me. Don't send them away."

The disciples stepped back. Jesus smiled as some parents brought their little ones so Jesus could hold them in His lap. The other children ran through the crowd to be close to Jesus. "I love each one of you," said Jesus. "You are important to Me." Then Jesus put His hand on each child's head and blessed them.

Jesus loves all people. He loves babies and children and teenagers and moms and dads and old people and all other kinds of people. Jesus loves you!

3

Tell about parents bringing their children to see Jesus. Clap your hands as you talk about how excited the children must have been.

When you talk about the disciples rudely stopping the children and sending them away, hold your hands up as if stopping traffic.

As you talk about how disappointed the children and their parents must have been, pretend to be wiping tears from your eyes.

Wave as if calling someone to come as you tell about Jesus asking them to bring the children.

Stretch your hands out in a welcoming gesture as you emphasize that Jesus loves people of all ages, and that children are very special to Him. He talked of the importance of having trusting faith like a child.

Shake hands with each child and touch their heads as you point out that the Bible tells us that Jesus lifted up the children and held them. He put His hands on them and blessed them.

Then stand with your hands stretched out on both sides and say, **Jesus loves each of us so much, He was willing to die for us on the cross to take away our sins. He did this because He wants us to live with Him as God's children in heaven.**

## RESPOND

Say, **The disciples' actions seemed to indicate that they didn't think children were part of the church. Jesus says you are!**

In the Apostles' Creed we say, "I believe in the Holy Spirit, the holy Christian church, the communion of saints, the forgiveness of sins, the resurrection of the body, and the life everlasting." These words are for you too. You are part of the holy Christian church because the Holy Spirit has brought you to faith. The church is not just a building; it is people of all ages, times, and nations who believe in Jesus. Sing "We Are the Church" (*LOSP*, p. 106).

Use pages 3 and 4 in the *Salvation* Student Book to continue to emphasize the welcoming love of Jesus. On page 4 the children are to draw a picture of themselves going to Jesus' open arms. They may also add pictures of family and friends. An option that would add an extra element of celebration and joy to the activity would be to take an instant-developing Polaroid picture of each child. (Have them stand sideways and stretch out arms as if running to Jesus.) Children may tape their photos to the page instead of drawing a picture. They can also trim off excess background from the picture if they wish and color in a background of trees and sky.

---

### Good News!

What good news! Jesus loves you! In this picture draw yourself running to see Jesus. He blesses you each day.

### Words to Remember

Follow the correct path and write the letters on the blanks to complete the Bible verse.

[Jesus said,] "Let the little children

C O M E   T O   M E ."

Mark 10:14

## WEEK 26-A

### Discovery Point

Rejoice! Celebrate the salvation we have through Jesus.

### Palm Sunday

Matthew 21:1–11

### Objectives

That by the power of the Holy Spirit working through God's Word, the students will

- know that Jesus was ready to die on the cross to take the punishment of their sins and the sins of all people;
- recognize that Jesus is the King over all, for He is true God;
- thank and praise Jesus in song and prayer for His great love.

### Day 1 Materials

- Green paper
- Tape
- Jake and Jenna puppets
- Blackline 26-A

### Day 2 Materials

- Flannelgraph materials
- Plain folded napkin
- Felt-tipped marking pen
- *Salvation* Student Book
- Holy Week poster

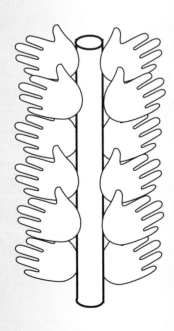

## INTRODUCE

Build anticipation and excitement for today's story. Tell the children that the people of Jerusalem had heard that Jesus was coming to their city. They wanted to welcome Him. They cut down palm branches to wave like flags. The people did this to prepare and get ready for Jesus' coming. **We are going to get ready for this Bible story. We will prepare our own palm branches.**

Have children roll green paper lengthwise to make a tube. Seal the tube edges with tape. Then they are to trace around their hands to make several hand prints. Cut these out with a scissors and tape them to the left and right sides of the paper tube. (See illustration.) Indicate times during the story and song when children are to wave these in celebration.

## DEVELOP

You may want to move desks together so that you can have a praise parade through the center of your room. Gather the children and say, **We're going to imagine what it was like on that special day when Jesus came to Jerusalem. Our classroom has a wall around it. Jerusalem had a wall around the whole city! To get in and out of our classroom, we open and shut the door. To get in and out of Jerusalem, they lifted and lowered a large gate.**

March a short distance, waving the palm branches. Stop and say, **Jesus usually *walked* from town to town. But on this day He rode on a donkey. A king who fights would ride a horse or chariot. A peaceful king would ride a slow and gentle donkey. Jesus is the King of Glory. He is the Prince of Peace.**

March a short distance, waving the palm branches. Stop and say, **The people placed their coats and robes on the ground before Jesus. It was their way of saying that Jesus was very special and important to them. They shouted "Hosanna," a cheering word that means "save us." The people did not know it yet, but that is exactly why Jesus was coming to Jerusalem—to die on the cross to save us from our sins. This was a special day for the people of Jerusalem. It is also a special day for you and me!**

Continue your praise parade, waving palms as you sing "Ho-Ho-Ho-Hosanna" (see the Supplemental Activities section in the Teacher Resource Book) or "The King of Glory" (*LOSP*, p. 77).

## RESPOND

Use the Jenna and Jake puppets to reinforce the concepts of the Bible story (and to help the children calm down after their celebration). Raise the puppet that is supposed to be speaking or place it in front of your face.

**TEACHER:** Why did the people of Jerusalem celebrate?

**JENNA:** I know! I know!

**JAKE:** I can tell you!

**JENNA:** They wanted to see Jesus. They knew He could make sick people well again.

**JAKE:** They wanted to see Jesus. They knew He had power to keep people safe in bad storms.

**JENNA:** They wanted to see Jesus. They knew He loved them and was kind.

**JAKE:** They wanted to see Jesus. They knew He spoke God's Word and truth.

**JENNA:** They wanted to make Jesus their King.

**JAKE:** They didn't know that Jesus was already the King of kings, the King of Glory!

**JENNA:** We can't see Jesus like the people of long ago, but we can praise Him as our King of Glory.

**JAKE:** We know we will see Jesus one day. He will come again, as the King of Glory, to take us to heaven! What a celebration that will be!

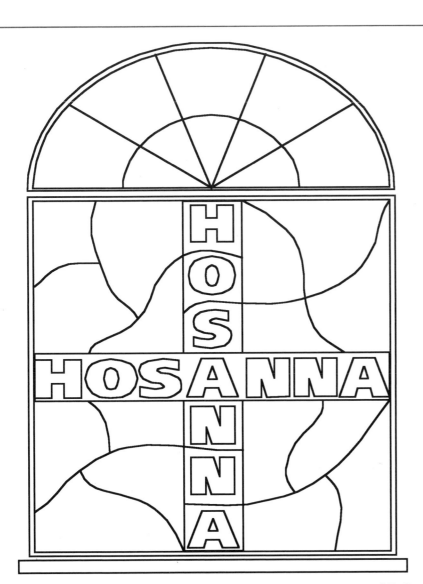

**Blackline 26-A**

## Worship Ideas

- The songbook and CD *Songs Kids Love to Sing 2* (available from Concordia Publishing House) have several songs about Jesus as King. Sing or listen to these joyful songs: "Kids of the Kingdom" (p. 38), "Oh, He's King of Kings" (p. 43), and "The King's Kids Are Prayin' " (p. 54).

- Sing "Hosanna! Hosanna!" (*LOSP*, p. 94, and on CD). Have the children stand whenever they sing the double Hosanna and be seated for the other words.

- There are several versions of hymnal liturgy that include the *Sanctus*, based on the Hosannas sung on Palm Sunday. Listen to or learn the song so that children can recognize it in church worship services and join in singing it.

- Add to the celebration this week by decorating your classroom. Distribute copies of Blackline 26-A. Let children color the stained-glass window pictures and display them in your room (perhaps on the windows). Suggest that children use a bright color such as yellow or orange to color the word hosanna because it is a cheering word. Point out that placing this word on the cross reminds us of two things: Jesus came on Palm Sunday, knowing He would soon die on the cross to save us; we can celebrate the cross, knowing Jesus arose on Easter!

## Bible Background

When nearing Jerusalem it was not unusual for pilgrims going to the festivals to break out into songs. (People sang Psalms 111–118, the Great Hallel or Hallelujah psalms.) Many people on Palm Sunday shouted the familiar "Hosanna," which means "save now." With these words they acknowledged Jesus as the true Messiah, coming into His kingdom.

This was not a triumphal entry in a splendid chariot with horses. Jesus rode on a lowly colt to show peace and mercy. He humbled Himself for us (Philippians 2:8–11). Jesus was about to complete His action to save the people—not as a leader of a mighty army that would overthrow the Romans, but by a cruel death on a cross. Now we, too, sing "Hosanna" to the One who also is our Savior!

# Day 2

## WEEK 26-A

### Words to Remember

*Blessed is He who comes in the name of the Lord! Hosanna in the highest! Matthew 21:9*

- Compare the second sentence of the Bible verse to the words of the angels at Christmas—"Glory to God in the highest" (Luke 2:14). Both are songs of praise. Christmas was the beginning of Jesus' mission on earth. Palm Sunday approaches the completion of Christ's mission for He knew He would die that week on the cross to redeem us.
- Practice the Bible words as a chant. Keep a steady beat, adding claps or rhythm sticks. Accent the boldfaced syllables (and note the extra syllable in the word *highest*).
  **Bless**-ed is **He**
  **Bless**-ed is **He** who **comes**
  **Bless**-ed is **He** who **comes** in the **name**
  **Bless**-ed is **He** who **comes** in the **name** of the **Lord!**
  Ho-**san**-na **in** the **hi**-igh-**est!**

### Extending the Lesson

- Learn about the differences between a donkey and a horse. Compare the size, shape, and color. Display books with pictures of each. **Why do you think a warring king would ride a horse and a peaceful king would ride a donkey?**
- Create a large praise parade mural. Use an overhead projector to enlarge a picture of Jesus riding a donkey on Palm Sunday. (Trace the picture of Jesus in the *Salvation* Student Book onto a clear plastic transparency. Use the overhead to enlarge the image, projecting it onto mural paper attached to a wall. Trace the projected image onto the paper with pencil.) Let children add to and color the mural. Attach to the mural the palm branches they made on Day 1.
- Ask your librarian to help you find books that show pictures of a variety of types of palm trees. Display these pictures in a learning center. Talk about foods that grow on some palm trees (coconuts, dates).

## INTRODUCE

Draw an eye on the board and ask the children what things they would have seen on that Palm Sunday when Jesus rode into Jerusalem. (Crowds of people, palm branches, coats on the path.) Draw an ear and ask what they would have heard. (Songs, shouts of hosanna, donkey hooves.) Draw a hand and ask what they might have touched. (Palm branches, which are sticky and can be heavy; the coarse bark of the palm tree.) Draw a heart and ask what they would have felt inside. (Joy, excitement.) Read aloud Psalm 100, a short psalm of celebration and praise.

## DEVELOP

Use flannelgraph figures (Teacher Kit) to retell the Bible story. As you tell the story include sound effects. Divide the class into four groups, giving each group a sound to make at the point in the story

### Palm Sunday
*(Matthew 21:1–11)*

Jesus and His disciples were on their way to the big city of Jerusalem. A large crowd of people followed them.

Jesus told two of His disciples, "Go into the little village nearby. You will find a donkey there. Untie it and bring it to Me. If a man asks why you are taking the donkey, tell him that I need it."

The disciples did just as Jesus said. The owner of the donkey was glad to help Jesus.

Jesus got on the donkey and began to ride into Jerusalem. It was a great day! Many people came from the city to welcome Jesus. Some people waved palm branches to celebrate. Others put their coats down on the road to make a soft path for Jesus.

Some people ran ahead. Some walked behind. The way was lined with people singing and shouting "Hosanna!" They said, "Blessed is He who comes in the name of the Lord! Hosanna in the highest!"

When Jesus got to Jerusalem, the whole city was wondering what the celebration was all about. Some people asked, "Who is this man?"

The crowd answered, "This is Jesus. He has come to save us. Hosanna!" We can sing praises to Jesus, the King of kings. He is our Friend and Savior too.

5

when you signal them. One group will make the sound of donkey hooves (clapping hands against thighs). Another group makes the sound of waving palm branches (whisper "swish-swish" or swish open hands against one another). The third group can be grown-ups, clapping their hands to honor Jesus as He passes by. The fourth group can be children, shouting "Hosanna!"

Point out that Palm Sunday was a happy day and also a dangerous day. The enemies of Jesus were upset. They said, "Look how the whole world has gone after Him!" (John 12:19). They would soon plan Jesus' arrest and death. **But Jesus already knew of the danger. He didn't run away. He didn't try to hide. He didn't even try to defend Himself. He wanted to die on the cross because He knew that was the only way He could save us. Jesus was punished for our sins. Jesus was willing to do this to take away our sins so that we are now forgiven children of God who will live with Him in heaven!**

Demonstrate these concepts with a simple visual that the children can try after your discussion. Hold up a plain square paper napkin and a dark-colored felt-tipped marking pen. Say, **This reminds me of what our sins do to our lives.** Press the marker near the folded corner of the napkin. Hold the pen down long enough so that the ink bleeds through all the layers. (Be sure to pro-

tect your table.) Say, **Sin soaks through our whole lives and messes things up. What would happen if I tried to wash out this spot?** (The napkin would be ruined.) **We can't do anything to get rid of the stain of our sins. Only Jesus can help us. He does this because He loves us.** (At the folded corner of the napkin cut out an *L* shape.) **I cut out the letter *L* to remind us of the *love* Jesus has for us.** Open the *L* shape to reveal a cross. **Jesus showed His great love for us by dying on the cross. He took our sins on Himself and gives us salvation and eternal life!**

Turn to pages 5 and 6 in the *Salvation* Student Book. On page 6 ask the children to connect the blue dots to make the shape of a crown. **On Palm Sunday, many people hoped Jesus was an earthly King who would fight their enemies and give them the food and things they wanted.** Now have children connect the red dots to make the cross. **Jesus came to Jerusalem for a different and far better reason. He knew He would die on the cross. He came to fight greater enemies than the people realized. Jesus came to fight sin, death, and the power of the devil. That is what we need more than anything else!**

Point out that the crown and cross make a new symbol picture called the *crown of life.* This symbol picture stands for heaven. **Jesus is the King, but He gives us the crown—the crown of life in heaven. He gives us His victory!**

Display the Holy Week poster in your worship center area. This poster, resembling a banner you might see in church, can be displayed for several weeks as you study the events of Holy Week. Frequently refer to the symbols pictured and the words and their meanings so that they become a familiar part of the children's visual and verbal vocabulary.

### Hosanna in the Highest!

God's Word says, "I will give you the crown of life" (Revelation 2:10). "When the Chief Shepherd [Jesus] appears, you will receive the crown of glory that will never fade away" (1 Peter 5:4). "Everlasting joy will crown their heads. Gladness and joy will overtake them" (Isaiah 35:10). We have this by faith in Jesus Christ! Hosanna!

### Words to Remember

Blessed is He who comes in the name of the Lord!
Hosanna in the highest!

Matthew 21:9

6

## WEEK 26-B

### Discovery Point

Rejoice! Celebrate the salvation we have through Jesus.

### Children Praise Jesus

Matthew 21:14–16

### Objectives

That by the power of the Holy Spirit working through God's Word, the students will
- know that Jesus loves them so much that He died on the cross for the forgiveness of their sins;
- thank and praise Jesus for His redeeming love;
- tell others of the salvation we have in Jesus.

### Day 3 Materials

- Mural paper
- Rhythm instruments
- Red, yellow, orange balloons
- Blackline 26-B

### Day 4 Materials

- Popped balloons
- Flannelgraph materials
- Mural paper
- Colorful round stickers
- Salvation Student Book

## INTRODUCE

Print the word *HOSANNA* vertically in large block or colored letters on the board or on chart paper. Ask, **What is this word and what does it mean?** (*Hosanna* is a cheering word that means "save us.") **When did the people sing and shout this word?** (On Palm Sunday as Jesus came into Jerusalem.) **Let's use this word to help us say a prayer to God.** Either write or prewrite these words as an acrostic. Read it to the children and then have them read it with you in prayer.

**H** elp us, dear Jesus.
**O** Lord, be with us.
**S** ave us from sin,
**A** nd help us to love You
**N** ighttime and daytime,
**N** ow and forever.
**A** men. Hosanna! Amen.

## DEVELOP

Say, **Actually, Palm Sunday was not the only day that people shouted Hosannas to Jesus. Almost every day during that Holy Week, Jesus went to the temple to teach and to pray. One day when He was in the temple, a group of children gathered around Jesus. They shouted Hosanna and sang praises to Him. The chief priests and leaders of the temple were indignant. In other words, they did not like the children to be making noise in the temple-church. But Jesus was happy to hear their songs. Jesus spoke up for the children. He was thankful to hear their praises. Jesus loves children. They are part of the church and members of God's family just like believers of all ages.**

## RESPOND

**Let's do like those children did long ago. Let's praise the Lord with a joyful noise.** Celebrate in the following ways.

Have the children make simple tunics. Cut lengths of mural paper that are about 4 feet long and 18 inches wide. Fold each tunic at the 2-foot center line and cut a large hole at the center of the fold so the tunic will fit over the front and back of the child. (See illustration.) Children may decorate the front with the word *Hosanna!* and other Christian messages and designs. Staple the sides of the tunic below the armhole once the child has it in place. Go to your church sanctuary to sing praises as the children did long ago.

Read Psalm 98:4: **Make a joyful noise unto the L**ORD (KJV).
Use rhythm instruments as you have a praise songfest. Encourage
children to sing enthusiastically. Sing several songs you have learned
that are on the Voyages CD.

Have a praise parade with red, yellow, and orange balloons.
Say, **The red reminds us of the love Jesus has for each of us; the
yellow reminds us of the glory of Jesus' death on the cross and
resurrection at Easter; and the orange reminds us of the joy we
have in Jesus.** After the parade, make more joyful noise by letting
the children pop their balloons at your signal. (Tell children that
you will pop the balloons for anyone who doesn't like to do so.)
Tell them you will collect the scraps in a plastic bag. (Save the balloon pieces for Day 4.)

To bring the celebration to an end (and to calm things down),
distribute Blackline 26-B. Ask what letter the hearts replace *(o)* and
have the children color the hearts red for Jesus' love. Ask what letter
the crosses replace *(t)* and color them yellow for the glory of God.
Then color the circular border orange to remember the joy that surrounds us through Jesus.

# Worship Ideas

- Make arrangements for the class to sing in a church worship service or chapel service, providing an opportunity for the children to make a joyful noise as they witness their joy in Jesus to others.
- Throughout the week, frequently sing "I Have the Joy" (*LOSP*, p. 62, and on CD).

# Bible Background

In Matthew 18:1 the disciples asked Jesus, "Who is the greatest in the kingdom of heaven?" Jesus called a little child and had him stand among them. He told His disciples, "Whoever humbles himself like this child is the greatest in the kingdom of heaven" (18:4). This faith relies not on our own efforts but on the efforts of our Savior. Later such faith led the children in the temple area to shout, "Hosanna to the Son of David" (21:15).

Jesus points out how these children fulfill an Old Testament prophecy, "From the lips of children and infants you have ordained praise" (Psalm 8:2). Again and again the Gospel writers reveal how Jesus became the fulfillment of prophecy. The people need search no longer. The Messiah has come! He has come to earn their salvation and ours.

Psalm 100:1

Shout for joy to the LORD!

## Words to Remember

*It is good to praise the LORD and make music to Your name. Psalm 92:1*

Read aloud Psalm 95; 98; or 100. Again and again we hear the words of celebration and praise that have been spoken for thousands of years.

## Extending the Lesson

- Play marching music as the children prepare for a praise parade by making paper banners and flags to carry.
- Make a chart comparing life for children in Bible times to life today for children. List ways things are the same and ways they are different.
- Provide materials so children can make their own rhythm instruments. Or ask the children to bring a household item from home that has a nice sound and can be used as an instrument. Remind children to get their parents' permission before they start banging on things in the kitchen or garage to listen to the various tones.

# Day 4

## INTRODUCE

Before class, scatter the scraps of popped balloons from Day 3 in your worship area or around the room. As you begin, comment on the mess and say, **When a celebration is over, people often feel sad, lonely, and let down as they look at the mess that is left behind. The party is over.**

**But it was different when Jesus went to Jerusalem on Palm Sunday. The parade was over, but the joy didn't stop. Children continued to sing their Hosannas in the temple. We sing our Hosannas and praise today. The joy we have in Jesus never ends. Because of Him it will continue forever in heaven. Let's look back again at that Holy Week long ago.**

### Children Praise Jesus

*(Matthew 21:14–16)*

The Lord went to the temple-church.
A crowd soon gathered 'round.
A group of children stood nearby
And made a joyful sound.

"Hosanna to the Son of God,"
The boys and girls did sing.
They shouted out their words of praise
To Christ our heavenly King.

The Savior listened carefully.
He loved to hear their song.
But then some men complained as if
The children had done wrong.

Christ Jesus praised the children's words.
What they had done was right.
He loves to hear our songs today.
Let's sing with all our might!

# DEVELOP

Use flannelgraph figures to show Jesus and children in the temple. Say, **The week after Palm Sunday, many people went to the temple in Jerusalem to see Jesus. They wanted to hear His words. Blind and crippled people wanted Jesus to heal them. Children sang Hosannas.**

**It was a happy time. But not everyone was happy. Some of the leaders complained. They didn't like all the noise and shouts of the children. But Jesus was happy. He loves us and wants to hear our songs and praise.**

Continue by reading the poem on page 7 of the *Salvation* Student Book. Then have the children read the poem aloud with you.

# RESPOND

Continue with the "Hosanna Hike" on page 8. Emphasize that Jesus wants to hear our prayer and praise wherever we are, at any time of day or night. Children are to write the missing word in each poem. **We have opportunities to pray and give praise to God, whatever we may be doing.**

Have the class create their own "Hosanna Hike." In advance, cut pictures from magazines that show people in a variety of situations. Tape them onto mural paper. (*Option:* Have children draw pictures of everyday activities on mural paper.) Say, **As we go through the days and weeks and months and years, we have many times and places to talk with God and about God.** Beside each scene, children are to write the words of a prayer. (This does not need to be in the format of a poem.) Children may then draw a path to connect the pictures of activities.

Share the joy in the Lord you have been celebrating all week. Give the children several colorful round stickers (available at office supply stores). Children may print "Joy in Jesus" on the stickers and give them to friends and family members to wear.

## A Hosanna Hike!

*Directions: We can praise God and pray to Him at all times, wherever we are. Draw a line to connect the pictures. Complete the poems.*

Science, math, and books to __read__, God has blessed our school, indeed.

For our blessings— clothes and toys— Praise God with a joyful __noise__.

Thank You, God, for giving __me__ Such a happy fam-i-l-y.

When I swing up to the __sky__, I praise God who lives on high.

At the beach or mountains __tall__, I see God's hand touches all!

When we camp out in the night, I thank God for stars so __bright__.

## Words to Remember

It is good to praise the LORD and make music to Your name.

Psalm 92:1

8

## Discovery Point

Jesus shows us His great love. He will forgive our loveless actions and will lead us to follow His ways.

## Jesus Washes the Disciples' Feet

John 13:1–17

## Objectives

That by the power of the Holy Spirit working through God's Word, the students will

- praise Jesus for coming to serve us, by saving us from sin, death, and the devil;
- believe that God enables them to serve others in love as they live as God's people;
- grow in kindness as they serve one another through the love of Jesus in their hearts.

## Day 1 Materials

- Towel, pan of water, bar of soap
- Flannelgraph materials
- Blackline 27-A

## Day 2 Materials

- Jake puppet
- Ball, box, cup
- *Jesus Washes Peter's Feet* Arch Book (Teacher Kit)

## INTRODUCE

Tell the children that today's lesson is about serving. **Serving is helping someone. Who would like to serve me by helping me with something?** Look at the show of hands, but do not choose a volunteer. Instead, drape a towel over one arm, set out a pan of water, and extend a bar of soap, saying, **I would like someone to wash my feet.** When children display surprise, hesitation, or even giggles, say, **Washing someone else's dirty feet would not be fun to do. It might even be embarrassing. It's the kind of job you might rather have someone else do. But this is exactly what the most important person ever was willing to do. Let's listen to today's Bible story.**

## DEVELOP

Use the flannelgraph figures that demonstrate this Bible story. (This setting will provide a good connection as later in the week you talk about another event of that evening—the Lord's Supper.) The Bible reference and page 9 of the *Salvation* Student Book can be used as a guide in telling the story.

When you have finished, ask, **Why didn't Jesus call a servant to wash the disciples' feet? That is what was usually done. Or why didn't Jesus ask one of His disciples to help? Jesus is Lord over all things, yet He did the work of a servant. Why?** (Jesus wanted us to see that serving others is important because it shows the love of God in our hearts.)

# RESPOND

Ask, **Why is it that we often fail to follow Jesus' example of serving others?** (We selfishly are most concerned with what we want; we get busy with other activities; we get forgetful or rude about helping; we do it only if there will be help or a reward in return.) **Let's talk to Jesus about this: Dear Lord, forgive us when we are selfish or self-centered. Help us to be helpers. Help us to be *joyful* helpers. Lead us to be humble servants like You. We can do this only through Your life-changing power. Amen.**

Chart the children's ideas of ways they can help each other at school and at home. Use these ideas to make a script for a demonstration skit. For each scenario, have one child narrate and two others demonstrate the helping action. (For example, the narrator can read, *You can be a servant. You can help someone pick up the crayons that just spilled on the floor.* The other two children can use props to demonstrate this.) You may want to present these scenes to another class, or you may want to make a video of the skits, allowing children, in turn, to take the videotape home to show their families what they learned about serving. Conclude with the statement, **God strengthens our faith through His Word and leads us to be Christian servants. As we serve each other with joy, we are also serving Christ Jesus!**

Read and work together on the blackline activity to further extend the servant concept.

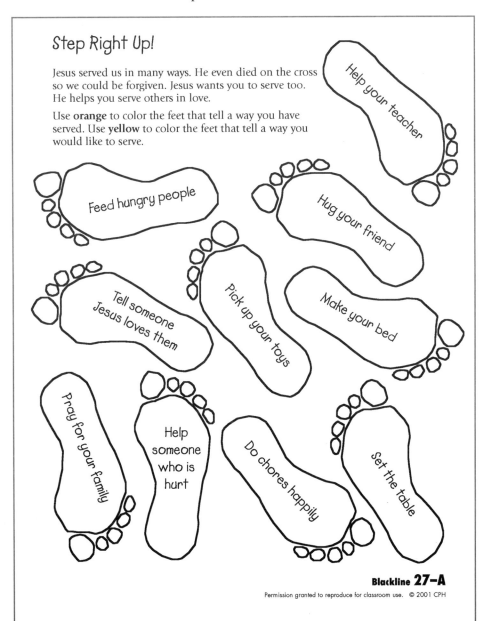

## Step Right Up!

Jesus served us in many ways. He even died on the cross so we could be forgiven. Jesus wants you to serve too. He helps you serve others in love.

Use **orange** to color the feet that tell a way you have served. Use **yellow** to color the feet that tell a way you would like to serve.

Help your teacher

Feed hungry people

Hug your friend

Tell someone Jesus loves them

Pick up your toys

Make your bed

Pray for your family

Help someone who is hurt

Do chores happily

Set the table

---

# Worship Ideas

- Pray together, **Dear Lord, sometimes I grumble and complain about helping others. Sometimes I try to get by without helping at all. Please forgive me. Help me to serve others joyfully because of the love of Jesus in my heart. I ask this for Jesus' sake. Amen.** Remind the children that Jesus says that when we serve other people, it is the same as serving Him. Then sing the following to the tune of "The Farmer in the Dell":

  **We'll serve the Lord with joy!**
  **We'll serve the Lord with joy!**
  **Here and there and everywhere!**
  **We'll serve the Lord with joy!**

- Sing "We Pray for Each Other," "Jesus Wants Me for a Helper," and "We Love" (*LOSP*, pp. 15, 33, 54, and on CD).

# Bible Background

During the three years of Jesus' earthly ministry, His disciples had learned to know Him as the Son of God and Messiah. Jesus had taught lessons about humility and service. However, the disciples still desired individual status and greatness (Luke 22:24). Against this background, Jesus reveals Himself as the servant Savior and provides a model for our motives in Christian ministry.

Jesus tells His disciples to wash one another's feet (John 13:14). Authority among Christians consists of love, humility, and service. We follow Jesus' example to do what He has first done for us: "We love because He first loved us" (1 John 4:19). His love inspires us to love others and to share the Good News of forgiveness and eternal life.

## Words to Remember

*Serve one another in love. Galatians 5:13*

Sing the five words of the verse using the first five notes of the musical scale. First, sing going up the scale. Then sing, coming down. Sing louder as you go up the scale and softer as you come down. Let children accompany the singing with Orff or other instruments based on a five-tone pentatonic scale.

## Extending the Lesson

- Talk with the children about people who serve them at home, at school, and in the community. Write thank-you notes to the custodian, lunch cooks, principal, pastor, police, firefighters, nurse, and others that serve. Make a list of ways the children could serve these helpers.

- Have children sit on chairs in a circle. Count feet by ones and then by twos. Take off shoes and socks, and count toes by fives and tens. **If you were washing feet today as Jesus did, how many feet and how many toes would you wash?**

- Emphasize that Jesus calls us to live not by rules, but by love. Again and again in the Sermon on the Mount (Matthew 5–7) Jesus looks at rules people have heard and says to go a step further—to show love by serving others. Looking at the rule "do not murder," Jesus goes further and says to make peace and not even get angry. Looking at the rule "do not break an oath," Jesus goes further and says don't swear at all. Looking at the rule "love your neighbor," Jesus goes further and says also love your enemies.

We can see this positive emphasis in the catechism's explanation of the Fifth and Seventh Commandments. (See Teacher Resource Book.) Looking at the rules "you shall not murder" and "you shall not steal," we know it is God's will that we serve someone in this way: "help and support him in every physical need" and "help him to improve and protect his possessions and income."

 # Day 2

## INTRODUCE

Use the Jake puppet. (Have him bounce up and down to accentuate his movements.) On a desk or table set out a ball, box, and cup. Stand behind this display with the puppet.

**TEACHER:** Hi, Jake! Please help me. Please put the ball into the box. *(Jake bounces off in the opposite direction, ignoring the teacher's request.)*

**TEACHER:** Jake!

**JAKE:** Oh, were you talking to me?

**TEACHER:** Yes. Please put the ball into the box.

**JAKE:** Sure thing! *(Jake puts the ball into the cup and bounces off.)*

**TEACHER:** Jake, come back. I asked you to put the ball into the *box!*

**JAKE:** Okee-dokee! *(Jake takes the ball out of the cup and places it on the table.)*

**TEACHER:** Jake, please watch me. *(The teacher picks up the ball and puts it into the box.)*

**JAKE:** Oh, the box! You want it in the box!

**TEACHER:** You remind me of the disciples in the Bible story we heard yesterday. Let me explain why.

### Jesus Washes the Disciples' Feet

*(John 13:1–17)*

The day was near when Jesus would die on the cross. Jesus and His disciples planned to eat one last supper together. They walked into town. They came to the house where they would celebrate the Passover meal. Their feet were hot and dusty from walking.

The disciples were seated. Jesus took off His coat, tied a towel at His waist, and put water into a pan. He knelt down and began to wash the disciples' feet.

The disciples were upset when they saw what Jesus was doing. This was the job of a servant. They thought, Jesus is our Lord. He shouldn't be doing this work.

When Jesus was about to wash Peter's feet, Peter said, "No, Lord. I will not let You wash my feet."

Jesus said, "If I can't wash your feet, you aren't letting Me show My love for you." Peter quickly changed his mind!

When Jesus finished, He said, "I am your Teacher and Lord, but still I washed your feet. I helped you. If you love Me, be kind and help each other. Love one another as I have loved you."

Jesus loves and forgives us too. He will help us to grow in faith and in kindness and service to others.

## D E V E L O P

Say, Remember the Bible story we had a few weeks ago? Two disciples, James and John, proudly wanted to be the greatest. Jesus had always taught them to serve one another with love and kindness. But one day James and John came to Jesus. They asked to sit beside Him when they reached the glory of heaven. They thought they were more important than the other disciples. This made the other 10 men very jealous and angry. Jesus said to all of them, "Whoever wants to become great among you must be your servant, and whoever wants to be first must be slave of all" (Mark 10:43–44).

Just like Jake, the disciples didn't seem to pay attention. They still didn't understand what Jesus wanted. They still did not serve and show kindness. They didn't obey Jesus' words (just like Jake didn't do what I asked). So Jesus demonstrated what He wanted. He knew that sometimes people learn best when they *see* what they are supposed to do. Just like I showed Jake by putting the ball in the box, Jesus showed His disciples by serving them. Use the Arch Book from the Teacher Kit to review the story of Jesus washing the disciples' feet. Point out that Jesus' words are also meant for us, His disciples today. **Jesus said, "I have set you an example that you should do as I have done for you"** (John 13:15). **Jesus wants us to live not by "rules we have to do" but by "love we want to do"** because of His love in our hearts.

---

### Serving Jesus with a Smile

*Directions: Draw a smiling face in each box by a picture that shows a happy server. Draw a cross in each box by someone who needs a change of heart, remembering that Jesus forgives our wrongs and puts joy back in our hearts. Jesus says when we serve others, we are also serving Him. So, "serve the LORD with gladness!" (Psalm 100:2 RSV).*

### Words to Remember
Serve one another in love.
Galatians 5:13

---

## R E S P O N D

Try this demonstration with the children. Except for four children, have the class form a circle. Tell the children to walk in a circle, with hands joined, as they sing this verse to the tune of "The Farmer in the Dell":

**We're following the Lord.
We're following the Lord.
Here and there and everywhere,
We're following the Lord.**

Having prompted the four remaining children, have them stand outside the circle with each one loudly saying one of these phrases:

I'm hungry.
I'm sick.
I'm lonely.
I need help.

After following this procedure for a short while, stop the group and ask, **Do you think we are really following what Jesus would do? What did Jesus do for people who were hungry, sick, lonely, or needed help? Would Jesus ignore them and keep moving on? What does Jesus want us to do?** Invite the four outsiders to join the circle. **Jesus wants us to reach out to others, to serve them, to show kindness. The Holy Spirit empowers us to live as people of God who are following the Lord.** Sing the song again.

Plan a service project the children can develop. Close by discussing together the events pictured in the *Salvation* Student Book, page 10, and follow the directions.

## Discovery Point

Jesus shows us His great love. He will forgive our loveless actions and will lead us to follow His ways.

## Jesus' Last Supper

Mark 14:12–26

## Objectives

That by the power of the Holy Spirit working through God's Word, the students will

- believe that all their sins are forgiven through Christ's body and blood, shed for them on the cross;
- know that Jesus gave the Lord's Supper to assure His followers of their forgiveness through Him;
- remember Jesus' love for them whenever they see the Lord's Supper celebrated.

## Day 3 Materials

- Keepsake item
- Flannelgraph materials
- Mural paper
- Blackline 27-B

## Day 4 Materials

- Celebration items
- Communion chalice and plate
- Pastor or videotape
- *Salvation* Student Book

## INTRODUCE

Show the children a keepsake item that is precious to you. Tell them who gave it to you or how you got it, why it is important to you, and what it helps you remember.

Then show the Bible and say, **God gives us His Word to keep in our hearts so that we will know and remember His love. God showed His great love for us by sending Jesus to be our Savior, who forgives us and offers us eternal life. God also gives us special means for remembering His love and grace in Christ. One of these is the Lord's Supper. Let's learn about when this special gift was first given, why it is still celebrated today, and what blessings from God it brings.**

## DEVELOP

Use the flannelgraph figures to set up the Upper Room scene similar to the setting for the Bible story presented earlier this week. Use page 11 in the *Salvation* Student Book and the Bible reference to tell the children the story of the institution of the Lord's Supper.

*Option:* Wrap aluminum foil around a paper cup and paper plate. Lift these up at the appropriate times when telling the story and then place them on your classroom altar as a reminder of the Sacrament. However, it is not advisable to act out the story with the children, offering bread and juice, because some children may think they are getting the actual Sacrament. It would also diminish the sacredness of the actual celebration. Put the emphasis on the children watching and remembering as their part of the celebration whenever the Lord's Supper is distributed.

## R E S P O N D

In advance, use a piece of mural paper to make an enlarged copy of Blackline 27-B. Starting at the bottom, fold each section back so that you can gradually reveal the sections one at a time. Begin with the first section, pointing out that the Lord's Supper is a *mystery*. It is something we cannot fully understand. Reveal the next section, pointing out that just like the first time with Jesus in the Upper Room, each time the Lord's Supper is celebrated in churches today there is wine and bread.

Unfold the next section and say, **The mystery is that Jesus gives His body with the bread and His blood with the wine. Jesus is in, with, and under the bread and wine. How does that happen? Jesus is true God. And it is a mystery we cannot completely understand, so we believe it by faith in our almighty God.**

Reveal the next section, showing the entire visual. **But there is more. Through the Lord's Supper, Jesus gives in a special way the gifts of forgiveness and salvation that He has won for us. Jesus says, "Do this in remembrance of Me"** (Luke 22:19).

Distribute copies of Blackline 27-B. Let the children color the shapes, letters, and backgrounds. Together, review the meaning of this visual.

## Worship Ideas

- Listen to a recording of the liturgy used in worship when the Lord's Supper is celebrated. Encourage the children to sing along with any words they know.
- Sing "This Is the Feast" and "Amigos de Cristo" (*LOSP*, pp. 95 and 23).
- Read aloud the Words of Institution said by the pastor before the celebration of the Lord's Supper. Help children to become familiar with these words. Ask them to listen for these words when they are in church on Sunday.

## Bible Background

The Passover festival commemorated God's power and grace in rescuing His people from slavery in Egypt. It also pointed to the rescue from sin that God would provide through Jesus. The spotless male lamb reminds us of Jesus, the spotless, sinless Lamb of God. The blood of the Passover lamb spread on the doorposts points to Jesus' blood on the cross. The lamb's blood on the door, saving the life of the firstborn son, portrays the blood of Christ, who saves us from eternal death.

As Jesus ate the Passover meal with His disciples, He was about to make that final, perfect sacrifice. Now was the time to institute the Lord's Supper, where Jesus' followers remember how His sacrifice rescues us from sin and damnation. In this meal believers receive Christ's body and blood for forgiveness and renewal in faith. His salvation is ours, and we are His!

## The Lord's Supper
## A Mystery

body     blood

forgiven     SAVED

## Words to Remember

[Jesus said,] "Do this to remember Me."
1 Corinthians 11:24 TLB

On chart paper, make a list of the many things children remember about Jesus from the Bible and as He blesses their lives today.

## Extending the Lesson

- Have the pastor show the children his portable Communion ware. He can explain that he uses it with people in the hospital or in convalescent homes so that they can celebrate the Lord's Supper even though they are unable to come to church.
- Show the children a piece of bread or wafer used in Communion. Explain that Jesus used this kind of hard, flat bread because they had been celebrating the Passover meal. At the Passover people used unleavened bread, which can be made quickly without yeast. Bread without yeast is not like the fluffy bread the children usually eat. God had told the people to make unleavened bread as they hurriedly prepared to leave Egypt when God delivered them from slavery. Jesus used elements from the Passover in a new way (a new covenant, a new testament). Jesus came to deliver all people from sin, death, and the devil by sacrificing His own body and blood.

Use this recipe to make unleavened bread. Mix the following ingredients:

2 cups flour
⅓ cup water
3 tablespoons melted butter
⅛ teaspoon salt
1 egg

Make a stiff dough and knead it. Roll the dough flat on a greased cookie sheet. Bake at 375 degrees until slightly brown. Cool and break apart to eat. May be topped with honey.

## INTRODUCE

Have the children guess what celebration is represented as, one at a time, you hold up a related item. (For example, candles for a birthday party, candy canes for Christmas, streamers for New Year's, etc.) Then hold up a picture of the chalice and bread plate (or the actual items) used in the Lord's Supper. After the children respond, say, **The Lord's Supper is really a *victory* celebration! Though some people might look sad as they think of sin and the cross, we can be very happy, knowing Jesus has won the victory over sin, death, and the devil. He gave His body and blood so that we have forgiveness and eternal life. This is a victory to celebrate joyfully! The Bible says, "Thanks be to God! He gives us the victory through our Lord Jesus Christ"** (1 Corinthians 15:57). **Let's learn more about the celebration.**

### Jesus' Last Supper

*(Mark 14:12–26)*

Jesus and His disciples were eating their last supper together. Jesus knew that it would soon be time for Him to suffer and die for the sins of the world.

During the meal Jesus took a piece of bread. He said a thank-You prayer to God. Then He gave each disciple a piece of it to eat. Jesus said, "Take and eat this bread. This is My body, which is given for you."

Then Jesus took a cup of wine and gave thanks to God. He handed the cup to His disciples, saying, "Drink from this cup all of you. This is My blood, which I give to take away your sins."

Jesus said His followers should have this special celebration often. Jesus said, "Do this to remember Me." This special meal is called the Lord's Supper. Christians today still celebrate it, receiving forgiveness through Jesus. We remember that Jesus died and rose again to save us so we may live eternally in heaven.

# D E V E L O P

Specifically talk about how the Lord's Supper is celebrated in worship today. Either ask the pastor to talk to the children about the significance and procedures for Communion or show a videotape recording of the Lord's Supper at a regular Sunday morning worship service. You might also take the children to the sanctuary and have them kneel at the altar as you show the Communion chalice and wafer plate and explain the celebration. In personal preparation for this lesson, it would be good to review the portion of the catechism (see Teacher Resource Book) that has explanations for questions about the Lord's Supper (the Sacrament of the Altar).

# R E S P O N D

After discussing the celebration of the Lord's Supper, say, **When you are older, you will celebrate the Lord's Supper too. Until that time, you can participate in this special celebration by remembering how much Jesus loves you and what He has done for you. You can fold your hands so that your thumbs cross. This cross will help you think about how Jesus died to forgive all your sins. You can remember Jesus' promise that you will live with Him someday in heaven.**

Turn to page 12 in the *Salvation* Student Book. Ask the children to draw a picture of something they can remember about Jesus during a celebration of the Lord's Supper. Talk first about the children's ideas for possibilities (Jesus on the cross, Jesus giving the Lord's Supper, Jesus with hands raised in blessing). After children have drawn and colored their pictures, let volunteers show and talk about what they have drawn.

## A Victory Celebration!

*What do you remember when you see the celebration of the Lord's Supper?*

### Words to Remember

[Jesus said,] "Do this to remember Me."

1 Corinthians 11:24 TLB

12

## WEEK 28-A

### Discovery Point

Jesus willingly suffered and died for us, so that we may receive forgiveness and eternal life.

### Jesus Prays in Gethsemane

Mark 14:32–42

### Objectives

That by the power of the Holy Spirit working through God's Word, the students will
- grow in their understanding of the enormous task that Jesus faced and completed;
- know that God listens to us when we come to Him with our troubles and our joys in prayer;
- share the selfless love of their Savior with others.

### Day 1 Materials

- Jake puppet
- House plants, rocks
- Blackline 28-A
- Yarn

### Day 2 Materials

- Flannelgraph materials
- *Salvation* Student Book
- Colored paper

## INTRODUCE

Either tell the following story in your own words or use the Jake puppet to tell the story. **Jake woke up early one day. It was 4:30 in the morning. It was still dark out. Jake felt terrible. He had never felt this bad before. He called out for his mom and dad. They could see that something was very wrong. They rushed Jake to the hospital. The doctor said Jake would need an appendix operation right away. Jake was worried. His mom and dad held his hand, said things to comfort him, and prayed with him. He felt better just knowing they were near.**

Jake's story reminds me of a story in the Bible. Jesus knew He would soon suffer and die. It would be painful, but it had to be done in order to save us. Jesus wanted to talk to His heavenly Father in prayer. He wanted his best friends to be near Him to comfort Him. Let's learn more about Jesus' prayer and Jesus' friends.

## DEVELOP

Gather the children around you. Set up a display of house plants and greenery to give the area in front of you the atmosphere of a garden. (If you use rocks in the suggested worship activities, add them to this garden scene.) Use the figures on Blackline 28-A to tell the Bible story. As you tell the story, set four paper figures in your garden scene. Set the disciples on their sides to show them sleeping. Turn Jesus around to show Him kneeling in earnest prayer. Include these elements in your discussion: Jesus' sorrow, the disciples' weakness, the comfort of prayer, Jesus' willingness to abide by His Father's will, His mercy toward His friends, the Father's comforting gift of an angel to strengthen Jesus.

Distribute copies of Blackline 28-A for the children to complete. Have them act out the Bible story in groups of four as you narrate it. Each child can be identified as one of the four characters in the story by placing the corresponding paper figurine on a 24-inch loop of yarn and wearing it around the neck.

# R E S P O N D

On the board or poster paper, print the four sections of Jesus' prayer as listed in Mark 14.

- *Abba*, **Father.** (A phrase indicating a very close relationship.)
- **Everything is possible for You.** (More than a statement of praise, this is also a statement of trust.)
- **Take this cup from Me.** (Jesus is pleading for help. The "cup" is the suffering and sorrow before Him.)
- **Yet not what I will, but what You will.** (He places what the Father wants above His own wants. He is willing to do what is necessary to take away the sin of the world.)

Point out that Jesus' prayer can be a model for our own prayers.

- Call on the Lord who loves you and cares for you as His child.
- Trust completely in His power and willingness to do what is best.
- Tell God your wants and needs. He will listen.
- Recognize that what He wants is better and more important than what you want.

Gather together and kneel in prayer as Jesus did. Each child speaks silently to God from the heart.

*Directions: (1) Cut on the three straight solid lines. (2) Fold on the dotted lines. (3) Color the pictures. (4) Overlap and glue together the small bottom flaps.*

| JESUS | PETER | JAMES | JOHN |

**Blackline 28–A**
Permission granted to reproduce for classroom use. © 2001 CPH

# Worship Ideas

- Point out that the Garden of Gethsemane was probably very much like a park, with trees, open grassy areas, and other plants. If possible, have your worship or prayer time in a grassy or wooded area. Learn stanza 1 of "Go to Dark Gethsemane" (*All God's People Sing* 105, available from CPH). Young children love this song because it pictures and tells the story so well. But it has many words you will need to explain first (such as *conflicts*, which one child puzzled over, thinking the word was *cornflakes*).

- Many artists show Jesus in Gethsemane, praying near a large rock. The Bible gives no indication if this was so. Point out that the Bible does say Jesus knelt to pray and had His face to the ground. But we can think about a rock in another way—as the strength of the Lord, on whom we rely. Read aloud Psalm 18:1–2. Jesus relied on the certainty of His Father, and He received comfort and strength. Then give each child a rock to decorate with acrylic paint. (These can be rocks added to the storytelling scene on Day 1. If you cannot find rocks of an appropriate size or smoothness, consider getting some from a nursery.) Praise God with a joyful noise by clapping the rocks together, with a partner, as you say the psalm verse and as you sing songs of praise and thanks for all that Jesus did for us.

# Bible Background

Jesus' prayer in the garden is one of the most poignant moments of spiritual struggle recorded in Scripture. Jesus, as true man, experienced the kind of fear and sorrow in the face of pain and hardship that is common to us. He was also fully aware of the divine wrath that would be poured out on Him as He carried the sins of the world—our sins—through suffering and brutal death. In intense agony, Jesus prayed that He might be spared this cup of suffering. Yet He faithfully accepted the will of His Father, was comforted and strengthened, and then demonstrated His love for all people.

When Jesus found His disciples asleep, He encouraged them to pray. So He also invites us, when we drift into spiritual slumber, to trust Him and call on Him for every need.

## Words to Remember

*Call upon Me in the day of trouble; I will deliver you, and you will honor Me. Psalm 50:15*

- Divide the class into three groups to practice the three sections of this verse. Help children to see the three-step process: go to God when you have problems; He will hear and help; thank and praise Him for what He has done.
- Relate the three parts of the verse to the Bible story. (1) When Jesus was troubled, He went to His Father in prayer; (2) the Father answered in the way that was best by strengthening Jesus for the task ahead; (3) Jesus honored the Father by completing the plan of salvation.
- Sing the Bible verse. See "Psalm 50:15" in the Supplemental Activities section of the Teacher Resource Book. You can also use the recording of it on the *Songs Kids Love to Sing* tape or CD, available from CPH.

## Extending the Lesson

- Set out a display of gardening magazines and catalogs. Talk about various types of gardens. Let children make a collage of gardens by cutting out pictures and using glue sticks to paste them at various heights and angles on a piece of poster paper.
- Pick up again on the rock theme. Give each child an irregular rock-shaped piece of gray paper. Ask children to make scribbles on the rocks as you name some of the sins we do. Have the children bring their paper rocks forward to place on a bulletin board or poster in the shape of a cross. Say, **It was for our sins that Jesus died on the cross.** Lead the children in a prayer of contrition and repentance. Then ask, **Can you think of a very large and important rock in the story of Holy Week?** (Give clues if needed: it was heavy to move, soldiers guarded it, an angel moved it.) Conclude by speaking of the joy we have in our risen Savior.

 **Day**

Begin today's lesson by teaching this little song, sung appropriately to the tune of "Are You Sleeping." Make the children aware of an important change in the pattern of the song: usually phrases are echoed, but this pattern changes in the line about the three disciples.

**Are you sleeping? *(Are you sleeping?)***
**James and John, *(Peter too,)***
**Stay awake and watch now *(Stay awake and watch now)***
**While I pray. *(While I pray.)***

---

## Jesus Prays in Gethsemane
### (Mark 14:32–42)

Jesus

Peter, James, and John

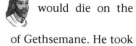
garden

It was Thursday evening, the day before  would die on the . 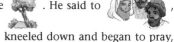 was with His disciples at the  of Gethsemane. He took His friends 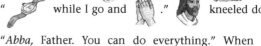 further into the . He said to , "  while I go and ."  kneeled down and began to pray, "*Abba*, Father. You can do everything." When  came back to , they were .  went away from them and began to  again, saying, "Take this cup from Me. But Your will be done." came back and again found asleep. So went away a third time to . When returned to the sleeping disciples, He said, "Couldn't **U** with Me **1** hour? Wake up! The time has come." could see the soldiers coming with and . knew He would be captured, and would soon die on the ✝ for the sins of the . But we also know the happy ending— came alive on Sunday.

13

## D E V E L O P

Use flannelgraph figures (Teacher Kit) to retell the Bible story. Be sure to have a nighttime setting, perhaps even adding stars to a darkened sky.

Review the story by reading the rebus on page 13 of the *Salvation* Student Book. Perhaps you can read the words and the children can "read" the pictures aloud.

## R E S P O N D

Continue with the puzzle on page 14 of the Student Book. It would be especially appropriate at this time to do some of the activities listed in the "Words to Remember" section of this lesson.

Continue with a prayer flip-book activity. Demonstrate to the children where they are to fold a piece of paper (see dotted line on the illustration). Then demonstrate cutting one half of this in half (as indicated by the solid lines) and cutting those halves in half again. This will give you a prayer-starter book with four flaps.

On the flaps, have the children print these prayer starters: *Thank You, God, for …; Praise God for He is …; Lord, give me …; Help me to …* Children may lift each flap and write the completion of the prayer on the space under the flap or draw a picture indicating their prayer. Allow time for children to share some of their completed prayers.

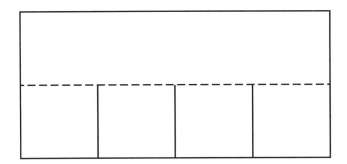

### Words to Remember

*Directions: What do you see in this garden? What letter is nearby? Look at the pictures below. On each blank line print the letter that is near each picture in the garden. Read the message from God's Word.*

## Call upon Me in the day of

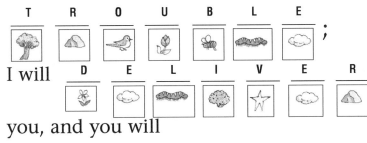

T R O U B L E ;

I will D E L I V E R

you, and you will

H O N O R **Me.** Psalm 50:15

14

## Discovery Point

Jesus willingly suffered and died for us, so that we may receive forgiveness and eternal life.

## Jesus Dies on the Cross

Portions of Matthew 27; Mark 15; Luke 23; and John 19

## Objectives

That by the power of the Holy Spirit working through God's Word, the students will

- know that Jesus willingly died for them, was buried, and became alive again;
- ask Jesus to forgive them when they sin and thank Him that He does forgive them;
- live as a redeemed child of God.

## Day 3 Materials

- Jenna puppet
- Lots of gray play dough
- Blackline 28-B
- Drinking straws

## Day 4 Materials

- Black fabric or streamers
- Flannelgraph materials
- Speech bubbles (Teacher Resource Book)
- *Salvation* Student Book

# INTRODUCE

Place a lump of gray play dough on each child's desk. (Mixing several colors of play dough together usually results in some shade of gray.) Then bring out the Jenna puppet, who is carrying a lump of gray play dough and staring at it.

**TEACHER:** Jenna, what are you doing?

**JENNA:** I'm staring at this lump—it looks like I feel.

**TEACHER:** You must be feeling awful! What's wrong?

**JENNA:** *I'm* wrong! I was looking at my mom's favorite necklace, and I broke it—beads everywhere.

**TEACHER:** Was your mom sad?

**JENNA:** She doesn't know about it. I hid it. And then I lied when she asked if I had seen it. Now she blames herself for losing it. Things just keep getting worse and worse.

**TEACHER:** I think you've learned something important. When we do something wrong, we sin. Feeling awful about it is called guilt. You tried to hide your sin. But we can never hide our sin and our guilt from Jesus.

**JENNA:** What can I do about it?

**TEACHER:** Why don't you talk to Jesus in prayer? Tell Him you are sorry. Thank Him that He was willing to die on the cross for you. And thank Him that He is willing to forgive you.

**JENNA:** Just remembering Jesus still loves me makes me feel a little better already. After I talk to Jesus, I'm going to talk to my mom. She knows about Jesus and forgiving too.

**TEACHER:** Let's learn more about God's plan to forgive and save us through Jesus.

# DEVELOP

Have the children bring their lumps of play dough as they gather around you in a circle. Say, **We are going to think about that Good Friday when Jesus died. He took our sins and our punishment to the cross.** Have the children quietly, one at a time, bring their lumps of play dough to the center of the circle and place them on the floor in the shape of a cross. Tell the story of Jesus' death and burial, using the Bible references and page 15 of the *Salvation* Student Book as your guide. As you are talking, slowly pick up the lumps and knead them together to form one large irregular oval shape. Then say, **We started with the shape of a cross. But the shape has changed. It reminds me of the happy ending of the story of Holy Week. How does this remind you of Easter?** (Lead the children to think of the play dough as representing the stone rolled away from the tomb on Easter. Jesus, true God, completed our salvation by defeating death, as well as defeating sin.)

# RESPOND

Distribute copies of Blackline 28-B for the children to color and cut out. As they do this, give each child two lumps of play dough pulled from the "stone." Children will use it as a base for the flowers they are making (see directions on the blackline page). Say, **Flowers remind us of Easter. Flowers come from seeds. They burst to new life out of the worthless covering of the seed. This can remind us of Jesus, who burst out of the lifeless tomb to new life on Easter. Even on a day when we think of the sad story of the cross, we also want to celebrate the happiness of Easter, which is not really the end of the story. It is the beginning for us, because in Jesus we receive eternal life!** Display the completed flowers on your classroom altar.

# Worship Ideas

- Read aloud the words of the thief on the cross in Luke 23:42. Then sing these words several times in worship and also several times during the lesson. (See *All God's People Sing* 146, available from CPH.) Emphasize that these are words for us to say too. Like the thief we are sinners, and like him we are saved.

- Talk about times in a church worship service that the pastor makes the sign of the cross (such as in Baptism or when a blessing is spoken). If you have not done so before, teach the children how to make the sign of the cross on themselves. Point out that this sign reminds us that Jesus' love surrounds us, from our head to our heart and over all parts of our body and our lives. It reminds us that we are His own people.

- Sing "Do You Know Who Died for Me?" (*LOSP*, p. 93, and on CD).

# Bible Background

Death by crucifixion is one of the most brutal forms of punishment. Even the ancient pagan world regarded execution by a cross with horror. It was a type of torture accompanied by a slow, painful death. In the Old Testament, idolaters and blasphemers were stoned to death. When the religious leaders demanded crucifixion for Jesus, they not only desired an agonizing death for Him but also wanted Him to bear the full shame of condemnation by God (Galatians 3:13).

Jesus willingly accepted this cruel punishment—the punishment we deserved because of our sin. He offers His life as atonement—full payment—for our offenses. He is our Substitute, our Mediator. In His sacrifice Jesus restores the broken relationship between humanity and God. His death means reconciliation, peace, and life (Romans 5:11; Colossians 1:22).

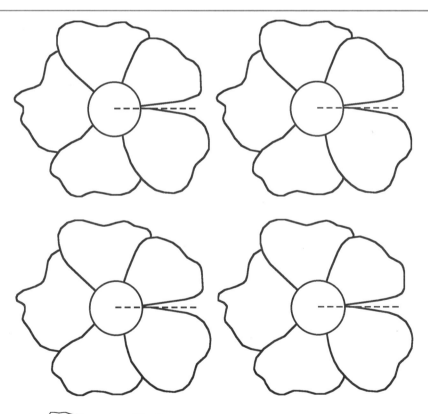

*Directions:*
1. *Color each flower.*
2. *Cut out the flowers.*
3. *Also cut on the dotted line that goes to the center of each flower.*
4. *Take two flowers and insert them together at the dotted lines. (They should cross each other in an X shape that gives the flowers fullness and dimension.)*
5. *Insert one end of a drinking straw into a lump of play dough.*
6. *Cut two small slits at the top of the drinking straw (stem). The slits should be opposite each other.*
7. *Insert one flower petal into the drinking straw slits to hold the flower upright.*
8. *Follow these directions to make another flower.*

**Blackline 28-B**

## Words to Remember

*Christ died for our sins. 1 Corinthians 15:3*
Repeat the Bible words several times as a chant, getting gradually softer each time and then gradually louder till you shout it triumphantly. You may want to signal the changes in volume by using hand motions.

## Extending the Lesson

- Give each child a sheet of graph paper that has large spaces. Suggest that the children use a variety of colors on the lines to make crosses. Suggest that the crosses be different sizes and placed at different locations on the page. Encourage children to add decorations around some of the crosses.

- Let children search the room for lines that come together to form a cross (such as the intersection of floor tiles, the crossing of window panes, etc.). Children may identify these places by attaching a piece of white removable paper tape on each cross.

- Use a calendar to review the events of the days during Holy Week (from Palm Sunday to Easter).

- Give each child a cross pattern cut from poster paper. They are to place the pattern at the center of a piece of paper and trace the cross with a piece of brightly colored chalk. Then brush the chalk dust outward with a cotton ball. Repeat this process using various bright colors of chalk. *Variation:* Children can move the cross to various positions on the paper, each time outlining it with a different color and then brushing it.

# Day 4

## INTRODUCE

Drape black fabric or black streamers on all crosses and pictures of Jesus in your classroom. Explain that on Good Friday we use the color black on altars and crosses in churches to help us think of Jesus' suffering and death. **Black can remind us of the three hours of complete darkness during the afternoon Jesus was on the cross. Black is often worn by people who are sad. But even more than that, we use black as a sign of respect and honor. We respect and honor Jesus for all that He has done for us out of His great love.**

### Jesus Dies on the Cross

*(Portions of Matthew 27; Mark 15; Luke 23; and John 19)*

"Crucify Him! Nail Him to the cross!" the people shouted. But Jesus did not hate them. Pilate, the ruler, wanted to please the people. He told the soldiers, "Take Jesus away. Nail Him to a cross." Jesus didn't hate Pilate. Jesus didn't hate the soldiers. Jesus loves all people.

The soldiers put a crown of thorns on Jesus' head. They hit Him. They made Him carry a heavy cross to a hill outside the city, where He was crucified. But Jesus continued to show love. Jesus prayed that God the Father would forgive His enemies.

Many people watched Jesus hang on the cross. Jesus' enemies laughed at Him. His friends cried for Him. Jesus loved them all because He is God, and God is love.

Jesus was on the cross for many hours. The sky became very, very dark. When Jesus knew that He had suffered everything to pay the penalty for our sins, He said, "It is finished." He breathed one last time and died. The earth shook. The Roman centurion leader of the soldiers said, "This man was truly the Son of God."

Jesus' friends took His body down from the cross, wrapped it in clean cloths, and buried it in a tomb. A large stone was rolled in front of the tomb's entrance.

Jesus' friends were sad. But they would not be sad for long. On Easter Sunday Jesus became alive again. Because Jesus died and arose again, we have forgiveness of our sins and the promise of eternal life in heaven!

## DEVELOP

Use flannelgraph figures to retell the story of Jesus' crucifixion. Discuss some of the details not previously mentioned. Today focus on the things Jesus said from the cross. Place speech bubbles, one at a time, on the flannelgraph scene to tell the seven statements of Christ from the cross. (See the Supplemental Activities section of the Teacher Resource Book for a page of these speech bubbles, which you can duplicate, cut out, and use.)

## RESPOND

Together look at page 16 of the *Salvation* Student Book. Say, **The many parts of the cross pictured here make me think of the many people Jesus saved by dying on the cross. That includes you and me! We belong together because we all belong to Jesus, our Savior! Let's help each other decorate our crosses.** Have each child choose a bright crayon. Allow a set amount of time for the children to mingle around the room, coloring in one section on each classmate's cross. As the children do this, play the recording of "God Loves Me Dearly" (on the Voyages CD) or other Christ-centered music. (If you have more than 30 children in your class, assign certain children to add colored outlines to the cross or add flowers around it; if you have fewer than 30, each child may complete the unfinished sections of the cross when seated again.) **Your pictures remind me that we are united together in Christ.** You may want to sing "We Are the Church" (*LOSP*, p. 106).

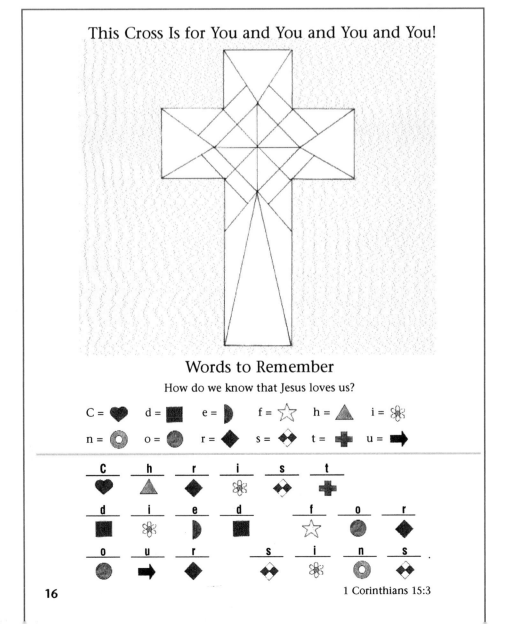

**This Cross Is for You and You and You and You!**

**Words to Remember**

How do we know that Jesus loves us?

16

1 Corinthians 15:3

# UNIT 8
# Alive

## Unit Overview

This unit of study and the accompanying Student Book are entitled *Alive*. This unit focuses on the very things that make Christianity unique. We have a living God who is with us all the time and everywhere. Christianity is based not on what we do, but on what Christ has done for us. The task He now gives us is to tell others what He has done. What joy we have in Jesus; what joy we have in the job He gives us—showing and sharing His love.

Send home copies of the family letter and Bible verse list for Unit 8 as you begin. (See the Teacher Resource Book.) This will let parents know what their children will be learning during the next few weeks. At the end of the unit, let the children take home their *Alive* Student Book. Encourage them to show their parents what they have learned. This is the eighth in a series of nine books that will cover the story of salvation through the Old and New Testaments. Also consider adding some of the following activities to your curriculum to make related connections between God's message of love and all that you do throughout the day.

## Worship Connections

This time of the year is a season of exuberant joy, which is often expressed in music. To help children understand, appreciate, and be involved worshipfully, introduce them to some of the musical instruments used in your church services. In addition to keyboard instruments (organ, piano, electronic keyboard), introduce the children to the use of guitar, trumpets, flutes, drums, stringed instruments, and so forth.

Invite guests to come into the classroom or sanctuary to demonstrate their music. Encourage the guests to include a song that the children can sing with instrumental accompaniment. Read aloud Psalm 150, noting that throughout history, a variety of musical instruments have been used to make a joyful noise unto the Lord. Consider inviting your guest musicians to accompany the children as they sing in a Sunday morning worship service. Praise the Lord joyfully!

## Community Building

- As you talk about Easter being the best news ever, play an Easter game that repeats the good news message. Roll up a newspaper and demonstrate how paperboys deliver newspapers by tossing them onto a driveway or porch. Have children stand in a circle. Toss a newspaper to a child, delivering the good news by saying, "Jesus is alive!" The person catching it should continue this pattern. *Variation:* Remembering that on Easter Day people were running around telling the good news of Jesus, break out of the circle formation and have children play the game while running.

- Play a Pentecost game similar to fruit basket upset. Using the names of the places people came from on Pentecost Day, assign each of the names to at least two children (if you have a small class, reduce the number of names used). Possibilities are Parthia, Media, Elam, Mesopotamia, Judea, Cappadocia, Phrygia, Pamphylia, Libya, Rome, Crete, and Arabia. Have children be seated except for one person in the center. When you say a name, children assigned that name are to switch seats. The person in the middle is also supposed to try to be seated. When you say *Pentecost*, everyone is to get up and run to a new place. **This can remind us that at Pentecost, the message of Jesus was spread to many places.**

## Tools for Witness

- This unit has a strong mission emphasis. Knowing that Jesus is our living Savior, we want to share the news with all people. Ask the children to bring in pictures from magazines, newspapers, or photos that show crowds of people. Display these pictures on a bulletin board titled "Look at All the People Jesus Loves." Over a week or two continue to build the display. Pray together that the people pictured may come to know this love that Jesus has for them.

- In contrast to a few people who think of a lettuce salad as lettuce and nothing more (not even dressing), most people like salads that have a mixture of flavors and textures. With the children watching, mix together various ingredients to make a salad (lettuce, croutons, carrots, tangerine slices, dried Chinese noodles, chopped boiled eggs, etc.). As you do so, compare the variety of ingredients to the variety of people in God's family of believers. We know that God loves all kinds of people from all over the world who are all ages and who are different from each other. God loves this mixture of people and calls us to do the same.

The one thing that brings everyone together in a salad is the dressing (pour it on). **What is the one thing that brings all kinds of people together in God's family?** (Jesus.) Distribute salad for all the children to eat. Suggest the next time they have salad at home, they talk about how God's family is a big mixture too—a mixture of people from different countries speaking different languages but loved and saved by the one true God. (There are many ordinary things around us that can help us think of Jesus!)

## Service Projects

Make plans to involve parents in a mission fair. Let them choose countries they are interested in or acquainted with. Suggest that they make a display of pictures, artifacts, food, and other things to share with the class. Spend part of one afternoon learning from each other. Pray together that God will bless people from all over the world by bringing them the Good News of Jesus, who is the only way of salvation (Acts 4:12). Set out a basket for freewill offerings that will be given as a gift to a mission overseas.

## Reaching Every Individual

Do not let printed words be a barrier for hearing the true Word of God. Always focus on faith formation and life transformation rather than mere information. God's Word is not just a detailing of facts; it is more a detailing of love—God's love for us in Jesus. Consider the abilities of the children in your class and adjust your use of the materials accordingly. Work together as a class, listing and spelling answers to assist, or have the children work together as partners. You may talk about rather than print responses. Choose whatever method is most effective. It is not the amount of material covered but rather its impact, empowered by the Holy Spirit.

The Holy Spirit led the disciples to speak in many languages on Pentecost Day. The Holy Spirit will also bless you as you share God's Word in a multiplicity of ways for a diversity of abilities and learning styles in the children in your class.

## Social Studies

- Social studies is a subject about people—where they live and what they do. Almost any aspect of social studies can, therefore, be related to our life in Christ and the need for all people to learn of Him as their Savior.
- Today, manuals and instructional brochures often are printed in more than one language. Display some of these side-by-side, showing the same illustrations but described in different languages. (Cosmetic companies based in Europe often have brochures in multiple languages.) Also display Bibles in several languages open to the same verse (perhaps highlight the verse). **God wants all people, speaking all languages, to hear the truth about salvation in Jesus.**

## Science

Set out a list of living and nonliving items. Determine what the characteristics are of each grouping and contrast them. Point out that living things grow, move, increase, and so forth. Consider how some of these characteristics apply to Jesus and His church. (Jesus moved, ate, and talked with the disciples after Easter. Jesus is alive and active in the world today, even though we can't see Him. The Christian church grew on Pentecost Day to 3,000 people, and it continues to increase as the Gospel is spoken around the world.)

## Mathematics

Work together to see the impact of many people speaking individually about the Gospel to just a few. Determine the number of people who would learn of Jesus if each child in the classroom told two people. Pray that God would bless your words and actions for the good of His kingdom.

Integrating the Faith

Alive

## Language Arts

Compare the title of this unit to the title of Unit 5. *Listen* implies learning and is passive. *Alive* implies action. Have the children help you make a list of action words (verbs) that tell what Jesus wants us to do as people of God (*do, go, grow, share, show, tell, help*).

## Fine Arts

As children work on projects or during study time throughout the day, play recordings of joyful Easter music. Also listen to recordings of music from various ethnic groups, sung in various languages.

## Technology

Make a list of types of transportation and communication technologies. Have the children suggest ways these could be used to spread God's good news. (For example, the Apollo 8 astronauts read from the Bible as they circled the moon. Their message was broadcast to people all over the earth.)

## Discovery Point

Jesus died and rose again so that, through the gift of faith, we are His children and have the assurance of life eternal.

## Jesus Lives!

Matthew 28; Mark 16; John 20

## Objectives

That by the power of the Holy Spirit working through God's Word, the students will
- celebrate that Jesus is alive and is true God;
- rejoice that because of Jesus' death and resurrection, they, too, will live in heaven;
- share their joy in the risen Jesus with others.

## Day 1 Materials
- Long strip of white fabric
- Christ's Tomb poster
- Blackline 29-A

## Day 2 Materials
- Flannelgraph materials
- *Alive* Student Book

## INTRODUCE

Hold up a long strip of white fabric. Ask (or tell the children if they are unsure), **How does this remind you of Jesus' birth?** (As a baby He was wrapped in swaddling clothes.) **How does this remind you of Jesus' death?** (When Jesus died on the cross, His friends wrapped His body in long strips of cloth and buried Him in a tomb.) **This cloth can remind us of Jesus' birth and death, the beginning and end of His life.** Having cut the poster of Christ's tomb in half, display the sad picture of Jesus' burial scene and continue with today's Bible lesson.

## DEVELOP

Say, **Jesus' friends were very sad when He died that Friday. They wrapped His body in clean cloth and buried it in a tomb. They rolled a large stone in front of the doorway. Then Jesus' friends went home. They would not visit the tomb on Saturday because that was the Sabbath, the day of rest. They would wait until the third day, Sunday, to return to the tomb to pour special perfumed oils on Jesus' body to honor Him.**

Point out that the burial scene is a sad picture, but it was not really the end of the story. Jesus died, but God's plan of salvation was not complete until Jesus arose to new life again on Easter Sunday. He is our living Savior. Place the Easter tomb over the burial scene and tell the events of Easter morning, using Matthew 28 and John 20 as your guide.

Then place the two pictures of the tomb side by side. Ask the children to compare the pictures, saying, **How are the pictures different from each other?** (Dark sky/sunrise, closed/open, sad/happy, death/life.) After listening to responses, say, **Jesus makes a big difference in our lives too. We don't have to be afraid or sad about death, because we know that death won't last forever. Jesus lasts forever. He will have a "resurrection day" for all believers when He takes us to live forever with Him in heaven! Because of Jesus, we are Easter people!**

# R E S P O N D

Examine the pictures on the border of the Easter half of the poster. Point out that these are pictures we often see at Easter time. They might remind us of spring. But much more important, each can give us a message about Jesus. As time is available you can discuss the symbolism of Easter flowers and Easter eggs (see "Extending the Lesson" activities). But today explain the picture of a butterfly. Demonstrate with a copy of Blackline 29-A. In advance, cut out the folded shape; color it light green on one side to look like a caterpillar; color the other side brown for the chrysalis; open the shape to reveal a butterfly and color it with bright patterns. Explain the life cycle of the butterfly. Then say, **This reminds me of Easter. The butterfly bursting out of the empty chrysalis shell makes me think of something else. I am reminded that Jesus burst out of the empty tomb to new and glorious life. The joyful sight of a fluttering, beautiful butterfly makes me think of the beautiful sights of Easter and our risen Savior!** Give the children copies of Blackline 29-A so they can make their own Easter butterflies.

## Worship Ideas

- Lead the class in an Easter cheer. Have them repeat the following lines:

  **What a celebration day!**
  **Jesus took my sins away!**
  **I will shout, "Hooray! Hooray!"**
  **I will shout it every day!**

- Play a recording of Handel's "Hallelujah Chorus." Point out that this is a victory song that tells us Jesus is King of kings and Lord of lords. Let the children wave colorful streamers in time with the music so that they can join in the celebration.
- Sing the Easter songs on pages 92–96 of *Little Ones Sing Praise* and any other Easter songs the children may know.

## Bible Background

By Hebrew counting, Jesus rose from the dead on the third day. The first day ended at sundown Friday. On the second day, until sunset Saturday (the Sabbath), Christ's body had remained lifeless. The third day began after the sun had set. On that day—Scripture does not tell at what hour—Jesus rose from the dead!

Jesus' resurrection proved His work of redemption: (1) He is the Son of God (Romans 1:4). (2) Everything else He said is true (Luke 24:6–8). We can be sure He will keep every promise He has made. (3) The Father has accepted Christ's death as a sufficient sacrifice for the sins of the world. God is satisfied; we are forgiven. (4) We will rise someday too. Because He lives, we shall live also.

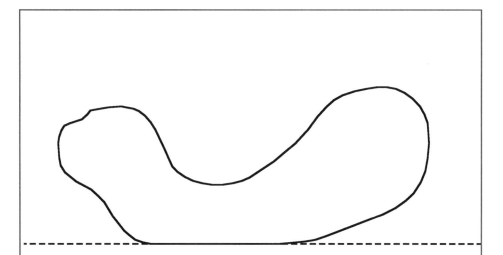

*Directions:*
1. *Color the shape light green (caterpillar).*
2. *Fold on the dotted line.*
3. *Cut out the shape, cutting through both layers of paper.*
4. *Color the other half of the shape brown (chrysalis).*
5. *Open the shape and turn it over. See the butterfly!*
6. *Color the beautiful butterfly.*

**Blackline 29-A**

## Words to Remember

*[Jesus says,] "Because I live, you also will live." John 14:19*

Emphasize that the Bible says Jesus gives His victory to us. Ask children to complete your statements, as follows.

- Because Jesus is without sin, in God's eyes we are _____ . (without sin)
- Because Jesus is holy, in God's eyes we are _____ . (holy)
- Because Jesus lives, you also will _____ . (live)
- Because Jesus' home is in heaven, your home will be in _____ . (heaven)

## Extending the Lesson

- Plant a small classroom garden in a plastic tub. Point out that the flowers will burst out of the shell of the seeds to new life. That reminds us of Jesus bursting from the grave and the new life He has and gives to us. Let children mark the spot where they planted their seeds by inserting into the soil crosses made from wooden craft sticks. On the crosses, each child can print "Jesus," a heart to stand for the word *loves,* and then the child's name.
- Today, children are used to finding chocolate and marshmallow inside an Easter egg. Ask, **What changes and grows to new life in a real egg?** (A baby chick.) **The baby chick pushes its way out of the shell. That makes me think of Jesus coming out of the rocky shell of the tomb. This picture of breaking out to new life is the real reason we celebrate with eggs at Easter.** Let children decorate and then eat cookies shaped like Easter eggs.

# INTRODUCE

Ask, **When you are excited about something, do you walk or run to tell someone?** (Usually run.) **To whom do you run to tell good news?** (Mom, Dad, friends, etc.) **What good news do you like to talk about?** (Winning a game, doing well in school, getting a gift, etc.) **In today's Bible story there is Good News and lots of people running to share that Good News.**

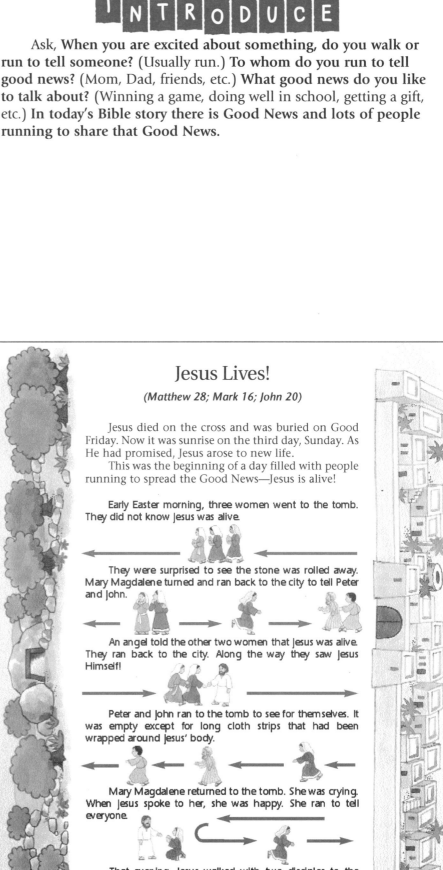

## Jesus Lives!

*(Matthew 28; Mark 16; John 20)*

Jesus died on the cross and was buried on Good Friday. Now it was sunrise on the third day, Sunday. As He had promised, Jesus arose to new life.

This was the beginning of a day filled with people running to spread the Good News—Jesus is alive!

Early Easter morning, three women went to the tomb. They did not know Jesus was alive.

They were surprised to see the stone was rolled away. Mary Magdalene turned and ran back to the city to tell Peter and John.

An angel told the other two women that Jesus was alive. They ran back to the city. Along the way they saw Jesus Himself!

Peter and John ran to the tomb to see for themselves. It was empty except for long cloth strips that had been wrapped around Jesus' body.

Mary Magdalene returned to the tomb. She was crying. When Jesus spoke to her, she was happy. She ran to tell everyone.

That evening, Jesus walked with two disciples to the village of Emmaus. Then they ran back to Jerusalem to tell the Good News—Jesus is alive!

## DEVELOP

Use flannelgraph figures to retell the Easter story. Emphasize the running back and forth between the tomb and the city of Jerusalem. (Use the story on page 1 of the *Alive* Student Book as your guide.) Ask, **Why was everyone so excited?** (Jesus was alive again.) **Why is that so important?** (Only God has such power. Because Jesus had such power for Himself, we know He has power for us. We can trust that all of the Lord's promises are true because He never fails to keep His word.)

## RESPOND

Use pages 1–2 of the *Alive* Student Book to review the events of Holy Week. Then say, **Like Jesus' followers long ago, let's run to share the Good News and praise the Lord!** Go to a large play area or gymnasium. Divide the class into eight small groups. Have four of the groups stand in the four corners of the room or play area. The other four groups stand near you at the center. Assign each group a corner and give them a message to share. At your signal, the groups run to their assigned corners, join hands, and shout the message you have given them. Then the corner people and the runners exchange roles and deliver a new message. Do this several times, giving messages such as **Jesus is alive; Christ has risen; our sins are forgiven; God loves us dearly; our Savior gave His life for us; Jesus conquered death; Jesus is true God; tell the Good News about Jesus.** Then gather together at the center and have the children repeat your words at the asterisk as you say this portion of the Second Article of the Apostles' Creed:

**I believe in Jesus Christ, * His only Son, our Lord, * who was conceived by the Holy Spirit, * born of the Virgin Mary, * suffered under Pontius Pilate, * was crucified, died and was buried. * He descended into hell. * The third day * He rose again from the dead. ***

*Option.* Read the Easter story in the Hear Me Read Big Book *Where Is Jesus?* (available from Concordia Publishing House). If you purchase the classroom set you will also receive a Teachers Guide pamphlet that provides extra ideas and activities for teaching this Bible story.

### Holy Week

*Fill in whatever is missing. Tell what is happening in each section.*

START
GOING TO JERU-SALEM

P A L M SUNDAY

THE TEMPLE

HOSANNA

JESUS LOVES

JESUS WASHES

SERVE

LORD'S SUPPER

YOUR WILL BE DONE

GOOD FRIDAY

JESUS LI V E S !

JESUS LO V E S !

**Words to Remember**
[Jesus says,] "Because I live, you also will live."
John 14:19

## Discovery Point

Jesus died and rose again so that, through the gift of faith, we are His children and have the assurance of life eternal.

## Jesus Appears to Thomas

John 20:19–31

## Objectives

That by the power of the Holy Spirit working through God's Word, the students will

- take any doubts they have to Christ to receive forgiveness and strength;
- rejoice in the many appearances of Jesus to His followers, which proved that He was alive;
- grow in their faith in the resurrection of their Savior.

## Day 3 Materials

- Gift-wrapped box
- Teddy bear
- Jenna puppet
- Flannelgraph materials
- Washable markers
- Blackline 29-B
- Paper punch
- Yarn

## Day 4 Materials

- *Alive* Student Book

# INTRODUCE

In a prominent spot, place a gift-wrapped teddy bear, with a large gift tag attached that has "Jenna" on it. Go to another part of the room and bring out the Jenna puppet.

**TEACHER:** Jenna, why are you over here? Didn't you see the nice gift I brought for you?

**JENNA:** I don't believe that it's for me. It's not my birthday. It's not Christmas or any other holiday.

**TEACHER:** You mean you *doubt* what I say? You don't *trust* me when I say it is for you?

**JENNA:** Sorry, Teacher. I *doubt* that the gift is for me. I guess I don't trust what you say because it seems too good to be true.

**TEACHER:** You sound a lot like a man named Thomas. He didn't trust the people who said Jesus arose from the dead on Easter. He doubted that Jesus was alive because it seemed too good to be true.

**JENNA:** Are you mad at me, Teacher, because I didn't trust you?

**TEACHER:** No, I'm not angry. That is why I will show you what is true. *(Open the gift box and have Jenna take out and hug the teddy bear.)*

**JENNA:** Oh, thank you! Tell me, was Jesus mad at Thomas for not trusting?

**TEACHER:** No, in fact, I was following Jesus' example just now. Jesus showed Thomas the truth so that Thomas would believe. Let's learn more about his story.

# DEVELOP

Use flannelgraph figures to tell the Bible story. Begin with the 10 disciples in the closed room the week before Thomas saw Jesus. Emphasize that Jesus had all power as God, even though He was also a man with a body to touch and scars from His wounds. Because Jesus is God He could appear and disappear wherever and whenever He wanted. Use the Scripture reading as your guide.

## R E S P O N D

The following activity will help children understand the terms *doubt* and *believe*. Use washable markers to draw a happy face on one palm and a sad face on the other palm of each child. Read the following statements (and others you create) and have the children respond, raising the happy-face palm if they believe it and the sad-face palm if they doubt it.

- It's (identify an unseasonal weather condition, such as snowing) outside.
- Today is my birthday.
- I went to college.
- My goldfish has a purse.
- Jesus loves me.
- The sun has turned purple.
- Children like recess.
- Jesus will take you to heaven.

Distribute copies of Blackline 29-B. Discuss each picture and have the children mark the boxes. Then have them cut out the picture in the last box, color it, and use crayons to print Thomas' creed on the back of the picture ("My Lord and my God!"). Punch one or two holes at the top of the picture, string yarn through the holes, and tie the yarn to make a pendant that shares a Gospel message.

## Do You Doubt or Trust?

Would you trust this bridge to hold you?

❏ Yes      ❏ No

Would you trust that this plane could fly?

❏ Yes      ❏ No

Would you trust Jill to fix dinner for your family?

❏ Yes      ❏ No

Would you trust Jesus to take away your sins?

❏ Yes      ❏ No

**Blackline 29–B**
© 2001 CPH Permission granted to reproduce for classroom use.

## Worship Ideas

- Read aloud Thomas' confession of faith: "My Lord and my God!" Say that this is a creed because a creed tells what you believe. Make a class creed by listing sentences the children volunteer that tell what they believe about God. (Edit any sentences that are not doctrinally correct so that the creed can be read as truth.) Then read the Apostles' Creed to the children, encouraging them to say with you any of the words they know.

- Place several natural objects (flowers, twigs, grass) on a table, pointing out that these are things God created. **What are some other things God created that wouldn't even fit on this table?** (Rivers, mountains, etc.) **Let's celebrate God's awesome creations, especially the plan of salvation He created for us through Jesus. Let's tell Him that He is great and almighty. The Book of Psalms in the Bible is filled with praises to God. I'm going to read parts of Psalm 148** (verses 7–13). **Every time I stop, you are to say, "Praise the Lord."**

## Bible Background

Late in the evening on the day of Jesus' resurrection, the disciples meet quietly in secret. The Roman governor had signed the execution order, and Jesus had been crucified. The disciples knew that they, too, could be arrested, charged, and punished.

Jesus comes in the midst of their fears. He shares His peace. He gives His forgiveness and salvation. He bestows the Holy Spirit on the disciples and confers His mission on them.

That mission has reached us. We hear God's absolution in Word and Sacrament in worship. By God's grace we and our students have also been graciously blessed, even though we have not seen the nail prints in Jesus' hands.

# Day

## Words to Remember

*I know that my Redeemer lives. Job 19:25*
Emphasize that we can say these words with complete confidence and certainty. We can be sure because Jesus spent 40 days talking with many disciples on different occasions. But more than that, our certainty is based on His Word as true and almighty God.

Invite an older group of children to come to your class to sing the Easter hymn "I Know that My Redeemer Lives." Cue your children so that they can sing along each time today's Bible verse is sung in the hymn.

## Extending the Lesson

Point out that the name *Thomas* means "twin." Explain that twins are two children born to a family at the same time. Point out that Thomas himself acted like two different people—once as a doubter and the next time as a firm believer. His behavior from one week to the next was the *opposite*. **What made the difference in Thomas?** (Jesus came to Thomas and gave him faith to believe.) **Jesus does the same for you and me. He comes to us in God's Word and through the power of the Holy Spirit.**

As you talk about Thomas' *opposite* behavior from one week to the next, make opposite art pictures. Fold a 9x12-inch piece of colored construction paper in half. This will serve as the background. Take a half sheet of contrasting colored paper. Cut out a design or picture. Save the scraps. Glue the cut-out design on one half of the background. Glue the scraps of paper in the opposite position on the other half of the background. You will have opposite (positive and negative) pictures.

## INTRODUCE

Use sign language for the name *Jesus* (middle fingers, back and forth, touching opposite palms). Say, **This is sign language for the name Jesus. The sign used for a person's name usually tells something important about them. What does this sign tell about Jesus?** (It indicates the nail marks on His hands from His crucifixion.) **Why is this important?** (Jesus' death on the cross and coming alive at Easter is the most important thing Jesus did for us. Because of this we have forgiveness and eternal life.) Sing several praise songs, making the sign language for Jesus each time His name is sung. Your choices could include "Jesus Loves Me, This I Know," "Jesus Is My Special Friend," and "There Is a Name I Love to Hear" (*LOSP*, pp. 42–44).

### Jesus Appears to Thomas
*(John 20:19–31)*

**NARRATOR:** After Jesus died on the cross and arose on Easter, many of His friends were in a house with the doors locked. All of a sudden Jesus was in the room with them.

**JESUS:** Peace be with you!

**ALL:** It is the Lord! He is alive!

**JESUS:** I have done all that I said I would do. Now I want you to go and tell the Gospel message.

**NARRATOR:** Then Jesus left. A short while later, Thomas came to see them.

**ALL:** We have seen Jesus! He is alive!

**THOMAS:** I doubt that. I don't trust your words.

**ALL:** But He was here, with us!

**THOMAS:** Unless I see Him and touch the nail prints in His hands, I will not believe it.

**NARRATOR:** A week later, in the same house, they were together again. This time Thomas was with them when Jesus appeared.

**JESUS:** Peace be with you. Thomas, come here. Touch My hands and the nail prints. Do not doubt it. Believe in Me!

**THOMAS:** My Lord and my God!

**JESUS:** You believe because you have seen Me. Blessed are those who have not seen and yet have believed.

**NARRATOR:** We believe that Jesus is our risen Lord and Savior! Praise God!

3

## DEVELOP

Use the script on page 3 of the *Alive* Student Book to act out the Bible story. Emphasize that Jesus gives us a special blessing when He says, "Blessed are those who have not seen and yet have believed" (John 20:29). **Jesus is talking about you and me when He says those words. The disciples were blessed to be able to see, hear, and touch Jesus. But He gives this *special* blessing to us because by faith we believe, trusting His Word that He is our living Savior and God. Let's thank Him in prayer: Dear Jesus, thank You for the special blessing You give to us. Even though we have not seen You, we hear Your words in the Bible. We know that someday we will see You face-to-face. We know that we will see You in heaven because You have promised to forgive our sins and because You have made us people of God. Forgive us when we doubt or question Your ways and Your will. Make our faith stronger each day and help us to live in faith. In Your holy name. Amen.**

## RESPOND

Look at the title on page 4 of the *Alive* Student Book. Say, **Thomas had doubted that Jesus was alive. He said, "When I see it, I'll believe it." God gives us faith to believe, even though we have not seen Jesus. That's why we can say together, "Since God said it, I believe it."** Together read the list of promises we have from God. Assure the children that we can trust these words completely and with absolute certainty.

Sing the title of this page to the tune of the first line of the Easter hymn "Jesus Christ Is Risen Today" (*LOSP*, p. 96). Be sure to add an *Alleluia*. Now use page 4 and this little song in responsive praise to God in this manner: the teacher will read a phrase listed beside the picture of Jesus, and the children will respond by singing the song:

**Since God said it, I believe it! Alleluia!**

---

### Since God Said It, I Believe It!

"I will always be with you."

"I listen to you pray."

"I forgive your sins."

"I give you what you need."

"I will take you to heaven."

"I will do what is best for you."

**Words to Remember**

I know that my Redeemer lives.
Job 19:25

4

## Discovery Point

Jesus completed His work on earth and sends His messengers out to share the Good News of forgiveness and salvation.

## The Great Commission

Matthew 28:16–20

## Objectives

That by the power of the Holy Spirit working through God's Word, the students will
- know that God loves all people and wants them to come to know Jesus as their Savior;
- praise God for His great love in sending Jesus to save all people from sin and eternal death;
- share Jesus with family, friends, neighbors, and "all nations."

## Day 1 Materials
- Great Commission poster
- Blackline 30-A
- Tape
- Length of paper
- Paint or markers

## Day 2 Materials
- Robed speaker
- *Alive* Student Book

## INTRODUCE

Let all the children have the opportunity to tell what job or jobs they would like to have when they grow up. Then say, **Jesus has given you a job to do right now! You don't have to grow up to do this job. Jesus wants you to be His messenger! What message can you tell? Jesus wants you to tell others what you know about God's love. You can do this job anytime, anywhere, throughout your whole life! Let's hear more about this important job we all have.**

## DEVELOP

Point out, **Jesus spent three years talking to His disciples about God's love and plan of salvation. But the disciples, just like you and me, didn't always understand. After Jesus died on the cross and arose at Easter, He spent 40 days with His disciples, helping them to see why He died on the cross and arose at Easter, helping them to get ready to be His messengers. On one of these days, they were on a mountain in Galilee, and Jesus spoke the words that we call "The Great Commission." This means "The Great Job Jesus Has Asked Us to Do." Let's listen to His words.**

Use the Great Commission poster to explain Christ's words. In advance cut apart the two rows of pictures and tape them together side by side to form one long strip. Fold the sections back and forth so you can gradually reveal one section at a time.
- *Go and make disciples of all nations.* First, Jesus tells us that He wants all people to know Him and be saved. Point out the importance of translating the Bible into all languages so that all people can hear God's Word. Praise God that the Gospel, originally written in Greek, has been translated into our own language so that we can hear the Good News of our Savior.
- *Baptizing them in the name of the Father and of the Son and of the Holy Spirit.* Baptism is a special gift from God, a special way that God blesses us with His grace and forgiveness. Baptism is not something we do; Baptism is something we receive. It is a gift from God.
- *Teaching them to obey everything I have commanded you.* Jesus desires that you hear, speak, and obey His Word. Living in Him and for Him is a way of life because of who you are (a child of God) and what you do (as God's messenger).
- *And surely I am with you always, to the very end of the age.* How can we do such a big and important job? We don't do it alone. Jesus is always with us, helping us, and He sends the Holy Spirit to empower us. Rely on Him. He is near.

# RESPOND

Ask the children, **How can you share God's message with people of all nations? You are just "kids." You can't fly all over the world telling people about Jesus! How can you help?** Children may respond that they can give offering money to support missions in other lands. Then note, **God has done an amazing thing for us in this day and age. He has brought people from all nations to us!** Lead a discussion that identifies people from other nations that now live in your neighborhood or go to your school. Perhaps some children even have family members that originally came from other countries. **We don't have to go far away to tell people about the love of Jesus! There are people all around us who need His love and salvation!**

Continue by distributing copies of Blackline 30-A. Children may color, cut, tape, and fold the sections to make a Great Commission booklet similar to the poster you used earlier. They may print this title on it: "The Great Commission—A Job for You!" Let the children work with a partner to read the words and explain the pictures. This will serve as a "rehearsal" so that they can later share this message with others.

As a class project, display a long, narrow section of paper (shelf paper or adding machine paper). Title this special mural "Jesus Loves All People." Using felt-tipped markers or paint, have the children draw stick people in all the colors available.

## Worship Ideas

- Sing the stanza of "This Little Gospel Light of Mine" (*LOSP*, p. 103) that says *all around the neighborhood, I'm going to let it shine.* Add new stanzas such as *all around our town and back* or *all around the U.S.A.* (or … *our Canada*) or *all around the whole wide world.*
- Learn the song "Go Tell" (*LOSP*, p. 104, and on CD). Then use the song in a special way to emphasize the message of each stanza. Speak stanza 1 to emphasize the word *tell*; sing stanza 2; shout stanza 3; and shake each other's hands or give hugs as you sing stanza 4.

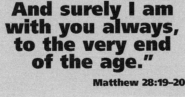

## Bible Background

Sometime during the 40 days between Jesus' resurrection and ascension, He told His disciples to travel to Galilee, the region in which Jesus had carried out much of His ministry. There He gave them the Great Commission. The disciples, then, returned to Judea prior to the ascension.

How can mere mortals "make" disciples (Matthew 28:19)? Jesus immediately provides the answer: "… baptizing them in the name of the Father and of the Son and of the Holy Spirit, and teaching them to obey everything I have commanded you" (28:19–20). *God* provides the power through Baptism and His Word! Those people who are given His authority to baptize, to preach, and to teach are serving as His instruments. We can go about that task joyfully, certain that Jesus is with us!

| "Go and make disciples of all nations, | baptizing them in the name of the Father and of the Son and of the Holy Spirit, |
|---|---|
| and teaching them to obey everything I have commanded you. | And surely I am with you always, to the very end of the age." **Matthew 28:19–20** |

**Blackline 30-A**

# WEEK 30-A

# Day 2

## Words to Remember

*Go and make disciples of all nations, baptizing them in the name of the Father and of the Son and of the Holy Spirit. Matthew 28:19*

Point out that these Bible words are printed on the first two sections of the poster and blackline activity. Evaluate the abilities of your students. Some of them may be able to learn verse 20 as well.

## Extending the Lesson

- Play a game similar to pin the tail on the donkey. Place a world map on a wall. Have each child write his or her name on a Post-It note. Blindfold each child, in turn, and have the child walk to the map and stick the name tag on the map. (If the child places it on an ocean, everyone says "splash," and the child moves the name tag.) Tell the child the name of the city, country, or continent where the name tag was placed. Also write that location on the child's name tag.

When the game is finished, provide time for the children to pray for the people in the place where they "landed." Remind them that God loves people everywhere. Pray that people everywhere may come to faith in Jesus as their Savior, so that they may have forgiveness and eternal life.

- Discuss ways to share God's message with others, in addition to a money offering for missions. Possibilities include make a card, send an e-mail, record a song (such as "I Love to Tell the Story"), compose a song (making up new words to a familiar tune), or design some type of art, all with a Christian message. Children will choose from this list and then prepare a message to share.

- Talk about maps and directions in social studies. On poster paper, make a large compass rose, with *north*, *south*, *east*, and *west* printed on the appropriate points. Draw a cross at the center. Attach the compass rose to your ceiling. Say, **This reminds us that Jesus wants people in all parts of the world— north, south, east, and west—to hear His Word and be saved.**

# INTRODUCE

If possible, take your class to a wide stairway inside or outside of your church or school. Have the children sit on the steps as you speak to them from the top of the stairway. Ask them to pretend that they are on a mountaintop. Point out that Jesus sometimes spoke to His followers on a mountain, as He did when He gave the Great Commission. Let the children guess why that was a good place to teach them. (Quiet, away from city noises, His voice would carry well so all could hear, everyone would be able to see Him.)

## The Great Commission

*(Matthew 28:16–20)*

After Easter, Jesus met His disciples on a mountain in Galilee. Jesus spoke about the job He was giving to His followers. And He promised always to be near with His power and blessings.

All power in heaven and on earth has been given to Me.

Where did Jesus get His power?

Go and make disciples of all nations, baptizing them in the name of the Father and of the Son and of the Holy Spirit. Teach them to obey everything I have commanded you. And remember, I am always with you, until the very end of time.

What should we say and do?

Who should we teach?

How can I do this important work?

5

## DEVELOP

Invite the pastor (or another church leader) to be your guest. (Ask him beforehand to wear a long robe.) Introduce the pastor and say that his robe reminds us that he will be telling you God's Word about Jesus. Have the pastor read Matthew 28:16–20 from a large Bible. Encourage him to talk to the children about the meaning of the verses or about their job as messengers for Jesus.

## RESPOND

Return to your classroom and talk about the training needed to be God's messenger. **Our pastor went to college and the seminary for many years to be a special messenger of God's Word. But you already know about Jesus and can already be His messenger. We can always learn more about Jesus, but as long as we know Him as our Savior, we never know too little. Just a few simple words about forgiveness through Jesus can be a very important message.**

Together look at page 6 of the *Alive* Student Book. This activity reminds us that simple words of God's love can be spoken anywhere, anytime. We have many opportunities each day. Inviting others to Sunday school and church is important. But here we are talking about a simple Gospel message to share right then and there. (Note: Answers may vary.)

### Messengers for Jesus
*Write what each child could say to share a simple message about Jesus.*

- What does that cross mean?
- Jesus is my Savior.
- Why didn't you fight back?
- Jesus wants us to forgive.
- Take one! No one will ever know.
- I want to follow Jesus' way.

### Words to Remember
Go and make disciples of all nations, baptizing them in the name of the ___Father___ and of the ___Son___ and of the ___Holy___ ___Spirit___ .

Matthew 28:19

# Day 3

## Discovery Point

Jesus completed His work on earth and sends His messengers out to share the Good News of forgiveness and salvation.

## Jesus Ascends to Heaven

Acts 1:1–12

## Objectives

That by the power of the Holy Spirit working through God's Word, the students will

- know that Jesus, true God and true man, returned to His home in heaven and will return to take us there too;
- trust in Jesus, King of kings, and in His promise to constantly be with us;
- be willing witnesses who share God's love with others.

## Day 3 Materials

- Jake puppet
- Flannelgraph materials
- Blackline 30-B

## Day 4 Materials

- Jenna puppet
- Alive Student Book

## INTRODUCE

Use the Jake puppet to introduce the story.

**TEACHER:** Jake, you are back from your trip! Did you have a good time?

**JAKE:** It was great. First, we spent a few days at Grandma and Grandpa's house. I wanted to stay even longer. But then we went to the beach. That was great too. I love to build sand castles and get splashed by ocean water.

**TEACHER:** What did you like best of all?

**JAKE:** Our trip was great. But the best part was coming home again.

**TEACHER:** Why was coming home the best?

**JAKE:** I like seeing other people and places. But I like my home the best—sleeping in my own bed, eating my mom's cooking, playing with my own toys, seeing my old friends, running with my dad and my puppy in the backyard. That's where I want to be!

**TEACHER:** What you are saying makes me think of today's Bible story. Jesus had been on earth for 33 years. He had important work to do. He died and rose again because He loves us and wanted to save us. But now it was time for Him to go home again. His work was finished. He was ready to return to His home in heaven and to His heavenly Father. But when Jesus returned home, He went in a very special way. Let's hear now what the Bible tells us.

## DEVELOP

Use the flannelgraph figures while using words such as these to tell today's story:

For 40 days after He rose from the dead, Jesus stayed on earth, visiting with His friends and showing Himself to many people. One day Jesus said to His disciples, "Come with Me. I am going to the Mount of Olives." The disciples walked with Jesus from Jerusalem to a sunny spot on the top of the hill.

Jesus said, "I am going to leave you. But don't be sad. I will come back someday to take you to My kingdom in heaven. I will go away, but I will not leave you alone. I will send My Holy Spirit to you. He will comfort you when you are sad. He will strengthen your faith and will help you to live and speak My Word. I want you to be My witnesses. Tell people what you know, what you have seen and heard, about God's loving plan of salvation."

Then Jesus raised His hands and blessed them. As He was blessing them, He began to rise up in the sky. The disciples watched in amazement, until a cloud covered Jesus and they could see Him no more. Still the disciples kept watching.

Suddenly two angels stood with them and said, "Why are you still looking up to heaven? Don't you know that Jesus has triumphed and is sitting on His throne at His heavenly Father's right hand? But He will come again in the same way that you have seen Him go."

The disciples knew that Jesus is true God and has all power. How happy they were. They walked back to Jerusalem, praising God and singing songs.

## R E S P O N D

Celebrate the majesty of this festival, which is sometimes ignored (perhaps because it falls on a Thursday in the church year calendar). Encourage the children to rejoice in the triumph and victory of our Lord. Sing "The King of Glory" (*LOSP*, p. 77, and on CD). After singing the song once, say, **This must be how the angels and heavenly hosts must have felt when Jesus returned to heaven!** Sing the song again, and then say, **This song is also our song for the day when Jesus returns to earth to take all believers to heaven. We don't know when that will be. But we do know that it will be the happiest day of all when we receive the crown of life—eternal life in heaven!**

Have a praise parade to emphasize the majesty of God. Sing songs like "Hallelujah! Praise Ye the Lord," "I Have the Joy," and "My God Is So Great" (*LOSP*, pp. 58, 62, 64, and on CD).

Distribute Blackline 30-B and let the children color and build a celebration picture of our King. Follow the directions on the page while listening to praise music.

King of Kings

*Directions:*
1. *Cut on the center line. Color all the pictures of a royal king.*
2. *Cut out the body of the king. Use a glue stick or tape to place Him on the throne.*
3. *Cut out the picture of Jesus. Glue or tape Him on the king's body. Jesus is our heavenly King.*
4. *Cut out and glue the crown on Jesus' head. Jesus rules over heaven and earth.*
5. *Cut out and glue the scepter to Jesus' hand. One day He will take all believers to His kingdom in heaven.*

**Blackline 30-B**

© 2001 CPH   Permission granted to reproduce for classroom use.

## Worship Ideas

- *Songs Kids Love to Sing 2*, available from CPH, has several songs appropriate for this lesson: "Heaven Is a Wonderful Place," "Kids of the Kingdom," and "Oh, He's King of Kings" (pp. 25, 38, 43). These songs are recorded on a tape and CD that accompany the songbook.
- Emphasize that Christ's victory is also our victory. Read aloud 1 Corinthians 15:57. Also point out that the "crown of life" that Jesus gives us is not a gold crown that sits on our head. Instead, it is the crowning glory of life in heaven, which will never end. Read aloud the last sentence of Revelation 2:10.
- Read Revelation 7:9–12 after explaining that this tells about the celebration of the heavenly hosts worshiping Jesus, the Lamb of God. Listen to a recording of (or invite an older class in to sing) the song "Worthy Is Christ" ("This is the feast of victory for our God") from the worship liturgy. Perhaps your class can join in singing a repeated phrase so that they will also feel comfortable doing so in a church worship service.

## Bible Background

In the 40 days since His resurrection Jesus had been explaining the true purpose of His coming—to save us from our sins (Luke 24:45–47). Even at this late date, however, the disciples remain fixated on His establishing an earthly kingdom (Acts 1:6). Jesus is gentle in His correction (1:7), not answering their question directly, but instead pointing to a higher goal—taking His salvation to the world. The itinerary He maps out will also become the outline of the Book of Acts: first close to home base (Jerusalem), then in the surrounding regions (the rest of Judea and Samaria), and finally to the ends of the earth.

The ascension does not mark a time when Jesus left His followers. Quite the contrary. The one Christ—both fully human and fully divine—is now omnipresent rather than in one location only, as Jesus chose to be during His humiliation on earth. Jesus is always with us!

## Words to Remember

[Jesus said,] "I am with you always, to the very end of the age." Matthew 28:20

Try this art activity to focus on Christ's ascension and promise. Have students glue various shades of sky-colored tissue paper scraps onto white paper by "painting" over them with white glue diluted with water. While the paper is still wet, have them randomly add pulled-apart cotton balls to form clouds in the sky. Once the paper dries, use a felt-tipped marker to print today's "Words to Remember" across the sky they created.

## Extending the Lesson

- Talk about "tri" words, each having something to do with the number 3. Possibilities: tricycle (3 wheels), triple (getting to third base in baseball), triplets (3 children born at the same time), Trinity (3 persons in 1 God). Ask, **How was each of the three persons of the Trinity involved in the Bible story?** (Father: Jesus returned to His Father in heaven; Son: Jesus is the Son of God who completed our salvation; Holy Spirit: Jesus promised to send the Holy Spirit to empower the disciples, and us, to be witnesses of God's love.)
- Create a Venn diagram, comparing Jesus as man and as God. The qualities of Jesus as man would include that He was born on earth, suffered pain, worked, got hungry, got sleepy, died. The qualities of Jesus as God would include that He was God's Son, lived a perfect life, loved everyone, took all people's sin upon Himself, rose from the dead. The overlapping sections of the diagram can state some names of Jesus such as Savior, Shepherd, Lord, and Redeemer.

# Day

## INTRODUCE

Use the Jenna puppet to introduce the story.

**JENNA:** Teacher, why did Jesus leave? The disciples sure needed His help! We sure need His help!

**TEACHER:** Well, first of all, remember that Jesus didn't leave us alone. He promises to send the Holy Spirit to our hearts. And Jesus promises to always be near us. We can't see Him anymore, but He is right here with us in this room.

**JENNA:** How can Jesus do that?

**TEACHER:** Because Jesus is God, He has all power. He can be everywhere at the same time, and nothing is impossible for Him.

**JENNA:** Tell me more about Jesus going back to heaven.

**TEACHER:** Well, first let me talk about when you learned to tie your shoelaces!

**JENNA:** Shoelaces! What does that have to do with Jesus?

---

### Jesus Ascends to Heaven

*(Acts 1:1–12)*

It was **40** days after [image]. "It is time for Me **2** go back **2** My home in heaven," said [image] to His [image]. "But [image] will send the Holy Spirit to help **U**." The disciples were [image]. They wanted [image] to stay with them. They walked to the top of the Mount of Olives, a hill near the city of [image]. [image] said, "I want you to do something for Me. Tell [image] all over the [image] about Me. And remember, [image] will always [image] with **U**." Then [image] began to rise [image] into the sky. The [image] watched [image] go [image]. They watched until a [image] covered [image] and they could not see Him anymore. Two [image] stood near them and said, "Why are you still looking for [image]? He has returned to heaven. But He will come again some day, just like He went away." The [image] were [image] now. They returned to [image] singing [image] to praise God.

7

**TEACHER:** Just wait and see. When you were younger, your mom and dad tied your shoelaces for you. Then they taught you how to do it yourself. They could have kept on doing it for you. But they knew it was time for you to learn and to grow. So now, tying shoelaces is your job.

**JENNA:** How does that remind you of Jesus?

**TEACHER:** Well, Jesus came to earth to save us. He did everything for us, by living and dying and living again. He taught the disciples (and us) about His salvation. He could have stayed around, doing all the teaching Himself (just like your mom and dad could keep on tying your shoelaces). But Jesus knew it was time for the disciples (and us) to learn and to grow in faith. So He gave them (and us) a job. Just like it is now your job to tie your own shoelaces, it is also your job to share God's love with other people and tell them about Jesus, our Savior. Let's learn more about Jesus right now.

## DEVELOP

Use the rebus on page 7 of the *Alive* Student Book to review the story. The teacher can read the printed words aloud while the children "read" the pictures.

## RESPOND

Say, **Jesus gives us the job to be His messengers, telling the message of salvation. Another word for this job is to be a "witness." Witnesses tell what they know. We can tell others that we know Jesus loves us, saves us, forgives us, and is always near to us.** Then ask, **Who first told you about Jesus? Whom can you talk to about Jesus?**

Read aloud Acts 1:8 to learn where Jesus wants His Word to be shared. He spoke to His disciples on the Mount of Olives, but we can modify the words to fit our own location. Jesus said to be witnesses in Jerusalem (your own town), Judea (your own nation), Samaria (nearby countries), and to the ends of the earth (all places in the world).

Children will more readily witness if they have had an opportunity to practice verbalizing what they can say. Ask for volunteers to act out these situations:

- You see a friend stealing something from your desk. What could you say?
- You see two younger children fighting over a toy. What could you say?
- One of your classmates is sad because their family pet has died. What could you say?
- A new child joins your class at school. What could you say?

Close by working together on the review activity on page 8 of the Student Book.

---

### What Was Witnessed?

Directions: Who? When? Where? What? Why? Can you answer these five "W" questions about today's Bible story? Write your answers on the fingers.

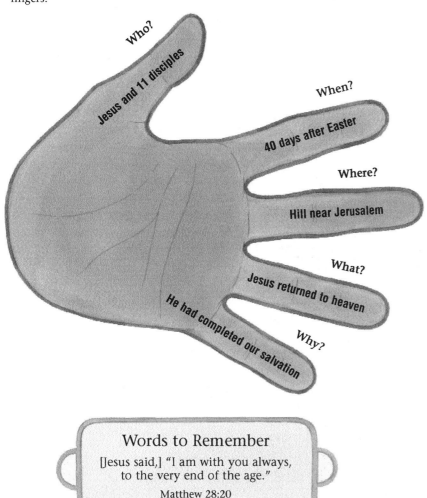

Who? — Jesus and 11 disciples
When? — 40 days after Easter
Where? — Hill near Jerusalem
What? — Jesus returned to heaven
Why? — He had completed our salvation

### Words to Remember
[Jesus said,] "I am with you always, to the very end of the age."
Matthew 28:20

## Discovery Point

The Holy Spirit works faith in the hearts of sinners so they are led to repent of their sins and receive forgiveness through the sacrifice of Jesus. The Spirit empowers believers to lead a life that witnesses boldly to God's love and grace.

## Pentecost

Acts 2

## Objectives

That by the power of the Holy Spirit working through God's Word, the students will

- rejoice that the Holy Spirit plants and grows faith in the hearts of God's people;
- recognize that the Holy Spirit works through God's Word and Sacraments;
- boldly speak about God's love in Jesus to others.

## Day 1 Materials

- Recorded message (from a pastor)
- Blackline 31-A
- Globe

## Day 2 Materials

- Three brown paper bags
- Box of cereal
- Hand weight
- Colored paper strips
- *Alive* Student Book

## INTRODUCE

Prepare to tell the Bible story by teaching the children a repeated response. First say, **We learned that 40 days after Easter, Jesus returned to heaven. We call that Ascension Day. Fifty days after Easter was Pentecost Day—another very special event. Pentecost was a day of noises and commotion. I'm going to have you make some of the noises as I tell the story.**

Divide the children into eight groups. One group is to make swooshing sounds to represent the sound of a great wind. Another group is to pat their hands on a desk or table to represent the sound of a huge crowd of people running. The other six groups are to say "Yes, Jesus Loves Me" in different languages. (See page 10 of the *Alive* Student Book, and teach the first line of the stanzas listed there.) After all groups have practiced their parts, have everyone make their sounds together at the same time. Tell them they are to make this noise each time you say "Holy Spirit" in the story. Give them a cutoff sign so that they know when to stop. Practice this a few times and then tell the story.

## DEVELOP

Say, **It was 50 days after Jesus arose from the grave, and 10 days after Jesus arose into heaven. His followers were in a large room together, waiting for the gift Jesus had promised to send. Suddenly there was the sound of a great wind. People from all over the city came rushing to find out what was happening. The sound led them to the house where the disciples were staying. This was the power of the Holy Spirit (pause) working to gather the people so they could hear God's Word.**

**The people wondered what was happening when they saw the followers of Jesus with flames of fire on their heads. This was a sign that the Holy Spirit (pause) was working in them, changing their hearts in faith and making them bold to speak.**

**The Holy Spirit (pause) made Peter brave, so he got up to speak about Jesus. But only people who spoke his language would be able to understand his words. So the Holy Spirit (pause) did another amazing miracle. He gave the disciples the ability to speak in other languages so that everyone could hear God's plan of salvation. The disciples spoke the languages of Parthians, Medes, and Elamites; of the people of Mesopotamia, Judea, Cappadocia, Asia, Phrygia, Pamphylia, Egypt, Libya, and Rome; and of Cretans and Arabs—all through the power of the Holy Spirit (pause).**

**Peter told the people that Jesus, who died on the cross, had arisen from the tomb because He is true God and is now in heaven. He explained that Jesus died to take away our sins. The Holy Spirit (pause) was at work in the people's hearts. They were sorry for their sins. They asked what they should do. Peter replied,**

"Repent and be baptized, every one of you, in the name of Jesus Christ for the forgiveness of your sins."

The Holy Spirit (pause) worked faith in the hearts of the people. That day 3,000 people were baptized in the name of the Father and of the Son and of the Holy Spirit (pause).

## R E S P O N D

In advance, make a recording of your pastor reading a Bible verse in the original Hebrew or Greek, followed by a reading of the same verse in English. After explaining and listening to the two versions, say, **We can be very thankful that we can hear the Bible in our own language. Someone who knows Hebrew [Greek] and our language had to translate the words or read them in one language and say what they mean in another language.**

Have the children do the activity on Blackline 31-A. Explain that the children are to be translators. They are to look at what each word means in the newly created language. Then they are to translate or change the words into English in order to hear the message of the Bible verse. Follow this with the first activity in the "Worship Ideas" section.

## What Is the Good News?

🍦 = in    ⭐ = and    🌴 = Believe    ♡ = be    🎀 = the

🐟 = Jesus    ⛵ = you    ➶ = Lord    🌻 = will    ☺ = saved

_____  _____  _____

_____  _____

_____  _____

_____  _____

_____  _____

*Directions: In order to understand the teacher's message, we need to hear it in our own language. Use this key to translate it. Write the matching words on the lines.*

## Worship Ideas

- Children like repetition and also unusual sounding words. Involve these factors in a responsive statement that emphasizes God's love for all people. You may want to hold a globe as you name cities and countries around the world.
  **TEACHER:** God loves people in Timbuktu.
  **CHILDREN:** And He helps us love them too.
  **TEACHER:** God loves people in Pakistan.
  **CHILDREN:** And He helps us love them too.
  **TEACHER:** *(continue with other locations)* God loves people in _____ .
  **CHILDREN:** And He helps us love them too.

- Give each child a brown paper lunch bag on which they are to draw a large simple stick person to represent themselves. Give the children crumpled and torn paper to put into the bags, saying, **This reminds us that we are filled with sin. Each day we do things that are wrong.** Gather around your classroom altar, place the crumpled papers on or around the altar, and say, **Jesus takes our sins away. He took all the guilt and punishment to the cross for us and blesses us with new life in Him.**
  Continue, **The Bible says "be filled with the Holy Spirit" (Acts 9:17).** Blow air into the bag and hold the top of the bag closed as you say, **We can't see the Holy Spirit, but we can see what He does. He fills our hearts with faith. He is with us wherever we go, leading us to live as God's people. Let's celebrate!** On the count of three, everyone can pop their bags.

## Bible Background

Pentecost, also known as the Feast of Weeks or the Feast of Harvest, was one of the three great festivals God had established for Israel already during their travels to the Promised Land (Leviticus 23:15–21). Celebrated 50 days after Passover (Pentecost comes from the Greek word meaning "50"), it attracted to Jerusalem thousands of Jewish visitors, many of whom would have stayed the entire period between the two festivals.

The miracle of Pentecost shows in a dramatic way the transforming power of the Holy Spirit. The Spirit works in our hearts, leading us to repentance and faith, ensuring us that God forgives all our sins and promises eternal life in Christ.

## WEEK 31-A

### Words to Remember

*Repent and be baptized, / every one of you, / in the name of Jesus Christ / for the forgiveness of your sins. Acts 2:38*

- Practice the four phrases of this verse, assigning each to one of four groups of children. Point out that the phrases answer these questions: What? Who? What? Why?
- Make an enlarged version of the Bible verse as shown on page 10 of the *Alive* Student Book. Cut large flames from red construction paper. Use black markers to print the words. Involve the children by letting them use yellow and orange crayons to color over the red background surrounding the words. Display these on a bulletin board.

### Extending the Lesson

- In advance cut sponges into the shape of a flame. Have students dip the sponges into yellow and orange or gold and silver tempera paint and press the shapes onto red paper at various heights and angles, overlapping the shapes. Discuss the festival color of red and its meaning. (Red makes us think of the excitement of a celebration; it also reminds us of the color of the flames that represented the power of the Holy Spirit.)
- Take the children to the church sanctuary if it has an eternal flame candle. Ask the pastor to discuss the purpose and meaning of that constant flame. Relate this to the Holy Spirit's work of constantly keeping faith alive and active in the lives of God's people and sparking that flame of faith in those who will hear about God's love from God's Word.
- Plan a Pentecost celebration with red balloons and red streamers. Have a cake decorated to read "Happy Birthday, Christian Church." Perhaps have a luncheon planned by parents that includes foods from a variety of other countries as a reminder that Jesus wants His Word to be spread to all people in every land. Sing "Amigos de Cristo" and "We Are the Church" (*LOSP*, pp. 23 and 106).

## INTRODUCE

In advance prepare three brown paper bags by placing a box of cereal in one, a piece of exercise equipment like a barbell hand weight in another, and a Bible in the third one. Display the bags and say, **Today we are going to talk about** *growing.* **In this first bag I have something that helps you grow bigger in size. What do you think is in here?** After responses, display the cereal. **The next bag has something that helps you grow stronger. What could that be?** After responses, show the hand weight. **The last bag has something that helps us grow in faith in Jesus. What could that be?** Display the Bible and say, **When we hear and read God's Word, the Holy Spirit is at work. The Holy Spirit gives us faith and helps us grow in faith. The Holy Spirit works through God's Word and through Baptism and the Lord's Supper, which also have God's Word with them. Let's hear again about the Holy Spirit at work on Pentecost Day and how faith grew in the hearts of the people.**

### Pentecost

*(Acts 2)*

After Jesus ascended into heaven, the disciples went back to Jerusalem. They waited for the Holy Spirit to come to them as Jesus had promised. They waited for 10 days.

On Pentecost Day, suddenly there was the sound of a mighty, rushing wind. But, amazingly, it was only a sound. They were also amazed to see what looked like a flame on each believer's head. These were signs that the Holy Spirit had come. But there was more!

People came rushing from all over the city to see what was happening. The Holy Spirit gave the disciples the gift to be able to speak the language of Egyptians, Arabs, Romans, and many others. People were able to recognize their own languages and listened carefully.

Peter and the other disciples bravely told the people about Jesus' death on the cross and that He had arisen at Easter. They explained that Jesus had done this to pay the punishment for the sins of the world.

As the people heard about God's love, the Holy Spirit worked faith in their hearts. That day, 3,000 people repented and were baptized.

The followers of Jesus continued to meet to worship God, hear His Word, share the Lord's Supper, and speak to Him in prayer. We are followers of Jesus too, hearing and living His Word in faith.

Print the word *AMAZING* on two large strips of colored paper. Tell the children what the word is, and say, **The power of the Holy Spirit was AMAZING on Pentecost Day!** Place the paper strips over your ears and review the *amazing* sound of a wind that brought a curious crowd of people together that day. Then place the paper strips over your eyes and review the *amazing* sight that people saw as flames like fire appeared on the heads of the followers of Jesus. Then place the strips over your forehead as you explain the *amazing* things that the people learned about Jesus, who is true God, who died on the cross and arose to life on Easter. Then place the strips over your heart as you tell the *amazing* work of the Holy Spirit in the hearts of the people as He led them to be sorry about their sins and as the Holy Spirit brought them to faith in the forgiveness of our Savior Jesus. Next hold a paper strip and wave it high in celebration as you tell of the *amazing* growth of the church that day as 3,000 people were baptized. (If you made the bulletin board with four flames, add the two AMAZING paper strips to the top corners of the display.)

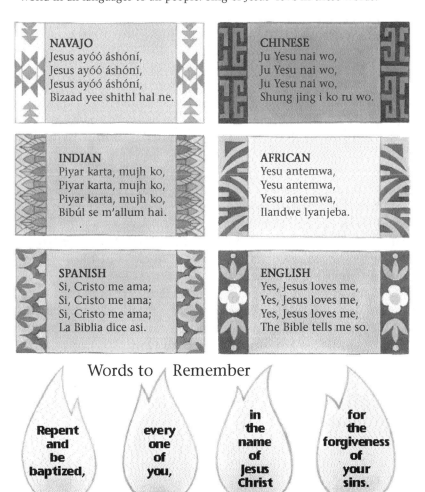

## Yes, Jesus Loves Me!

Jesus wants the Gospel message of God's love to spread around the world in all languages to all people. Sing of Jesus' love in these words.

**NAVAJO**
Jesus ayóó áshóní,
Jesus ayóó áshóní,
Jesus ayóó áshóní,
Bizaad yee shithl hal ne.

**CHINESE**
Ju Yesu nai wo,
Ju Yesu nai wo,
Ju Yesu nai wo,
Shung jing i ko ru wo.

**INDIAN**
Piyar karta, mujh ko,
Piyar karta, mujh ko,
Piyar karta, mujh ko,
Bibúl se m'allum hai.

**AFRICAN**
Yesu antemwa,
Yesu antemwa,
Yesu antemwa,
Ilandwe lyanjeba.

**SPANISH**
Si, Cristo me ama;
Si, Cristo me ama;
Si, Cristo me ama;
La Biblia dice asi.

**ENGLISH**
Yes, Jesus loves me,
Yes, Jesus loves me,
Yes, Jesus loves me,
The Bible tells me so.

### Words to Remember

Repent and be baptized, every one of you, in the name of Jesus Christ for the forgiveness of your sins.

Acts 2:38

10

On the board or chart paper draw a circle with a cross in the center. Say, **Pentecost is not the end of the story. The Bible tells us that the Christian church grew and grew. "The Lord added to their number daily those who were being saved"** (Acts 2:47). **Soon there were 5,000 Christians and then more and more.** Draw a circle around the first one and say, **The church was growing in number of people and in their faith. The Bible says the people continued to grow in the teachings of God's Word.** Print "teachings" at the top of this circle and fill the remainder of the circle with stick people shapes (children can help you). Then add another surrounding circle and say, **The people worshiped together every day at the temple church, and they grew in faith.** Print "worship" at the top of this circle and fill it with stick people. Continue in the same way, adding two more circles, labeling them "Lord's Supper" and "Prayer," and filling them with stick people as a reminder of the church growing. **God continues to bless His people. The Christian church has grown to millions of people. God wants the whole world to know Jesus as its Savior.**

Emphasize that God wants each of them to hear His Word and grow in faith through the power of the Holy Spirit. Read the special words in 2 Timothy 3:14–15 that encourage us to continue in what we have learned about our Savior, even from the time we were little children.

Discuss page 9 of the *Alive* Student Book. Then point out on a map the location of the places indicated on page 10. Read the words of the stanzas and encourage the children to try to read them and sing them with you. **After hearing these new words, I am glad that I can hear that "Jesus loves me" in my own language. I'm sure people in other parts of the world are happy to hear this message in the language they speak!** Encourage the children to try singing some of the stanzas with family members or friends when they take the booklets home.

## Discovery Point

The Holy Spirit works faith in the hearts of sinners so they are led to repent of their sins and receive forgiveness through the sacrifice of Jesus. The Spirit empowers believers to lead a life that witnesses boldly to God's love and grace.

## Jesus Changes Paul

Acts 9:1–20

## Objectives

That by the power of the Holy Spirit working through God's Word, the students will

- rejoice that God has called them to faith and forgiveness, changing them as sinners into saints through Christ Jesus;
- grow in their desire to tell others the Good News of God's love in Jesus for all people;
- show their faith through their words and actions.

## Day 3 Materials

- Paper bag
- Clothing items
- Blackline 31-B

## Day 4 Materials

- Flashlight, batteries
- Jake and Jenna puppets
- *Alive* Student Book

## INTRODUCE

Display a paper bag containing several clothing items. Say, **Today we are going to talk about *change*. I can change the way I look by putting on a hat.** Take a hat from the bag, preferably a funny or interesting one, and place it on your head. **I can change the way I look by taking off [or putting on] my jacket.** Take off your jacket and place it in the bag. **I can change the way I look by changing my shoes.** Take a pair of shoes from the bag, sit down, and switch shoes. **In our Bible story we will hear about a man who changed, but he still looked the same. He was changed on the inside. Jesus changed his heart. Let's hear how this happened.**

## DEVELOP

Have the children stand with you in a circle. Ask them to imitate your actions as you dramatically tell the story. (This will help them to focus on the details and progression of the story.) First, bounce up and down a little, pretending that you are holding the reins of your imaginary horse as you ride, saying, **My name is Saul, but you probably know me by my other name—Paul. I'm in a hurry, traveling from Jerusalem to Damascus. I've heard about people there who believe that Jesus was crucified, but then He came alive again at Easter. They believe that He is their Savior. I don't like those Christians. I'm going to arrest them and make them my prisoners. We'll see if Jesus can help them now.**

Fall to the ground and shade your eyes as if looking up at a bright light. **What's happening to me? Where is that light coming from? Who is that talking to me? It is Jesus Himself! He wants me to stop fighting against Him. He wants me to go to towns and cities and tell people that He is their crucified and now-living Savior.**

Stand up, eyes closed, arms stretched out as if trying to feel your way. **Jesus told me to go to Damascus and wait for His messenger. But I am blind now. My friends and helpers must lead me by the hand and show me the way.**

Sit down. **I have been waiting for three days. I wonder what God's plan is for me. My friends want me to eat. But I know I can't eat or drink anything till I hear the Lord's message.**

Stand up, arms lifted in praise. **Praise God! He sent the prophet Ananias. He blessed me and said, "Be filled with the Holy Spirit." He baptized me. I can see again. I can't wait to tell people the truth about Jesus. He is our Savior and God!**

# RESPOND

Ask, **What changed Paul?** (Jesus.) **When Paul changed, he still looked the same. What was different about him?** (Now he believed in Jesus. He stood *for* not *against* Jesus. Now his actions were different, because now he lived for Jesus.) **The Lord has changed you too. He has forgiven your sins and has given you faith. What difference does Jesus make in your life and in how you live?** (Discuss what your life as a child of God is like in Christ and through the power of the Holy Spirit, as you live in obedience, showing love to others, and worshiping God in all circumstances.)

Distribute copies of Blackline 31-B and follow the directions to make "stand-up books." When finished, read the story together. Talk about the ways that Roberto's story is like Saul's story. **God continues to change the hearts of people today. He can use you to tell others about His love.**

*Directions: Cut on the solid lines. Fold on the dotted lines. Use a glue stick to attach the backs of side 2 and side 3. Attach the backs of side 4 and side 5. Attach the backs of side 6 and side 7. Attach the backs of side 8 and side 1. You will have a stand-up book you can turn to read the story.*

**Blackline 31-B**

# Worship Ideas

- God used Paul to share the Gospel with people in many places. God can also use us, right where we are today. He wants us to speak of Jesus and live for Him. Sing several of the songs from the "Witness" section of *Little Ones Sing Praise* (pp. 99–106).

- Point out that Paul was not one of Jesus' 12 disciples. Jesus made a special appearance after His ascension into heaven in order to call Paul to faith. Point out that instead we call Paul one of the apostles. An apostle is *one who is sent.* Jesus sent Paul with a special task to preach to the Gentiles, taking the Gospel to the non-Jewish as well as the Jewish people (Acts 9:15). **Praise God that Jesus came to save the whole world!** Sing "Jesus Loves the Little Children" (*LOSP*, p. 94, and on CD).

# Bible Background

Paul was once a Pharisee named Saul, thoroughly trained in the Mosaic Law. His personal mission was to study and obey the commandments of God and teach others to follow the covenant regulations. The Christian message threatened the core of his convictions, so Saul attempted to destroy both the message and the messengers.

Later, in Paul's epistles, we learn that he thought he was doing God's will in persecuting the Christian church, but he learned that he was wrong—dead wrong! Paul was fighting God, denying and trying to destroy God's plan for the salvation of the world. He was, by his own admission, the "worst" sinner (1 Timothy 1:15). Yet Paul is no different from any other person; we are all sinners in the sight of God. Through Baptism and God's Word the Spirit has converted us too. Forgiven, we—like Paul—have been called to a new life of service in God's kingdom.

# Day 4

## Words to Remember

*If anyone is in Christ, he is a new creation.*
2 Corinthians 5:17

- *A new creation* implies change. It also implies getting rid of old, sinful ways. Have the class help you make a list comparing *old, sinful ways* to *a new creation.* **Jesus changes us through the power of the Holy Spirit working in God's Word. This is not a change in how we look. It is a change in how we live. As new creations, we live for Jesus!**

- Discuss the word *repent* and its forms (repented, repentance, etc.). Emphasize that repenting involves changing. Repentant change involves turning away from sin (sorrow and contrition) and turning to a life in Christ (following His ways as His new creation). We don't do this on our own—God calls us to repentance. He empowers this change in us.

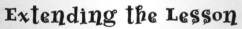

## Extending the Lesson

- Have children draw four simple faces to retell the day's story. The first shows angry Paul, who hated Christ and Christians; the next shows that he was blinded by the light of Christ's presence; the next shows him miraculously receiving his sight again; and the last shows him happy, knowing his Savior and seeing with his heart ("I see! I understand! I believe!") as well as with his eyes.

- Briefly refer to the history of the Bible times. On a map show the tiny country where Jesus lived. Point out that people in those days did not know how big the world is. Their world consisted of the countries in the Roman Empire that surrounded the Mediterranean Sea. Circle this area on the map. This is the area where the apostle Paul and other followers of Jesus traveled and taught. No one knew at this time about China or America. But in time God would lead people to spread His Word throughout the world.

## INTRODUCE

In large letters on the chalkboard or on two separate posters print "BEFORE" toward the left of the room and "AFTER" to the right. Explain that we are going to think a lot about *befores* and *afters.* Hold up a flashlight (with no batteries); try flicking it on several times. When nothing happens, say that this is a *before* flashlight. Then put batteries into the flashlight, turn it on, and ask, **What happened *after* I put in the batteries? Why did the batteries make a difference?** (The batteries gave power to the light.)

**Remember the *before* and *after* story of Saul? Afterward, most people called him Paul or even St. Paul. You and I have a *before* and *after* story too. Before we were changed, we were sinners, and afterward we became saints. What makes the difference?** (Jesus.) **Jesus is the power that changes us. Now we are saints, without sin, because Jesus took our sins away! Now I can call you St. _____ .** (Name off all the children, identifying each one as saint.) Then say, **Let's have Jenna and Jake remind us again of St. Paul's *before* and *after* story.**

## Jesus Changes Paul
### (Acts 9:1–20)

After Jesus returned to heaven, many people heard and believed that Jesus was their Savior. The Christian church grew and grew.

But not everyone loved Jesus. One such person was Paul (also called Saul). Paul thought believers in Jesus were wrong. Paul tried to have them thrown in jail. He even had some of them killed.

One day something happened that changed Paul completely. He was traveling to a town to arrest Christians. Suddenly a light from heaven shone so brightly that Paul fell to the ground. A voice said, "Why are you hurting Me?"

Paul asked who was speaking. The voice answered, "I am Jesus. Get up, go to the city, and wait. You will be told what to do next." When Paul stood up, he couldn't see. He friends took him by the hand and led him into the city.

For three days Paul sat alone, not eating or drinking anything. Then Jesus sent a Christian man named Ananias to Paul. Ananias blessed Paul.

Immediately Paul could see! Ananias said, "Jesus has special work for you to do. Stand up and be baptized."

Paul was a changed man. Jesus changes our hearts, too, by forgiving our sins and making us people of God!

# DEVELOP

Review the story using the Jenna puppet as you stand near "BEFORE." Use Jenna to tell about Paul before his conversion. Then move toward "AFTER," and have the puppet Jake tell about Paul after he met Jesus on the road.

Next, review the story by having the children physically identify your statements as BEFORE and AFTER Paul came to faith by standing next to the printed word. Statements can include the following:

- He put believers in Jesus into prison. (Before)
- He was baptized. (After)
- Jesus spoke to him in a bright light on the road. (Before)
- He told many people the truth about Jesus, the Savior. (After)
- He hated Christians. (Before)
- He didn't know that he was really fighting against God. (Before)
- He became a missionary, traveling to many countries to tell the Good News about Jesus. (After)

# RESPOND

Point out that God wants us to share His message with others. He gives us many opportunities each day to share His love by our words and our actions. Turn to page 12 in the *Alive* Student Book. Study the four situations pictured. Talk about what you, as a child of God, could say to each of these people as you share the love of Jesus in your words and by your actions. Let volunteers suggest possible responses. Print these on the chalkboard so children can copy the words into their books.

---

## Live a New Life for Jesus!

What could you say or do to show Jesus' loving-kindness to the people in the picture? Write your message on each arrow.

**Let's forgive each other like Jesus does, and then let's play together.**

**I think God sent me here today so I could help you.**

**Jesus gives us different blessings. Let's play something we can *all* do.**

**God wants us to take good care of all the animals He has made.**

## Words to Remember
If anyone is in Christ, he is a new creation.
2 Corinthians 5:17

12

271

## Discovery Point

God works in the lives of His people, leading them to reach out to others with the Gospel message and the love of Jesus.

## Paul Travels as a Missionary

Acts 9:26–31; 11:19–26; 16:22–36;
1 Timothy 4:12

## Objectives

That by the power of the Holy Spirit working through God's Word, the students will
- know that the Holy Spirit empowers God's people to speak His Word throughout the world;
- rejoice that God wants all people to be saved through Christ Jesus;
- realize that they can support missionaries through their prayers, offerings, and encouragement.

## Day 1 Materials

- Bible costumes or flannelgraph materials
- Jake and Jenna puppets
- Blackline 32-A

## Day 2 Materials

- Crackers
- Peanut butter or soft cheese
- Plastic knives
- Paper plate
- Wooden craft sticks
- *Alive* Student Book

## INTRODUCE

Ask the children to help you make a list of things that friends do together. Also ask, **Why is it good to have a friend with you when you go someplace new? Why is it good to have a friend help you with something that is difficult? In the Bible, we see that Paul always had friends with him as he traveled around doing God's work. Let's learn about Paul, his job, and his friends.**

## DEVELOP

If you have Bible costumes, have one child be Paul and three others act as his friends. Otherwise, display flannelgraph figures to help children distinguish the changing sets of characters.

- **Paul and Barnabas (Travels).** Explain that after Paul came to faith through the message of Jesus, he went to Jerusalem to join the disciples. But they were afraid of him, thinking it was a trick to infiltrate and destroy them. But Barnabas proved to be a true friend. He defended Paul and spoke well of him, telling how he preached fearlessly in the name of Jesus. Paul and his friend Barnabas began their missionary travels to other countries to tell the Gospel. For a year they "taught great numbers of people" in Antioch (Acts 11:26). They went to the island of Cyprus, where the Roman proconsul sent for them "because he wanted to hear the word of God" (Acts 13:7). And one time in Galatia "almost the whole city gathered to hear the word of the Lord" (Acts 13:44).

- **Paul and Silas (Troubles).** Explain that on another missionary trip, Paul traveled with his friend Silas. But things did not always go well. One time they were thrown in jail. But even there they prayed together and sang songs to the Lord. That night there was an earthquake. They could have escaped when their chains broke loose, but their first thoughts were to save the jail keeper. They saved his life by stopping him when he was going to kill himself. And they gave him the good news that he was saved eternally through Christ. The jailer and his whole family were baptized in the name of Jesus.

- **Paul and Timothy (Teachers).** Another friend and fellow traveler was a young man named Timothy. Timothy learned about God's Word from his grandmother, Lois; his mother, Eunice; and Paul, his teacher. Paul treated Timothy like he was his own son and encouraged him to join in spreading God's Good News. Read aloud Paul's words to Timothy in 1 Timothy 4:12 and 2 Timothy 3:14–15. Use these words to encourage the children in your class, pointing out that no one is too young to serve the Lord.

## RESPOND

Use the Jenna and Jake puppets to continue the lesson.
**JENNA:** I'd like to be a missionary like Paul and Barnabas and Silas

and Timothy when I grow up. I'd like to travel to lots of different countries. But I don't think I can.

JAKE: Why not?

JENNA: I get carsick, seasick, and airsick. So traveling is not for me.

JAKE: You don't have to travel to other countries to serve the Lord. You could become a pastor, teacher, or director of Christian education right here when you grow up.

JENNA: But it's taking too long to grow up. What can I do right now?

JAKE: You can talk about Jesus and His blessings wherever you are and whatever you are doing. We're talking about Him right now!

JENNA: I'm good at talking. I just need to remember to talk about Jesus, instead of always talking about myself.

JAKE: Good idea! And you can also let your money do the talking.

JENNA: What does that mean?

JAKE: Well, the offerings you give at church help to spread the Word of God here at home and around the world.

JENNA: Something else I can do is pray. I'll pray that God will bless what I say and do so that more people can know about Jesus.

Distribute copies of Blackline 32-A. Have the children suggest ways they can use each item depicted to share God's Gospel and love with others. Depending on the ability of your class, children can either work independently and then share answers or you can work together and list answers for them to copy onto the page.

## Worship Ideas

- Each day this week focus on a different continent. Pray for the people in the countries and cities located there. Perhaps sing a praise song originating from that part of the world or write words about Jesus to fit a melody from that area.

- Focus on the word *travels*. Paul's travels were for a specific purpose—to tell people about Jesus. Today, our travels are often during a vacation, but even there we take Jesus with us and can share His Gospel in simple but effective ways.

## Bible Background

Paul's life and ministry provide evidence of the power of the Holy Spirit. As he traveled to Damascus, Paul was determined to destroy the Christian message and the messengers. Then he became a messenger who dedicated his life to proclaiming that Christian message! The Spirit changed Paul's zeal—once used to persecute Christians—into a zeal for the Gospel. God uses every kind of person in His mission! God can use anyone for His instrument because the power of the message comes from God Himself.

Witnessing to the grace of God in Jesus Christ became Paul's singular purpose in life. He desired to reach his fellow Jews first, but he recognized and obeyed the Lord's call to preach to the Gentiles. All have sinned and deserve death, but the Gospel brings life and salvation to all (Romans 3:22–24; 6:23).

| Spread the Gospel  *Write words or draw pictures to show how you can use these to share the good news and the love of Jesus.* | |
|---|---|
| ♫ | |
| (praying hands) | |
| $ | |
| (smiling face) | |
| (pencil) | |
| (holding hands) | |

**Blackline 32–A**
Permission granted to reproduce for classroom use. © 2001 CPH

273

# Day

## Words to Remember

*The LORD your God will be with you wherever you go. Joshua 1:9*

Have children help you make a list of the places they go during the week, such as the soccer field, the mall, fast-food restaurant, and so forth. Talk about opportunities they have to demonstrate their love for Jesus or to share His love with others.

## Extending the Lesson

• Provide materials so children can make cards with words of encouragement to send to overseas missionaries and their families. Addresses can be obtained by calling LCMS World Mission at 1-800-433-3954.
• Tie in social studies units on transportation or communication means, noting how these have been used in the past and are used today to spread the Good News of Jesus to the whole world.

## INTRODUCE

Give each child a plastic knife and a cracker with a dollop of peanut butter or soft cheese in the center. Say, **You can "spread" the peanut butter [cheese] over the cracker and eat it.** As they do so, say, **Sometimes people say we are to "spread God's Word" or "spread the Gospel." What do you think that means?** Listen to responses. Then emphasize that just like they spread the peanut butter [cheese] to the edges of the cracker, God wants us to spread the Good News about Jesus to the ends of the earth. **You can spread God's love in your own home and your neighborhood by what you say and do in the name of Jesus.** Discuss specific ways this can be done. Read Jesus' words aloud from Acts 1:8. Also read Acts 19:20.

### Paul Travels as a Missionary
*(Acts 9:26–31; 11:19–26; 16:22–36; 1 Timothy 4:12)*

After  had  ,  , and

He appeared to a man named  and brought him to faith.
**Paul**

 told  to go around the  telling people

they are saved through  .  traveled with his friend

 . They traveled by  . They traveled by  .
**Barnabas**

They told people about forgiveness of sins and eternal life through

 .  also traveled with  . Many people were
**Silas**

 to hear about God's love. Some were angry and mean. Once

 were even thrown into  . But even

there,  sang 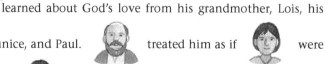 to praise God. A young person named

 learned about God's love from his grandmother, Lois, his
**Timothy**

mother, Eunice, and Paul.  treated him as if 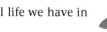 were

his own son. joined Paul in missionary travels to tell people

about the forgiveness of sins and eternal life we have in .

13

## D E V E L O P

Make a small puppet stage with a paper plate and two wooden craft sticks. Use marking pens and perhaps glued-on fabric to make Paul and Barnabas puppets from the two craft sticks. Draw a horizontal center line on the paper plate that stops within one inch of the edges. Color blue sky above the line and green grass below it. Cut along the center line and insert the two puppets through the opening. Move the puppets from one side to the other as you read through the list of places Paul traveled to in his missionary journeys. **God gave Paul a special job—to spread God's Word of salvation around the world. With friends, Paul traveled to**

| | |
|---|---|
| Antioch | Macedonia |
| Athens | Pamphylia |
| Berea | Perga |
| Corinth | Philippi |
| Cyprus | Phoenicia |
| Derbe | Rhodes |
| Ephesus | Samothrace |
| Galatia | Tarsus |
| Iconium | Thessalonica |
| Lystra | Troas |

**and many other places.**

## R E S P O N D

Explain that after Paul left a place, he often wrote letters to the Christian people there to remind them of what they had heard and learned about Jesus. He wanted them to know the truth and to continue in God's Word. Hold an open Bible as you read the people to whom Paul wrote: the Romans, Corinthians, Galatians, Ephesians, Philippians, Colossians, and Thessalonians. See if anyone recognizes these names. **These are the names of some of the books of the Bible. These books of the Bible are actually letters that Paul wrote to the people to help them better understand the truth about God and salvation. These letters are for all God's people. We can read these 2,000-year-old letters today! Paul was led by the Holy Spirit to speak God's truth to us through these words.**

Discuss the missionary scenes on page 14 of the *Alive* Student Book. Talk about where each scene takes place and what the people are doing. Have the children write a letter to a pastor, teacher, or missionary, thanking them for spreading the Gospel. Then pray together that God would bless the missionaries as they speak of Jesus so that more people will come to know Him as their Savior.

---

### Missionary Travels Today

People today continue to go from place to place wherever people need to hear about Jesus. What do you think these missionaries say to the people they meet? What can you say to the people you know?

### Words to Remember

The LORD your God will be with you wherever you go.

Joshua 1:9

14

## Discovery Point

God works in the lives of His people, leading them to reach out to others with the Gospel message and the love of Jesus.

## Paul and His Nephew

Acts 23:12–24

## Objectives

That by the power of the Holy Spirit working through God's Word, the students will
- know that their help comes from the Lord, who has delivered them from the greatest enemies of sin, death, and the devil;
- share the Good News and love of Jesus, starting with their families;
- know that God blesses their actions, even the small, ordinary things they do in His name.

## Day 3 Materials

- Flannelgraph materials
- Yarn
- Blackline 32-B

## Day 4 Materials

- Sidewalk chalk or poster paper
- Family pictures
- *Alive* Student Book

## INTRODUCE

Use the Jenna puppet to introduce the story.

**TEACHER:** Jenna, you have a big smile today! Why are you so happy?

**JENNA:** Because I forgot my book bag this morning.

**TEACHER:** I would think that would make you feel sad.

**JENNA:** Well, I did feel sad at first. But my big brother saw my book bag on the table and brought it to school for me. I love my big brother!

**TEACHER:** It's always a good thing when family members help one another. The Bible says, "Do everything in love" (1 Corinthians 16:14).

**JENNA:** Sometimes we don't act so loving in my family. Sometimes my brother teases me or I get mad at Mom. But we always have God's love and forgiveness. That makes a big difference in my family.

**TEACHER:** Let's learn something about everyone's family. If you have a brother stand up. *(Then have those children be seated, and continue this line of questioning as you ask about sisters, parents, grandmothers, grandfathers, aunts, uncles, and cousins.)*

**JENNA:** My family helps me. I want to learn to be a helper too.

**TEACHER:** Today we will hear about a boy who helped his Uncle Paul. God blessed his actions so that Paul could continue to spread the Gospel.

## DEVELOP

Use flannelgraph materials to tell today's story. Instead of background scenes, use long strips of yarn to divide your flannelgraph board into five areas. Start with the boy overhearing the plot to murder Paul. Move the boy to the next section, where Paul is in jail. Move the boy to the next section, where Paul tells the centurion (a soldier in charge of 100 soldiers) to take the nephew to see the commander (a soldier in charge of 1,000 soldiers). Move the boy to the commander's section, where he takes the boy by the hand and kindly asks what the problem is. Move Paul and the commander to the last section, where over 400 troops have gathered to sneak Paul to safety at the governor's palace, protecting him as he leaves town that night.

## RESPOND

Point out that the boy (not named) in the story was very brave as he helped save his uncle's life. **We might not have such important work to do. But we can help the people in our family each day by** sharing God's love with them, even in little ways. Emphasize that sharing Jesus doesn't have to mean preaching or telling Bible stories. Simple statements can be touching reminders of God's love, such as saying, **"I'll pray for you"** or **"God has really blessed us"** or **"I thank Jesus that you are my dad"** or **"Take this—God has given me plenty."** Our *actions* can also tell about living as a child of God. God leads us to help others and to "do everything in love." Ask how the children could be helpers in these situations.

- Your mother is busy getting supper ready, and your little sister is crying because she can't get her shoes on.
- Your dad is trying to clean the garage, and you can see a lot of your toys lying on the floor.
- Grandma wants to read the newspaper, but she left her glasses in her bedroom.
- Your big brother is trying to study for a test.
- Your uncle looks sad and grumpy.

Then say, **Jesus is our best helper. He made us free from the punishment of sin by dying on the cross and arising at Easter. He forgives us and helps families forgive each other when they hurt one another. He helps us show kindness to each other. Jesus helps us "do everything in love."**

Distribute Blackline 32-B and have children follow the directions. This will remind them to bring pictures of their families tomorrow.

## Worship Ideas

- Sing "Jesus Wants Me for a Helper," "God Chose Me," or "We Will Help the Little Children" (*LOSP*, pp. 33, 107, 109). Then sing "Jesus Is My Special Friend" (*LOSP*, p. 43, and on CD), reminding children that the good we do is possible only because Jesus has taken our sins away and the Holy Spirit empowers us to live as God's people.
- Count off on your fingers as together you try this finger play. Raise your fingers high and wiggle them on the last two lines.

**Five little helpers sat down to play.**
**The first one said, "Did you help today?"**
**The second one said, "I made my bed."**
**The third one said, "I helped Uncle Fred."**
**The fourth one said, "I buttoned baby's dress."**
**The fifth one said, "I cleaned up my mess."**
**Then up jumped the helpers to shout, "Hooray!**
**God helps us to help others every day!"**
Adapted from *Fingers Tell the Story*, © 1989 CPH.

## Bible Background

God had revealed to Paul, "You must also testify in Rome." However, forces were at work trying to prevent this from happening. Following his third missionary journey, Paul is mobbed by angry Jews who believe, incorrectly, that he desecrated the temple by bringing Gentiles into it. This was one offense for which the Romans would permit the Jews to execute a man—but not without a trial—so the Romans take Paul into protective custody. More than 40 Jews then vow to kill him when he is transferred for the trial.

Somehow Paul's nephew learns of this plot. The commander takes the young man's word seriously, and Paul is escorted out of Jerusalem to the safety of Caesarea, the headquarters of Roman rule for Samaria and Judea. Paul would continue to speak the Gospel message, later testifying in Rome. God works in many and different ways to accomplish His purposes.

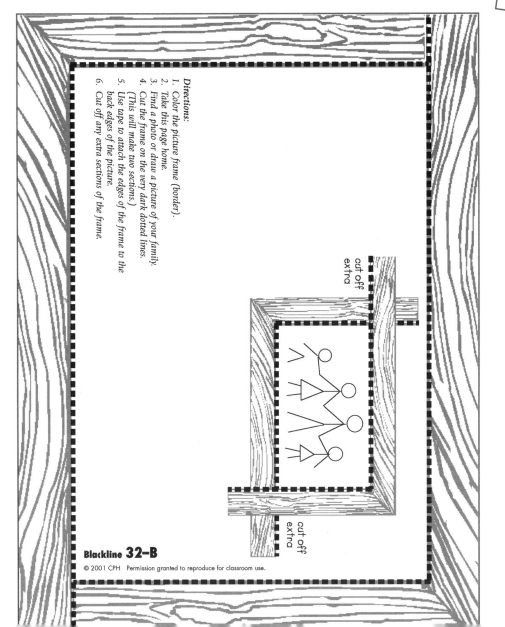

*Directions:*
1. *Color the picture frame (border).*
2. *Take this page home.*
3. *Find a photo or draw a picture of your family.*
4. *Cut the frame on the very dark dotted lines. (This will make two sections.)*
5. *Use tape to attach the edges of the frame to the back edges of the picture.*
6. *Cut off any extra sections of the frame.*

cut off extra

cut off extra

**Blackline 32-B**

## Words to Remember

I have had God's help to this very day. Acts 26:22

Have the class list some of the ways that God has helped them. Encourage them to be specific. Thank God in prayer. Then sing "This Is the Day" (*LOSP*, p. 53, and on CD).

## Extending the Lesson

- Expand on some of the lesson concepts by reading the Big Book *Jesus Helps Me to Help Others* by Carolyn Bergt, available from Concordia Publishing House.
- Have a sibling hour one day. Invite brothers and sisters to come to class to play, hear a story, share a snack, and give thanks to God in prayer for each other.
- Invite some of your family members to school to visit and get to know the children. Or show photographs of family members. Tell a short story about each person and how God has used them to help you in your life.

 **Day** 11

# INTRODUCE

Take the children outside for today's story presentation. You will be using sidewalk chalk to make large words and numbers, at least three feet high, on a length of sidewalk or playground blacktop. (If this is not possible, print the letters and words on individual posters and place them on the floor of a long hallway or around the gymnasium.). **We need lots of room to retell this exciting story.**

# DEVELOP

Have the children gather around you as you print a large number "40." Demonstrate the number by having four children each hold up 10 fingers. Talk about the 40 mean men who made plans to ambush and murder one man, Paul. Point out why they hated him so much—they were enemies of Jesus, and since Paul was a follower of Jesus, that made Paul their enemy too.

Run with the children to a spot farther down the sidewalk. Stop

### Paul and His Nephew
*(Acts 23:12–24)*

Many people listened and believed what the apostle Paul told them about Jesus, our Savior who died on the cross and arose on Easter to save us. But some people who didn't like Jesus didn't want Paul to talk about Jesus. In one town, Paul was thrown into jail. His enemies made a secret plan to kill him. But God had other plans.

Paul's young nephew heard about the secret plan. He ran to warn his uncle. Paul called for the Roman centurion, who took Paul's nephew to see the commander.

This whole adventure was very scary. But God helped the boy to be brave and the commander to be kind. Though he was a very busy and important man, the commander stopped to listen to the boy. He took the boy by the hand and asked what was the problem.

When he heard about the secret plan, the commander said, "We won't let that happen." He ordered over 400 troops to guard Paul, taking him to safety in another town. The commander even wrote a letter to the Roman governor, asking him to continue to protect Paul.

God used a young boy to help Paul be able to continue to speak God's Word. God blesses us with people who help us learn about Jesus. God can use you as His helper too.

15

and write "jail." Explain that Paul's young nephew heard about the evil plan and ran to warn his uncle, who was in jail.

Walk a short distance, stop, and print "centurion." Explain that a centurion was a Roman soldier in charge of 100 other soldiers. Paul called to the centurion and asked him to take Paul's nephew to see the commander because he had something important to tell. God was with them, guiding and blessing them, because, amazingly, this important soldier listened to a prisoner (Paul) and took the nephew to a leader who was even more important.

Walk a short distance, stop, and print "commander." (A commander was in charge of 1,000 soldiers.) Point out that the commander was a very, very important man. But the boy had a very important message. God was with him and led the commander to listen. The commander took the boy by the hand to calm his fears and considerately asked, "What is it you want to tell me?" He listened to what was secretly planned and refused to let it happen.

Motion for your group to tiptoe, escaping to some distant spot. There print the number "400." Explain that the commander thought about the 40 evil men, and then ordered 10 times as many guards to protect Paul. That very night they led Paul away to another town. The commander sent along a letter to the Roman governor to ensure Paul's safety.

Now ask, **What kept Paul safe? Was it because his young nephew was brave? Was it because the commander was a powerful man? Was it because there were so many soldiers to protect**

**Paul? The reason Paul was safe was that God was with him. God had a plan and purpose for Paul that no one could destroy. Praise God that His care and protection watches over us too!**

## RESPOND

Point out that in this Bible story there were secret plans, military plans, but the most important plan was God's plan. And God's greatest plan of all was sending Jesus to die on the cross and arise at Easter so that we could have forgiveness and eternal life. **This is the plan that Jesus wanted Paul to tell people. And because of God's care, Paul continued to spread this Gospel message for years and to many more people.** Help the children to see that perhaps they may never have to be as brave as Paul's nephew, or perhaps they can't travel and preach like Paul, but they can still spread the love of God, starting with their families. The home can be the training ground for future witnessing in other spheres. We need to see the home as the starting point for talking about Jesus as part of our daily lives. This can happen in the simple things we say and do.

On poster paper make a three-part chart with these titles: "Someone Helped Me," "I Helped Someone," "God Helped Me." In advance, write the names of all the children in the third column. Tell the children to write their names in a column every time one of these statements is true for them. Ask, **Why do you think I've already written all of your names in the last column?** Because God has already helped us in so many ways and continues to do so.

Continue by using pages 15 and 16 in the Student Book.

Display the family pictures the children have brought today. Pray for all families and for willingness to help and serve them. Then do the following action poem together.

**I'm a helper from head to toe;**
*(Touch your head, then your toes.)*
**I'll help in any way that I know.**
*(Turn around.)*
**My eyes can see what can be done;**
*(Make "binoculars" with hands over eyes.)*
**When you need help, I'll come at a run.**
*(Run in place.)*
**My ears can hear when you are sad;**
*(Cup hands behind ears, make a sad face.)*
**With happy words I'll make you glad.**
*(Point to mouth, then smile big.)*
**My hands can work and clap and play;**
*(Hold out your hands, palms up.)*
**And I can fold them when I pray.**
*(Fold your hands.)*

---

### Spreading the Good Word (God's)

*In each of these story scenes, neither person is saying something wrong. But one of the people is sharing the news of God's love. Use a light-colored crayon to fill in the white area around the words that speak of the Lord.*

Our new baby is so cute.

I'm so thankful to God for her happy smile.

This food tastes yummy!

God gave us a perfect day for our picnic.

Please don't cry, Mommy.

Aunt Lucy had faith in Jesus. We know she is in heaven with Him.

Grandma, they smell so good!

God filled the world with beautiful things for us.

### Words to Remember
I have had God's help to this very day.
Acts 26:22

## Unit Overview

This unit of study and the accompanying Student Book are entitled *Praise.* It is a fitting conclusion to this year, in which you have surveyed the Old and New Testaments, seeing God's plan for our salvation unfold and recognizing His hand in our daily lives.

In this unit, children will study several psalms. Then they will see how these relate directly to the life of one individual (Elijah) and also to their own lives. They will learn about the church at the time of the tabernacle, the temple, and today. The unit will conclude in celebration of God and His gracious promises.

Send home copies of the family letter and Bible verse list for Unit 9 as you begin. (See the Teacher Resource Book.) This will let parents know what their children will be learning during the next few weeks. At the end of the unit, let the children take home their *Praise* Student Book. Encourage them to look at all nine books of this series and show their parents what they have learned. Consider adding some of the following activities to your curriculum to make related connections between God's message of love and all that you do throughout the day.

## Worship Connections

In your lessons about worship at the tabernacle and temple, talk about the annual celebration of the Passover. Ask, **What special celebrations do we have in our church during the year?** (Christmas, Easter, and so on.) You may want to discuss the why and how of these events.

Discuss family celebrations such as birthdays and anniversaries. Then point out the special events in our own lives that are celebrated at church, such as weddings and funerals. Note that though these are not always performed in a church, **Why do God's people want to celebrate these events in His house?** (It reminds us that God is a part of all that we are and do. We want His blessing and hope to be a part of these events.) **Why can the funeral of a Christian be called a celebration?** (We celebrate that the person was saved by Jesus and is now in heaven.) Point out that these celebrations are often beginnings and endings when we want our family with us—and that includes our church family.

Also talk about the two celebrations that we call *Sacraments*—Baptism and the Lord's Supper. **In Baptism we are celebrating that God has called someone into His** family and washed away the person's sins through the blood of Jesus. We are celebrating a new brother or sister in Christ. At the Lord's Supper we are celebrating the forgiveness that we receive through the body and blood of Jesus Christ.

Visit your church sanctuary and talk about things you might see unique to each celebration discussed.

## Community Building

Encourage the children to identify lots of reasons to celebrate during the final month of the school year. Celebrate big things like finishing your math book early so you can spend more time on math games. Celebrate little things like having a perfectly round apple with no soft spots in your lunch bag. Establish a special celebration ritual, perhaps changing the words of a praise song to include the day's celebrated items. Make a classroom banner that children can add to daily with pictures of things to celebrate. Emphasize that these celebrations praise not the gift but the Giver of all good things—the Lord Himself.

Celebrate all the children in the class. Display a sheet of mural paper listing the names of everyone in the class (or place one name on each page of a blank book). Ask everyone to write what they celebrate about each individual in the class. Say, **Let's make sure everyone has a nice long list. If you see that someone has a short list, add to it right away to cheer them on.** Thank God for the blessing of your classroom's Christian community.

## Tools for Witness

Have each child make several button covers to share with others outside of your classroom. This is a simple way to share a message about Jesus. Cut out 3-inch circles of colored paper. Snip a 1-inch slit near the top of the circle, so that a jacket or shirt button can be inserted through the slit. Use colorful marking pens to print the following message in code. (It says, Jesus loves you; I do too.) Encourage children to distribute these to family members, friends, and neighbors. You may want to surprise another class with button covers or give one to your school principal, pastor, and lunchroom cooks.

## Service Projects

This is a unit of celebration and praise to the Lord. Point out, though, that there are many people in the world who may not feel like celebrating. One way we can celebrate is by sharing our blessings with them to cheer them up. Choose a project like a collection of food, personal hygiene items, clothes, or blankets. Onto each item have the children attach a colorful piece of paper that says, *Don't thank me—thank the Lord!*

## Reaching Every Individual

Many of the psalms speak of God as our hiding place and shelter. This feeling of safety and security should permeate the time during which your children learn about and worship the Lord. It is important that children do not feel that reading skills or memorization abilities affect their relationship with the Lord and their ability to know Him. Our relationship is based totally on the saving grace of Christ Jesus. Because of Jesus we are loved, redeemed, and accepted fully by God.

During the time you study God's Word, all children should evidence a sense of success—not based on their own efforts, but based solely on the victory that is Christ's, the victory He gives to us! See 1 Corinthians 15:57. What a reason to celebrate!

Help children to know that their individual worth is not based on how fast they run, how well they draw, or how tall they are. God created giraffes and spiders, cheetahs and turtles, hippos and cranes, animals and people of all colors, sizes, and skills. God accepts us for what we are—people who are new creations in Christ, clothed in His righteousness. In Christ we are one—there are no differences!

## Science

Discuss temperature and the varying melting points of different substances. Note that a much greater heat is needed to melt metals such as gold, silver, or bronze than to melt something like chocolate. Using chocolate as an example, pour melted chocolate into candy molds and dip pretzels in chocolate to candy-coat them. Relate this to the process metalworkers use to mold metal into decorative shapes or to coat something with metal, as was done in the building of the tabernacle, temple, and perhaps your own church sanctuary.

## Mathematics

As you talk about the many things God provides for us, calculate together the number of breakfasts, lunches, and dinners that God blesses you with in a year. Have a clothes inventory. Ask children to count the number of shirts and blouses they have in their closets or cupboards at home and print the number on a piece of paper. (No names—no comparing to see who has more.) Collect the slips of paper and use a calculator to get a quick classroom total. Then praise and thank God for His many blessings.

## Social Studies

As you learn about the skilled craftsmen who worked on the tabernacle and temple, invite local craftspeople to your classroom to give demonstrations. Weavers, sculptors, wood-carvers, and stained-glass artisans would relate especially well to the kind of ornamentation done for your own church sanctuary.

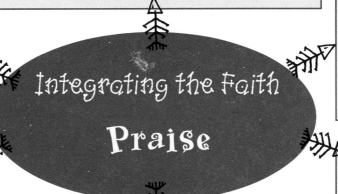

Integrating the Faith

## Praise

## Language Arts

Have the children help you make lists of synonyms to describe the greatness or power or kindness of God. Use these words in a praise prayer. Or make lists of antonyms and use them in sentences to make contrasting descriptions such as, "God is always *energized;* He is never too *tired* to help us."

## Fine Arts

Work as a group to write a "piggyback" praise song. Compose new words for a familiar tune. Then sing it to praise God. The words do not need to rhyme. But it is easier to sing if the lines have the right number of counts (syllables). Use a tune such as "Yankee Doodle," "Row, Row, Row Your Boat," or "Twinkle, Twinkle, Little Star."

## Technology

This unit talks about praising God with voices and instruments. But it does not really discuss *electronic* instruments. Have a visitor demonstrate an electronic keyboard and the variety of sounds it can produce. Thank God for people who have developed such instruments. Sing a praise song that has at least four stanzas, using a different setting on the keyboard with each stanza.

## Discovery Point

Our great God has blessed us in many ways throughout His creation and in making us a new creation through Christ Jesus. We praise and thank Him!

## God Blesses Us

Psalms 24 and 95

## Objectives

That by the power of the Holy Spirit working through God's Word, the students will
- appreciate God's care for them and the wonder of His creation, preservation, and salvation;
- rely on His care and concern for His people;
- share God's blessings and His Good News with others.

## Day 1 Materials
- Paper crown
- Blackline 33-A

## Day 2 Materials
- Paper crown
- Walking stick or picture of Jesus as the Good Shepherd
- Large rock
- Drawing paper
- *Praise* Student Book

## INTRODUCE

Display a paper crown you have made or purchased. Ask, **Who wears a hat like this?** (Kings and queens.) **What do kings and queens do?** (Rule over people, make laws, protect the people.) **Today we will learn more about how God is our King. Where is the kingdom that God rules over?** (He rules over heaven and earth; He rules in the hearts of all believers.) **God is called the King of Glory.** Explain that glory means majestic, awesome, and deserving praise and honor. **Today we will praise God—the King of Glory.** Sing "The King of Glory" (*LOSP*, p. 77) now and as a repeated chant throughout the lesson.

## DEVELOP

Print the word *psalm* on the board and explain, **A psalm is a song to God in the Bible.** Hold up a Bible opened to the very center and say, **The psalms are easy to find. There are 150 of them in the very center of the Bible.** Have the children imitate your motions as you read portions of Psalm 24.

**The earth is the LORD's, and everything in it** (sweep arms in a wide circle), **the world, and all who live in it** (point to individuals);

**For He founded it upon the seas and established it upon the waters** (make wavy water motions).

**Who may ascend the hill of the LORD? Who may stand in His holy place** (point up high)?

**He who has clean hands and a pure heart** (place both hands over heart), **who does not lift up his soul to an idol or swear by what is false** (move head and hand to indicate "no").

**He will receive blessing from the LORD and vindication from God his Savior** (make the sign of the cross).

(On the remaining verses, indicate number 1 with a raised index finger whenever you say *LORD*, place upstretched fingers beside your head to form a crown whenever you say *King*, and lift arms high on the word *glory*.)

**Lift up your heads, O you gates; be lifted up, you ancient doors, that the King** (crown) **of glory** (lift arms) **may come in.**

**Who is this King** (crown) **of glory** (lift arms)? **The LORD** (#1) **strong and mighty, the LORD** (#1) **mighty in battle.**

**Lift up your heads, O you gates; lift them up, you ancient doors, that the King** (crown) **of glory** (lift arms) **may come in.**

**Who is He, this King** (crown) **of glory** (lift arms)? **The LORD** (#1) **Almighty—He is the King** (crown) **of glory** (lift arms).

## RESPOND

Ask, **Why can we call God the King of creation?** (He made the world and still preserves the things in it.) Reread Psalm 24:1. Then distribute Blackline 33-A. Ask the children to color all the things made by God Himself. Then point out the man-made things the children did not color, noting that they were made from materials that God made in the first place (such as the clay and wood that people use to make bricks and buildings). **We praise and thank God for all the blessings He has given.**

Continue, **We call God the King of creation. We also call Him the King of Glory. How did God show that Jesus is the King of Glory, even when Jesus was a tiny baby?** (Angels announced His birth; Wise Men came to worship the newborn King; He fulfilled the prophecies of the promised Savior King.)

Then reread Psalm 24:4. Point out that none of us can do this perfectly. We use our hands to do wrong things; our hearts are sinful; we do not always obey God's will. That is why Jesus, the King of Glory, entered our world, and on Palm Sunday entered Jerusalem, so that He could die on the cross to take away our sins. **Pilate placed a sign above Jesus' head on the cross. It said Jesus was the King of the Jews. But Jesus is much more. He is the King of Glory, who rules over heaven and earth!** You may use page 1 of the *Praise* Student Book today or tomorrow to review Psalm 24, or use it in your Worship Time.

**Blackline 33–A**
Permission granted to reproduce for classroom use. © 2001 CPH

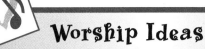

## Worship Ideas

- Read, sing, or listen to a recording of the first stanza of "Beautiful Savior." Or consider inviting an older group of children into your classroom to sing the stanza to your class. Ask your class to listen carefully for the words *king of creation* and *crown*.
- *Songs Kids Love to Sing 2* has several songs with the words *king* or *kingdom* in the title ("Kids of the Kingdom," "Oh, He's King of Kings," and "The King's Kids Are Prayin' "). This songbook and CD or audiocassette recordings are available from Concordia Publishing House.
- Begin your worship in the narthex of the church sanctuary by reading Psalm 24:7–10. Then open the church doors (much like opening the gates mentioned in the psalm) and have the children follow a processional cross into the sanctuary as they sing "The King of Glory." Once seated in the church, worship God by singing other songs of praise.

## Bible Background

Psalms 22–24 are considered messianic psalms, giving us pictures of the Savior as the One who suffered, who guides and gathers, and who is glorified. Psalm 24 was written by David as a processional liturgy, either for the occasion of the return of the ark of the covenant to Jerusalem or for a festival commemorating the event. The New Testament church has long used this psalm in celebration of Christ's ascension into the heavenly sanctuary on high.

Psalm 95 is often known as the Venite, which is Latin for the word *come*. This is a call to worship the one true God. The ancient pagan world had many gods for many places and purposes. But the true God, we are reminded, is above all the man-made gods—the Lord is King above all. He alone is our Maker, who has great and effective power.

## Words to Remember

*Come, let us sing for joy to the LORD. Psalm 95:1*

- Use this as your call to worship each day this week. As the children gather at the classroom altar, begin your worship with songs of praise, just as the Bible verse suggests.
- Listen to a recording of the Venite from the worship service liturgy in the hymnal. Or invite an older group of children to come in and sing it to your class.

## Extending the Lesson

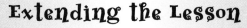

- Make a life-size praise display. Have each child lie down on a large sheet of mural paper. Assign partners to trace around one another's body. Then have the children fill in their shapes with printed words, pictures they draw, or magazine cutouts of things for which they give praise and thanks to God.
- Have each child draw a simple side view of a lamb, glue cotton balls on the shape, and print his or her name above the picture. Gather these together to make a "flock" on a bulletin board. Add these words: "He is our God and we are the people of His pasture, the flock under His care" (Psalm 95:7).
- Take a nature hike with your class. Have them identify things that God has made. When you stop to rest, read aloud Psalm 24 or Psalm 95.

# Day

## INTRODUCE

Display the crown you used on Day 1 and say, **Today we will hear another psalm that talks about God as our King. But this psalm gives us two other pictures. One is of God as a shepherd.** Display a long walking stick or a picture of Jesus as the Good Shepherd. **A shepherd takes care of his sheep. We are like a flock of sheep because God takes care of us.** Display a large rock. **The other picture the psalm uses is of God as a rock. Can you think of a way that God and a rock are alike?** (Both are strong.) **Let's learn more about Psalm 95—a song of praise to God.**

### God Blesses Us
*(Psalm 24:1, 7–10)*

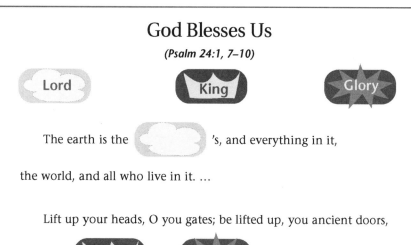

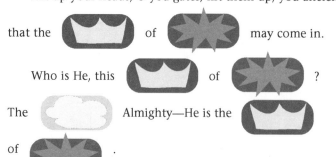

1

## DEVELOP

Say, **Verse 1 begins Psalm 95 by telling the main reason we praise God. We praise God because of salvation. Do you remember a shorter word that begins with the same sound and means the same as salvation?** (Saved.) **How did Jesus save us?** (By dying on the cross to take away our sins.) **Why did Jesus save us?** (Because He loves us and wants to take us to heaven someday.) **Let's praise the Lord!** Have the children imitate your motions as you say the psalm.

**Come** (make a beckoning motion), **let us sing for joy to the LORD; let us shout aloud** (cup hands around mouth) **to the Rock** (pound one fisted hand onto the open palm of other hand) **of our salvation** (make the sign of the cross).

**Let us come before Him with thanksgiving** (fold hands) **and [praise] Him with music and song** (pretend to strum a guitar or play a piano).

**For the LORD is the great God** (lift arms in a wide-sweeping gesture), **the great King above all gods** (point upwards).

**In His hand are the depths of the earth** (reach low), **and the mountain peaks belong to Him** (touch fingertips to make mountain shapes).

**The sea is His, for He made it** (make wavy motions), **and His hands formed the dry land** (pretend to mold clay).

**Come, let us bow down in worship** (bow from the waist), **let us kneel before the LORD our Maker** (kneel);

**For He is our God and we are the people of His pasture, the flock under His care** (give yourself a hug).

Use page 2 of the *Praise* Student Book to review this psalm.

## RESPOND

Have the children draw a picture similar to the illustration as a reminder of the three things we remember about God in Psalm 95. (Better yet, do a three-dimensional project using a real rock, with a bent chenille wire [pipe cleaner] taped across the rock and a crown cut from gold metallic paper taped over that.) Say, **God is like a rock because He is strong. We can be sure that He is near us and cannot be moved. God is like a shepherd who guards and guides us. God is our King of kings who has forgiven us through Jesus and will take us someday to the Kingdom of heaven.**

Point out that the Lord's Prayer ends with words to praise the glory and greatness of God. Practice saying this conclusion together. Then say the entire Lord's Prayer, inviting children to speak any of the words they know with you. Have everyone stand for the conclusion of the prayer and speak these words together with a loud voice: *For Thine is the kingdom and the power and the glory forever and ever. Amen.*

### Psalm 95:1–7

1. Come, let us [ ] for joy to the LORD;
Let us [ ] aloud to the [ ] of our salvation.

2. Let us come before Him with thanksgiving
and [praise] Him with [ ] and song.

3. For the LORD is the great God, the great [ ] above all gods.

4. In His [ ] are the depths of the "[ ]",
and the [ ] peaks belong to Him.

5. The [ ] is His, for He made it,
and His [ ] formed the dry [ ].

6. Come, let us [ ] down in worship,
let us [ ] before the LORD our Maker;

7. For He is our God and we are the [ ] of His pasture,
the [ ] under His care.

### Words to Remember

*Directions: Circle the first line of Psalm 95 above. Those words can be your Bible "Words to Remember." You may even want to try all of the first verse!*

## Discovery Point

Our great God has blessed us in many ways throughout His creation and in making us a new creation through Christ Jesus. We praise and thank Him!

## God Is Great

Psalms 77 and 46

## Objectives

That by the power of the Holy Spirit working through God's Word, the students will
- rely on God's help and protection in all troubles;
- recognize that He has delivered them from the greatest of evils—sin, death, and the power of the devil;
- know the comfort and peace that comes only from our great God.

## Day 3 Materials
- Picture of earth
- Drawing paper
- Blackline 33-B
- *Praise* Student Book

## Day 4 Materials
- *Praise* Student Book

## INTRODUCE

Display a picture of the earth. You may reproduce the globe in the Teacher Resource Book (Supplemental Activities section) but color it in with green land and blue water. Say, **When God made the world, everything was perfect.** Crush the picture. **Sin brought evil and trouble into the world—storms, wars, accidents, illness, and other dangers.** Smooth out the picture. **But even when we have problems, we can remember that God is still with us. Even though there will be trouble in this world, God can help us. Let's hear what the psalm writer says about our God Almighty.**

## DEVELOP

Ask the children to close their eyes and picture in their minds some of the things that the psalmist talks about. Read the portions of Psalm 77 that are printed on page 3 of the *Praise* Student Book. Read verses 14–19a with lots of drama, emphasizing key words. Then read the last two lines quietly, changing the mood and pace of your voice.

After reading the verses, provide paper so the children can draw a picture of something they saw in their minds as you were reading. Display the pictures. Read the psalm section again, having the children add sound effects (either making their own "whooshing" and "crashing" sounds at your signal or using rhythm instruments such as drums and cymbals). Point out the quiet comfort and peace we have in the last two lines as we remember that God is there, though unseen, like a shepherd guarding His sheep.

# RESPOND

Reread Psalm 77:11–12 and say, **Remembering what God has done in the past can help us remember that He is with us now.** Point out that the psalmist is talking about the miracle of the parting of the Red Sea in verse 19. Use Blackline 33-B to review other Bible stories that show God's greatness. Ask children to tell about the four pictures (Noah's ark in the great flood, Jesus stilling the storm, the walls of Jericho crumbling, the lions quieted around Daniel). Then have children draw a picture of God's greatest defeat of evil. Children can show a Good Friday or Easter scene. **Jesus has saved us from the worst evils of all—sin, death, and the power of the devil. Praise the Lord!**

## God Is Great!

*Draw a picture to show how Jesus delivered us
from the very worst evils—sin, death, and the power of the devil.*

## Worship Ideas

- In this *Praise* unit sing a lot of songs to praise the Lord. Review songs learned during the past year and try some new ones too. Sing songs of thanksgiving for all God has done. Sing songs that speak of God's greatness, such as "My God Is So Great" (*LOSP*, p. 64, and on CD) and "Psalm 8" (*LOSP*, p. 50).
- Point out that many of the psalms were used as part of the liturgy—the form of worship used regularly on the Sabbath Day. Learn several parts of the liturgy commonly used in your Sunday worship. The Offertory ("Create in me a clean heart …," based on Psalm 51) may be a good starting place.

## Bible Background

Psalm 77, a psalm of Asaph, seems to be written in a time of great distress. The writer wrestles with God in prayer. The emphasis in the first portion of the psalm is on the anguished struggle of faith to hold on to God when there seems to be no evidence of His preservation or protection. But in verse 11 and the following, the psalmist receives strength in looking at what God has done in the past, knowing God will again intervene at the right time and in the way He sees as best. He notes that we cannot see God's footprints (v. 19), but we know He is there watching, guarding, and guiding.

A subtitle for Psalm 46 says this psalm was written for the director of music. We no longer have the melodies used originally to sing the psalms. But many form the basis of new songs (such as "A Mighty Fortress Is Our God"), and some have been given new melodies or psalm tunes. Psalm 46 is a triumphant confession of trust in God's almighty power. The psalm reminds us that God, not some unconcerned distant deity, is active in our lives. As the psalmist says, God is ever-present (v. 1) and is with us (vv. 5, 7, 11).

## Words to Remember

*God is our refuge and strength. Psalm 46:1*
Point out that God protects us from the worst of evils—sin, death, and the devil. He does this through the death and resurrection of Christ Jesus. Jesus has won the victory and continues to help us with our daily battles. Sing "I'm in the Lord's Army," remembering that we daily fight temptation, and we can win through the help of the Lord. (Ephesians 6 reminds us of ways the Holy Spirit equips us to fight these battles.) In all of this, our strength, fortress, and weapon is Jesus Christ and His Word of salvation.

## Extending the Lesson

- Provide materials that children can use to build forts, castles, and walled cities. Provide boxes or large building blocks for this purpose. On a smaller scale, these can be made from play dough.
- Discuss some of the dangers Martin Luther faced as he wrote the song "A Mighty Fortress Is our God." This was a time when he had been placed on trial and declared an outlaw, wanted dead or alive. Luther knew that his help and protection had to come from God. He rested, assured in the knowledge that Christ had felled his greatest enemies when the Lord died on the cross. In this context explain more of the stanzas of Luther's hymn. Though it is a difficult song, young children do like to learn and sing at least portions of this triumphant hymn.

# Day

## INTRODUCE

Print the word *fortress* on the board. Ask if anyone knows what a fort or fortress is and what is its purpose. Listen to responses. Then show pictures of castles with high walls. Say, **Another word for a fortress is a** *refuge.* **A fortress often has strong, high walls to** *wrap* **around buildings or even around a whole town to protect the people inside. The Bible calls God a fortress and a refuge. That doesn't mean God has strong, high walls. It means that He wraps His love and care around us. He is our protection and shelter.**

**Even if our troubles don't go away, God is with us to comfort us and help us live with our troubles. And because Jesus takes away our sins and makes us people of God, we will someday live with Him in heaven, where there will be no problems, no pain, only joy and love through Jesus! Let's hear what the psalm writer says about God, our fortress.**

God Is Great!
(Psalm 77:11-20a)

11 I will remember the deeds of the LORD; yes, I will remember Your miracles of long ago.
12 I will meditate on all Your works and consider all Your mighty deeds.
13 Your ways, O God, are holy. What god is so *great* as our God?
14 You are the God who performs *miracles;* You display Your *power* among the peoples.
15 With Your *mighty* arm You *redeemed* Your people, the descendants of Jacob and Joseph.
16 The waters saw You, O God, the waters saw You and *writhed;* the very *depths* were *convulsed.*
17 The clouds *poured* down water, the skies *resounded* with *thunder;* Your arrows *flashed back and forth.*
18 Your *thunder* was heard in the *whirlwind,* Your *lightning lit up* the world; the earth *trembled* and *quaked.*
19 Your path led through the sea, Your way through the *mighty waters,* though Your footprints were not seen.
20 You led Your people like a flock.

## DEVELOP

Turn to the selected psalm verses that are printed on page 4 of the *Praise* Student Book. Teach children the Bible "Words to Remember" (in italics). Then read the psalm antiphonally, having the children softly chant the repeated words at the beginning of each verse and the teacher reading the remainder of the verse.

Read the psalm again, but change the procedure. Have the children sing the first line of "A Mighty Fortress Is Our God" before each verse in place of the repeated chant.

## RESPOND

Point out that God is great and has great power. The psalm reminds us that God has power over storms, over nations, over evil. But He does not always use His great power in dramatic ways. He chooses whatever way and time will be best for His people.

Tell a story about the prophet Elijah, whom we will study more next week. (Consider adding sound effects to dramatize the story.) Explain that Elijah was having troubles. **In fact, he was ready to give up. He said, "I have had enough, LORD"** (1 Kings 19:4). **He had forgotten that God is our fortress, who wraps His love and care around us.**

Continue by explaining that God told Elijah to wait on a mountain till the Lord passed by. **First, there was a powerful wind. But God was not in the wind. Next, there was a tremendous earthquake, but God was not in the earthquake. Then, there was a roaring fire, but God was not in the fire. After that, Elijah heard a gentle whisper. God used a still, small voice to speak.** This story reminds us that God can use His great power, but He also works in quiet ways to bring us comfort and peace. Close by reading the words of peace Jesus gives to us in John 14:27.

### Psalm 46:1-3, 6-7, 10-11

*Directions: The first six words of Psalm 46 are special Bible "Words to Remember." Repeat these words together softly at the beginning of each verse as your teacher reads the psalm.*

*God is our refuge and strength,* an ever-present help in trouble.

*[God is our refuge and strength.]* Therefore we will not fear, though the earth give way and the mountains fall into the heart of the sea,

*[God is our refuge and strength.]* though its waters roar and foam and the mountains quake with their surging.

*[God is our refuge and strength.]* Nations are in uproar, kingdoms fall; He lifts His voice, the earth melts.

*[God is our refuge and strength.]* The LORD Almighty is with us; the God of Jacob is our fortress.

*[God is our refuge and strength.]* "Be still, and know that I am God; I will be exalted among the nations, I will be exalted in the earth."

*[God is our refuge and strength.]* The LORD Almighty is with us; the God of Jacob is our fortress.

# WEEK 34-A

## Discovery Point

God loves us and graciously blesses our life here on earth. He supplies our need for salvation and eternal life through Jesus. Our almighty God rules over all and uses His great power for our good.

## God Always Provides

1 Kings 17:1–16

## Objectives

That by the power of the Holy Spirit working through God's Word, the students will
- feel secure that God is always with them and can help them in all things;
- know that God always provides for their needs, especially their need of a Savior;
- thank and praise God for His goodness and blessings.

## Day 1 Materials

- *Praise* Student Book
- Flannelgraph materials
- Blackline 34-A
- Colored paper

## Day 2 Materials

- Jake puppet
- Costume or stick puppet
- *Praise* Student Book

# INTRODUCE

(Note: This week we will study stories about the Old Testament prophet Elijah that relate to the psalms studied last week, demonstrating once again why we praise and worship the Lord.) Point out that last week the class used Psalm 24 to worship and praise God because He provides what we need day-to-day. Together read the portions of that psalm printed on page 1 of the *Praise* Student Book. Then say, **In the psalm we just read, we called God *the King of Glory*. Today we will hear the story of a king named Ahab who forgot this. Ahab thought he was a very powerful king himself. But God soon showed Ahab who truly has the power. As the psalm verse says, "The earth is the LORD's, and everything in it." We will see that God has control over the weather, the animals, the rivers and streams, and so much more.**

# DEVELOP

Use the flannelgraph materials to tell the Bible story dramatically. Display figures representing King Ahab and Elijah on a grassy green background. Under this background have a barren desert scene ready. Also have available a strip of blue fabric for the brook and several simple black birds. Say, **Ahab was the king of Israel. But he was an evil king and led the people to worship idols. God sent the prophet Elijah to warn Ahab and the people about their sins. Elijah said, "Stop worshiping idols. They are false gods. Pray only to the true God, who has power over heaven and earth." But Ahab would not listen. He did not want to hear the truth. The king became angry at Elijah. Elijah warned the people, "God will stop sending rain to this land. No rain will fall, and no plants will grow. You must repent and change your ways."**

Remove the fertile scene, revealing the barren desert scene. **Elijah's message came true. For a long, long time no rain fell. Wells began to dry up. Plants did not grow. The people were running out of food and water. They would learn that their idols could not help them.**

**But what would happen to God's faithful helper Elijah? The Lord had a plan to give him what he needed. God told Elijah where to find a brook that still had flowing water. God also provided food. Ravens brought bread and meat to Elijah every morning and evening.** Add the brook and show the birds flying to and away from Elijah.

**God took care of Elijah in a spectacular way. God takes care of us too. He uses farmers, factory workers, grocery store clerks, and Mom and Dad to bless us with the food and drink we need. We thank Him for His good gifts. And when we forget to thank Him or are ungrateful, He calls us to repentance. He offers us forgiveness through His best gift—Jesus.**

# RESPOND

Review the story using Blackline 34-A. First have the children make raven puppets as directed on the blackline sheet. Have the children act out the Bible story as you narrate it. You will need actors for the parts of Elijah and King Ahab. All the other children will use the raven puppets to bring bread and/or meat to Elijah. (Children will put the food shapes into the birds' mouths and then deposit them near the Elijah character.)

Say, **God blesses us with all good things. Sometimes we forget to thank Him. God also provides for our greatest need—forgiveness. He forgives us for being unthankful. He forgives all our other sins for Jesus' sake. Let's praise and thank God for His great gifts to us.** Sing several thank-You songs such as "The Lord Is Good to Me" (*LOSP*, p. 16).

## Worship Ideas

- Remembering that the earth is the Lord's and everything in it, sing "Oh, Who Can Make a Flower" and "Who Made the Sky So Bright and Blue" (*LOSP*, p. 74, and on CD). Mention that God used birds in a very special way to help Elijah. Ask, **How does God bless us through birds today?** (They sing for us; drop seeds that grow into plants; provide eggs; and some, such as chickens and turkeys, are eaten as food.)
- Play a guessing game of blessings. Say, **I am thinking of a blessing from God.** Give the children two clues. (Include items in addition to food.) Ask, **How can we say God blesses us with our homes and clothes since it was your mom or dad who bought these things?** (God blesses us through those people in our lives who help us.) Sing songs of thanks to God.

## Bible Background

After Solomon's death, the kingdom of Israel was fractured by hostility and rebellion. It became two nations. The northern tribes, often called Israel, refused to acknowledge Solomon's son Rehoboam as ruler. Many of their kings led them into idolatry and Baal worship. Some time later God called Elijah to speak His word of judgment to Ahab, king of the northern tribes. Elijah announced God's punishment upon the land: no dew or rain in the years ahead, except at the prophet's command. We see God's control over His creation as He rules over the weather, and He uses elements of His creation—ravens—to provide for His prophet in a manner that goes against their nature (ravens tending to be *takers* rather than *givers* of food).

The drought, intended to call the people to repent of their idolatry and disobedience, creates a hardship for many, including a poor widow. God purposely changes His provision plans, directing Elijah to receive his daily food from this widow. Her situation seems so hopeless that she is about to prepare a final meal for herself and her son and then die. In a miraculous way God provides for them. God continues today to provide all that we need (Matthew 6:33; Romans 8:32).

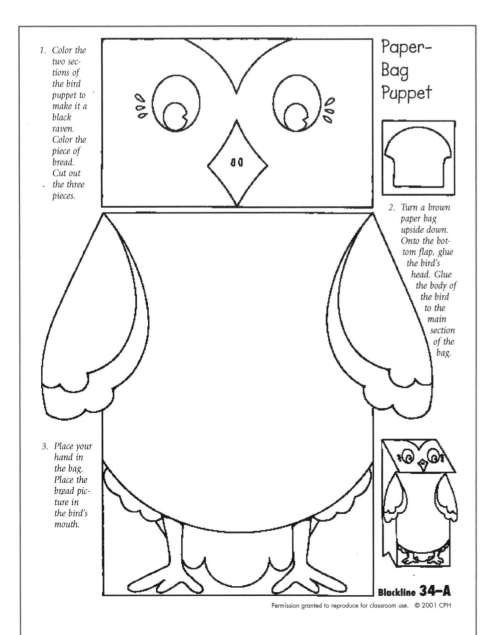

1. Color the two sections of the bird puppet to make it a black raven. Color the piece of bread. Cut out the three pieces.

Paper-Bag Puppet

2. Turn a brown paper bag upside down. Onto the bottom flap, glue the bird's head. Glue the body of the bird to the main section of the bag.

3. Place your hand in the bag. Place the bread picture in the bird's mouth.

**Blackline 34-A**

Permission granted to reproduce for classroom use. © 2001 CPH

## Words to Remember

*The eyes of all look to You, and You give them their food at the proper time. Psalm 145:15*

- Use these words as a lunchtime prayer each day this week. Together with the children plan actions to accompany the words.
- Depending on the ability level of your class, consider also learning Psalm 145:16: "You open Your hand and satisfy the desires of every living thing."
- One way to show your thankfulness to God is by sharing the gifts He gives. Collect food or money to share with a food pantry for the poor in your community.

## Extending the Lesson

- Use the water cycle picture in the Teacher Resource Book and the following experiment to see God's plan for caring for us through the processes of evaporation and rain. (Note that God has power over these processes, as seen in the Bible stories of Noah's ark, Jesus stilling the storm, and His sending the drought and later restoring rain as He declared through Elijah.)
- Set out a shallow pan of water. Check on it over the next few days to note the progress of the evaporation. Say, **Water evaporates when droplets of water float into the air. The droplets are so tiny that they are invisible to us. When the droplets in the air cool and come together, they form larger drops that fall as rain. This is God's plan, continuing to provide water over and over again.**
- Use the reproducible in the Teacher Resource Book that shows the steps involved in getting bread to our tables. Emphasize that God is blessing us through the many people involved in a process that begins with His creation—soil, water, wheat. You may also want to discuss the process of how we get cotton or wool clothing, how we get materials for home building, and so forth.

 **Day**

## INTRODUCE

Use the Jake puppet to introduce the concept that God blesses us by giving people to help us.

**TEACHER:** God has given us many helpers. Jake, can you think of someone who has helped you today?

**JAKE:** My mom did. I usually fix myself a bowl of cereal for breakfast. But today Mom got up early and fixed French toast with powdered sugar!

**TEACHER:** Mmmm! Sounds good. Any other helpers today?

**JAKE:** Yes, my cousin Enrique spent the night with us. This morning I couldn't find my shoes.

**TEACHER:** You must have found them. I see you have them on.

**JAKE:** Actually, Enrique found them by the back door. I left them there last night because they were muddy. That reminds me of another helper.

**TEACHER:** Who would that be?

**JAKE:** My dad. He saw I was in a hurry, so he cleaned the mud off my shoes.

### God Always Provides
*(1 Kings 17:1–16)*

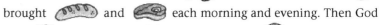

| Ahab | Baal | Elijah | Widow |

 was a wicked king. He did not love God. He prayed to the idol  . The people of Israel prayed to  too. God's helper, the prophet  , warned the people, "God will not send any  until I say so." God kept His promise. The land became dry. There was little food. King  prayed to  . But  could not help. God helped  . God told him where to find water to drink in a  . God sent 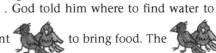 to bring food. The 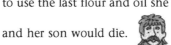 brought  and  each morning and evening. Then God sent  to a little  . He met a  who was going to use the last flour and oil she had to bake 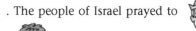 to eat. Then she and her son would die. 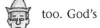 told the that God promised to help them. Every day when she went to her kitchen, there was always new flour and oil to bake a new loaf of . It was a miracle! God took good care of , the , and her son. God takes good care of you and me. He blesses us now and eternally.

5

**TEACHER:** God has blessed you with a lot of helpers. Today we'll hear how God blessed a family and Elijah as they shared food and helped each other.

## DEVELOP

As you tell the story from the widow's perspective, wear a costume or headpiece yourself or have a costumed child pantomime the actions of the widow. Another option is to attach a female flannelgraph figure to a wooden craft stick to make a stick puppet. Say:

I am a widow lady in the town of Zarephath. I was ready to give up. I just couldn't find any food for my son and me. You see, there had been no rain for three years, so very little wheat grew for making bread. We were starving. I only had a small amount of oil and flour left—just enough for a small bit of bread for my son and me. After that, with no food left, we would die.

I was gathering sticks to build a fire to bake the last bit of bread. That's when I met Elijah. He looked hungry. He asked for a drink of water and some bread. I told him that my son and I were going to eat the very last of the food.

Elijah told me not to be afraid and to trust the Lord. He said I should make bread for the three of us and that God would make sure we did not run out of flour and oil.

God kept His promise. Every day when I looked in the cupboard there was enough oil and flour to bake bread for the three

of us. Each day I would use it all up, and the next day there would be enough for more bread. God kept making more and more each day. God had sent Elijah to help me, and we shared God's blessings with Elijah.

## RESPOND

**Let's thank and praise God Almighty for all that He has done for us.** Say together the portions of Psalm 95 that are printed on page 2 of the *Praise* Student Book.

Continue with page 6 of the Student Book. Ask children to draw a cross at the center of the page as a reminder of the great blessing of salvation we have in Christ Jesus.

Refer to the Fourth Petition of the Lord's Prayer ("Give us this day our daily bread"). Review that these words mean more than bread and also more than food. Read aloud the explanation from the catechism that answers the question *What is meant by daily bread?* List some of these items on the board. Then make a "thank-You garden." Provide yellow paper so children can draw and cut out a circle for the center of a flower. On this they are to print *God's Gifts.* Next provide red or pink paper that children may use to make heart shapes to attach as petals to the yellow center. Ask children to write a word or draw a picture on each petal, telling of something for which they give thanks to God. (Let them refer to the list you printed on the board.)

Next provide green paper that the children are to use to make a cross shape, which is to be attached to the flower as the stem and leaves (see illustration). On the cross children are to print *Jesus, Our Savior.* Display the flowers on a bulletin board after using the words printed on them in a thank-You prayer.

God Cares for Me

*Directions: Draw pictures to show gifts from God.*

God cares for me.
See the food He gives.

God cares for me.
See the home He gives.

God cares for me.
See the clothes He gives.

God gives me more than I need.
I can share with these people.

### Words to Remember

The eyes of all look to You,
and You give them their food at the proper time.

Psalm 145:15

God's Gifts

Jesus, Our Savior

## Discovery Point

God loves us and graciously blesses our life here on earth. He supplies our need for salvation and eternal life through Jesus. Our almighty God rules over all and uses His great power for our good.

## God Shows His Power

1 Kings 18:16–46

## Objectives

That by the power of the Holy Spirit working through God's Word, the students will
- confess their faith in God and in His power and presence in their lives;
- trust God to use His power for good in their lives;
- love the Lord above all else.

## Day 3 Materials

- Large rock
- *Praise* Student Book
- Flannelgraph materials
- Blackline 34-B

## Day 4 Materials

- Clear glass of water
- Paper clouds
- *Praise* Student Book

## INTRODUCE

Display a large rock and tell the children that you are going to have a contest between the rock and some children. Choose a volunteer to run a race with the rock. Ask the children, **Who do you think will win this contest?** Run the race and then ask why the rock lost. Next have a jumping contest and an eating contest (using the same line of questioning). Then say, **Today's Bible story has a contest between an idol made out of stone and our God. Who do you think won that contest?** Listen to responses. **We know God is the true God above all others because we can look at the things He has done. He blesses us. He has done many miracles. His power is great. Let's praise God for His almighty power.** Say together the portions of Psalm 77 printed on page 3 of the *Praise* Student Book.

## DEVELOP

Continue the story of Elijah, using flannelgraph materials. You may have to make extra pieces from paper or fabric to represent the two altars and the fire from heaven. Say:

**King Ahab, Queen Jezebel, and the people of Israel worshiped false gods. God punished them by not sending rain for a very long time. He wanted the people to know that He is true God. His prophet Elijah said to the king, "Let's have a contest to see who is the true God. Tell the people of Israel and the priests of the idol Baal to meet me on Mount Carmel." The people said, "This will be a good contest."**

**On Mount Carmel, Elijah gave the rules for the contest: "Your prophets will build an altar and pray for fire to come down from heaven to burn the sacrifice. I will do the same. Then you will see who is the true God who has the power to answer prayer."**

**The prophets of Baal went first. They prayed all morning and all afternoon. They shouted. They danced. They even hurt themselves, hoping Baal would notice them and answer their prayer. But Baal was just made of stone. Baal couldn't hear. Baal couldn't do anything.**

**Then it was Elijah's turn. He built an altar and even poured water on it—three times. He prayed a short prayer: "O Lord, show these people that You are the only true God." Immediately God sent fire down from heaven. The fire burned up the sacrifice, the wood, and even the stones and the water! The people saw the power of the Lord and worshiped Him as the true God.**

# R E S P O N D

Say, **God wants us to love Him above all things. At first that sounds simple to do. After all, we don't pray to a stone statue like the people in our Bible story. But wait! Whenever we treat other things like they are more important than God, we are worshiping a false God. We need to have God as number 1 in our lives.**

Discuss some of the things and people that are important in our lives. God has blessed us with so much. But when we love these things more than God, we are breaking the very first of His commandments. God calls us to repent of this sin. He wants to forgive us for Jesus' sake. Work together on copies of Blackline 34-B to develop this concept.

Close with a prayer: **Dear Lord, I need Your forgiveness and help. I don't always do Your will. I don't always put You first in my life. Help me to change. Give me a strong faith. Help me to live as Your child. In Jesus' name. Amen.**

---

## What Comes First in Your Life?

When you put God *first* in your life, what will you love above all? Circle those things and draw a connecting line to the number 1.

The other pictures show many things that you and other people may like. God blesses us in many ways. It is not wrong to like those other things, unless they become more important to you than God.

As a reminder that Jesus, the Savior, is number 1 in your life, use a crayon to change the large number 1 into the shape of a cross. Jesus is most important because only through Him do we have forgiveness and eternal life.

**Blackline 34-B**
© 2001 CPH  Permission granted to reproduce for classroom use.

## Worship Ideas

- If available, hold up a trophy. Point out that when a team wins a tournament, the players often shout, "We're number 1!" Ask the children what this means. Then point out that God is number 1 above all things because He is the best. **Can you tell me why we say God is the best?** Point out that God is truly number 1 over all things, and He wants to be number 1 in our hearts. In prayer, ask for forgiveness for times when we don't put God first and for help to serve only Him.
- Sing "My God Is So Great" (*LOSP*, p. 64, and on CD) and other praise songs that speak of God's power, might, and greatness.

## Bible Background

As Elijah had announced the drought (1 Kings 17:1), so he was to transmit to Ahab the word of the Lord that alone could terminate it. After more than three years of famine, desperate Ahab sought out the prophet. Elijah insisted on an arrangement that would let Israel know the power of God and the wickedness of King Ahab and his family (18:18–19).

Of course, Baal could not answer the prayer of his prophets, as Elijah fully knew. However, Elijah arranged the "contest" to demonstrate this truth to the people. The people responded in faith to this demonstration (18:39), and God sent the promised rain.

For his sacrifice Elijah rebuilt the altar of the Lord, using 12 stones, one for each of the tribes descended from Jacob. In this way he called attention to the covenant unity of Israel as people of God in spite of the nation's political division. The Lord is their God and ours!

# WEEK 34-B

## Words to Remember

*Love the Lord your God with all your heart and with all your soul and with all your mind.* Matthew 22:37

- Add motions to the Bible verse to help focus on its meaning. During the first phrase of the verse, point up high with index finger raised to indicate "God is number 1." On the words *with all your heart*, point to your heart with your two index fingers. On the words *with all your soul,* place your hands on the opposite shoulders (indicating loving God with your whole self). On the words *with all your mind,* clasp your hands on top of your head.
- Print each word of the Bible verse on a separate index card or sheet of paper. Place them in order on a pocket chart or chalkboard tray and together read the verse aloud. Have a volunteer leave the room. Ask another child to switch the position of two of the cards. Have the volunteer return. Ask, "What moved?" The volunteer is to put the words in the proper sequence and then read the verse aloud. Repeat the activity with new volunteers. Perhaps change more than two cards if children can take on the challenge.

## Extending the Lesson

- The story of Elijah shows God working to bless him in amazing ways. Ask the children to draw a picture of some of their favorite events in Elijah's life. Perhaps, as a class project, they might enjoy making a life-size mural of Elijah's altar and the fire coming down from heaven.
- Discuss the purpose of a sacrifice on an altar. (It was an offering, given as a plea for forgiveness or in grateful thanksgiving.) **Why don't we burn sacrifices on an altar anymore?** (Because Jesus is the full, final, and complete sacrifice for our sins. His sacrifice on the cross is all that is needed—He brings the gift of salvation. We continue to give offerings in grateful thanksgiving. But now our offerings are usually money gifts to share the message and kindness of Jesus with others.)

# INTRODUCE

Hold up a glass of water. Ask, **How do you think the water got into the glass?** (You put the glass under a faucet and turned on the water.) **I have the power to turn the faucet on and off. God has much greater power. He turns the rain on and off! No person can do that. Today we'll hear how God used His mighty power again, turning rain off and on.**

# DEVELOP

In advance prepare three paper cloud shapes. One is the size of your hand, one the size of a computer screen, and the third as large as possible on mural paper.

## God Shows His Power
### (1 Kings 18:16–46)

*Directions: Color what God sent to answer Elijah's prayer. Color what God sent to save us from our sins.*

King Ahab and the people of Israel worshiped Baal, a god they had made themselves from gold and stone. God's prophet Elijah challenged them to a contest to see who the true and almighty God really is. They met on top of Mount Carmel.

The prophets of Baal prayed and shouted and danced all day. But of course, their god could not hear them. Their god could do nothing at all. Their god was just a rock.

Then Elijah built an altar. He placed wood and a meat sacrifice on it. He poured water over it and dug a ditch around it. He filled the ditch with water. Then Elijah said a short prayer. He asked God to send fire from heaven so that all the people could see that our God is the one and only true God.

Immediately, fire came down from heaven. The fire burned up the sacrifice and wood. The fire even burned up the water and the stones. The people were amazed. They shouted, "The Lord is God! The Lord is God!"

7

Explain that God had just sent fire from heaven to Elijah's altar on Mount Carmel. The people had acknowledged the Lord as the true God. Now, after three dry years, it was time for the rain to return. Elijah asked his servant boy to look toward the sea and report back if he saw any rain clouds. (You may want to have a child act the part of the servant.) The boy saw nothing. Elijah sent the boy out to look seven times. On the seventh time, the boy said he saw a cloud in the distance, but it was only about the size of a person's hand. (Display the first cloud you made.)

Elijah knew that God would work quickly. He told King Ahab and the people to hurry down the mountain before the rain stopped them. Display the second cloud and then the largest cloud, noting that quickly the sky was filled with dark clouds. The wind began to blow, and the rain began pouring down. King Ahab was driving his horse and chariot at top speed down the mountain. But, as the Bible says, "the power of the LORD came upon Elijah," and Elijah ran past the king and his chariot and raced down the mountain ahead of him! **Time and again God showed His power to Elijah through great miracles.** Praise God together in the words of Psalm 46 printed on page 4 of the *Praise* Student Book. **These words remind us that God has power over mountains and seas, over nations and earthquakes. We can trust that God will guard us. He is our refuge and fortress.**

# RESPOND

Emphasize that God has used His great power to take away our sins and to change us into people of God. He shares His power through the outpouring of the power of the Holy Spirit. We now have power to love Him, serve Him, and live for Him.

Display the three cloud shapes you made. On the smallest cloud print the words *The power.* On the next one print *of God is …* Then have the children help you fill up the last cloud with words that describe our almighty God. (Awesome, majestic, remarkable, loving, forgiving, miraculous, enormous, etc.) Keep this display up for at least a week, letting children add words to it as they think of other descriptions. Use these words in prayers of praise. (Use a few each day, circling the ones you have mentioned.)

Review the Bible story, using pages 7–8 of the *Praise* Student Book. The children can complete the pictures.

*Option.* As you focus on having God first in our lives, discuss the following scenarios and possible responses.

1. Charles wants to play with his video games. His mother wants him to get dressed to go to church. Charles is trying to decide: What is more important—playing video games or worshiping the Lord?

2. Tanya saw her neighbor, old Mrs. Johnson, drop her bag of groceries on the driveway. But if she goes to help, she will miss the ice cream truck that is going by. Tanya is trying to decide: What is more important—eating ice cream or sharing the loving-kindness of Jesus with someone?

3. Cindy sees that the new kid in her class has no one to play with. The other kids don't like him because he wears torn and shabby clothes. If Cindy is a friend to him, her other friends will laugh at her and tease her. Cindy is trying to decide: What is more important—what her friends think or what God thinks?

---

At last, the people knew that the Lord is God, and He alone is powerful and mighty. He alone deserves our worship and praise. Now God was ready to return rain to the dry land so that plants and animals could again live and grow.

Elijah sent a servant boy to the edge of the mountain to look at the sky. Six times he returned, saying he saw no clouds. The seventh time, he said he saw a little cloud, a long way away. The cloud was only the size of a man's hand. Elijah told the people they must hurry down the mountain because, after waiting three years, the rains were about to come pouring down.

Quickly the sky filled with clouds, and the rains came down. King Ahab was driving his horse and chariot quickly down the mountain, going back to town. God gave special power to Elijah. He was able to run so fast that he ran right past the king and his horses.

The rains turned the dry land to green hills with grass for the sheep, cattle, and goats to eat. The waters helped the trees and crops to grow food once more for the people. God's great power continues to bless us today!

*Directions: Show the plants growing and rivers flowing as God returned the rains to Israel. Also draw and color the gifts of food God gives to you daily.*

## Words to Remember

Love the Lord your God with all your heart
and with all your soul and with all your mind.

Matthew 22:37

8

## Discovery Point

We worship and praise God Almighty, our Creator and Savior. The family of God worships together in church as well as individually. We can worship God in a variety of ways and places.

## Worship at the Tabernacle

Exodus 25 and 36

## Objectives

That by the power of the Holy Spirit working through God's Word, the students will

- grow in a desire to worship God for all His gifts, especially the gift of Jesus, the Savior;
- recognize the church as a special place to worship God and to see themselves as part of their church family;
- worship God with praise and joy in all situations and locations.

## Day 1 Materials

- Jake and Jenna puppets
- Red, blue, and purple cloth
- Wood and leather objects
- Faux gemstone beads
- Silver, gold, and bronze objects
- Blackline 35-A

## Day 2 Materials

- Clocks and watches
- Long scarf or sash
- Props from Day 1
- *Praise* Student Book
- Worship the Lord poster

## INTRODUCE

Use the Jake and Jenna puppets to introduce the lesson.

**JAKE:** Hi, Jenna! I missed seeing you at church yesterday.

**JENNA:** We went out of town for the weekend. We went to church at my Uncle Tony's house. He set up extra chairs in the family room. Neighbors on his street and from other places came over. A pastor talked about God and read from the Bible. We all sang hymns as Aunt Julia played the piano.

**JAKE:** I guess that does sound like church to me. But why did they meet in a house?

**JENNA:** Uncle Tony says the people want to build a special church building someday, but they don't have enough money yet. Aunt Julia says they may not have a church building, but they have what is needed to have a church.

**JAKE:** What is that?

**JENNA:** They have God's Word and people who believe in God. She says that church is not a building—a church is people.

**TEACHER:** You are right, Jenna. Today we will hear about people of God in the Bible who worshiped God wherever they traveled. Since they moved so much, they did not have a church building, so they built a tent church.

**JAKE:** But even a tent can have what it takes to be a church—God's Word and God's people!

**JENNA:** Now you've got the idea!

## DEVELOP

Explain, **Today we will look at how the people of Israel worshiped God long ago. They were traveling for years in the desert between Egypt and the Promised Land. God knew that the people needed a special place to gather in worship where they could hear God's Word and praise God together. God gave Moses instructions for building a tent-church. It was called the tabernacle.**

**The people wanted to give the very best they had so that God's house would be beautiful and would honor Him. Some people brought expensive red cloth, blue cloth, and purple cloth—the colors used for a king.** Show swatches or strips of red, blue, and purple fabric and pass them around the class. **The people brought the best building materials they had, such as wood and leather and gemstones.** Show a nicely finished wooden object, something made from leather, and stone beads. Again, let children handle the objects. **The people brought expensive metals such as silver, gold, and bronze.** Pass around jewelry or decorative housewares made from these metals. A copper object can be used if you do not have bronze. **The people brought so many good gifts—much more than was needed. Moses had to ask them to stop—enough is enough!**

The people had *given* their best. Then they *did* their best—sewing, carving, building. There were artists, carpenters, and stonemasons. Everyone worked hard to build the tabernacle and the objects in it such as candlesticks, altars, and the ark of the covenant. When it was finished, the tabernacle was beautiful. A large cloud covered the tabernacle. The glory of God filled the tent-church. God's people came together to worship the Lord. Wherever they traveled, they took the tent-church with them. They knew God was always with them, in every place they went.

Distribute copies of Blackline 35-A for the children to color.

# R E S P O N D

Point out that in many ways the people of God today are like the people of God long ago. Print this as a list or in a circular fashion connected by arrows: **(1) We worship God. (2) But sometimes we don't honor Him … (3) because we are sinners. (4) And because we are sinners … (5) Jesus died for us. (6) So … (1) We worship God.** Point out that we are back to the beginning of our list. **God is very patient with us as we continue to make mistakes. He forgives us. But He also helps us, through the power of the Holy Spirit, to change our ways and to grow stronger in faith and in our faith life.**

## Worship Ideas

- Say, **We tell each other "I love you" in many different ways. We might say the words. We might give a loving hug. We might help someone in a loving way. God tells us "I love you" too. Listen to how God shows His love for us.** From a Bible read 1 John 4:9–10. **God shows His love for us through Jesus.** Read aloud 1 John 3:1. **God shows His love by calling us His own dear children and by preparing a place for us in heaven to live with Him eternally. How can we tell God "I love You"?** Listen to their responses. Then sing and pray to the Lord.
- Sing about your love for the Lord. Sing "Say to the Lord, I Love You," "Love, Love, Love," "There Is a Name I Love to Hear," "My Best Friend Is Jesus," "We Love" (*LOSP*, pp. 18, 30, 44, 45, 54, and on CD).

## Bible Background

At the time of the exodus, God chose a nation to be His own. From this nation He would send the Messiah—the Savior. At Sinai He gave His people the Ten Commandments (Exodus 20). The remainder of the Book of Exodus and the pages of Leviticus, Numbers, and Deuteronomy detail numerous additional laws and rituals for God's chosen people. The tabernacle became the central point of their worship. God gave detailed instructions for the construction of the tabernacle and its furnishings (Exodus 25–40).

The tabernacle, the furnishings, and the rituals all served as means by which the people remembered God's redemptive acts. He called them as His own people; He rescued them from slavery in the land of Egypt; He preserved them for years in the wilderness; He accepted their sacrifices for their sins; and He would send the Savior, whose death the Father would accept as the complete sacrifice for the sins of all people of all times.

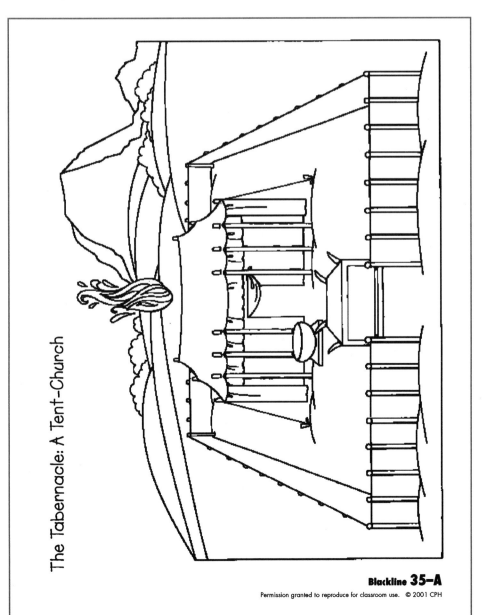

The Tabernacle: A Tent-Church

**Blackline 35-A**

Permission granted to reproduce for classroom use. © 2001 CPH

## Words to Remember

*Rejoice in the Lord always. I will say it again: Rejoice! Philippians 4:4*

This Bible verse begins and ends with the same word. Ask the children if they can think of any other words we repeat often when we speak or sing about the Lord. Sing some of these songs that joyfully repeat praises: "Rejoice in the Lord Always," "A Hymn of Glory Let Us Sing," "Hallelujah! Praise Ye the Lord," "Praise Him, Praise Him," "Hosanna! Hosanna!" (*LOSP,* pp. 52, 56, 58, 68, 94, and on CD).

## Extending the Lesson

- Help students write thank-you notes or cards to professional and volunteer church workers in your congregation, thanking them for sharing God's Word.
- Have children make simple invitations for an upcoming worship service at your church. Place the invitations inside helium-filled balloons. Encourage children to tie the balloons to the mailbox or front door of friends and neighbors to spread the news.
- Locate old catalogs of church products that contain pictures of the variety of church furnishings available. Let children cut out pictures, glue them to make a collage of pages, and staple these together to make a book titled *Church Buildings—Inside and Out.* Put an *X* next to any picture that looks like something in your own church sanctuary. Discuss the use and purpose of some of the more unique items pictured.

# Day 2

## INTRODUCE

Display a number of clocks and watches, all set at different times. Say, **I brought all these clocks and watches so that I would know when it is the best time to worship God.** Examine each watch or clock, read the time displayed, and ask if this would be a good time to praise and worship the Lord. Come to the conclusion that *right now* is always a good time to praise the Lord. **Wherever we are, whatever the time of day, we know God is with us and blessing us. So wherever and whenever, it is always a good time to worship God.** Worship the Lord, singing a favorite song of praise such as "Psalm 8" (*LOSP,* p. 50, and on CD).

## DEVELOP

Say, **As the people of Israel traveled from place to place in the wilderness, they were able to worship God wherever they were because they took their church with them! How did they do that?**

### Worship at the Tabernacle

*(Exodus 25 and 36)*

When the people of Israel were traveling in the wilderness for many years, God told Moses how to build a tabernacle. This would be a special place to remember and worship God for all He had done.

The people did as God had said. They brought gifts of gold, silver, and bronze. They brought cloth in beautiful colors of blue, red, and purple. They brought wood, leather, and gemstones. The people brought so many gifts for the Lord that Moses had to ask them to stop!

Then the artists, builders, and carpenters got busy. They did the very best work they could. That was their special gift of thanks to God.

At last the tent-church was finished. A cloud covered it, and the glory of God filled the tabernacle. God's people joyfully worshiped God at the new church. We worship God in our church too, thanking Him especially for the gift of our Savior, Jesus. We can worship God wherever we are! He is everywhere and always hears us!

(Their church was a tent that they could pack up, move with them, and set up again somewhere else.) Act out the building of the tabernacle. A sash can be tied around the teacher's forehead to indicate the character of a builder. The children can be given props to pantomime their parts. Say:

I was so excited when Moses told us about God's plan. I like to build things, and I especially like the idea of building a place to worship God. I can hardly wait to start working on the tabernacle.

Let's see … We'll need brightly colored fabric for the tent walls and curtains. They should be the color of kings because God is King of kings. Have volunteers bring fabric pieces forward.

Thank you for your gifts. Now, we'll need strong wood to build poles to hold up the walls and make the furniture. We will need soft leather and valuable gemstones to decorate the building. Who can bring these gifts? Volunteers bring forward wood, leather, gems.

We want the very best for the Lord. So let's cover the candlesticks, plates, altars, and tables with the finest metals—gold, silver, and bronze. Volunteers bring metal items forward.

Stop! We have enough gifts! We have more than we need! Now we must get to work. Builders, carpenters, weavers, and artists can all do their best work for the Lord. Volunteers step forward and pretend to hammer, cut, or weave.

At last it is the Sabbath Day, the seventh day, the day we set aside to worship the Lord. Have all the children gather around to kneel and pray. **Dear Lord, as the people of Israel did so long ago, we want to give You our very best to thank You for giving Your very best—Jesus—to be our Savior. Our gifts are small compared to the gifts of forgiveness and eternal life You give to us. We thank and praise You in Jesus' name. Amen.**

## R E S P O N D

Point out that the people of Israel gave God their best, such as gold and silver. **How can you thank and worship God with the best that you have?** Emphasize that our gifts do not have to be gold or silver or even money. **Your gift to God may be something you do well. It may be the gift of time, or the gift of a talent.** If children are unsure what gifts they have to give, make suggestions to start the discussion. (The children can give their songs to Jesus; someone good in art can make a beautiful picture of Jesus; remembering that Jesus says that whatever we do for others we are doing for Him, we can give up some of our time to help others; if someone has a special skill like playing basketball, they can dedicate that skill to God by playing in a considerate and honest manner; writing talent can be used to create poems or prayers.) **All we do and say and think can be dedicated in worship to the Lord.** Read aloud Colossians 3:17 and 23.

Together discuss page 10 in the *Praise* Student Book, noting ways we worship God in our churches today. Then say, **I want to add something to what I said earlier. I said that the people of Israel were able to worship God anywhere because they took their church with them. That is true, but there is more! We don't have to be in church to worship God! We can worship God wherever we are—with other people, with our families, or even by ourselves.** Display the Worship the Lord poster. Point out the picture of the tabernacle and of the present-day church building. But then note other places where people can worship the Lord. Have the children help you make a list of places in addition to school, home, and your own room. (We can worship God in prayer and praise on the playground, at the grocery store, at Grandma's house, on vacation, etc.) Talk about what words you might say in these situations to praise or petition the Lord. (Continue to refer to this poster throughout this unit.)

### God's People Worship

*Directions: Can you find these people in the picture? Draw a line to show where each one is. How is each person worshiping God in church?*

### Words to Remember

Rejoice in the Lord always. I will say it again: Rejoice!

Philippians 4:4

## Discovery Point

We worship and praise God Almighty, our Creator and Savior. The family of God worships together in church as well as individually. We can worship God in a variety of ways and places.

## Worship at the Temple

1 Kings 6 and 8

## Objectives

That by the power of the Holy Spirit working through God's Word, the students will

- identify the church as both a place to worship and the family of believers who gather to worship;
- grow in respect and appreciation for God's house;
- gladly worship and praise God, our Creator, Savior, and Sanctifier.

## Day 3 Materials

- Various items in paper bags
- Sand blocks, drums, rhythm sticks, bells
- Other rhythm instruments
- Blackline 35-B
- Colored pencils

## Day 4 Materials

- *Praise* Student Book
- Items from church

# INTRODUCE

In advance prepare several paper bags, each containing items for a specific use. For example, put baking items in one bag (egg beater, mixing bowl, measuring cup), hair-care items in another bag (comb, brush, shampoo), repair or building tools (hammer, nails, saw, screwdriver), swimming pool items (goggles, fins, beach ball), and in the last bag put items used in a worship service (hymnal, collection plate, altar cloth). Display items from each bag separately, asking, **Can you guess what these things are used for?** After the last group of items is identified, say, **Yes, these are items we use in church. We use these things to help us worship. What does it mean "to worship"?** (To hear and learn about God's Word and then respond in prayer, songs, thanksgiving, and in living for Jesus.) **Today we'll learn more about worship long ago and worship today.**

# DEVELOP

Distribute the following rhythm instruments to the children: sand blocks, drums, rhythm sticks, and bells. (Other instruments may also be included.) Children will be anxious to use the instruments, so begin by worshiping God in song. Sing "I Have the Joy" (*LOSP*, p. 62, and on CD). Have the children play their instruments only on the sections repeated four times in each stanza. Then have the groups use their instruments at your signal to help you tell the story. Say:

**Once the people of Israel were through with their travels and were settled in the Promised Land, it was time to build a new church. King Solomon had a large, beautiful house. Now he wanted to build a large, beautiful house for the Lord. King Solomon lived in a palace; the special building where people would go to worship the Lord was called the temple.**

**Solomon used the best wood to build the temple. Many carpenters sawed the wood.** Signal the children with sand blocks.

**Solomon used the best stone to build the temple. Stonecutters cut large stones from the earth. Stone movers pushed the heavy stones into place.** Signal children to sound the drums.

**Many artists carved beautiful pictures in the wood and stone. They covered the pictures with gold.** Signal the rhythm sticks.

**In the temple room called the Most Holy Place, they set the ark of the covenant. Everyone worked very hard to make the temple the very best.** Signal children to sound the bells.

**It took thousands of workers seven long years to build the temple. When it was finished King Solomon said, "Everyone come! Let's celebrate! Come to the temple to worship the Lord."** Signal all instruments to play.

**The woodworkers came to worship.** Signal the sounding of sand blocks. **The stone workers came to worship.** Add the sounding of the drums. **The artists came to worship.** Add the sounding of the

sticks. **All the people came to worship.** Add the sounding of the bells.

King Solomon stood up before all the people and prayed to God: **"Dear Lord, You are wonderful! You keep all Your promises. Now watch over this temple and these people. Hear our prayers. Help us when troubles come. Forgive us when we sin. Bless Your people, Lord. May we love and obey You always. Amen.**

King Solomon's prayer can be our prayer too. **Fold your hands and pray silently as I say the prayer again.** Repeat the prayer, changing the word *temple* to *classroom*.

# RESPOND

Point out the picture of Solomon's temple on the Worship the Lord poster. Then say, **We want to give our best in thanks to the Lord. We want our church buildings to be beautiful to honor the greatness of God. But much more important than the church building is the people. When God looks at us as we worship, He is not looking at the windows or the paintings or the chandeliers. God is looking at our hearts and the faith we have in Jesus as our Savior. Because of Jesus, we are children of God the Father. We are brothers and sisters in Christ and one big church family.** Distribute Blackline 35-B and colored pencils. Instead of coloring in the sections, print a word of praise and thanks to God in each section. Work together to make a list of possibilities.

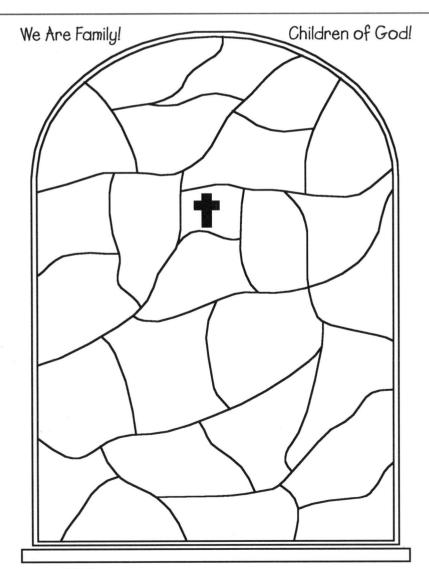

We Are Family!    Children of God!

**Blackline 35-B**

## Worship Ideas

- Consider ways to worship the Lord with things that children especially like. For example, praise God with balloons. Stand in a circle for prayer. Have volunteers say sentence prayers. At the end of each prayer have all children give a cheer for God by raising their balloons and shouting, **Hosanna! Hallelujah!**
- Children like to bounce balls to each other. Stand in two lines. Have a child say the first word of a selected Bible verse. Then that child bounce passes the ball to the opposite child in line. That child says the next word in the verse and continues the process to completion.
- Children love to make pictures and write messages. Build a "praise wall" in the hallway outside your classroom. Let children fill the wall with illustrations and messages about Jesus to witness to passersby. Let children continue to add to the wall throughout the week.

## Bible Background

The construction of the tabernacle allowed it to be moved from place to place. After the nation of Israel had become firmly established in the Promised Land during the reign of King David, God gave instructions for a permanent structure—a temple—to be built by David's son Solomon (1 Kings 5:5).

Like the tabernacle, the temple served as the focal point for worship, which focused on God's redemptive acts. We find a detailed description of the building, its construction, and its furnishings in 1 Kings 5–8. Amid the simple dwellings of the people of that day, the building may have seemed extravagant. However, the extravagance of such a magnificent structure pales when compared to the extravagant love God had bestowed on His chosen nation and continues to shower on us, His chosen people today (1 Peter 2:9).

# Day 11

## Words to Remember

*I rejoiced with those who said to me, / "Let us go to the house of the LORD." Psalm 122:1*

Divide the class in half. Have the two groups stand opposite each other, and then have one group say half of the Bible verse to the other group and vice versa. Repeat this, but switch phrases. Use the same process with a different alignment of groups (such as boys and girls).

## Extending the Lesson

- Take the class to the cornerstone of your church building. Explain that a cornerstone is often the main stone or even the foundation stone in a building. Read aloud 1 Peter 2:5–7a. Point out that Jesus is our cornerstone—the most important part of our lives. Talk about why He is so important in all things and how everything in our life depends on Him.
- Provide empty boxes, cardboard tubes, colored paper, wooden blocks, and other materials. Let children work together to build models of churches.
- Let the children sing and move, pantomiming the actions of this song sung to the melody of "Here We Go 'Round the Mulberry Bush":

**This is the way we cut the wood,
Cut the wood, cut the wood.
This is the way we cut the wood
To build our temple-church.**

Add your own verses (such as carve the stone, melt the gold, shine the brass, sew the drapes; place the ark).

## INTRODUCE

Point out that Solomon was King David's son. God had told David that his son, not he, should build the temple. So David began to store up things that his son could use to build the temple-church. **What kind of things do you think David may have gathered?** (Perhaps wood, stone, candlesticks, cloth, etc.) **Let's think again about the building of the temple.**

## Worship at the Temple
*(1 Kings 6 and 8)*

**NARRATOR:** God chose King Solomon to build a special place where His people could worship. It would be called a temple.

**FIRST WORKER:** We must cut the stones carefully. They must fit together well.

**SECOND WORKER:** The walls will be so beautiful—carved cedar wood and covered with gold.

**NARRATOR:** Thousands of people helped make the temple. They worked hard. They did their very best for the Lord's house.

**SOLOMON:** We will put the golden ark of the covenant in the Most Holy Place of the temple.

**NARRATOR:** The people worked for seven years. Finally the temple was finished.

**SOLOMON:** Come, everyone! Let's celebrate! Let's worship the Lord!

**NARRATOR:** God was pleased. The glory of the Lord filled the temple.

**SOLOMON:** We thank You, O God. You keep all Your promises. Watch over this temple. Hear the prayers of Your people. Help us when troubles come. When we sin, forgive us. May we love and obey You always.

**NARRATOR:** Solomon and all the people worshiped at the temple for seven days. Then they worshiped for another week! We, too, have much for which we are thankful, especially God's blessings and grace in Christ Jesus.

## DEVELOP

Sing the following story song to the melody of "The Farmer in the Dell." Then sing the song a second time, having the children echo your words after each line.

**The wise King Solomon—**
**He took a thousand men.**
**He sent them to get wood and stone**
**And brought them back again.**

**They worked for seven years**
**And built an awesome place.**
**The temple-church was beautiful.**
**God's glory filled the space.**

**The king called one and all**
**To sing and pray and praise.**
**"O Lord, You are most wonderful.**
**Our worship now we raise."**

Review the story, using pages 11–12 of the *Praise* Student Book.

---

### Come to God's House!

*Directions: Review the Bible story, placing these words in the correct spaces: TEMPLE, SEVEN, ISRAEL, WORSHIP, GOLD, STONES, GLORY.*

```
1.  [ ][S][ ][ ][ ][ ][ ]
2.    [O][ ][ ][ ][ ]
3.      [L][ ][ ][ ][ ][ ]
4.        [O][ ][ ]
5.  [ ][M][ ][ ][ ][ ]
6.      [O][ ][ ][ ][ ][ ]
7. [ ][ ][ ][ ][N]
```

1. Solomon was king of **ISRAEL**.
2. The **STONES** for the temple walls had to be cut carefully.
3. When it was finished, the temple was filled with God's **GLORY**.
4. The walls were carved and covered with **GOLD**.
5. The **TEMPLE** took seven years to build.
6. The people of Israel had a wonderful place to **WORSHIP** the Lord.
7. The people worshiped for **SEVEN** days. And then they stayed another week to worship.

### Words to Remember

I rejoiced with those who said to me,
"Let us go to the house of the Lord."
Psalm 122:1

---

## RESPOND

In advance, with the permission of the pastor and church custodian, gather together several items from your church sanctuary and place them all on a step at the center of the chancel area. Bring your class to the church and seat them near the chancel. Say, **The temple King Solomon built was a beautiful place to honor and worship God. We have a beautiful house of worship too.** One at a time, examine the articles you have gathered. Ask the children how the item is used or why we have it in church. Then let a volunteer respectfully put the item back in its place.

Talk about *why* we worship God in church. **First of all, this is what God wants. In the Third Commandment He says, "Remember the Sabbath Day by keeping it holy." God wants us to set aside one day of the week to gather with other believers, to worship, and to rest.** Point out that we can worship God anytime, but we especially set aside Sunday because Jesus rose from the grave on a Sunday. **It's like celebrating Easter every week. Why is Easter so important?** (Because we have a living Savior who took the punishment for our sin in His death on the cross. He has defeated death as well and ensures that we, too, will have life eternal by grace through faith in Him alone.) **This is our main reason for worshiping God—because we want to praise and thank Him for His great goodness to us.** In celebration, provide time for the children to circulate, greeting each other as brothers and sisters because in Christ we are the family of God.

# Day 1

## Discovery Point

God has blessed us in the past, especially through Jesus, our Savior. God continues to bless us daily, and His promises extend faithfully to fulfillment in eternity.

## Praise the Lord!

Psalms 148 and 150

## Objectives

That by the power of the Holy Spirit working through God's Word, the students will

- think about the greatness and grace of our God;
- speak and sing praises to His name;
- live, in all that they do, to the glory of the Lord.

## Day 1 Materials

- Fresh flower
- Rock
- Bird or other pet
- Clear glass of water
- Blackline 36-A
- *Praise* Student Book

## Day 2 Materials

- Jake and Jenna puppets
- Small Bible (optional)
- *Praise* Student Book
- Rhythm instruments

## INTRODUCE

Display a living flower, a polished rock, a bird (or other pet), a clear glass of water. Say, **We know that God created these things. But today we are going to look at psalm verses that say these things** *praise the Lord.* **How can a flower praise God? What about a rock? It can't think about God; it can't think at all! How can a rock praise God?** Explain that all creation shows God's glory. All things created show how wonderful the Creator is. When we see plants, rocks, animals, and other things, we see how wise and powerful God is. **Why can people praise God in a special way?** (Because we can know God through Jesus and His Word; we can speak and sing about how wonderful God is; we can share the Good News of God's love with other people.)

## DEVELOP

Point out that all year long the children have been learning about the goodness and greatness of God. As the year nears its end, it is fitting that we close the year with praise and thanks to God. Read aloud the portions of Psalm 148 printed on page 13 of the *Praise* Student Book. Then ask, **What word did you hear over and over again?** (Praise.) Tell the children that you will read the psalm again. Every time they hear the word *praise,* they are to "explode" out of their chairs (meaning they jump up with raised arms and then sit down again).

Assign children to be the parts of creation mentioned in the psalm. For example, one individual or small group can be *sea creatures,* someone else can be *lightning and hail,* and so on. Tell the children that when they hear their part of creation mentioned in the psalm, they are to jump up and shout, "Praise the Lord!"

# R E S P O N D

Use copies of Blackline 36-A to write a new psalm together. Choose elements of creation not mentioned in Psalm 148 and print them in the blanks (according to categories listed in parentheses). On the board, print the words suggested by the children so that spelling does not become an issue or obstacle. Use your completed psalm, reading it together to praise God.

## Worship Ideas

As a review of songs learned throughout the year, have the following "praise project." Look at the list for one of the Voyages music CDs. Have the children number a sheet of paper according to the number of songs on the CD. They will be using this sheet to vote on the songs they would like to sing. Read through the list of song titles and numbers. Children are to place an X next to the number of any song they would like to sing. Gather their sheets. Tally up the votes (or have a group of children tally them). Sing those songs that the children especially like. (Perhaps sing any song that got eight or more votes.) You may want to try this process over several days.

## Bible Background

Psalm 148 is a call to all things in creation to praise the Lord. Psalm 150 is a call for the orchestra and choir to praise the Lord. These psalms are a fitting ending to this year and a prelude to the great praises to be sung in heaven for the fulfillment of God's great promise of the Savior Jesus Christ, who brings us eternal life:

*Then I looked and heard the voice of many angels, numbering thousands upon thousands. ... "Worthy is the Lamb, who was slain, to receive power and wealth and wisdom and strength and honor and glory and praise!" Then I heard every creature in heaven and on earth and under the earth and on the sea, and all that is in them, singing: "To Him who sits on the throne and to the Lamb be praise and honor and glory and power, for ever and ever!" (Revelation 5:11–13).*

### A New Psalm

Praise the Lord!

Praise God for the earth and all things in it. Give glory to God, all you (plants)

_____

_____

and (animals) _____

_____ .

Praise the Lord, all things created afar in God's universe--(planets)

_____ .

Praise God when you are at (places) _____

_____ .

Praise God with (people) _____

_____

Praise God at all times, when you (things you do)

_____ .

Praise the Lord, all people, places, and things, for the Lord created the heavens and earth.

The Lord is ruler over all! Praise the Lord!

 **Day 2**

## Words to Remember

*Let everything that has breath praise the* LORD. *Psalm 150:6*

Use your own *breath* to praise the Lord. Blow up eight balloons. Use a felt-tipped marking pen to write one word of the Bible verse on each balloon. Mix up the balloons and let children place them in the proper order. (Balloons add a festive note to this subject of praise.)

## Extending the Lesson

Each day this week, post several sheets of paper with categories listed at the top. Under each category children may list things for which they praise and thank God. Use the listed items in a praise prayer at the close of each day. Suggestions follow.

- Post three lists, one with a circle at the top, one with a square, and one with a triangle. Children may list blessings that have these shapes (such as an orange, house, and mountain).
- Post three sheets for listing *persons, places,* and *things* for which they praise God.
- Post a variety of sheets of colored paper. Children may list things they are thankful for in each color.
- Post a titled sheet for each of the major classifications of vertebrate animals: fish, amphibians, reptiles, birds, and mammals. If you have not studied these in science, choose familiar categories such as fish, birds, and bugs.
- Post sheets for various food groups such as fruit, vegetables, meat, dairy foods, and grains.

## INTRODUCE

Use the Jake and Jenna puppets to introduce the lesson. If possible, have Jenna hold a small Bible.

**JENNA:** Hey, Jake. Today we are going to hear Psalm 150. Listen to these great words: "Praise God in His sanctuary." *Sanctuary* means "the church."

**JAKE:** I know that.

**JENNA:** And then it says, "Praise Him in His mighty heavens."

**JAKE:** So it's saying we can praise God *in* church and also everywhere *out* of church.

**JENNA:** Right, inside and outside. *(Hold Jenna curled up tight on the word* inside *and hold her stretched wide on the word* outside.*)*

**JAKE:** And when I think of church I think of a lot of "ups and downs," like stand up, sit down, stand up, sit down.

### Praise the Lord!

*(Psalm 148)*

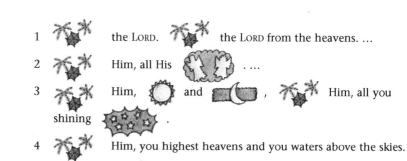

13

JENNA: Oh, Jake, you are so silly.

JAKE: Actually, this *in* and *out* and *up* and *down* makes me think of a song that praises God! Let's sing "Happy All the Time" (*LOSP*, p. 59, and on CD; add the motions).

## DEVELOP

Tell the children that you are going to read the psalm that Jenna was talking about. **Here are three things to listen to: (1) each verse says the word *praise* at least two times; (2) the psalm writer asks all the instruments in the whole orchestra to join in praising God; and (3) at the end he asks the whole choir—everything that has breath—to praise the Lord.** (Explain that a lyre is a handheld harp.) Read aloud Psalm 150 from a Bible.

Turn to page 14 of the *Praise* Student Book. See how many of the instruments the children can identify. Point out the old and new styles of trumpets, harps, and flutes.

## RESPOND

Noting that Psalm 150 calls on the orchestra and choir to join in praising God, let the children respond as an orchestra, using rhythm instruments. They may also respond as a choir, singing selected songs from the Voyages CD. Consider having a "praise march" around the room in celebration of all that the Lord has done for us in Christ. The children will sing and play their instruments.

(Note: If you don't have rhythm instruments available, use this time to allow children to make their own. Glue sandpaper to wood blocks to make sand blocks; seal rice in empty, clean soda cans to make maracas; attach "jingle bells" to the edge of paper plates to make tambourines; make drums from empty coffee cans or oatmeal boxes, using pencils for drumsticks.)

### Praise with Instruments and Choirs *(Psalm 150)*

*Can you name some of these instruments? Can you circle the ones that may have been used in Bible times? Place an X next to instruments you have heard used in church to praise the Lord.*

### Words to Remember

Let everything that has breath praise the LORD.

Psalm 150:6

14

## Discovery Point

God has blessed us in the past, especially through Jesus, our Savior. God continues to bless us daily, and His promises extend faithfully to fulfillment in eternity.

## God's Eternal Promises Continue

Selected Scripture Verses

## Objectives

That by the power of the Holy Spirit working through God's Word, the students will

- know that God blesses us as He continues to fulfill His promises;
- trust that God will always keep His promises;
- praise God for His faithfulness and constant love.

## Day 3 Materials

- Paper heart shapes
- Blackline 36-B

## Day 4 Materials

- Unshelled peanut
- *Praise* Student Book

## INTRODUCE

Say, **When people make promises, we either believe or doubt the promise.** Play thumbs-up, thumbs-down to illustrate this point. Explain, **If the promise I tell you is believable, show thumbs-up. If you doubt the promise could be kept, show thumbs-down.**

**(1a) Your friend says she has a koala bear living in her purse. (1b) Your uncle, the zookeeper, says he will bring a koala bear to your birthday party.**

**(2a) Your baby brother says he will read a book to you. (2b) Your mom promises to help you with your math homework.**

**(3a) Your little sister promises to build a tree house for you. (3b) Your dad says he will set up a tent for you in the backyard.**

Talk about the scenarios and how the first person in each pair is unlikely to be able to do what they say. **We trust a promise if the person and the promise are *trustworthy*, that is, worthy or deserving of our trust. We know God's promises are trustworthy because He can do all things and has always kept His word. Today we'll look at some of the promises of God that are trustworthy.**

## DEVELOP

Before class begins, copy these Bible references onto five heart shapes: Jeremiah 31:34; Nahum 1:7; Matthew 28:20; Isaiah 65:24; Luke 10:20. Place the hearts in your Bible to mark the verses.

Say, **We've learned so many things from God's Word this year. What we have learned is important for all the days of our lives. I've marked a few very important promises that we all want to remember. God makes every one of these promises to you. He shows us His great love for us through the saving power of Jesus. He is able to do anything He says because He is God!**

Read Jeremiah 31:34. This promise is possible because Jesus took away our sins by His death and resurrection. This promise is the starting point in our relationship as children of God, and it makes all other promises of God possible and certain.

Read Nahum 1:7. Ask, **Why does God want us to be safe?** (He loves us.) **In this world we will have problems like accidents, storms, and illness. But Jesus has conquered the worst problems of sin, death, and the devil. When will we have complete safety in the Lord?** (In heaven.)

Read Matthew 28:20. Ask, **Why is this promise so comforting? When might this promise be extra special to you?** (When you are lonely, worried, or afraid.)

Read Isaiah 65:24. Here God promises to hear and answer even before we have spoken. Ask students to identify times in the past when God answered a prayer.

Read Luke 10:20. If you have a red-letter edition of the Bible, show the children that these are the words of Jesus. By faith in the saving power of Jesus, we have a place ready and reserved for us in heaven. Jesus has prepared a place for us and will return to take all believers to live with Him eternally. We can be certain of this because this rests on His word, not ours, and because He has always been true to His word.

# R E S P O N D

Discuss: **What happens when things go wrong and it's hard to trust God's promises to be with us and help us?** Remind the children that God does not say we will never have troubles. He does not say He will do whatever we want and do it right away. **He does say that at the right time He will do what is good. Sometimes it is hard for us to be patient. Sometimes it is hard for us to see what good God can bring out of a bad situation. We need to trust Him and His timing.** You may want to read Psalm 130:5 and Romans 8:28.

Distribute copies of Blackline 36-B. Follow the directions. Encourage children to display this reminder of God's promises in their homes.

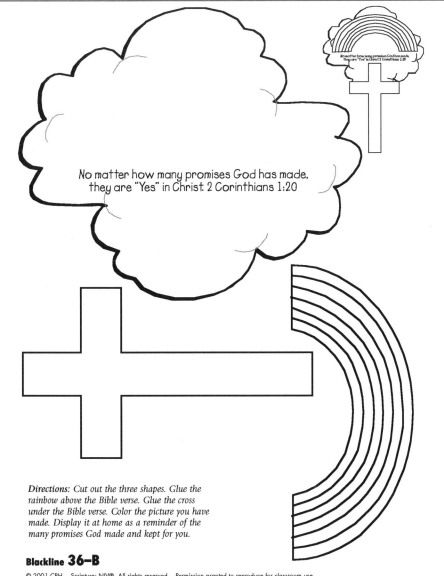

*No matter how many promises God has made, they are "Yes" in Christ. 2 Corinthians 1:20*

*Directions: Cut out the three shapes. Glue the rainbow above the Bible verse. Glue the cross under the Bible verse. Color the picture you have made. Display it at home as a reminder of the many promises God made and kept for you.*

**Blackline 36-B**

# Worship Ideas

- Set out classroom textbooks you have used this year in science, math, and reading. When students are gathered in the worship center, say, **Since it's the end of the year, let's vote on which one of these subjects is the most important to know.** After voting, say, **Actually, not one of these subjects is the most important.** Hold up a Bible. **This has what we need to know most of all. Only here can we learn that God loves us and sent Jesus to save us from sin so that we may live as God's children.** Ask why this is so important. (It is needed every day of our lives. Only in Jesus do we have eternal life.) Sing "Let Me Learn of Jesus" (see the Supplemental Activities section in the Teacher Resource Book). This song tells about God's action in the past, present, and future.

- Tie a red string around the top of your index finger. Point out that some people do this to help them remember something. **What other things do people do to remember something important?** (Make a list, write it on a calendar, enter it into a computer file.) **God never forgets. He always remembers His promises. And He doesn't need a red string, long list, or calendar to remind Him. We can always trust Jesus to keep His promises.** Sing "I Am Trusting You, Lord Jesus" (*LOSP*, p. 24, and on CD).

# Bible Background

This lesson discusses five promises from the Lord. But there are so many more given in His Word. Here is a sampling of the certain hope we have in God.

*My unfailing love for you will not be shaken. Isaiah 54:10*

*Fear not, for I have redeemed you; I have summoned you by name; you are Mine. Isaiah 43:1*

*The Holy Spirit, whom the Father will send in My name, will teach you all things. John 14:26*

*The LORD gives strength to His people; the LORD blesses His people with peace. Psalm 29:11*

*I will heal My people and will let them enjoy abundant peace and security. Jeremiah 33:6*

*You will rejoice, and no one will take away your joy. John 16:22*

## Words to Remember

*No matter how many promises God has made, they are "Yes" in Christ. 2 Corinthians 1:20*

This lesson focuses on five important promises God makes and keeps. This Bible verse reminds us that God's promises to us number more than five, and we can trust all of them with certainty. We have this certainty in Christ because He fulfilled God's promise of a Savior and has restored our relationship as children of God. (Many Bible bookstores carry little books that list some of the promises of God. You may want to show one of these to the class and read some of the additional blessings God has promised and supplied. Or choose some from the "Bible Background" section.)

## Extending the Lesson

- The rainbow is often used as a symbol for the promises of God. Students will probably remember that God made the first rainbow as a sign of His promise to Noah. In science class this week, investigate the rainbow. What colors make a rainbow? When is a rainbow most likely to appear? What causes a rainbow's different colors? Use prisms to see "rainbows."
- Encourage families to look at their baptismal certificates and talk about the many promises made at the time of Baptism. In Baptism, God promises to make us His children. Parents promise to teach little ones about Jesus, the Savior. Sponsors of the baptized person promise to pray for him or her. Suggest that Baptism certificates be framed and hung as reminders of these special promises.
- Suggest a "promise picnic" to families this week. Tell families to set a date for their family picnic. Make this picnic a top priority—a promise to be kept, no matter what! If bad weather prevents an outdoor picnic, hold the picnic indoors. Use your picnic basket, spread a blanket on the floor, and enjoy your unique picnic. (A few plastic ants can add to the fun!) Talk about God's faithfulness in keeping His promises to your family.

## INTRODUCE

Put an unshelled peanut in your pocket before class begins. Tell students, **I have something in my pocket no person has ever seen before. I promise this is true! Do you believe me?**

Show the peanut shell. **Sometimes it's hard to believe someone's words because you can't figure out how it could be true. But inside this shell are peanuts that have never been exposed to the light of day and have never been seen by any person's eyes.** Crack open the shell and show the peanuts that are being seen for the very first time.

**I made a promise to you about something unseen. But there was an explanation. It was not really so amazing. But God's promises are amazing. And God keeps His promises because He is all-powerful. He is God and can do all things.**

### God's Eternal Promises Continue
*(Selected Scripture Verses)*

I will forgive their wickedness and will remember their sins no more. Jeremiah 31:34

The Lord is good, a refuge in times of trouble. He cares for those who trust in Him. Nahum 1:7

I am with you always, to the very end of the age. Matthew 28:20

Before they call I will answer; while they are still speaking I will hear. Isaiah 65:24

Rejoice that your names are written in heaven. Luke 10:20

## DEVELOP

Review the promises of God studied yesterday. Have the children help you with this promise poem. After you say two lines, the children are to repeat this phrase: **I know and believe God's promise is true.** Use some type of signal to cue students when it is time for them to speak.

**God says He forgives**
**And makes your heart new.**
*I know and believe*
*God's promise is true.*

**God cares and He helps**
**When troubles pursue.**
*I know and believe*
*God's promise is true.*

**You're never alone**
**For God is with you.**
*I know and believe*
*God's promise is true.*

**God listens to prayers**
**From me and from you.**
*I know and believe*
*God's promise is true.*

**He'll take us to heaven**
**When our life is through.**
*I know and believe*
*God's promise is true.*

Read the poem again to the class, having students identify the promise referred to in each stanza. (God promises forgiveness, care and protection, to always be with us, to hear and answer prayer, and to take us to heaven.) As you examine individual poem stanzas, also look at the corresponding Bible verses, printed on page 15 of the *Praise* Student Book.

## RESPOND

Discuss these situations and our trust in God's promises: **A tornado destroyed Tammy's home, but no one in her family was hurt. Did God keep His promise of protection?** Yes, but perhaps not in the way Tammy wanted. God chose to save the family members. He can bring blessings even out of disasters.

**Even though Troy prayed about it, his dad still lost his job. The family moved to a new neighborhood and joined a new church. Did God keep His promise to answer prayer?** Yes, but God answered it in the way that was best for the family. They may not see it now, but they can trust God's plans to give them hope and a future in this new place. Read Jeremiah 29:11.

**Mariah's uncle died of cancer. He was only 25 years old. Why didn't God help him?** God did help him, though not in the way Mariah may have expected. God took her uncle from the pain of this world to heaven, where there is no sickness or pain.

**Tony is in a wheelchair. He can't walk, but he sure can tell funny jokes. His mother prays and prays for a miracle. She wonders why God doesn't help her son.** God promises to be with us in the midst of our troubles. Sometimes He doesn't take the trouble away, but He can help us live with the problem. He can bless us in other ways. Trust that He knows what is best.

Ask, **If someone asks if you will go to heaven someday, what can you say?** After listening to responses, emphasize that heaven is not a wish and is not something we accomplish. **We know absolutely, positively that we are going to heaven because Jesus has promised it to us. And like all that He says, this promise is certain. We can trust the word of Jesus.** From a Bible read Hebrews 10:23; Joshua 23:14; and the last half of Psalm 145:13. These verses remind us that God is faithful, dependable, and trustworthy. Have students work on page 16 of their books to discover another Bible verse that reminds us that God never changes—we can be sure that He does what He says He will do, including taking us to heaven. "Jesus Christ is the same *yesterday* and *today* and *forever."*

---

### God Is Faithful and Unchanging

*Directions: Complete the puzzle and read the Bible words that remind us we can be absolutely certain that Jesus will keep His promise to us. Look at the yellow boxes. Below each one, print the letter that comes next in the alphabet.*

## Jesus Christ is the same

| x | d | r | s | d | q | c | x |
|---|---|---|---|---|---|---|---|
| y | e | s | t | e | r | d | a | y |

| | s | n | c | x |
|---|---|---|---|---|
| and | t | o | d | a | y |

| e | n | q | d | u | d | q |
|---|---|---|---|---|---|---|
| and | f | o | r | e | v | e | r |  .

Hebrews 13:8

### Words to Remember

No matter how many promises God has made,
they are "Yes" in Christ.

2 Corinthians 1:20

16